Pakistan at Seventy

This handbook examines Pakistan's 70-year history from a number of different perspectives. When Pakistan was born, it did not have a capital, a functioning government or a central bank. The country lacked a skilled workforce. While the state was in the process of being established, eight million Muslim refugees arrived from India, who had to be absorbed into a population of 24 million people. However, within 15 years, Pakistan was the fastest growing and transforming economy in the developing world, although the political evolution of the country during this period was not equally successful. Pakistan has vast agricultural and human resources, and its location promises trade, investment and other opportunities. Chapters in the volume, written by experts in the field, examine government and politics, economics, foreign policy and environmental issues, as well as social aspects of Pakistan's development, including the media, technology, gender and education.

Shahid Javed Burki is an economist who has been a member of the faculty at Harvard University, USA, and Chief Economist, Planning and Development Department, Government of the Punjab. He has also served as Minister of Finance in the Government of Pakistan, and has written a number of books, and journal and newspaper articles. He joined the World Bank in 1974 as a senior economist and went on to serve in several senior positions. He was the (first) Director of the China Department (1987–94) and served as the Regional Vice-President for Latin America and the Caribbean during 1994–99. He is currently the Chair of the Board of Directors of the Shahid Javed Burki Institute of Public Policy at NetSol (BIPP) in Lahore.

Iftekhar Ahmed Chowdhury is a career Bangladeshi diplomat and former Minister of Foreign Affairs in the Government of Bangladesh (2007–08). He has a PhD in international relations from the Australian National University, Canberra. He began his career as a member of the civil service of Pakistan in 1969. Dr Chowdhury has held senior diplomatic positions in the course of his career, including as Permanent Representative of Bangladesh to the United Nations in New York (2001–07) and in Geneva (1996–2001), and was ambassador to Qatar, Chile, Peru and the Vatican. He is currently a visiting senior research fellow at the Institute of South Asian Studies, National University of Singapore.

Asad Ejaz Butt is an economist trained in Canada. He is currently the Director of the Shahid Javed Burki Institute of Public Policy at NetSol (BIPP) in Lahore. Before joining the BIPP, Mr. Ejaz was a member of the Economics faculty at the University of Central Punjab. He has worked as a consultant, most notably working with the United Nations Development Programme (UNDP) on its sustainable development goals (SDG) agenda for the province of Punjab, and with ICF International, Canada, on energy efficiency and policy analytics.

Europa Emerging Economies

The Europa Emerging Economies series from Routledge, edited by Robert E. Looney, examines a wide range of contemporary economic, political, developmental and social issues as they affect emerging economies throughout the world. Complementing the *Europa Regional Surveys of the World* series and the *Handbook of Emerging Economies*, which was also edited by Professor Looney, the volumes in the *Europa Emerging Economies* series will be a valuable resource for academics, students, researchers, policy-makers, professionals, and anyone with an interest in issues regarding emerging economies in the wider context of current world affairs.

There will be individual volumes in the series which provide in-depth country studies, and others which examine issues and concepts; all are written or edited by specialists in their field. Volumes in the series are not constrained by any particular template, but may explore economic, political, governance, international relations, defence, or other issues in order to increase the understanding of emerging economies and their importance to the world economy..

Robert E. Looney is a Distinguished Professor at the Naval Postgraduate School, Monterey, California, who specializes in issues relating to economic development in the Middle East, East Asia, South Asia and Latin America. He has published over 20 books and 250 journal articles, and has worked widely as a consultant to national governments and international agencies.

The Islamic Republic of Iran
Reflections on an Emerging Economy
by Jahangir Amuzegar

**Argentina's Economic Reforms of the 1990s in Contemporary
and Historical Perspective**
by Domingo Cavallo and Sonia Cavallo Runde

Handbook of Small States
Economic, Social and Environmental Issues
edited by Lino Briguglio

Pakistan at Seventy
A handbook on developments in economics, politics and society
edited by Shahid Javed Burki with Iftekhar Ahmed Chowdhury and Asad Ejaz Butt

Pakistan at Seventy

A handbook on developments in
economics, politics and society

*Edited by Shahid Javed Burki with
Iftekhar Ahmed Chowdhury and Asad Ejaz Butt*

Routledge
Taylor & Francis Group

LONDON AND NEW YORK

First published 2019
by Routledge
2 Park Square, Milton Park, Abingdon, Oxon OX14 4RN

and by Routledge
52 Vanderbilt Avenue, New York, NY 10017

Routledge is an imprint of the Taylor & Francis Group, an informa business

First issued in paperback 2021

Europa Commissioning Editor: Cathy Hartley

Editorial Assistants: Eleanor Catchpole Simmons, Lucy Pritchard

British Library Cataloguing-in-Publication Data
A catalogue record for this book is available from the British Library

Library of Congress Cataloging-in-Publication Data
Names: Burki, Shahid Javed, editor. | Chowdhury, Iftekhar Ahmed, editor.
Title: Pakistan at seventy : a handbook on developments in economics,
    politics and society / edited by Shahid Javed Burki with Iftekhar Ahmed Chowdhury.
Description: Abingdon, Oxon ; New York, NY : Routledge, 2019. | Series:
    Europa emerging economies | Includes bibliographical references.
Identifiers: LCCN 2018054328 (print) | LCCN 2019002378 (ebook) | ISBN
    9780429426810 (ebook) | ISBN 9781857439847 | ISBN 9780429426810 (ebk)
Subjects: LCSH: Pakistan–History.
Classification: LCC DS382 (ebook) | LCC DS382 .P27 2019 (print) | DDC
    954.9105–dc23
LC record available at https://lccn.loc.gov/2018054328

ISBN: 978-1-85743-984-7 (hbk)
ISBN: 978-1-03-209210-2 (pbk)
ISBN: 978-0-429-42681-0 (ebk)

Typeset in Times New Roman
by Taylor & Francis Books

Contents

Illustrations

Figures

Tables

Boxes

Foreword

Shahid Javed Burki and Iftekhar Ahmed Chowdhury, his colleague at the Institute of South Asian Studies (ISAS) at the National University of Singapore, have done a commendable job in compiling this book whose chapters have been written by experts from several fields. The book was assembled to mark the 70th anniversary of the birth of Pakistan. It is a collaborative effort mounted by the ISAS and the Burki Institute of Public Policy (BIPP). The BIPP is a successor institution to the Institute of Public Policy that I helped Javed Burki to set up 10 years ago. At the time I was Vice-Chancellor of Beaconhouse National University, Lahore.

The primary objective of setting up the Institute of Public Policy (IPP) in 2007 was to publish an independent report on the state of the economy every year, along with a special well-researched report on a burning topic of the day. The topics chosen included the economic cost of domestic terrorism and energy shortages; the growing sense of deprivation in the province of Punjab; and the economic and financial consequences of the 18th amendment to Pakistan's Constitution. This tradition of publishing independent reports on the state of the economy continued after the IPP was transformed into the BIPP. Several authors who have contributed chapters for this volume were involved in writing some of the IPP/BIPP reports.

This is a timely and thoughtful book. It examines Pakistan's 70-year history from a number of different perspectives. The past seven decades have not been easy for Pakistan. People seldom realize how precarious the situation was for Pakistan at the time of its birth. Unlike India, its sister state born one day after Pakistan came into being, Pakistan did not have a capital, a functioning government or a central bank. There was also a serious shortage of trained manpower. While the state was in the process of being established, eight million Muslim refugees arrived from India. They had to be absorbed into a population of 24 million, bringing the total to 32 million.

When Pakistan conducted its first census in 1951, one out of every four citizens was a refugee. It is testimony to the first generation of Pakistani leaders that within 15 years Pakistan was the fastest growing and transforming economy in the developing world. Several Western development economists wrote books on Pakistan's extraordinary performance in the 1960s. They suggested that the country could serve as a model for the economic advance of the rest of the developing world.

However, the political evolution of the country during this period was not equally successful. In the very first decade of Pakistan's existence, a basic democratic principle was violated when East Pakistan was denied its due share in the political power structure in proportion to its population, which was larger than that of the four provinces of West Pakistan combined. In order to resolve the deadlock over constitution-making, an artificial parity was created between East and West Pakistan in 1955 by merging the four West Pakistan provinces into a single unit and giving equal numbers of seats to the two provinces. In a genuine democratic framework, imbalances in population are often accommodated by having an upper house, or Senate, with equal representation from all provinces.

This injustice was further compounded by General Muhammad Ayub Khan when he promulgated the Constitution in 1962. He had come to power in October 1958 after abrogating the 1956 Constitution, just a few months before the first general elections under this constitution were able to be held in February 1959. The new Constitution concentrated all powers in the hands of a President, who was indirectly elected through 80,000 'basic democrats'. Ayub Khan also retained his military position by assuming the lifelong rank of a Field Marshal. Under this Constitution, Ayub Khan drastically reduced the quantum of provincial autonomy by exercising all effective powers through nominated governors rather than giving them to elected assemblies. This created serious political fault lines which ultimately led to the split with Bangladesh and the break-up of the country in December 1971.

The second major cause of the failure of democracy can be attributed to the dominant role of the military in the country's power structure. The first war between India and Pakistan over Kashmir broke out within a year of Pakistan's birth. The foundations of a 'security state' were laid from the very outset. The next two India–Pakistan wars in 1965 and 1971 were fought when Pakistan was under army rule and further reinforced the paramount supremacy of defence and national security in the national agenda. That is why even the short periods of civilian rule that were allowed by the Establishment were largely overshadowed by the military's influence on key policies.

These chronic problems of political instability and difficult civil military relations were compounded by many external problems over which Pakistan had no real control. The Soviet invasion of Afghanistan in December 1979 virtually converted Pakistan into a melting pot of many global fault lines with serious consequences for the stability of the country's security and economy. By gradually overcoming these problems, the citizens of Pakistan showed resilience and its leadership at various times displayed both determination and imagination.

Of the many themes covered in the book, I would like to highlight four. The first of these is Pakistan's remarkable endowments, all of which could help to speed up the pace of economic development and social improvement. Pakistan has the world's largest contiguous irrigated area. The available water needs to be put to productive use and not wasted on producing low-value crops. How should this be done in terms of government policy and farmers' incentives? The 1988 report of the National Commission on Agriculture, which I chaired as Minister of State for Food and Agriculture, provides answers to these questions. However, many of the recommendations in this report have not yet been implemented.

Human resources constitute an endowment that, put to good use, can produce impressive results for the economy and society. If neglected, a country's youth can create the kind of convulsions that have rocked the Arab world for more than a decade. However, the youth can be turned into economic and social assets. With a large and steadily growing population, Pakistan needs to develop an approach that will provide its youth with the education and skills they need to become productive participants in the modern economy. Pakistan's youth aspires to a better life. We should make a real effort to provide it to them.

I agree with the thrust of the sectoral analysis provided in this book that greater and better use should be made of some of Pakistan's traditional skills, especially those found in the area that is generally referred to as the 'golden triangle' and includes the cities of Lahore, Gujranwala, Gujrat and Sialkot. This area has long been known for its metal and wood craftsmanship. We should take advantage of the way the global production system is being restructured so that the enterprises located in this geographic region become integrated into the various supply chains that constitute the system of global industrial development.

The third conclusion reached by several authors with which I agree is that Pakistan's policymakers should be mindful of the enormous changes that are occurring in the global environment in which we must operate. Pakistan is not as well integrated into the global economic system as it should be. Only if we make an effort to become a more active player in the world economy will we be looked at in a more positive light. Given that the international trading system is under stress because of the preference of the present US administration for bilateral agreements rather than multilateral arrangements, we will need to reorient our trade policy and build stronger trading links with Europe and with Asian and African countries.

I also fully agree with the book's conclusion that the location of Pakistan is exceptionally advantageous. The country occupies a geographic area that could help to turn Pakistan into an important corridor for international commerce. With the China–Pakistan Economic Corridor (CPEC), we can now regard this geographic location, which has hitherto been a liability, as a valuable asset. Carefully implemented, the planned investment by the People's Republic of China in developing Pakistan's infrastructure and linking our production system with its own will provide handsome dividends for the country. The connectivity with the world that would result from the investments planned under the CPEC initiative should help us to expand significantly the volume and value of our exports. A higher exports-to-GDP ratio would help us to deal with our perennial external resource problem.

I concur with the basic thrust of the book that Pakistan's future looks promising. The country has many advantages and several rich endowments that can be put to good use to enable its population of approximately 208 million to make rapid economic progress, achieve social peace and realize political stability. We are ready once again to raise our rate of growth well beyond 6 per cent per annum to perhaps as much as 8 per cent. However, that will require serious efforts on the part of policymakers, business leaders and the nation as a whole.

Economic growth is the sum of three factors: growth in population, location of population, and growth in productivity. We have achieved the first two factors, but not the third. With the population still increasing at the rate of 2.4 per cent per annum and urbanization accelerating at twice that rate, productivity needs to grow by more than 5 per cent per annum in order to climb on to a higher growth trajectory. Some of this can happen automatically as people relocate from the countryside to towns and cities. However, the public and private sectors will need to invest in those activities that can promote sustained increase in productivity. We need, for instance, to improve the reach of communication infrastructure to deliver farmers' produce to processing centres. We need to improve the quality of education and skills development of our youth so that they can move into higher productivity jobs. We need to accommodate in the modern sectors of the economy the million or so well-educated women who enter the workforce every year.

This book provides much food for thought and effective action by those involved in managing the complex process of economic change. I hope that it will be widely read and followed in the country.

Sartaj Aziz is a development economist who served as adviser on foreign affairs to the Prime Minister of Pakistan between 2013 and 2016. He was then appointed as Deputy Chairman of the Planning Commission until the end of the government's tenure in June 2018.

Acknowledgements

As both Pakistan and India approached the 70th year of their independence, the Institute of South Asian Studies (ISAS) at the National University of Singapore decided to support the writing of two edited books that would reflect on the developments that have taken place in the two countries since their birth in 1947. I mention Pakistan before India since it was born one day before its sister state. The date 14 August was set as Pakistan's birthday in order to allow Lord Louis Mountbatten, British India's last Viceroy, to swear in Muhammad Ali Jinnah as the country's first Governor-General. After performing that function, Mountbatten flew back to New Delhi to be sworn in on the following day as independent India's first Governor-General.

Since the ISAS did not have a senior resident scholar from Pakistan, the Pakistan book was assigned to Iftekhar Ahmed Chowdhury from Bangladesh who was a full-time resident fellow at the ISAS. Chowdury worked for a number of years in the civil service of Pakistan prior to the country's independence. He served his country as its Minister of Foreign Affairs before taking up residence at the ISAS. He asked me to join him in this enterprise. I was a visiting fellow at the institute spending six to eight weeks every year in Singapore.

We decided to divide the production of the book by having Chowdhury manage the logistics of this work while I was to select the contributing authors and edit their chapters. Svlvia Tieri, Chowdhury's research associate, was enormously helpful in managing the production of the book during the first phase of the project. She helped both Chowdhury and I to organize and conduct a workshop in Singapore in the winter of 2017 at which several contributing authors presented the material they were preparing for the book. A follow-up seminar was held in Lahore at the Burki Institute of Public Policy (BIPP) in the spring of 2017 for most of those who did not attend ISAS workshop in Singapore.

The BIPP's work was handled with great competence by Asad Ejaz Butt, my associate, who not only co-authored with me a chapter in the book but was closely involved in editing the entire volume. He was also in direct communication with the editors at Routledge. I am enormously grateful to all of these individuals for making possible the production of what I believe will be an important contribution to Pakistan studies.

Shahid Javed Burki
Potomac, Maryland, USA
October 2018

Contributors

Shahid Javed Burki is an economist who has been a member of the faculty at Harvard University, USA, and Chief Economist, Planning and Development Department, Government of the Punjab. He has also served as Minister of Finance in the Government of Pakistan, and has written a number of books, and journal and newspaper articles. He joined the World Bank in 1974 as a senior economist and went on to serve in several senior positions. He was the (first) Director of the China Department (1987–94) and served as the Regional Vice-President for Latin America and the Caribbean during 1994–99. He is currently the Chair of the Board of Directors of the Shahid Javed Burki Institute of Public Policy at NetSol in Lahore.

Iftekhar Ahmed Chowdhury is a career Bangladeshi diplomat and former Minister for Foreign Affairs of Bangladesh (2007–08). He has a PhD in international relations from the Australian National University, Canberra. He began his career as a member of the civil service of Pakistan in 1969. Chowdhury has held senior diplomatic positions in the course of his career, including Permanent Representative of Bangladesh to the United Nations in New York (2001–07) and Geneva (1996–2001), and was ambassador to Qatar, Chile, Peru and the Vatican. He is currently a visiting senior research fellow at the Institute of South Asian Studies (ISAS), National University of Singapore.

Daud Ahmad is a retired World Bank member of staff with extensive experience of development and transport in East Asia, particularly China.

Mahmood Ahmad is adviser to the Shahid Javed Burki Institute of Public Policy at NetSol, Lahore, Pakistan, and Visiting Researcher at the Center for Water Informatics and Technology, Lahore University of Management Science. He is also a consultant to a number of international organizations, including FAO, the World Bank, the Asian Development Bank, USAID, JICA, the Aga Khan Foundation, the Mercy Corps and Shore Bank. He retired from FAO as Senior Policy Officer (Water), FAO Regional Office, Cairo, Egypt, after serving for 24 years providing policy support to countries in the Near East.

Khaled Ahmed is a political analyst and consulting editor of *Newsweek* Pakistan.

Kulsum Ahmed is Practice Manager in the Environment and Natural Resources Global Practice of the World Bank.

Masood Ahmed is a theoretical physicist.

Ziad Alahdad is the former Director of Operations and Lead Energy Specialist, World Bank.

Asad Ejaz Butt is an economist trained in Canada. He's currently the Director off the Burki Institute of Public Policy in Lahore. Before joining BIPP, Mr. Ejaz was member of the Economics faculty at the University of Central Punjab. He's also taken a number of consultancy assignments, most notably working with the United Nations Development Programme (UNDP) on its SDGs agenda for the province of Punjab and with ICF International, Canada on its energy efficiency and policy analytics division.

Ayub Ghauri is a business leader in the IT, education, electronic media and fashion sectors.

Riaz Hassan is Australian Research Council Professorial Fellow and Emeritus Professor, Department of Sociology, Flinders University, Australia.

Ishrat Husain is a former Dean of the Institute of Business Administration and a former Governor of the State Bank of Pakistan. He has worked at the World Bank.

Farrukh Iqbal works for the World Bank.

Farah Jan is a PhD student in Political Science, Rutgers University, USA.

Jehangir Karamat is a retired general, diplomat and former Professor of Political Science, National Defense University, Pakistan.

Shahid Kardar is a former Governor of the State Bank of Pakistan.

Nasreen Kasuri is the founder and Chair of Beaconhouse School System.

Aziz Ahmad Khan was High Commissioner of Pakistan to India (2003–06), and Pakistan's ambassador to Afghanistan.

Subrata K. Mitra is Professor and Director, Institute of South Asian Studies, National University of Singapore, and Visiting Research Professor, National University of Singapore.

Shahid Najam is Vice-Chairman of the Shahid Javed Burki Institute of Public Policy, Pakistan.

Muhammad Saleem Ahmad Ranjha is a Founding Director of Akhuwat and Federal Secretary of Benazir Income Support Program.

Shirin Tahir-Kheli is Senior Fellow, Foreign Policy Institute, Johns Hopkins University School of Advanced International Studies, USA. She served in senior positions at the White House and the Department of State for three US Presidents, including as Special Assistant to the President and as the first ambassador for women's empowerment. She has a PhD from the University of Pennsylvania and a BA from Ohio Wesleyan University.

1

An overview

Shahid Javed Burki

Introduction

This chapter, in addition to providing an overview of the content of this volume, explains why the editors, Iftekhar Ahmed Chowdhury and I, decided to collaborate on a book entitled *Pakistan at Seventy*. Both of us are associated with the Institute of South Asian Studies (ISAS), National University of Singapore, as senior research fellows. The institute decided to observe the 70th anniversary of the birth of Pakistan and India by sponsoring two volumes, one on each country, in which a number of contributors would be invited to write on the fields in which they specialized. This project was preceded by the publication of two working papers on Pakistan and India, respectively. The study on Pakistan was written by me, and that on India by Subrata Kumar Mitra, the director of ISAS. My study was published on 14 August 2017, Pakistan's birthday, and that by Mitra one day later, to coincide with the birth of India, Pakistan's sister state.[1] This overview will take a thematic approach rather than discussing each chapter in turn.

The Pakistan story

Chapter 2 in this volume, 'The Pakistan story', is based on the above-mentioned working paper on Pakistan but was rewritten and expanded to serve the purpose of introducing this book. It provides a brief overview of the country's turbulent political and economic history. It makes the point that as Pakistan enters the eighth decade of its existence as an independent state, its situation can be better appreciated if we look at how the country has travelled the distance from the time of its birth to the present 70 years later. Economists call this method of studying the present in terms of the past 'path dependence'.

The founding of Pakistan coincided with the arrival of eight million Muslim refugees who had to be accommodated in a population reduced to 26 million following the departure of six million Hindus and Sikhs from the country. The 14 million people who crossed the hastily demarcated border between India and Pakistan in a short period of time was perhaps the largest movement of people in human history. It has been suggested that such a large dislocation of people might not have occurred had the British exit from its former

Indian colony been better planned and not opted for what the historian Stanley Wolpert has called its 'shameful flight'.[2] The fact that such a large number of people were absorbed by Pakistan into a small population was a remarkable feat accomplished by a government that was still in the process of being formed in a new capital that had yet to be built.

Pakistan's difficulties were exacerbated by the hostile stance adopted by India's inaugural government, which was led by Prime Minister Jawaharlal Nehru, who bitterly opposed the partition of the Indian subcontinent. New Delhi seemed determined to strangle its sister-state at birth – or so the people and the government of Pakistan believed. The Indian government cut off the supply of power to Lahore, at that time Pakistan's largest city. The city was receiving some of its power requirements from a coal-fired plant that was now on the other side of border. India also attempted to block the flow of water into the irrigation system that watered agriculture in Pakistan.[3] Two years after the birth of Pakistan, New Delhi imposed a trade embargo on Pakistan that resulted in a significant structural change in the economy. The severing of trade ties also broke the bond that had once tightly linked the economies of the two countries that were now independent India and Pakistan. Following the trade blockade, Pakistan went on its own way and developed an economy that became totally independent of India.

This chapter, by taking a long-term view of the development of the economy, endeavours to dispel the notion that Pakistan has been an economic failure while India has enjoyed considerable success. With an average rate of growth of 4.6 per cent per annum during the period 1947–2017, Pakistan was one of the fastest expanding economies in the developing world. By the time the country celebrated its 70th birthday the size of its economy was 25 times larger than at the time of its birth. The size of the industrial sector had increased one hundredfold. In 2017 the population was 6.5 times its size at the time of the country's birth. The number of people living in poverty in 1947 was estimated at 20 million. Seventy years later, when the population had increased by 176 million persons, the proportion of the poor in the population had declined from 80 per cent to 20 per cent. This was another aspect of the positive developments that have taken place since 1947.

There are a number of 'what ifs?' in telling the Pakistan story. This chapter asks 'what would have happened to the community of Indian Muslims had the British not partitioned its Indian colony into predominantly Hindu India and predominantly Muslim Pakistan?' 'What would have happened if Karachi not been chosen as Pakistan's first capital?' 'What would have happened had Pakistan followed India in quickly adopting a constitution?' What would have happened if Liaquat Ali Khan, Pakistan's first Prime Minister, had not been assassinated in October 1951?' 'What would have happened if relations between India and Pakistan had not soured to the point where most economic contacts between the two countries were suspended and have remained that way for almost 70 years?' 'What would have happened if Sheikh Mujibur Rehman, whose political party won the first election in the country's history in 1970, had been allowed to become Prime Minister?'

In the concluding part of the chapter, I offer some thoughts about what could happen to the country in the eighth decade of its independence and what Pakistan might look like when it celebrates its 80th birthday in 2027.

Politics, theory and practice

The first part of the volume concludes with Chapter 4 by Shirin Tahir-Kheli. She is a US citizen of Pakistani origin and has served in a number of senior positions in the US government. She was her adopted country's ambassador to the United Nations (UN) and now acts as a consultant for a number of Washington-based think tanks. She and I collaborated on a short book on Pakistan's relations with the United States.[4]

Tahir-Kheli picks up on my analysis of Pakistan's troubled start, noting the absence from the Pakistani political scene of a 'first leader' who could have taken the country forward. In Jawaharlal Nehru India had such a person, and he served as Prime Minister from 1947 to 1964. 'Pakistan was in particular need of an overarching father figure/first leader to draw together the myriad parts of a tribal or parochial society to help the nation to navigate between the competing interests of regions and to propose the compromises necessary for the establishment of a vibrant and successful state', she writes.

Pakistan suffered not one but two blows soon after the country's birth. Muhammad Ali Jinnah, the country's founding father, died on 11 September 1948. Three years later, Liaquat Ali Khan, the country's first Prime Minister and Jinnah's acknowledged second-in-command, was assassinated. Why he was murdered remains a mystery to this day. However, his death left a void that politicians were unable to fill for decades to come. 'Political Science literature gives great credibility to the importance of leadership in nation building', continues Tahir-Kheli. 'The histories of many nations of the post-colonial era demonstrate the need for early agreement on the rules of the game following independence. In Pakistan's political development, the process was made complicated by Liaquat's death'.

What exactly is the role that leaders play in the lives of nations, especially at their formative stage? Tahir-Kheli answers this question by borrowing from the reflections of Condoleezza Rice, the former US Secretary of State, with whom she worked at the White House during the presidency of George W. Bush. Rice points to the importance of institutions in nation building, calling them the 'scaffolding for democracy'. According to Rice, a more 'ethnically homogenous population is likely to find it easier to achieve stability. And if civil society – all the private, non-governmental groups, associations, and institutions in the country – is already well developed, the scaffolding for the new democracy is stronger.'[5] In the late 1940s Pakistan did not have such a scaffolding, nor does it now.

When the process of institutional development goes off track it hinders political progress. This is what happened in Pakistan. Unlike India, Pakistan did not inherit a well-developed system of governance. When the British vacated the subcontinent they left behind a well-functioning system of government in New Delhi supported by the renowned Indian Civil Service (ICS), once described as the 'steel frame' upon which London had built its Indian administrative structure.[6] That was not the case in Pakistan. The new country inherited a number of ICS personnel but did not have politicians with experience of governance. India started from a stronger base since a large number of the members of the Indian National Congress – the party of Mahatma Gandhi and Jawaharlal Nehru – had served in provincial administrations that enjoyed some autonomy. The only Muslim-dominated provincial government was in the province of Punjab, but there the Unionist Party governed. The Unionists had opposed the idea of Pakistan. It is not surprising that in politically weak Pakistan, within a few years of the founding of the state, the military was welded to the steel frame of the civil service. The result was a system that proved to be durable but which inhibited political development.

Tahir-Kheli and Jehangir Karamat examine the role of the military in Pakistan's politics in their respective chapters. Karamat, a former Chief of the Army Staff from 1993 to 1996, is well placed to write on the subject. In Chapter 6, 'Sustained political progress: the supportive role of the military', Karamat makes five important points. First, the military leadership, in filling its ranks at all levels, has moved away from the approach adopted by the British when they used what is now Pakistan as the main recruiting ground for their army in India. 'From its inherited legacy of selective recruitment based on the lore of the "martial tribes" during the British colonial era, the military now recruits from across the country and from all segments of the population and without discrimination', he writes. In this respect the military represents the citizenry it defends. However, that does not imply that the military and the institution's leadership has bought the increasingly conservative Islamic ideology Pakistan seems to have adopted. The military was protected from the palpable moves towards Islamic conservatism that resulted from the policies adopted and actions taken by one of its own leaders, General Muhammad Zia ul-Haq, Pakistan's third military President. This was possible because military's strong training institutions that mould and train those who join the armed services are able to infuse in the new recruits' culture and beliefs.

Second, the military's role in Pakistan goes beyond the task of defending the country's borders. Karamat argues that the military, largely on account of the areas in which it must have a strong presence, has gotten involved in the activities that are not its primary responsibility. 'The military facilities in the remote areas are the only ones available to the population there and these include education and health facilities', he writes.

Karamat's third point will be of particular interest for those studying Pakistan's political progress and its international relations. While the military, having directly governed the country for almost half of its life, has pulled back, it is believed by many that it still wields considerable influence on policymaking in many areas. Some observers and analysts are convinced that the military encouraged the judiciary to remove Prime Minister Nawaz Sharif from office in July 2017 and forced the courts to order the National Accountability Bureau to investigate how the deposed leader was able to accumulate expensive assets abroad. Sharif's removal was conducted under Article 62 of the Constitution which stipulates that whoever holds the position of Prime Minister must display good conduct and character. 'The bell is now tolling for Mr. Sharif', declared the influential weekly the *Friday Times* in an editorial. 'Every time he has hand-picked an army chief or the Inter-Services Intelligence (ISI) chief, both have wilted under pressure from their institution to stand up to him and establish their independence.' In fact, in order to describe the power play that was under way when this article was being written, the magazine coined the term 'Miltablishment' to identify those institutions that were refusing to be guided by elected leaders.[7]

Karamat would like to see the contacts between the civilian and military authorities be formalized. He was responsible for the creation of the Council for Defense and National Security (CDNS) while he was the army chief and Farooq Leghari was President. The CDNS laid the basis for several future institutional developments. Karamat writes approvingly of the appointment of the National Security Adviser, the establishment of a National Security Secretariat and the creation of a National Security Council. This was done during the third tenure of Prime Minister Sharif.

Karamat's fourth point relates to the numerous important contributions that the military has made to economic development. This is particularly the case in the long-troubled tribal areas bordering Afghanistan. Finally, he points to the successful operations launched by the military to clear the tribal areas of the sanctuaries established by a number of terrorist organizations. There is some resentment among the military circles that this costly effort – costly in terms of the lives lost – was not appreciated by the United States. In fact, as I point out in Chapter 10 which looks at Pakistan's external relations, many of those in senior positions in Pakistan were unable to comprehend why the new US President, Donald Trump, had launched an attack on Pakistan in his statement of 21 August

2017 at the same time as announcing his administration's new Afghan policy. Trump continued to attack Pakistan as he headed towards the first anniversary of his presidency. In his first tweet of 2018, he condemned 'Pakistan's deceit' in responding to American pleas for cooperation.

Religion, as might be expected in a country created to 'save Islam' in the South Asian subcontinent, has played an important role in Pakistan's political history. Riaz Hassan, an Australian sociologist of Pakistani origin, covers this subject in Chapter 5, 'Islam, society and politics in Pakistan'. The idea of Pakistan was opposed by most religious parties as the British began the process of disengaging themselves from their Indian colony. Among conservative elements in political Islam, the objective was to move towards the creation of an Ummah, a worldwide Islamic political entity. According to this line of thinking, nationalism such as that espoused by Jinnah, stood in the way of developing the Ummah. However, once Pakistan won independence, the Islamists turned their attention towards creating an Islamic Pakistan. Initially this fight was led by Alama Abul ala Maududi, a highly respected Islamic scholar whose reputation extended beyond Pakistan. While Maududi had founded his organization in a city that went to India when the province of Punjab was partitioned, he moved to Pakistan after the country was created. Had he stayed on in the Indian Punjab he might have been able to help the community of Muslims that remained behind. As Hassan has discussed elsewhere, there are some ways in which the Indian Muslims have fared less well compared to those who were to become citizens of Pakistan and Bangladesh.[8]

Maududi and his party focused their attention on turning Islam into an exclusive religious entity that would admit as Muslims only those who followed their interpretation of the religion. One of the targets of their campaign was the Ahmadiya community, the followers of Mirza Ghulam Ahmad who had claimed prophethood in defiance of Islam's strong adherence to the concept of Khatam-e-Nabuwat, namely that the Prophet Muhammad was the last in a long line of prophets. An anti-Ahmadiya movement launched by Maududi in the mid-1950s resulted in violence and led to the proclamation of martial law in Punjab. This marked the first time that the military was called out to enforce civil power. Two decades after this episode, Prime Minister Zulfikar Ali Bhutto obliged the national assembly to adopt a resolution declaring the Ahmadis to be non-Muslims. Bhutto, a secular-minded politician, took this step to curry favour with the Islamists. The same approach was followed by General Zia ul-Haq, who wrested power from Bhutto.

The role of Islam in Pakistan – in its political system and in the way it defines the nation itself – remains unfinished business in the country. There are a number of issues that have yet to be resolved, including the question of 'who is a Muslim?' While the Pakistani parliament voted to declare the Ahmadis as non-Muslims in 1974, the status of the Shiites remains a source of contention. Should the state impose on its citizens what the majority – or those who are more militant and prepared to resort to violence to have their way – believe are the basic tenets of Islam? If force is to be used, should that involve the military and if that were to happen would it result in the armed forces re-entering the political domain?

These questions surface regularly and affect Pakistan's political and economic progress. In November 2017 protesters seized control of the main highway interchange that connects the twin cities of Islamabad and Rawalpindi. At the heart of the protest was a proposal by the Minister of Law and Justice, Zahid Hamid, to make a small change to the oath administered to the members of the national assembly upon taking their seats. The protest caused chaos in both cities. Following an order by the high court to clear the intersection, the government tried to force the demonstrators to leave. The government failed in its attempt and asked the military for help. However, army leaders formally asked the civilian authority to clarify the role of troops in the event of further civilian unrest. It was 'apparently concerned about losing public support'.[9] The main protest leader, Allama Khadim Hussian Rizvi, told journalists at the site of the protest that the group would negotiate only if the government removed Hamid from office. The government, after initially resisting the protesters' demands, capitulated and allowed Hamid to resign from his post.

Hassan goes on to distinguish between two strands of Islam that have impacted Pakistani politics: Sufism and Scripturalism. 'The conflict between these two traditions of Pakistan Islam is now manifesting itself in the increasing violent sectarian conflicts as well as the ethnic-based insurgencies in Pakistan that are posing a serious threat to the country's social and political stability', he writes.

In recent years, the media in Pakistan has made significant contributions to political development, a subject covered in this volume by Khalid Ahmed, one of Pakistan's most accomplished journalists. He began his professional career as a member of Pakistan's Foreign Service but left to take up journalism. He was one of the main contributors to the Lahore-based news magazine, the *Friday Times*. Ahmed has written extensively on the subject of the rise of Islamic extremism in the country including a book on which he worked as a visiting scholar at the Washington-based Woodrow Wilson Institute.[10] In Chapter 7 he traces the development of the media in the country and shows how it is now contributing to the country's drift towards extremism. He notes that following independence, Pakistan's print media mainly appeared in English but this domination was soon lost to Urdu as its status as the national language became unchallenged. With the domination of TV, both Urdu and English in the print media have suffered a decline. English is now read by a very small percentage of the population, while Urdu dominates the print market.

Owing to the rise of the new middle class and rural to urban migration, the segment of the population that mans the army, the media and educational institutions remains conservative and is heavily involved in religious politics. Anyone who is not perceived to be deeply conservative is condemned as 'liberal'. Following the rise of the middle class, a similar concern has been voiced by the seasoned liberals in India. Urdu journalism is controlled by madrasas, the 'proxy warriors' or state-sponsored militias, the conservative middle class, and the army, and most of this control is spontaneous. However, rebellious journalists can be punished not only by the Taliban, al-Qaeda and society at large, but also by the solidly middle-class army officers.

An increasing number of young men from conservative rural-based families have joined organized underground groups with affiliations to international terrorist outfits in order to implement their agenda of change through violence. They threaten and kill journalists whom they consider to be un-Islamic. In addition, college and university campuses are dominated by religious parties who oppose tendencies towards free expression in the media.

The polarity between the English- and Urdu-language press (unlike India, there are no English TV channels in Pakistan except for the state-owned 'external publicity' stations) is now extreme, if not mutually hostile. What gets published in English can't be published in Urdu.

Extremism has grown out of nationalism and ideology and finds natural expression in Urdu. With its rational-sequential discourse the English language is not a good vehicle for nationalism and extremism. The trend for condemnation by politicians of English-medium education has sprung from this clash of idioms.

A weak economy affects the efficiency of the free media which can only survive under capitalism and as 'business'. It is easy for a conservative army to control the media through handouts of cash and other material benefits, especially since the recipient is already wedded to the same conservative worldview. Rebels can be killed via 'proxy warrior' elements. The army is also said to kidnap 'liberal' bloggers who use the media to propagate their worldview.

Just as Pakistan's fourth military President, the liberal General Pervez Musharraf, could not punish the conservative army officers who tried to kill him, it is also difficult to defend the punishment of killers under 'blasphemy law' in the Urdu media. Anyone opposing the law is considered to have blasphemed. The media remains divided and opposition to blasphemy law can only be voiced in English.

The polarization between army and government has had a negative effect on the freedom of the media. Almost half of all the TV channels are vigorously anti-government. In the past, such 'politically' partisan TV channels opposed the government but not as vehemently as they do now, as a result of the alleged cash handouts and backing from the army where, incidentally, the military's Inter-Services Public Relations operation has a big budget. In August 2018 Imran Khan was elected as Prime Minister of Pakistan, and supporters of his party, Tehreek-e-Insaf, adhere so clearly to this view of affairs that it has become public knowledge.

Pakistan's dependence on the outside world

Part 2 of this book examines Pakistan's evolving relations with the world. It should be stressed that much that has taken place in Pakistan during the past 70 years is the outcome of the way the country has reacted to the world beyond its borders. Pakistan's relations with India, the United States, China, Saudi Arabia and Afghanistan are covered in depth in this volume. The impact of Pakistan's policymaking on the other countries is examined in Chapter 9. The assumption is that policymaking with respect to one has had an influence on the others. The theoretical underpinning of the analyses of these relationships is provided by Iftekhar Ahmed Chowdhury, the co-editor of this volume.

In Chapter 8 Chowdhury maintains that we live in a rapidly changing world. Old paradigms of international relations are shifting. Traditional alliances are changing. Tensions in many parts of the world are increasing. At the same time some hotspots and flashpoints are cooling down. Age-old linkages are being loosened. However, Pakistan remains a country very much in focus. Indeed, for a variety of reasons, throughout its chequered history, it has continued to attract global attention for both positive and negative reasons. Chowdhury seeks to explain the nature of Pakistan's relations with the rest of the world as clearly as possible, and he considers whether some general extrapolations might be made regarding the behaviour of other states in a comparable milieu.

Chowdhury examines a number of foreign policy models to fit Pakistan's external relations. Some models are more relevant for developed countries, and others for developing countries. The chapter concludes that in the case of Pakistan, its socio-economic features reflect those of both developed and developing countries intertwining with a complexity that renders any single model of analysis difficult. Consequently, Chowdhury argues that what evolved would most appropriately apply to Pakistan. It was a 'model mix', with empiricism as the dominant factor.

Chowdhury identifies the three-fold objectives of Pakistan's external policy. The first is to close up the power gap with India; the second is to access the external resources it requires to facilitate the country's growth and development; and the third is to expand its manoeuverability in terms of policymaking, while keeping its 'sense of sovereignty' intact.

These objectives have led Pakistan to follow policies that rest upon on four pillars. The first of these pillars is its relationship with the United States in particular, and the West in general. The second is its 'all-weather' ties with China. The third is its linkages with the Islamic countries. The fourth is its interactions with multilateral bodies, in particular with the United Nations and the International Monetary Fund (IMF).

The chapter goes on to describe and analyse in broad strokes each of these pillars, before identifying the centrality of South Asia. The Partition of 1947 and British colonial policies have caused the historical relations among South Asian states to be fraught with distrust. The division of colonial India was planned in haste and consequently there a number of conflicts took place between the two major protagonists in the region, India and Pakistan. These included the irredentist issues over Kashmir and the failure to anticipate and reconcile the fissiparous problem of Bangladesh which led to the war of 1971.

The chapter concludes by advancing a concept of 'trilateralism' between India, Pakistan and Bangladesh. It seeks to emphasise how this novel idea could help not only to reduce tensions but also to enable the South Asian nations to progress in a 'flying geese formation' paradigm for the benefit of all South Asian peoples. For now, this idea may seem beyond reach, but it is worth trying.

As Chowdury indicates in his analysis, ever since its birth 70 years ago, Pakistan has been more dependent on the outside world for support than is the case for most developing countries. One of the main reasons for this is the country's inability to access its own resources to finance development. For this reason the volume examines Pakistan's relations with the countries which had the resources or the interest to provide capital to it. Before dealing with inter-country relations, however, we identify some of the influences on the making of foreign policy.

In Chapter 9, Aziz Ahmad Khan, a former Pakistani diplomat who served as ambassador to Afghanistan and as High Commissioner in India, looks at the development and changing parameters of Pakistan's foreign policy. He begins by recollecting that the initial framework for Pakistan's foreign policy was articulated by the father of the nation, Muhammad Ali Jinnah. He declared that 'our foreign policy is one of friendliness and goodwill towards all the nations of the world'. Pakistan pursued this policy by adhering to the UN Charter, fostering good relations with all UN member states, supporting human rights, and seeking peaceful resolutions to all disputes.

Khan distinguishes several influences on the making of foreign policy: those in leadership positions; experienced diplomats serving in senior positions in the Ministry of Foreign Affairs; some think tanks that focus on the formulation of foreign policy; and last, but not least, the positions adopted towards Pakistan by the countries of interest to Pakistan. The focus of his chapter is on the first three.

Khan discusses the contributions to the making of foreign policy by some of the other leaders who followed Jinnah. They also left their imprint on Pakistan's relations with the world. Liaquat Ali Khan, Pakistan's first Prime Minister, pointed Pakistan in the direction of the United States, visiting Washington even though he had also been invited by Moscow. General Ayub Khan, Pakistan's first military President, signed a number of formal agreements with the United States. These included the Central Treaty Organization (CENTO) and the Southeast Asia Treaty Organization (SEATO). In fact, Pakistan was the link between these two treaties. Zulfikar Ali Bhutto who served Ayub Khan as a minister pulled Pakistan away from the United States and brought it closer to China, a policy for which the ground was prepared by the former general, President Yahya Khan. This swing towards China was to have significant consequences for the country. The two military leaders who followed Bhutto moved the focus back to the United States. However, relations with Washington were never easy. Khan explains what lay behind these individual preferences.

There was also considerable analytical input in the design of foreign policy, mostly from those who had served the country as ambassadors. The members of the Foreign Service acquired both experience and knowledge of the outside world. Some of the institutions linked to the Foreign Ministry played an important role in the making of policy. However, Khan points out that it is only in recent years that politics have entered the foreign policy arena. This was not the case when the men in uniform were in charge and were able to bring about sharp changes in the making of policy without paying much attention to public opinion.

The India–Pakistan rivalry dominated South Asian politics for 70 years. Pakistan's foreign policy was shaped and guided by its (in)security concerns vis-à-vis the India threat. On 28 and 30 May 1998 Pakistan tested six nuclear devices in the mountains of Balochistan, thereby officially becoming a nuclear weapons state. In Chapter 12 Farah Jan explores a range of factors and events that led to the decision by Pakistan to invest in nuclear weapons technology in order to acquire the bomb. The basis for Pakistan's quest for nuclear weapons is directly linked to its rivalry with India. The decision was based on Pakistan's need for internal balance, or what international relations scholar John Mearsheimer would call self-help, against India. The relationship between India and Pakistan over the past 70 years has consistently been marked by conflict, and for this reason Pakistan needed to maintain a defence capability comparable to that of India. Thus, possession of a nuclear deterrent became the inevitable response to this problem.

Jan argues that nuclear weapons have had a significant impact on the India–Pakistan rivalry. Nuclear weapons have cemented the status quo, by intensifying the mutual vulnerability dilemma whereby both countries are capable of destroying what the other values, marked by a heightened perception of threat and distrust on both sides. However, the major point of conflict – the issue of Kashmir – between the two nuclear rivals remains unresolved, over which both sides have revisionist aims. Pakistan's revisionism is spatial in nature and is unsatisfied with the status quo in Kashmir. India's revisionism is positional, is linked with the Chinese influence in South Asia and the region at large and is unsatisfied by playing second best to China in its regional hegemony ambitions.[11]

Up until Pakistan's 70th birthday, Islamabad looked to Washington for support. Help came when the United States took an interest in Pakistan for its own strategic reasons. This changed when Donald Trump became President of the United States. Even before Trump took up residence in the White House, Pakistan's relations with the United States were complex. There were many ups and downs; relations cooled and warmed depending mostly on Washington's strategic needs. On three occasions, the United States walked away, leaving Pakistan to its own devices. This happened in 1965 when Pakistan fought one of its many wars with India; in 1988 when the Soviet Union pulled out of Afghanistan and Pakistan was not needed any longer as a partner to keep in check the advance of Communist power in Asia; and in 1998 when Pakistan defied US pressure not to test nuclear weapons and indicated its intention to develop and accumulate a large arsenal of nuclear bombs along with the medium-range missiles that could launch them.

The United States reached out to Pakistan in September 2001 when it sought Islamabad's support in opposing the Taliban regime in Kabul. The Taliban had not only encouraged the Al-Qaeda leader Osama bin Laden, to establish a base in Afghanistan, but also looked the other way when bin Laden's supporters launched devastating terrorist attacks on the United States. Pakistan provided the support the United States needed but Washington felt it did not do enough. In 2017 the United States threatened not only to leave Pakistan again but to punish it as well. Nicki Haley, the US ambassador to the UN and a person of Indian descent, suggested that India should 'keep an eye' on Pakistan. In early 2018 Washington announced the suspension of most aid including military assistance to Islamabad.

Washington's earlier departures worked since they were the result of what the Americans regarded as missions accomplished In the late 1960s Washington saw that it had succeeded in blocking the advance of Communism in Asia. In the late 1980s it was happy with the humiliation suffered by Moscow in its Afghanistan adventure. In the late 1990s the United States was taking what it believed was a principled position on the spread of nuclear weapons. This time around – the occasion of the fourth US exit from Pakistan – it appeared that the rift between the two countries had deepened to the point that the Americans would stay out for a very long time. Also, it was very unlikely that the new Afghan policy would work and that the country would be pulled together again and governed from Kabul.

As I discuss in Chapter 10, Washington's stance with respect to Pakistan has added another difficult dimension to Islamabad-New Delhi relations. The US position articulated by President Trump on 21 August 2017 with reference to Washington's new approach towards concluding its involvement in Afghanistan suggested that Pakistan was one of the main reasons for America's difficulties in that country. In 2017 Trump singled out Pakistan's alleged support for terrorist organizations including al-Qaeda as a factor in Washington's inability to extract itself from Afghanistan where it had been militarily engaged for more than 16 years. The US–Afghan conflict is the longest war the United States has fought in its history. Islamabad believes that Washington supports the New Delhi view on Pakistan and terrorism and therefore the United States has avoided negotiations with Islamabad that might bring about an improvement in its relations with its northern neighbour.

The military solution on which the United States embarked in early 2017 was unlikely to bring peace to Afghanistan. A negotiated settlement was needed. In it the groups that have rebelled against Kabul will have to be brought in as full partners in the process of governance. China was likely to play the role of a leader in this effort, working with a number of other countries in the area, most notably Pakistan, Iran and Turkey. In a book co-written with two colleagues from the ISAS in Singapore we suggested a mechanism involving a number of countries in the area to oversee the preparation and implementation of a programme aimed at bringing durable stability to Afghanistan.[12]

It appears that Pakistan's difficult relations with the United States may influence its growing links with China, with which Islamabad has maintained a steady relationship. There have been no ups and downs in this relationship as was the case with relations with the United States. That said, the reason why the two countries stayed steady on their course had a great deal to do with their own strategic compulsions. Pakistan initially reached out to Washington – Liaquat Ali Khan, the country's first Prime Minister, chose to go to Washington rather than to Moscow upon being invited by both – in order to obtain badly needed financial and military support. Capital was needed to speed up the pace of economic development. Military assistance was required to balance India's growing military strength. However, it soon became clear to the Pakistani leadership that the United States was less inclined to pay much heed to Pakistan's needs. It was much more interested in pursuing its own interests. This approach found clear expression in

Donald Trump's slogan, 'America First'. Beijing, on the other hand, was much more interested in basing its contacts with Islamabad with the clear intention of not allowing any surprises to affect the relationship.

China has helped Pakistan in a number of ways. The form that Beijing's help took is detailed at some length in *Eating Grass* by Feroze Khan who worked in the military unit that kept a close watch on Pakistan's efforts to acquire nuclear weapons.[13] The title of the book draws on the statement by Prime Minister Bhutto when in 1974 India exploded a nuclear device. Bhutto declared that Pakistan would match India's nuclear weapons programme even if that meant the country would 'eat grass'. Pakistan's perennial resource shortage meant that sacrifices would have to be made in order to match India. A quarter of a century later, by testing six nuclear devices, Pakistan delivered on Bhutto's promise.

Now, once again, China is reaching out to the world but this time in a different way. Compared to its overtures to the West following the visit by President Richard Nixon in 1972, China's new opening has a different geographic orientation. Then Pakistan played an important role. It is once again involved as Beijing is opening itself to the West in a different way. It has put its faith in land-based commerce to provide a different set of stimuli to its economy. What the World Bank in a 1993 study called the 'East Asian miracle' model has run its course.[14]

Work associated with the One Belt, One Road initiative is progressing steadily in Pakistan. Results will become visible in the next few years as China's initiative knits together the countries of Central and West Asia. While Trump's approach to South Asia would result in diminishing his country's presence in the subcontinent, that of China would increase significantly. It is also unlikely that the United States would succeed in building up India as a counterforce to the growing strength of China. Rex Tillerson, the US Secretary of State, described what his government was trying to achieve in Asia as Trump set out on his Asia trip in November 2017. He proposed a 'free and open Indo-Pacific' area in which Australia, India, Japan and possibly even Vietnam would help to counter China's maritime expansion. However, the idea is bankrupt if America is opposed to free and open trade. As *The Economist* reported on Trump's Asia visit, 'an administration more clear-eyed about what is at stake for America would have taken more seriously China's belt-and-road initiative, linking Asia by land and sea to the Middle East and beyond'.[15]

In Chapter 11 Farah Jan discusses Pakistan's relationship with Saudi Arabia over the past 70 years. Jan delineates Pakistan's relationship with Saudi Arabia along three central themes: religion, economy and security. After tracing the history of the Pakistan-Saudi Arabia alliance, Jan focuses on the critical junctures and major events that have impacted, defined and frustrated this relationship, first addressing the religious dimension and its related security implications starting in the 1960s, through the Afghan war, and beyond. In contrast to the religious, historical and cultural bond, the economic and security side of the relationship were and remain transactional in nature. The chapter investigates how the security and migrant labour needs of Saudi Arabia (with remittances topping US $7 billion and 1.9 million Pakistani workers in the Kingdom) initiated and cemented this partnership.

The chapter elaborates on how great power politics in South Asia and the Middle East shaped and constrained the perceptions of common interests between Saudi Arabia and Pakistan. It addresses the turbulence of the formative days of Pakistan-Saudi relations, expanding on the regional context that prompted Pakistan to sign the Baghdad Pact in 1955, which led to King Saud openly criticizing Pakistan in a meeting with Prime Minister Nehru during the Suez Canal crisis in 1956. The chapter then focuses on the early

1960s when Ayub Khan visited Riyadh and discussed the critical defence and security needs of Saudi Arabia, paving the way for a long-term training and advisory role for Pakistan with Saudi Arabia's Internal and Defense Ministries. The defence and security relationship is then traced from 1961, when Pakistan supplied arms to the Saudi-backed loyalist forces in Yemen, and later in 1967 signed the first official agreement to train Saudi armed forces. The chapter expands on the mutual commitment of Pakistan to the territorial integrity of Saudi Arabia, and vice versa, and how Kashmir remains a cornerstone of this understanding. There follows a discussion on the absence of a formal alliance treaty, and explains the observable resilience and evolution of this relationship in the face of regional and systemic transitions. The chapter concludes with a short assessment of how this long-lasting relationship might be affected by some of the policies adopted by the new Crown Prince, Mohammad bin Salman. MBS, as he is commonly referred to, has hardened his country's stance towards Iran as Pakistan is attempting to base its relations with the Shiite neighbour on solid footing.

Economic development and the importance of good governance

In Chapter 16 of this volume, Farrukh Iqbal, who after retiring from the World Bank accepted the position of director of the Karachi-based Institute of Business Administration, has provided a chapter on 'Recent economic developments and prospects', in which he offers a balanced view of the current situation in Pakistan and its future prospects. Iqbal notes that the rate of growth in the economy picked up and averaged 4.5 per cent during the period 2014–17. In discussing the immediate future, Iqbal reflects on the loosening of fiscal strings that might result following the general election that took place in November 2018. On a positive note, he also considers the likely impact of the investments that are coming into the country as a consequence of the China–Pakistan Economic Corridor (CPEC), the subject of Daud Ahmad's contribution to the volume (see Chapter 13). The CPEC investments could add US $13 billion to Pakistan's gross domestic product (GDP) in the first seven years following its inception. The programme may 'crowd in' other investments as the community of investors take cognizance of the full potential of the CPEC. However, while noting the positive impact of the Chinese programme, Iqbal is concerned about whether the significant amount of additional power generation could be carried to the areas of high demand. 'There remain concerns about the technical and financial ability of Pakistan's power distribution companies to pass through the increased power supply in an efficient and timely manner', he says.

Ishrat Husain who, like several other contributors to this volume, spent a good part of his working life at the World Bank, has written on economic governance. Upon taking early retirement from the Bank, he returned to Pakistan and was appointed Governor of the State Bank of Pakistan, the country's central bank. After serving there for six years, he assumed the post of Director of the Institute of Business Administration. In 2006–08 he chaired the National Commission for Government Reforms that 'made exhaustive recommendations in the structure, human resource policies, business practices' in the federal, provincial and local governments (see Chapter 17 in this volume). The report was well received but not implemented. Husain believes that the report found its way to the government's shelves where it rests along with so many reform documents prepared by other Commissions, Task Forces and Committees. Once again powerful interests who would have been hurt had the proposed reforms been implemented prevailed.

Husain argues that Pakistan's relatively poor performance in recent years is the result of poor governance. The quality of governance has deteriorated over time. He believes that it was not the stop-and-go flow of foreign funds that produced the roller coaster ride in the performance of the economy but the way in which the country was governed that is the most important determinant of that performance. He cites a 2003 IMF study that found a statistically significant impact on GDP per head across 93 countries in which the quality of governance was used as a determining variable. This explained 75 per cent of the variations between countries in income per head. A 2010 Asian Development Bank study shows that developing Asian economies with government effectiveness, regulatory quality and rule of law scored well above the global mean. Husain believes that if sweeping government reforms are not possible, what may be more practical is a limited approach that deals sequentially with the various government institutions, starting first with those that have greater impact on the economy and are more consequential for the lives of the citizenry.

Locating funding in appropriate quantity and that did not impose an excessive long-term burden on the government and hence on the people has been an important preoccupation of policymakers in Pakistan. Following the passage of the 18th amendment to the Constitution, policymakers in the provinces will also have to pay attention to the financial side of the development equation. The amendment adopted in July 2015 devolved a number of functions that were previously the responsibility of the federal government. However, devolution did not come with financial planning. The provinces have been left to their own devices to find the resources that added to those available from the federal government's 'divisible pool'. The pool is the money that Islamabad collects on behalf of the provinces and then distributes according to a formula worked out by the National Finance Commissions. The Constitution requires these Commissions to be appointed by the President every five years. Chaired by the federal finance minister they have representation from all the provinces.

Social underdevelopment

It is widely recognized both within and outside the country that Pakistan has done poorly in maintaining development appropriate to its large and rapidly growing population. The underdevelopment of the country's large and young human resource will have serious consequences for its future. The population census carried out in early 2017 produced some findings that surprised many policymakers, economists and demographers. It showed the population to be much larger than was generally assumed. Estimated at 208 million, Pakistan's population is growing at a rate much higher than the government had factored into its activities. The *Pakistan Economic Survey, 2016–17* assumed the rate of population growth at 1.8 per cent.[16] The census estimated it at 2.4 per cent, a rate 33 per cent larger than the government's working assumption. This means that Pakistan has not arrived at the stage of demographic transition already reached by other South Asian nations, in particular Bangladesh.

As discussed in a study I co-authored with Riaz Hassan, there is much Pakistan can learn from the experience of Bangladesh. The impressive demographic transition of that country owed a great deal to the improvements in the economic social situation of the country's female workforce. The development of the garment industry played an important role; it provided not only jobs for women but also increased the incentive for families to send their daughters to school. These developments contributed significantly to reducing the rate of human fertility in the country. Bangladesh's total fertility rate is close to reaching the replacement rate.[17]

As a result of the rapid rate of growth over the last several decades, Pakistan has one of the world's youngest populations. The median age is estimated at only 24 years which means that 104 million people in the country are below that age.[18] The country's youth have aspirations which, if not met, can result in the type of social turbulence witnessed the Middle East. There the youth were behind the Arab Spring of 2011 that resulted in the overthrow of a number of long-enduring authoritarian regimes. It also contributed to the Syrian Civil War that has been the most costly conflict in terms of lives lost since the Second World War. Meeting the youth's hopes would mean equipping them with the skills to participate in the modern sectors of the economy. The four authors who have contributed chapters to Part 4 of this volume share the view that the persistent weakness of the Pakistani state means that the private entrepreneurs need to step forward to educate the country's youth as well as to improve its health care. The incentive for private involvement is not entirely for making profit. As Adil Najam, a scholar of Pakistani origin, has pointed out in his work on philanthropy in Pakistan, private giving is an important part of the development of private enterprise in health and education.[19]

Chapter 21, 'Private sector in education', by Shahid Kardar, and Chapter 22, 'Educating and employing women', by Nasreen Kasuri, provide data on the dismal state of education in the Pakistan. Kardar is currently the Vice-Chancellor of the private Beaconhouse National University and Kasuri is the founder of the Beaconhouse School system, one of the largest educational institutions in the world. There are 286,200 students enrolled in institutions located in 35 cities. The two authors cite a number of statistics to highlight Pakistan's poor performance in educating its population, in particular its women. Of the 775 million illiterate adults in the world, 50 million live in Pakistan. The literacy rate for those aged 10 years and above is estimated at 60 per cent, 70 per cent for boys and 49 per cent for girls. Female literacy in rural areas stood at 38 per cent compared to male literacy at 63 per cent. In urban areas the figures were 69 per cent for females and 82 per cent for males. The UN 2016 *Global Education Monitoring Report* suggests that Pakistan is at least 50 years behind its primary education targets and more than 60 years behind its secondary education targets. The 2017 *Global Human Capital Report* ranks Pakistan's Human Capital Index at 125, compared with Sri Lanka at 70, Nepal at 98, India at 103 and Bangladesh at 111. Women's education needs special attention.

This situation is of concern to policymakers both in Islamabad and the provincial capitals. Over the years, a number of policy statements have been issued and a number of programmes were drawn up but little progress has been made. The main reason is poor implementation in part because of the level of corruption in the provincial education departments that have the responsibility for carrying out government's policies. In the 1990s the World Bank, in association with a number of Western donors, launched the multi-billion-dollar Social Action Programme (SAP) with the aim of jump-starting social development in the country. The SAP, after making several poor starts, was abandoned largely because of corruption. Some of this was the result of political interference: powerful politicians used SAP resources to hire workers for political activities, siphoning off money that was should have been used to employ teachers and health workers.

Chapter 22 begins with an expression of hope: 'When Nobel Peace Prize Laureate Malala Yousafzai was designated as a United Nations Messenger of Peace by the UN Secretary-General Antonio Guterres in April 2017, the highest honour to have been bestowed on a global citizen, it underscored the importance of girls' education.[20] While the story of resistance and courage of this particular girl has inspired the world and is symbolic of the struggle for education, particularly of females, it is not uncommon in

Pakistan ... Physicists, microbiologists, fighter pilots, neurosurgeons, bankers, army generals, urban planners, psychiatrists, industrialists, mountain climbers – the list keeps growing'. She could have also included in the list Sharmeen Obaid-Chinoy, the female film producer and director who twice brought home Pakistan's only Oscar award. Meanwhile, Pakistan's former Prime Minister, Benazir Bhutto, was the first woman to lead a Muslim country. These successes notwithstanding, as the figures cited above suggest, Pakistan has a long way to go before it can be comfortable with the state of women's education and their participation in the workforce. Kasuri focuses on two aspects of the problem, both requiring greater investment by the public and private sectors: increasing the supply of well-trained female teachers and increasing the density of schools in rural areas.

In Chapter 19 Ayub Ghauri, one of the brothers behind the success of NetSol, Pakistan's largest IT firm, provides data on the poor coverage of the health sector by both the state and private providers. He believes that improvements are needed in all areas of health care. The state needs to invest more of its resources in expanding the coverage of health care among the citizenry, and distinction has to be drawn between the needs of different segments of the population and different parts of the country. For instance, poor coverage in the countryside has added to the impulse to move to urban areas where health facilities are more readily available.

Ghauri believes that the quality of care can be improved considerably by introducing IT into managing the health sector. Some of what he is suggesting became the basis of what in the United States is called 'Obamacare'. Under the appropriately titled Affordable Care Act (ACA), the state in the US intervened more robustly into the health sector by making it mandatory to obtain insurance. With the pool of the insured having been expanded, the cost per person for insurance companies became lower, and this had a powering effect on insurance coverage. Even then the poor could not buy insurance; they were given government subsidies to lower the cost. Physicians were required to use IT to maintain patient records. This made it easier for those needing health care to move between providers. Ghauri believes that there is scope for the adoption of ACA-type coverage in Pakistan to improve the provision of better health care to the country's citizens, and the private sector could play an important role in this.

In Chapter 20 Muhammad Saleem Ranjha discusses a microfinance programme in Pakistan that is different from those that have gained popularity in several parts of the world. Ranjha holds a senior position at Akhuwat, a microfinance institution that adheres strictly to *Sharia*, or Islamic law. Akhuwat, a non-governmental organization, has introduced a different way of bringing the private sector to the task of providing to the poor the services they cannot access in order to aid the poor. Microfinance is a rapidly growing segment of the world's financial system. Global growth is expected to reach 15.6 per cent in 2016–20. The sector has also done well in Pakistan. Growth in the country was facilitated by the passing of Microfinance Institutions Ordinance of 2001 that regulated the entities working in the area. The law was adopted a year after the establishment of Khushali Bank, the country's first microfinance institution. However, it was felt that an institution that did not charge interest was needed to reach the poor who were also deeply religious and wanted to abide by the Islamic injunction to avoid *riba*, the practice of charging, or promising a fixed rate of return on loans. There was increasing recognition of the role that *Sharia*-compliant instruments of microfinance could play in reaching the poor.

The word Akhuwat is derived from Arabic and means 'brotherhood'. According to Ranjha, the organization was founded in 2001 to replicate the bond of brotherhood that was exemplified by the Prophet Muhammad by establishing a bond between the people of

Medina and his followers who had left Mecca in order to escape harassment and persecution from the citizenry of the place of the prophet's birth. In the model the Pakistani institution adopted, 'the rich help their poorer brethren to get on their feet and become self-sufficient', says Ranjha. Akhuwat is currently running two types of programmes in the areas of microfinance and social development. The microfinance programme includes group loans, individual loans and participation in increasing the institution's reach. 'Every borrower receives a small donation box when he or she receives a micro-loan. The borrower displays the donation box in shops where customers can see it. Whenever the borrower or his customers put money in the donation box, they become Akhuwat donors', explains Ranjha.

Some problems that need government's attention

Part 5 of this volume deals with two problems that Pakistan must contend with if it is to achieve a reasonable level of growth that can be sustained over time and that is also inclusive in that it reaches all segments of the population and all parts of the country. The first is the environment and the second the availability of adequate amount of water for human consumption as well as for various productive purposes.

On departing from Islamabad recently, the co-editors of this volume noticed that the temperature showed 77 degrees Fahrenheit and that the atmosphere was 'cloudy'. When we descended from the Kalarkahar plateau, the temperature showed 80 degrees Fahrenheit, and the air was now 'misty'. However, as we approached Lahore the thermometer climbed to 84 degrees Fahrenheit and the air was now said to be 'smoky'. By now visibility was quite poor. It was clear to us that the smoke that hung in the air was the result of human activity. We could see the farmers burning the residual crops in their fields, causing smoke to rise into the air. Some distance from the Islamabad-Lahore motorway, we could see small kilns burning soft coal to produce baked bricks. The traffic picked up as we approached Lahore, and we noticed that there were now more motor rickshaws than cars and buses. Most of the rickshaws were belching dark smoke from their exhaust pipes.

The damage that pollution is doing to Pakistan is well illustrated by some of the figures shown in a recent report by the World Health Organization (WHO) about the ill-effects on health resulting from the poor quality of air most Pakistanis now breathe. According to the WHO, the mortality rate in Pakistan attributed to household and ambient pollution per 100,000 of the population was 87.2 in 2012. At that time the population of Pakistan was 178 million, which means that 155,000 deaths in that year could be attributed to atmospheric pollution. A comparison of this number with the deaths related to terrorist activities is revealing. In the 14-year period between 2003 and 2017, Pakistan lost 62,574 people to terrorism. This means that on average the county has been losing 4,500 persons a year to violence. However, air pollution is taking 30 times as many lives.

Global warming has begun to receive some attention in Pakistan and other parts of the developing world since the UN Climate Change Conference held in Paris, France, in December 2015. The plan that was agreed at Paris has created some momentum towards international action to prevent the globe from a climate catastrophe. However, atmospheric pollution caused by actions nearer the ground is not achieving as much attention. Some of the solutions are simple but need both people's awareness as well as the government's ability to enforce regulations. I will use an example from my experience working on the China desk for the World Bank to illustrate this point.

In 1987 China was still relatively underdeveloped. I noticed after walking through the city that I had a bad taste in my mouth and was told that it was because of pollution in the air. To avoid breathing in the foul air, I tied a handkerchief around my face; on removing it I noticed that there were dark spots in front of my mouth and nose, and complained about the air quality in the city. I was asked if I could bring in some World Bank experts to study the matter and offer advice.

The experts came and one of their simple recommendations was that the heaps of sand and soil that were lying around the many construction sites in the city should be covered with plastic sheets. Beijing is subject to strong breezes which waft sand and dirt into the air and the coal residue adheres to these particles. A notice was published a few days later in the *People's Daily*, the official newspaper of the Chinese Communist Party, ordering that all construction material should be fully covered. My World Bank colleagues and I drove around the city and found that there was total compliance to the government's order. While such a quick response by the population to the directives issued by the authorities may not be expected in Pakistan, there has to be greater attention given to getting people to act. This is the plea Kulsum Ahmed makes in Chapter 23.

Kulsum Ahmed, formerly of the World Bank, who took early retirement from the institution in order to focus on Pakistan's environmental problems and the challenges the country faces, is passionate about Pakistan as well as about improving the country's physical environment. The focus of her work is on the formulation of public policy at the national as well as at the international level. At the national level she has been identifying air pollution and solid waste disposal as the areas that deserve the attention of the government as well as that of civil society.

In 2017 the problems caused by air pollution were particularly visible to the millions of people who live in Lahore and several other large cities near the capital of Punjab. A heavy smog descended on Lahore and the urban areas around it and stayed there until the rains arrived in mid-November. According to an article that appeared in *The Economist*, 'As South Asians gasp for breath, governments sit on their hands'. The periodical's focus was on New Delhi but Lahore also received a mention. 'Delhi's autumnal pollution is of a more dangerous kind. Its 25 million people suffer under a seasonal plague that afflicts the Indo-Gangetic Plain from the city of Lucknow in the east all the way to Lahore, Pakistan to the west.' The governments in both countries were to blame. 'India is not alone among its neighbors in being so neglectful. Just like Delhi, Lahore has flailed feebly at tackling toxic air', continued the article. 'Only when public anger over the stink mounted in recent weeks did the city government reveal that it had bought six pollution monitors some time ago but had not yet installed them. As in India, Pakistan's state governments have been wary of forcing farmers, a crucial vote bank, to curb their pyromania.'[21]

As Mahmood Ahmad points out in Chapter 24, which looks at problems associated with water and offers solutions to them, the same set of issues are behind another environmental problem facing Pakistan: the predicted water shortages are less obvious but will do a great deal of damage to the health and economic well-being of most of the country's citizens. Ahmad, who works as an adviser to the Burki Institute of Public Policy, devoted a large part of his career to examining water issues in several parts of the Middle East. He is recognized as one of the world's most knowledgeable experts on water problems in drylands across the globe. He offers a well-informed analysis of the circumstances that pushed Pakistan from a situation of 'plenty' at the time of the country's independence in 1947 to that of 'stress' in the early 2000s, and, finally, to 'scarcity' beginning in 2010. 'On a global scale, over the next 15 years, almost half of the world's population will be living in areas that are running out of water', he writes. Many of these millions of people deprived of wholesome water will be citizens of Pakistan. There is work to be done. Ahmad quotes UN estimates that annual expenditure of US $50–60 billion will be needed until 2030 in order to avoid future shortages. However, he believes that while finding additional resources and using them wisely is necessary, much more needs to be done.

While the effects of global warming are well documented, Ahmad points to some other features of the Pakistani situation that differ from similarly affected other countries. 'The increase in the number of tube wells in the Indus Basin has been phenomenal, and are now estimated at 1.5 million units, accounting for half of all farm irrigation requirements – supplementing 34 million acre feet of surface water that reaches farmlands'. However, this resource is not being well managed. 'This massive growth is leading to groundwater depletion in urban, peri-urban and rural areas that could also be irreversible if a policy of unsustainable water use continues.'

What is contributing to Pakistan's steady drift towards another environmental catastrophe is not different from what is affecting other parts of the economy and polity. It is a combination of poor governance, crowding of institutions in the narrow space that needs to be well managed, and lack of political will to introduce proper pricing to regulate the use of water so that efficiency becomes the guiding principle. Ahmad believes that these are not insurmountable problems. Overcoming them would assure Pakistan a better future: this is one of the themes that is repeated in several chapters in this volume.

The final word

The point made by the editors in Part 6, which concludes this volume, is that there are both unique and normal features in Pakistan's development as a nation state. Pakistan is one of two countries – the other being the State of Israel – whose foundation has its basis in religion. Could religion lead to nationhood? I published a book three decades ago entitled *Pakistan: A Nation in the Making*.[22] Although Pakistan came into being as a state on 14 August 1947, it had not yet become a nation. That this did not happen was demonstrated less than a quarter of a century later when much blood had been shed but the country's two wings remained disunited. Muhammad Ali Jinnah, the country's founding father, had argued that India comprised not one but two nations – one Hindu and the other Muslim. He demanded a separate state to accommodate the latter while recognizing that the state he sought could not accommodate all of British India's 100 million Muslim population. However, when a bloody civil war led to the secession of East Pakistan and the emergence of independent Bangladesh, there was ample proof that religion was a poor basis for defining a nation. Did the departure of Bengal make Pakistan a nation? This question cannot be answered even now with certainty. Pakistan continues to deal with forces of secession. This is particularly the case in the restive province of Balochistan.

There are other reasons why religion is a poor basis for nationhood. Serious disagreement about the role of religion in politics prevented Pakistan from drafting a constitution. After two attempts, it settled on a constitutional framework in 1973 – more than a quarter of a century after its birth. The Constitution has survived for almost half a century but has not been fully accepted by all segments of the population. For many of the country's inhabitants the role of Islam in the way the country is governed needs to be more visible and pronounced. However, the Islamists wield sufficient disruptive power to defy international pressure which urges the suppression of those who have introduced the use of terror as an instrument of coercion.

In evaluating Pakistan's situation in geopolitics, we suggest that this country merits careful study and understanding. This is not only because of its large and young population – the sixth largest in the world with a median age of only 24 years – but also because there are more Muslims as its citizenry than in any other country. How the followers of Islam will define their relations with the West is a fundamental question of our time. Part of the answer relates to the geographic location occupied by Pakistan, and its neighbours Afghanistan and the troubled and contested state of Kashmir.

Notes

1 Shahid Javed Burki, 'Pakistan Is 70: What If?' Working Paper No. 266, Institute of South Asian Studies, National University of Singapore, 14 August 2017. See also Subrata K. Mitra, 'Indian Democracy at 70', Working Paper No 267, Institute of South Asian Studies, National University of Singapore, 15 August 2017.
2 Stanley Wolpert, *Shameful Flight: The Last Years of the British Empire in India*, New York, Oxford University Press, 2014.
3 Who was responsible for the attempt to block the flow of water from India to Pakistan is a question that is still being debated by historians. See Daniel Haines, *Rivers Divided: Indus Basin Waters in the Making of India and Pakistan*, New York, Oxford University Press, 2017.
4 Shahid Javed Burki and Shirin Tahir-Kheli, *Pakistan Today: The Case for U.S.-Pakistan Relations*, Johns Hopkins University School of Advanced International Studies, Foreign Policy Institute, Washington, DC, 2017.
5 Condoleezza Rice, *Democracy: Stories from the Long Road to Freedom*, New York, Twelve, 2017, p. 11.
6 Philip Mason, *The Men Who Ruled India*, New York, W. W. Norton, 1985.
7 'Nawaz Sharif's Options', *Friday Times*, 3–9 November 2017, p. 1.
8 Riaz Hassan, *Indian Muslims Struggling for Equality of Citizenship*, Melbourne, Melbourne University Press, 2016.
9 Pamela Constable, 'Anti-Government Protests in Pakistan Enter 2nd Day, But Most Are Peaceful', *Washington Post*, 27 November 2017, p. A9.
10 Khalid Ahmed, *Sectarian War: Pakistan's Sunni-Shia Violence and its Links to the Middle East*, Karachi, Oxford University Press, 2012.
11 John J. Mearsheimer, *Conventional Deterrence*, Ithaca, NY, Cornell University Press, 1985.
12 Shahid Javed Burki, Iftekhar Ahmed Chowdhury and Riaz Hassan, *Afghanistan: The Next Phase*, Melbourne, Melbourne University Press, 2016.
13 Feroze Khan, *Eating Grass: The Making of the Pakistani Bomb*, Stanford, CA, Stanford Security Studies, 2012.
14 The World Bank, *The East Asian Miracle: Economic Growth and Public Policy*, New York, Oxford University Press, 1993.
15 See www.economist.com/asia/2017/11/04/donald-trumps-agenda-in-asia-is-a-mystery.
16 Government of Pakistan, *Economic Survey, 2016–17*, Islamabad, 2017.
17 Shahid Javed Burki and Riaz Hassan, 'Pakistan's Demographic Situation as Revealed by the 2017 Census', South Asian Studies, National University of Singapore, 2017.
18 Shahid Javed Burki, various articles contributed to the Pakistani newspaper, the Express *Tribune*. These articles appear every Monday.
19 Adil Najam, *Portrait of a Giving Community: Philanthropy by the Pakistani-American Diaspora*, Cambridge, MA, Harvard University, Global Equity Initiative, 2007.
20 Malala Yousafzai collaborated with a foreign journalist to write her memoir. See Malala Yousafzai and Christina Lamb, *I Am Malala: The Girl Who Stood Up for Education and Was Whot by the Taliban*, New York, Little Brown and Company, 2013.
21 'Banyan. Under a Cloud: As South Asians Gasp for Breath, Governments Sit on their Hands', *The Economist*, 18 November 2017, p. 23.
22 Shahid Javed Burki, *Pakistan: A Nation in the Making*, Boulder, CO, Westview Press, 1986.

Part I
Politics, theory and practice

2

The Pakistan story

Shahid Javed Burki

Introduction

It is impossible in just one chapter to outline the complete history of a single nation. This is particularly the case with Pakistan, which was founded on the notion that religion could (and in fact should) be the basis of nationhood. That was the approach adopted by Muhammad Ali Jinnah's All-India Muslim League. Its campaign for a separate homeland for the Muslim community of British India was not unlike that of the Zionists which led to the creation of a homeland for the world's Jewish community. In fact, Pakistan and Israel are the only two countries in the world that came into existence in order to accommodate people of a particular faith. However, there is one important difference between the two religions: the world's Jewish population is small enough – estimated at some 13 to 15 million people – to fit within the boundaries of a single state. That is of course not the case with the world's Muslims who at 2010 numbered 1.6 billion people. As events unfolded in South Asia following the departure of the British from India, the subcontinent's 100 million Muslims clearly could not become the citizens of one contiguous state.

This chapter will focus on a number of key events in the history of the state of Pakistan. These, I hope, will illustrate how Pakistan has progressed from a country with a highly uncertain future to the one that holds out the promise to become a model for the rest of the Muslim world. This chapter will highlight some of the main landmarks of Pakistan's history: its difficult beginning; its impressive economic performance; its shaky political progress; the challenge to the state's authority by a number of non-state actors; and finally the country's often troubled relations with some of its immediate neighbours. The chapter also touches upon a number of issues not usually covered in most Pakistan studies. These include some of the 'what ifs' in the history of Pakistan; for example, what might have happened if, upon leaving the subcontinent, the British had not decided to partition the country on the basis of religion. The chapter also speculates on the direction in which the country may now be headed.

A difficult beginning

The campaign for the creation of a Muslim state in British India began in 1940 with the passage of the Lahore Resolution, moved by A. K. Fazlul Haque, Bengal's most popular and powerful Muslim leader. Jinnah presided over the annual meeting of the All-India Muslim League held in Lahore, the capital of Punjab, which, after Bengal, was the most populous Muslim-majority province in British India.[1] Recently historians have suggested that Jinnah's call for the establishment of a Muslim state was primarily aimed at gaining political rights for the Muslim community in an independent India that would also have a vast Hindu majority. According to this line of argument, Jinnah did not actually want an independent Muslim state to be created by the British at the time of their departure from the Indian subcontinent. He only wanted to ensure that the Muslim community in an independent India would have political rights that would be at least commensurate with their numbers in the population. 'Only after the elections of 1937, when its overtures to the Congress had been rebuffed did the Muslim League adopt a new line', wrote Ayesha Jalal in her account of Jinnah's stance. 'In 1940, a mere seven and half years before partition, it formally demanded independent Muslim states, repudiating the minority status which separate representation necessarily entailed, and asserted that Muslims were a nation.'[2] This position came to be known as the 'two nations' theory.

Other than suggesting that India was home to two nations, Jinnah did not spell out what kind of a nation-state he would create if the British agreed to his call for the establishment of a Muslim country. The British were preparing for what Stanley Wolpert, a historian who has written on the Partition of British India, later described as a 'shameful flight'.[3] It was 'shameful' because the bloodbath and the mass dislocation of people that followed Partition could have been avoided. Jinnah had not prepared himself to deal with the situation that developed once the British had left the subcontinent. Following the birth of Pakistan, Jinnah was anxious to focus on nation-building. He made it clear that he did not want religion to become the basis of the Pakistani nationhood. In his oft-quoted speech of 11 August 1947 to the Constituent Assembly, Jinnah seemed 'suddenly to awaken from a dream, looking at the hall packed and steaming with eager, perspiring faces all turned towards him for inspiration, orders, instruction, on every minute question of how to build a new state'.[4] Although he had given some thought to what kind of political structure the new country should have, he had not considered the type of economy that he wanted Pakistan to develop. Given his background – he was born into a merchant family in Karachi – it is likely that he would have left the economy largely in the hands of the private sector. However, as in its politics, Pakistan went on a roller coaster economic ride. It experimented with socialism (under Prime Minister Zulfikar Ali Bhutto, 1971–77) and an Islamic system (under President Zia ul-Haq, 1977–88) before settling for a system based on public-private sector partnerships and an economic system dominated by the military and civilian bureaucracies.

On 14 August 2017 Pakistan celebrated the 70th anniversary of its birth, one day before its sister state India. The reason why Pakistan came into existence one day before India was to allow Lord Louis Mountbatten, British India's last Viceroy, the necessary time to administer the oaths of office to the two successor governments. Since the date 15 August had already been set as India's Independence Day, Mountbatten agreed with Muhammad Ali Jinnah, who was to become Pakistan's first Governor-General, to bring forward the establishment of Pakistan by one day. On 14 August the Viceroy flew to Karachi, which had been chosen as the capital of the new country, and swore in Jinnah.

Mountbatten then flew back to New Delhi where he was sworn in as independent India's first Governor-General.

The creation of Pakistan can be viewed as an experiment in nation-building. A number of questions were asked when Jinnah was campaigning to have the British carve out a separate state for British India's Muslim community. Prior to Partition, India had a population of 400 million people, of whom 100 million were Muslims. About 75 million Muslims were concentrated to the north-west and north-east of the country, while the remaining 25 million were clustered together in the provinces where the Hindus formed the majority. What would be the sense of separating the two religious communities when no amount of geographic engineering could create a state that would accommodate all of British India's Muslims? If a state were to be created, what would be the basis of its nationhood? Jinnah had campaigned on the basis of religion and culture, calling the Hindus and the Muslims two separate nations. Would this be the basis of the nationhood of Pakistan?

In the event, Partition resulted in the deaths of one million people and the movement of 14 million people across the hastily demarcated India–Pakistan border. Eight million Muslims entered Pakistan from India, while six million Hindus and Sikhs travelled in the opposite direction. This was to be the largest movement of people in human history over such a short period of time – barely four months. It had profound consequences for Pakistan, which reverberate some 70 years later. Within a few months, Pakistan had gone from being a country with 65 per cent of the people being Muslims to one in which they made up 95 per cent of the population. Jinnah may not have intended that to be the case but the country he had created was now prepared to be 'Islamized.' This has happened to some extent.

Pakistan had a shaky economic start. It had to accommodate eight million refugees into a population of 24 million. It had to install a new government in a new capital. It had to deal with a hostile government in New Delhi that cut off electricity supplies to Lahore and threatened to block the flow of water into the canals that emanated from the headworks that were now in India. The biggest shock to the Pakistani economic system occurred in 1949, when New Delhi opened a trade war against Pakistan to punish its neighbour for not following it to devalue its currency with respect to the US dollar. The last act was to have a profound impact on Pakistan and changed the structure of its economy.

Despite such inauspicious beginnings, Pakistan did surprisingly well in building its economy. In 2017, as shown in Table 2.1, having grown at an average rate of 6.5 per cent per annum since its birth in 1947, Pakistan's economy was 25 times larger than in 1947. Since the population has increased six and half times, income per head is four times as large. The output of the industrial sector is 300 times as large. The proportion of people living in poverty (although apparently not the total number) has declined significantly. The urban population is one hundred times its size in 1947.

Although Pakistan has been an economic success, the same cannot be said of its political development. Unlike India, Pakistan was unable to develop a political system that would accommodate all segments of the population. Since its establishment in 1947, the country has come under military rule at intervals for 33 years in total. Successive governments have adopted three Constitutions, the first borrowed heavily from that of India and promulgated in 1956. Like India, Pakistan was to be a parliamentary democracy. The Constitution was abrogated two years later after the military intervened and introduced martial law. In 1962 Field Marshal Ayub Khan introduced a presidential form of government that survived while he remained in power. He was removed from office by the military junta after 11 years at the head of the government. The secession of East Pakistan from Pakistan in 1971 prompted a civil war that resulted in the establishment of the

Table 2.1 How Pakistan has changed in 70 years

Indicator	1947	2017	Δ
Population (total, millions)	32	208	6.5x
Urban population (total, millions)	1.5	150	100x
Urban population (% of total)	4	50	-
Population of Karachi and Lahore (combined total, millions)	0.9	35	40x
GNP (2017 US $)	12	300	25x
GNP per head (2017 US $)	375	1442	3.8x
Agricultural output (2017 US $)	24	60	2.5x
Agricultural output (% of GDP)	75	20	-
Industrial output (2017 US $)	0.24	72	300x
Incidence of poverty (total, millions)	22.5	54.0	2.4x
Incidence of poverty (% of population)	70	18	-

Source: author's estimates.

independent People's Republic of Bangladesh. What was left of Pakistan went on to promulgate the country's third Constitution in 1973, indeed the country has survived two military takeovers and periods of extreme political instability.

The ideological moorings and profile of today's Pakistan are not the same as those envisioned by Muhammad Ali Jinnah, the country's founder, when he began his campaign to create an independent state for the Muslim population of British India. Seventy years after the country's birth on 14 August 1947, it is about one-half of its original size. Originally Pakistan consisted of two parts, separated by about 1,000 miles of India's territory. The tensions between the two wings of Pakistan came to the surface soon after the country became independent. There was a dispute about the representation for the eastern wing (Bengal) in the national legislature. Since the east had a larger population, it was eligible for a majority of seats in the National Assembly (NA). This was, however, not acceptable to the country's political and military establishment that also dominated the western part of the country. Under pressure, Bengal agreed to the system of parity, with each wing having an equal number of representatives in the NA. The parity formula was the basis of the Constitutions of 1956 and 1962. To operationalize it, the provinces in the western wing were merged into what came to be called the 'One Unit of West Pakistan'. Constitutionally the country had two provinces, East and West Pakistan, with both having equal representation in the national legislature. The West Pakistanis wanted Urdu to be the national language; those in East Pakistan sought equal status for Bengali. In March 1948 Jinnah travelled to Dhaka, the capital of East Bengal, and announced that Urdu was to be the new state's national language. The Bengalis rebelled against the idea; their reaction led to the 'language riots'. Furthermore, there was concern that the Bengalis were not receiving their legitimate share of the capital and revenues flowing into the country as export earnings and foreign assistance. The resource issue became intense as the Planning Commission started working on the fourth Five-Year Plan which was to cover the 1970–75 period. As a result, Bengali resentment rose against the western wing.

In December 1971, after a bitterly fought civil war, the eastern wing of the original country won separation from the western part and became the independent state of Bangladesh, with strategic help from India. However, that is not the only change from Pakistan's original design. In the already cited speech given on 11 August 1947 before he became the independent nation's first Governor-General, Muhammad Ali Jinnah laid out his dream for the country he had founded when Britain decided to partition its Indian colony. His strong preference was to have Pakistan become what in today's parlance would be described as a liberal Western-type democracy. That did not happen but may occur if the progress made since 2008, when the military finally gave up political power under pressure from civil society, is sustained.

Today, 70 years after the country's birth its political system is once again under considerable stress. An elected prime minister was removed from office on charges of accepting payments from a foreign company headed by his son. At late 2018 Shahid Khaqan Abbasi faced imprisonment if an ongoing investigation by the National Accountability Bureau reached the conclusion that some of his wealth lodged abroad was acquired by corrupt means. If that were to occur and resulted in a political upheaval would the military stay on the sidelines and let politics take its course?

Pakistan also has to deal with considerable tensions with two of its four neighbours. Afghanistan maintains that it can only stabilize once Pakistan stops aiding the terrorists operating in its territory. India has the same set of complaints; attributing the trouble in its part of the disputed state of Jammu and Kashmir to intervention by Pakistan. The United States, while not a neighbour, has openly threatened Islamabad with action if it fails to move decisively against terrorists operating from its territory. There is, in other words, considerable uncertainty about the future as Pakistan begins the eighth decade as an independent state.

Some 'what ifs?' concerning Pakistan

Sometimes the 'what if?' questions help to bring under focus the most salient features in history. According to Robert Cowley, the historian who has done pioneering work in this area, the 'what if' approach 'can be a tool to enhance the understanding of history, to make it come alive ... History is properly the literature of what did happen; but that should not diminish the importance of the counterfactual. What if can lead us to question long-held assumptions. What ifs can define true turning points.'[5] This is certainly the case with Pakistan. Using Cowley's approach, I will ask the following 'what if?' questions in order to help us to better understand Pakistan's history:

1   What would have happened if the British had not agreed to partition the Indian Empire?
2   Where would Pakistan be today if it had written and adopted a constitution soon after gaining independence, just as India, its sister state, did? The Indian Constitution was ratified on 26 November 1949 and came into force on 26 January 1950.
3   Where would Pakistan be today if it had located its capital at or near today's Islamabad rather than in Karachi?
4   How would Pakistan have developed as a nation-state had its relations with India not deteriorated from the time the two countries were born?
5   Could Pakistan have survived in its original form if Pakistan, the country's eastern wing, had been fully accommodated into the country's political and economic systems?
6   What would have happened had Zulfikar Ali Bhutto, the country's first elected Prime Minister governed as a liberal democrat and not veered towards authoritarianism?

Many more 'what if?' questions can be asked, and in the discussion that follows I will seek answers to some of them.

Whenever Pakistan faces what appears to be an existential crisis, the question arises whether the more than 200 million Muslims who now make up the country's population would not have been better off had British India not been partitioned into two states, a Hindu-majority India and a Muslim-majority Pakistan.[6] In 2017 it was estimated that nearly 14 per cent of India's population was Muslim, making it, with 170 million citizens of that faith, the world's third-largest Muslim community. The largest Islamic societies are Indonesia and Pakistan. Bangladesh is the fourth largest. Had India not been partitioned, it could today have a population of 1.7 billion, with Muslims numbering more than 500 million, a proportion of about 34 per cent.

Had Partition not taken place, the Indian administrations would be struggling to satisfy the political and economic aspirations of such a large body of Muslims. As the political scientist Subrata Kumar Mitra has pointed out in his work on the evolution of the Indian political system, the large proportion of Muslims in the country's population would not have facilitated the development of strong democratic institutions. Also, with the leadership concerned with as to how to serve the interests of the people who follow a faith which is in great turmoil in the early decades of the 21st century, India would not have been held out as an example of political progress which the other South Asian nations could emulate. Partition served well the overall interests of the South Asians. However, as Riaz Hassan points out in Chapter 5, the Indian Muslims have done less well in general than the non-Muslims in India.[7]

After independence, India quickly moved to draft and promulgate a constitution. This was accomplished within two years of winning independence. However, it took Pakistan more than a quarter of a century and two failed attempts before it finally managed to agree on what now *appears* to be a durable document for governance. I have italicised the word 'appears' since it cannot be said with total certainty that the Constitution promulgated in 1973 will survive and that the country's powerful military will not be tempted to intervene once again. It is possible that the roller coaster political ride on which Pakistan embarked soon after gaining independence could have been avoided had the country adopted and followed a legal framework for good governance. However, it struggled to achieve this owing to the difficulties resulting from the Partition of British India.

In 1958 General Ayub Khan, at that time the Commander-in Chief of the Army, abrogated the Constitution that had been adopted two years earlier after a great deal of debate. The role of Islam in politics was the most contentious issue. It was resolved through the adoption of a preamble to the Constitution that maintained that sovereignty would rest not with the people but with Allah. The general who went on to become Pakistan's first military leader abrogated the 1956 Constitution and gave the country a new system which appeared to give some legitimacy to an authoritarian style of rule.[8] Ayub Khan was overthrown by General Yahya Khan, the head of the army, who followed his predecessor's approach and also abrogated the 1962 Constitution. The new military leader would have liked an elected NA to draft another constitution. However, the assembly elected in December 1970 was dominated by the East Pakistan-based Awami League which, by proclaiming a six-point plan for governance, had campaigned for the granting of much greater autonomy to the country's eastern wing. Zulfikar Ali Bhutto, a young and highly ambitious politician from the province of Sindh, led the newly created Pakistan People's Party (PPP) to victory. The PPP won 81 out of the 138 seats allocated to the province. That was not acceptable to the political elite in West

Pakistan nor to the powerful military. Their resistance led to civil war and the eventual creation of Bangladesh as an independent state.

The arrival of eight million Muslim refugees from India and the movement of six million Hindus and Sikhs in the opposite direction unsettled the country and entirely changed its demographic structure.[9] In terms of the proportion of the population not born in the country, there is no other precedent in human history to equal Pakistan's case in 1947. When it took its first census in 1951, one-fourth of the country's population was made up of refugees.

Nearly three million refugees from India travelled to the new capital, Karachi, and to other neighbouring cities in south Sindh. They went there in search of government jobs and in the hope that proximity to the authorities would make it easier to integrate. In 1947 Karachi was a small port-city with a population of 400,000. It was much smaller than Lahore, the capital of Punjab province. Although Lahore had the physical infrastructure to accommodate the nascent government, it was deemed to be situated too close to the border with India, with which relations were strained. Had some other city in Punjab, such as Rawalpindi, been chosen as the national capital, that is where most of the refugees would then have gone, and it is possible that Pakistan would not have had to deal with the ethnic problems which were to turn Karachi into one of the world's most violent cities.[10] It would also have facilitated the creation of a different economic structure for the country.

The refugees who settled in Karachi took up posts in the still-formative government or set up businesses in and around the city. Most of these people had previously lived in the urban areas of the Muslim-minority provinces of British India. Very few were involved in agriculture. Pakistan-India economic and commercial relations were severed when New Delhi refused to accept Karachi's decision not to devalue its currency with respect to the United States dollar as was done by all other members of what was then called the Sterling Area (now the Commonwealth). Without this, greater opportunities for industrial development and commerce might have arisen for Pakistan. The Indian decision was to profoundly affect the direction of economic development in Pakistan.

Another 'what if' concerns India-Pakistan strategic relations. In 2006 I was invited by the US Institute of Peace to write a paper on the resolution of the Kashmir dispute. In it, I suggested that the Kashmir issue had cost Pakistan a great deal. It diverted resources to defence that could have been used for economic development. It also brought terrorism into the country when its military, having supported radical Muslims to fight and expel the Soviet Union from Afghanistan in the 1980s, turned the attention of these militants towards Kashmir.[11] In the circumstances, I suggested that Pakistan should distance itself from the situation and make no further efforts to bring about a change in the status quo. Prior to publication, the paper was read by General Jehangir Karamat who was then Pakistan's ambassador to the United States, and by President Pervez Musharraf. The latter told me: 'You write regularly about Pakistan for the Pakistani newspapers. Why don't you write about your main findings in your columns? I want the people to realise how costly it has been for us to remain involved in Kashmir.' His reaction came as a surprise, because he had been behind the Kargil War in north Kashmir in 1999 when Pakistani troops captured the Kargil Heights but were driven back by a strong Indian response. The Kargil War hindered efforts initiated by the then Prime Ministers of India (Atal Bihari Vajpayee) and Pakistan (Nawaz Sharif) to improve relations between their two countries. At December 2018 relations between the two countries remained strained.[12]

In a special report published by *The Economist* to mark the 70th birthday of both Pakistan and India, the conclusion reached about the future of relations between what it called 'hissing cousins' was accurate but not encouraging. 'Sadly, reconciliation may become even harder as time goes by. For young Indians in Kolkata or Bangalore, Pakistan is no longer viewed as a lost cousin but simply as a bothersome distant neighbour. Younger Pakistanis follow the news from India more closely, but are increasingly alienated by their neighbour's rightward, Muslim bashing drift.'[13]

Another 'what if?' examines the country's history in terms of the 19th-century 'great man theory', according to which history can largely be explained by the impact of great men. This was popularized by the Scottish writer Thomas Carlyle and developed further by Herbert Spencer. According to Spencer, great men were the product of their societies. Of the 13 men and one woman who left their mark on Pakistan, two were particularly notable. The first was Prime Minister Zulfikar Ali Bhutto who governed from 1971 to 1977, and the second was his successor, General Zia ul-Haq, who ruled from 1977 to 1988 as Pakistan's third military President. Had Bhutto governed as a democrat and not veered towards authoritarianism, Pakistan may have avoided martial law, consolidated liberal democracy as the prevailing form of governance, and continued with the spectacular rate of economic growth begun under Ayub Khan. Had General Zia not imposed his personal religious piety on Pakistani society, the country would have been saved from the advance of Islamic extremism.

Evolution of the economy and the political system

Economists have acknowledged that there is a strong relationship between political stability and economic progress. This is certainly the case in Pakistan. Two academics – economist Daron Acemoglu from the Massachusetts Institute of Technology, and political scientist James Robinson from Harvard University – collaborated to write *Why Nations Fail*, in which they explored the way in which political and economic systems interact with each other. They divided institutions into two categories: exclusive and inclusive. According to the authors, if a country has an inclusive economic system in which the rewards of growth are equitably distributed in a reasonable manner, it must also have an inclusive political system which permits the equal participation of all segments of the population and all areas of the country.[14] Pakistan's history has many examples to show that these two authors are correct in positing these relationships. Field Marshal Ayub Khan had to give up power once the people came out on the streets to protest that they had not benefited much from the growth achieved during what the military ruler had called the 'decade of development' (namely the period 1958–68). Perception about economic discrimination was also the reason why in 1971 the people of East Pakistan fought a civil war and won independence for their province and became the nation of Bangladesh. The Bengalis had felt for over a quarter of a century that they had suffered economic deprivation at the hands of the political establishment in West Pakistan.

Economic and political development in Pakistan has been uneven over the last 70 years. As shown in Table 2.2, high rates of economic growth were recorded in the 1960s and 1980s. Martial law was imposed during both periods and this brought about political stability. Meanwhile, there were large inflows of external capital, mostly from the United States. Washington, in pursuing its strategic objectives in the geopolitical arena in which Pakistan is located, was prepared to give generously to Islamabad. However, when the US strategy changed and Pakistan's importance waned, Washington ceased to offer aid. Each period of rapid growth was followed by brief interludes of near-democratic governance and a loss of economic momentum. Each time, the rate of economic growth declined by almost two percentage points.

Table 2.2 Annual growth rates of GDP, population, and per head GDP (% per annum)

Year	GDP	Population	Per head GDP
1950–60	3.1	2.4	0.6
1960–70	6.8	2.9	3.8
1970–80	4.8	3.0	1.7
1980–90	6.5	3.2	3.3
1990–2000	4.6	2.4	2.1
2000–10	4.7	2.3	2.3
2010–16	4.0	2.0	1.9

Source: Economic Surveys, Government of Pakistan.

The military ruled Pakistan for 33 of the first 70 years of the country's existence; military men were presidents during the periods 1958–69, 1969–71, 1977–88 and 1999–2008. Even when they did not control the government, they influenced policymaking in other important areas.

To a considerable extent, Pakistan's relations with its four neighbours – Afghanistan, the People's Republic of China, India and Iran – were heavily determined by the thinking of, and inputs from, the men in uniform. The furthest that the military has withdrawn from the centre-stage to the backbench was noticeable in recent years, when elected men governed at the federal and provincial level. The boisterous press and television have also acted as overseers of the country's political development. The Lawyers' Movement of 2006–07 also demonstrated the power of protest that would be very hard for the military to ignore. The movement was launched when the former President of Pakistan, General Pervez Musharraf, removed Chief Justice Iftikhar Chaudhry from office. Pakistan's lawyers protested that 'due process' had not been followed by the military President and that the independence of the judiciary was being compromised. The legal community won the argument by taking to the street. Musharraf got the message, and held a national election in which the political party he had supported lost and the PPP won. The President resigned and was succeeded by Asif Ali Zardari, the PPP chairman who went on to govern for five years. It appeared that the military had finally decided to back away from politics.

The decision by the Supreme Court on 28 July 2017 to remove Nawaz Sharif from his post as Prime Minister had the tacit support, it is believed, of the military leadership. Commenting on Sharif's removal, Salman Masood of the *New York Times* maintained that 'the Pakistani military has seldom been able to wield as potent a mix of policy control and popular acclaim as it does now. The fragile democratic system … again appears to be on shaky ground'.[15] Sharif had always had a difficult relationship with the military establishment. His earlier tenures were cut short either by the military operating behind the scenes (in 1993) or by its direct intervention (in 1999). According to Masood, 'During his most recent tenure, Mr Sharif had an uneven relationship with the military. His overtures of more openness toward India, Pakistan's long-time foe, backfired as generals spurned his efforts.'[16]

Political periods in Pakistan's history

There are several distinct periods in Pakistan's history. In all of these, the country's citizens witnessed the country being ruled interchangeably by civilian and military leaders:

1   1947–51: The settling down was delayed because of the death of Muhammad Ali Jinnah in September 1948 and the assassination of Liaquat Ali Khan, the country's first Prime Minister, in October 1951. Had the country's first Prime Minister not been killed, he may have succeeded in overseeing the introduction of a constitution and thus promoting the rule of law in Pakistan.

2   1951–54: Pakistani politics was militarized for the first time with the entry of General Ayub Khan as Minister of Defence in the federal cabinet. The General agreed with the Americans that Pakistan would join the two international defence pacts – the Central Treaty Organization (CENTO) and the Southeast Asia Treaty Organization (SEATO) – they had organized to stop the Communist regimes in Moscow and Beijing from extending their influence over Asia. A Constitution was finally promulgated in 1956 but the politicians continued to squabble.

3   1958–62: A *coup d'état* led by Ayub Khan established the first military administration. The 1956 Constitution was abrogated in 1958 and a new Constitution with a presidential form of government was promulgated in 1962. Ayub Khan promoted himself to the rank of Field Marshal and went unchallenged for more than a decade.

4   1962–69: Rapid economic progress occurred during what the military called the 'decade of development'. However, widespread unhappiness with the inequitable distribution of the incremental national income led to Ayub Khan's removal from office by the military.

5   1969–71: Pakistan's second military government, led by General Yahya Khan, took office but failed in its attempt to draft another constitution. The civil war in East Pakistan led to the creation of Bangladesh. The forced departure of General Yahya Khan and the political ascent of Zulfikar Ali Bhutto followed.

6   1971–77: Bhutto introduced socialism by nationalizing large industrial, financial and commercial enterprises owned by the private sector. This signalled a fundamental departure from the private sector-oriented model of economic development that had been pursued during the Ayub Khan era with great success. Bhutto, after having drafted a Constitution for Pakistan that gave the country a parliamentary system of governance, wanted to move towards a presidential form of governance. For that to happen, he needed a large majority in the National Assembly. With that in view he allegedly rigged the elections held in 1977. This led to demonstrations against him and his removal by the military.

7   1977–88: The third military government was established by General Zia-ul-Haq, who held office for 11 years. Bhutto was executed in April 1979 on the charge that he had ordered the murder of a political opponent. The military government sided with the United States and organized the opposition to the Soviet Union's invasion of Afghanistan. It also introduced Islam into the country's economic and political governance. Zia was killed in an unexplained aeroplane accident in August 1988.

8   2008–July 2018: Two elections, five years apart, brought some stability to the political system. The civilian government, headed by the PPP, remained in office from 2008–13, followed by another civilian government, this time led by the Pakistan Muslim League (Nawaz) that won a decisive victory in 2013. However, on 28 July 2017, the Supreme Court declared Sharif ineligible for the office of Prime Minister.

Some of the details of the practices by the Sharif family came to light as a result of the revelations made in the 'Panama papers'. The publication of the papers caused global shock waves, and led to the resignation of Iceland's Prime Minister as well as causing considerable embarrassment to David Cameron, the British Prime Minister. From the released material it appeared that some members of the Sharif family had set up a number of shadow enterprises in Panama to hide the nature and scope of a number of real estate transactions undertaken by Sharif's sons, Hassan and Hussain, and his daughter, Maryam. The transactions involved the purchase of luxury apartments in London. The Minister of Finance, Ishaq Dar, who had successfully steered the Pakistani economy through difficult times was also implicated in the 'Panamagate' scandal.

As the 'Panamagate' scandal gained currency, Imran Khan, the Pakistani cricketer-turned-politician and leader of the Tehreek-e-Insaf party, forced the Supreme Court to take up the matter. He had threatened a 'million supporters march' into Islamabad if the judges did not take up the case. In response, the court ordered the establishment of a six-member Joint Investigation Team (JIT) to probe the matter and report back to the court within 90 days. This was done and a detailed report was duly submitted by the JIT. It was widely expected that the judges would order inquiries to be made by some of the government agencies with the necessary authority to examine whether the erstwhile Prime Minister, his children, and some of his associates (former Minister of Finance Ishaq Dar, for instance) had acted in ways that could lead to their conviction for wrong-doing. The court-ordered investigation found that there was a 'significant disparity' between the declared wealth of the Sharif family and the assets it owned in London and the Middle East. The verdict was delivered on 28 July 2017 when the five-member bench declared that Sharif should vacate his seat in the National Assembly and must relinquish his post as Prime Minister.

On 13 April 2018 the Supreme Court issued another verdict according to which Nawaz Sharif's disqualification was for life unless the National Assembly was able to amend the clause under which he had been debarred from holding an elected position. It can be argued, as was done in the foreign press, that, with the removal of Sharif as Prime Minister, Pakistan may have entered another period of political instability. No elected Pakistani Prime Minister has completed his or her full five-year term in office. However, the opposite case could also be made. According to the *Washington Post*, 'the historic ruling while hailed by Sharif's opponents as a victory for Pakistani democracy, threw the country's political future into turmoil'.[17] At a news conference, Imran Khan viewed the Supreme Court judgment as 'the beginning of a new era in the history of Pakistan' in which there would no longer be 'two types of laws, one for the weak and one for the wealthy and powerful. In this new era, justice will reign supreme. It is a victory for the entire nation.'[18]

What could have been?

Now that economists have accepted the notion that the performance of any economy – developed, underdeveloped or emerging – is influenced by politics, it would be interesting to determine what would have been the case had Pakistan been politically stable throughout its 70-year history. Before moving towards that analysis, another important fact about stability needs to be noted. It is needed not only in domestic systems, but is also required at the global level. Following the election of Donald Trump to the US presidency, policy analysts predicted that the series of shocks delivered to the world economic and political order would result in instability that would be costly for the global economy. Individual nations striving to stabilize their own domestic politics must hope that they will have the good fortune to operate within a stable and rule-bound global system.

In order to consider how Pakistan might have fared had it enjoyed greater stability as a nation-state, we should first note that during the course of the country's 70-year history, there were three periods of relative political stability. These occurred in the 1960s, the 1980s and the early 2000s. During all three periods, the country was under the rule of the military. Simultaneously, the rate of economic growth was relatively high. While Ayub Khan was in office the rate of growth was close to 7 per cent per year. When General Zia ul-Haq was in charge, the rate of GDP averaged about 5 per cent per annum, and stood at roughly the same rate when General Pervez Musharraf dominated the political system. However, the high rate of economic growth during military rule should not lead to the conclusion that martial law is good for economic development. In Pakistan's case, the military rulers were able to quickly align public policymaking with American strategic interests in the geographic space of which Pakistan is an important part. This alignment brought generous American financial support for the capital-poor country. However, stability resulting from civilian rule can also bring in the needed capital. Political uncertainty has resulted in a significant amount of capital flight from the country. Political stability would bring this money back.

It should be possible to do some simple arithmetic to show how much income was lost owing to political instability during the periods between military rule. However, before doing that calculation, we should point out one more aspect about the rule of the military. Taking 1960 as the starting point, a sustained rate of growth of 6.5 per cent a year would have meant that the size of Pakistan's GDP would have reached US $1.1 trillion rather than the actual $300 billion it achieved in 2017. Political stability could have turned Pakistan into a trillion-dollar economy by 2017. In other words, the price the country has paid for political instability can be estimated at $800 billion, more than 2.5 times the current size of the economy.

This rate of high, sustained GDP growth would most probably have had a negative effect on the rate of population increase. This has been the experience of most countries; high increases in GDP usually coincide with lower fertility rates. The size of the population in 2017 would have been 180 million rather than the 208 million estimate provided by the census conducted in early 2017. This would have produced a per head income of US $6,000 rather than the $1,450 estimated for 2017. On average every Pakistani citizen has potentially lost $4,550 of income per year on account of political instability. A heavy price has been paid for political turbulence.

There were other kinds of costs. Two of these are worth identifying. One, sustained high rates of growth would have increased the level of investor confidence in the country. Economists correctly identify confidence as an important determinant of growth. A higher confidence in the economy would have drawn more investment capital from both domestic and foreign financiers. With more private sector resources flowing into the economy, Pakistan's dependence on external finance would have been reduced. Two, with national and personal incomes at higher levels, the country would have invested more in developing the social sectors of the economy. More resources would have flowed into education and health. Political stability would not only have made the average Pakistani man or woman more affluent but also more educated and healthier.

However, the conclusion to be drawn from this 'what could have been' analysis is not that the military needs to win power to bring about political stability. In fact, the opposite is the case. Pakistan's political development was not helped but delayed by military interventions. These prevented the country from developing the institutional infrastructure necessary for political progress. What gives me hope for the future is that this delayed development of democracy-supporting institutions may have finally begun to happen. Various components of a working and durable democracy are now asserting themselves, speeding up the process of political progress and thus setting the stage for rapid economic advances.

Pakistan at 80: the next 10 years

A number of notable historians have examined Pakistan's economic past.[19] As Pakistan celebrates the 70th anniversary of its birth, it would not be inappropriate to speculate about its future. Where will Pakistan be when it celebrates its 80th birthday in 2027? This is a particularly difficult question to answer for a country such as Pakistan where so much remains unsettled even after 70 years of its existence as an independent entity. Pessimism is a widespread indulgence for Pakistanis who think about their country. The following comments by a highly respected scholar of Pakistani origin who is now an American citizen but who returns frequently to his homeland, reflect this situation: 'This trip has been even more disturbing for me than the last few', he stated following a recent visit to Pakistan. 'The level of decay and deterioration here in the very fabric that defines human and social behaviour is unbelievable! The rot here is much deeper than even I had assessed before. Alas, such is our sorry state and we seem condemned here to this horrible fate. I guess the only option for people like us is to continue doing whatever good we can and pray for a miracle.'

The 'Panamagate' episode highlighted at least two features of the Pakistani political landscape that concern all those who are concerned about the country's future. The first factor is the important role that the military continues to play in the life of the country. It is noteworthy that two members of the JIT came from the military intelligence services. The second factor concerns the steady deterioration of the institutional infrastructure needed for a maturing political and social entity. As discussed earlier, having come under pressure from elements of civil society, in particular the lawyers of Pakistan, General Pervez Musharraf held elections. The elections brought parliamentary form of government back to Pakistan. Once the civilian government was in place, Musharraf resigned and left the country. Does this mean that for the moment the military is finally out of politics? That may not be the case. There is some speculation that the military may have had a hand in the way the 'Panamagate' crisis was handled. If that is the case, Pakistan will revert to its historical path; if not and the military was mostly a bystander in these events, the country may have taken another step forward in terms of its political development.

The JIT report also highlighted some of the country's institutional failings. Pakistan has become an institutional graveyard, burying many institutions that have critical roles to play in developing the country and modernizing its society. There are a number of examples of the effect that politics has had on the institutional structure. The judicial system is weak, a characteristic which the country shares with other South Asian nations. At the federal level the Planning Commission, as well as various provincial planning and development departments, were once deeply involved in formulating policies and carrying out project appraisals. This is no longer the case. Most projects in the US $60 billion[20] China–Pakistan Economic Corridor (CPEC) were included in the programme without being subjected to evaluation about their economic and financial viability.[21] While in post, Bhutto methodically dismantled the institutional structure built by Ayub Khan. He also dissolved Pakistan's civil service that had its roots in the renowned Indian Civil Service, once called the 'steel frame' of the British Raj. An independent and merit-based system of bureaucracy served Pakistan well during the post-independence years. It is also the reason for India's success in building a modern political system. By nationalizing large segments of the modern parts of the economy, Bhutto also did away with the dynamism of the Pakistani private sector that had powered the economy for a number of years, especially during Ayub Khan's time in office. The elaborate systems put in place to ensure the accountability of officials in public service have not delivered what they were supposed to ensure – a fact pointed out at some length by the JIT report. There are, in other words, many reasons for backing those who are pessimistic about the country's future.

Pessimism is a self-fulfilling premise. As economists have discovered, the level of confidence about the future is a major contributor to the pace and scope of development. This is true at both the micro and macro levels. Stock markets value individual stocks on the basis of how they rate their future. Confidence also dictates the level and direction of investment by the private sector. Prevailing sentiment about the country affects the amount of investments by private players. Changing the narrative about Pakistan – focusing on some of the positives rather than being totally preoccupied with the negatives – will invite more capital into the economy from both local and foreign entrepreneurs. If there is truth in the findings presented in the JIT report, even those who occupy senior positions in the government are inclined to invest their wealth outside the country's borders. Given all this, are there reasons to be optimistic about the future?

A number of positives should begin to figure in the way the economy's future is assessed. The most important of these is demography. The 2017 census provided estimates of the size of the population, its rate of growth, and its age distribution. Preliminary estimates released by the Bureau of Statistics suggest that with a population of almost 208 million that is growing at a rate of 2.4 per cent a year, the country is sitting on a demographic time bomb. Without a decline in the rate of increase, the population could increase to 400 million by the year 2050 at which point Pakistan would have overtaken the United States and become the world's third most populous country. However, even this seemingly looming disaster has some positive attributes. With a median age of 24 years the population is very young. I have estimated elsewhere that some 75 per cent of the population of large cities – those with more than five million people each – is below the age of 25 years. The city youth is better educated and the women among them have done surprisingly well in acquiring the skills needed by the modern sectors of the economy. Economists correctly believe that the next global growth thrust will come from South Asia but that the countries in this region will not follow the pattern of East Asia's 'miracle economies'. Instead, they will provide modern services to the world's ageing population.

Pakistan also has its location as an asset. Sitting north-west of India, and between the resource-hungry China and resource-rich Middle East and Central Asia, Pakistan could facilitate the free flow of land-based commerce. This is the reason for China's investment of large amounts of its resources in the CPEC. In fact, the CPEC is an important component of its new development paradigm.

There is no doubt that the Pakistani economy has turned a corner, moving from a sluggish to a reasonably fast rate of economic growth. It has successfully dealt with some of the stresses that it came under in the immediate post-military era. The economy is now moving forward at a sustainable rate of growth of 5.5 per cent per year, two percentage points higher than the rate at which it was growing during the 2007–14 period. It is estimated that between 2017 and 2027 the rate of growth could average 6.5 per cent per year. Investments being made by China will certainly help to accelerate this rate of growth. If that were to happen, the size of the economy could be 90 per cent larger than the level reached in 2017, and the income per head 63 per cent higher.[22]

Notes

1 There are numerous academic works on the founding of the state of Pakistan. An early authoritative account is by Khalid bin Sayeed, *Pakistan: The Formative Phase, 1857–1948*, Karachi, Oxford University Press, 1991.
2 Ayesha Jalal, *The Sole Spokesman: Jinnah, the Muslim League and the Demand for Pakistan*, London, Cambridge University Press, 1985.
3 See Stanley Wolpert, *Shameful Flight: The Last Days of the British Empire in India*, New York, Oxford University Press, 2006.
4 Stanley Wolpert, *Jinnah of Pakistan*, New York, Oxford University Press, 1984, p. 337.
5 Robert Cowley, *The Collected What If? Eminent Historians Imagine What Might Have Been*, New York, Putnam, 1999, pp. xiii–xiv.
6 The 2017 census of Pakistan estimated the size of the country's population at 207.7 million.
7 Subrata K. Mitra, *Politics in India: Structure, Process, and Policy*, London, Routledge, [2011] 2017.
8 Riaz Hassan (ed.), *Indian Muslims: Struggling for Equality of Citizenship*, Melbourne, Melbourne University Press, 2016.
9 The author estimated these numbers while working at Harvard University under the supervision of the economic historian Alexander Gerschenkron. The conclusions drawn from this work were published in Shahid Javed Burki, *Pakistan under Bhutto, 1971–77*, London, Macmillan, 1980.
10 Steve Inskeep, in *Instant City: Life and Death in Karachi*, New York, Penguin Books, 2012, has provided an insightful account of the development of Karachi.
11 Shahid Javed Burki, *Kashmir: A Problem in Search of a Solution*, United States Institute of Peace, Washington, DC, 2007.
12 Shahid Javed Burki, *South Asia in the New World Order: The Role of Regional Cooperation*, London, Routledge, 2011.
13 Special Report: 'India and Pakistan: Hissing Cousins', *The Economist*, 22 July 2017, p. 12.
14 Daron Acemoglu and James A. Robinson, *Why Nations Fail: The Origins of Power, Prosperity, and Poverty*, New York, Crown Business, 2012.
15 Salman Masood, 'Nawaz Sharif, Pakistan's Prime Minister, toppled by corruption case', *New York Times*, 28 July 2017, p. A7.
16 Ibid.
17 Pamela Constable and Shaiq Hussain, 'Pakistan's High Court Removes Prime Minister from Power', *Washington Post*, 29 July 2017, p. A10.
18 Ibid.
19 Shahid Javed Burki, *Changing Perceptions, Altered Reality: Pakistan's Economy under Musharraf, 1999–2006*, Karachi, Oxford University Press, 2007. See also Parvez Hasan, *Pakistan's Economy at the Crossroads: Past Policies and Present Imperatives*, Karachi, Oxford University Press, 1998.
20 While a smaller figure was mentioned initially when China and Pakistan signed the agreement to begin work on the CPEC, the estimate is being revised as the projects included in the programme are identified and developed.
21 Shahid Javed Burki Institute of Public Policy, *The State of the Economy: China-Pakistan Economic Corridor*, Lahore, 2018.
22 These are the author's estimates based on his ongoing work on Pakistan's future.

3

Unintended consequences

The long shadow of Partition on Pakistan and India

Subrata K. Mitra[1]

Introduction

The Partition of 1947 was not imposed on the Muslim League and the Indian National Congress who were the main stake-holders for Pakistan and India – the two states which emerged from the division of British India. The Muslim League was the main driver of the process. Led by 'secular' Muslims such as Muhammad Ali Jinnah (the *ulama* had stayed out of the Pakistan movement) the project was meant to secure Muslim rights. This was the leitmotif for the politics of the League. It tried, unsuccessfully, to protect Muslim interests in the face of the perceived danger of Hindu preponderance in independent India. Having failed to secure a guarantee for a legitimate share of office in a united India, in the face of Congress inflexibility, the League eventually moved on to the idea of a territorial state – a homeland for Muslims of India. Partition, which was meant to protect Muslim rights, ended up doing the opposite for many. A substantial number of Indian Muslims were left behind in India where, at 10 per cent of the population, they formed a smaller minority group, having formerly made up 25 per cent of the population. Furthermore, with the loss of powerful Muslim-majority provinces such as Punjab and Bengal, there were no longer any strident regional voices in the Indian federation to defend Muslim interests.

The state of Pakistan that finally emerged did not meet initial expectations.[2] Nor was Pakistan meant to produce an Islamic state. Partition was meant to be a solution to violence, not a cause of violent confrontation with neighbouring India. The fact was that soon after independence Pakistan and India got locked into a Cain and Abel fratricidal war over Kashmir and never managed to solve it, and so the unfolding of the Pakistan idea led ultimately to the decline of the liberal constitutional order. Partition, loss of the Eastern Wing and militarization were all unintended consequences of an idea which looked most promising at the time.

Partition, acrimonious and violent, has cast its malevolent shadow over the two states, poisoning their relations, severely affecting the status of their minority populations and stymieing the evolution of South Asia as a cohesive, orderly region.[3] If Pakistan has paid a heavy price for Partition, the same is also true for India. Both 'distant' neighbours have been affected, but in contrasting ways, and in consequence have developed ominous, radically different, national narratives around the tragic events of 1947. The principle on which Partition was enacted and the manner of its implementation have adversely affected the nature of state formation in both Pakistan and India. Based on this sombre intro-spection, we ask, what lessons does Partition hold for the present politics and future developments in both Pakistan and India, and how might they overcome the negative consequences of Partition?

Instead of indulging in nostalgia for pre-Partition India, trading in culpability or pro-viding a detailed historiography of the events surrounding Partition, this chapter seeks to show how Pakistan and India can overcome the lingering trauma of Partition. The unrequited sorrow, rage and memories of the unspeakable violence of Partition have become the 'chosen trauma' which informs the perception and behaviour of each succes-sive generation.[4] A resolution of the contradictory feelings of a desire for greater intimacy but with a persisting dread of proximity is possible only through the combination of a radical change in the mindset as well as innovative institutions – both binational as well as multilateral, such as the South Asian Association for Regional Cooperation (SAARC). This might ease the transition from the deadly impasse to a normal relationship based on power-sharing and the apportioning of responsibility for the environment, security and other public contacts between the two neighbours.[5]

Unintended consequences

The violent consequences of Partition were unintended. They were not the product of a deliberate plan. The evolutionary trajectory can be explained in terms of a combination of chance, choice and contingency. According to Merton,[6] these unintended consequences can be attributed to five constituent factors. The first and most important of the causes refers to the ignorance of the full set of variables that are causally related to the phe-nomenon under question. When one is unaware of the comprehensive set of factors that have an impact on the outcome, one can find oneself facing consequences that were not factored into the model. Thus, the unfolding geopolitics of post-war coalitions spread to Asia and pitted Pakistan as a Western ally against India which sought to emerge as a third pole of non-aligned powers. The second cause of unanticipated outcomes arises from the prognosis of future behaviour based on past assumptions. The radical collapse in law and order in the areas immediately affected by Partition was not anticipated as all three stakeholders – the League, the Congress and the British – assumed that once Par-tition was conceded life would continue as usual and the normal mechanisms of law and order would prevail. Third, short-term calculations on the part of leading actors form the basis of critical decisions that affect posterity to the detriment of long-term interests which eventually surface as the cause of avoidable suffering. The hunger for office on the part of the leaders of Congress and members of the League led to hasty decisions being made, oblivious to the danger of accepting religion as the basis of state-formation without any iron-clad guarantees for minorities, which subsequently led to tremendous problems for them and caused waves of panicky refugees to flee in both directions. The fourth cause points towards the adoption of basic values at variance with the customary ones. The two-nation theory as the basis of Partition is a case in point, and will be discussed in depth below. Finally, 'self-fulfilling prophecies' or the fear of consequences of phenomena that have yet to happen, lead to the point where defensive measures reinforce the presumed cause, and so the dispute escalates. The fear of attacks by the adversaries on both sides of the religious divide appears to have reinforced the stockpiling of weapons by Muslim, Sikh and Hindu communities which added to the intensity of the violence that marked Partition. We will analyse these causes of the unintended consequences of Partition below.

The founding fathers of Pakistan had designed a state that they thought would be viable, and would not unravel while it was still developing. In spite of the jubilation that saluted its birth, Pakistan's road to democracy and stability was no easy ride. The first unintended consequence of Partition was the great mass migration, perhaps the largest in human history. Based on his own calculations, Javed Burki suggests that there were 14 million refugees:

> [E]ight million Muslims moved into Pakistan while six million Hindus and Sikhs moved in the opposite direction. Of those who came to Pakistan, 2.5 million were Urdu-speaking and mostly from the urban areas of Muslim minority provinces of British India while the remaining were from Punjab. The first group went to Karachi since that's where Pakistan located its first capital. They were looking for urban jobs and were correct in believing that most of these would be in government service. They dominated the government and public policymaking until the Ayub Khan era (1958–69) during which the process of 'indigenization' was launched. The population movement made Pakistan much more Muslim than was the case in the areas that became part of the new country – from 65 per cent Muslim in early 1947 to 94 per cent in 1951 when the country conducted its first census.[7]

Two-nation theory: a flawed design

The unravelling of Pakistan in 1971–72 needs to be understood in terms of the fatal flaw in the basic design of the state. The original idea behind Partition was simply to cut the land mass into two and leave the Muslim League and Congress in charge of both parts in the hope that all would be well afterwards. That this is not how things turned out has to be seen as the consequence of a flawed design. The assertion of the hegemony of Islam as the core concept of the state of Pakistan and its mirror opposite – the denial of a public role for Hinduism in the rump that was to become the Republic of India – have both proved to be inadequate as bonding mechanisms for the multiple groups that were packed into the two new sovereign states. The Urdu-speaking Sunni elite led by the Muslim League could not appropriately accommodate the diverse Pakistani peoples, and this had tragic consequences for the integrity of the state. On the Indian side, the Nehruvian state secularism denied any public role to Hinduism, although much to the discomfiture of the ranks of the Hindutva brigade a concept of Hindu Rashtra is an oxymoron. This secularism has not resolved India's inter-community problems – aggravated today by the divisive ideology of Hindutva, now ominously sweeping across the land and accelerating the pace of distrust and confrontation between India and Pakistan.

The consequence of the original flawed design can be seen in the national narratives that have grown around the Partition of the two now-distant neighbours. Both states are radically different to one another. In the historiography of the Partition, Pakistan showcases Partition as a major foundation stone in the evolution of Islam in South Asia and the *raison d'être* of a homeland for Muslims. For India, it marks yet another episode of loss, and a vivisection of 'Mother India' in the litany of Islamic aggression dating from the original Arab invasion of Sind in 712 AD. Partition revives the memory of this continually bleeding wound on the Hindu psyche. The two opposing narratives have become the source of distrust, hatred and bitter rivalry between the two states.

The two-nation theory which argued that Hindus and Muslims were two distinctly different nations who should each have their own homelands, was contested among Congress leaders and never got legitimacy in post-colonial India. However, the idea was the bedrock upon which Pakistan was built.[8] India's institutions were modelled according on a different brand of secularism, which specified that state and religion were separate entities; that the state should take a neutral attitude towards all religions, and so on. Pakistan, however, adopted Islam as the core value of the state. Jinnah valiantly proclaimed that in the Islamic state different religious communities would continue to enjoy their rights to ritual and practice, for Pakistan was to be a state for Muslims and not an Islamic state.[9] However, his demise put paid to this notion. Jinnah's followers, lacking his charisma and without deep roots in the political soil, drew on Islam and the military for their own political survival. The result was fresh waves of outmigration, which caused the percentage of Hindus among the population to dwindle rapidly. The Indian story is different. The Muslim population, after the first waves of outmigration, held its own in India; it eventually increased from 11 per cent post-independence to more than 14 per cent, whereas the percentage of the Hindu minority of Pakistan – once substantial in certain areas that became Pakistan – shrank to a negligible number.[10] Indian secularism in practice has had a relatively benign effect on plurality. Despite such iconic cases as the destruction of the Babri Mosque by a fanatic Hindu mob in Ayodhya in 1992 and the Hindu-Muslim riot in Gujarat in 2002, on the whole the Muslim community, which lost its leaders in 1947 when they migrated to Pakistan, has emerged over the last 70 years from the early desolation to national prominence in many fields,[11] which shows what minorities can achieve when a constitutional level playing field is available to them.

At critical junctures in the emergence of the state of Pakistan, the decisions made by the elite in charge, led to a path dependency that pointed towards the second break-up that took a concrete, violent shape in 1971. Following the first Partition, the Muslim exit from India and the Hindu and Sikh exit from Pakistan, and the process of Bengali alienation and the militarization of Pakistan which led to the inability of the political system to accommodate Bengali interests, and the effect of the Kashmir conundrum, all of these accelerated the process of the second Partition of Pakistan. The initial design of forcing an idea of Pakistan onto a territory where political structures at the level of region and locality were intact, jealous of their identity and watchful of their autonomy, led to alienation and eventually open rebellion. Within a very short time, the rulers of the nascent state of Pakistan lost a solid political base of support which left a void in terms of legitimacy, and this, in turn, drew the army into the position of leadership.

History has demonstrated that Pakistan and India – despite coming into the world as sister nations, born simultaneously from the events of 1947 – have taken very different political paths. This difference can be articulated at two levels. When compared to each other, they are found to have produced two divergent forms of statehood: they have adopted contrasting types of national identity, and (consequently) have developed two systems of political institutions which differ strongly from one another. In addition to this reciprocal incongruence, India and Pakistan also differ in their supposed destinies; the reality of their evolution contradicts that which in 1947 seemed a logical development of the events, namely a cohesive, stable Pakistan and a divided, unravelling India.[12]

The primordial seeds of such contrasting and controversial political developments were sown at the very moment of Partition. Partition, in the way it was brought about, attributed to each of the two nascent polities a very distinct national identity, the two being divergent from each other having been built on diametrically opposite theories of the nation. However, the political development of the two countries has been unexpected. Although created as a religiously homogeneous home for the Muslims in South Asia, Pakistan still struggles with centrifugal forces and chronical instability; the heterogeneous India, on the other hand, in spite of its political inconsistencies, seems to hold far more firmly.

In order to appreciate this point, we need to reanalyse the history of Partition in light of the exposed narrative, highlighting its repercussions on the 'idea of Pakistan' and 'the idea of India' which accompanied the formation of the two states and their consequent political development. More specifically, we need to analyse the series of events that led to the Partition of British India in 1947, and those which followed, as well as the waves of Muslim exit from India and the Hindu exit from Pakistan, further compounding the memories of violence. Equally important is the issue of political development in Pakistan where the ruling Muslim League, bereft of its mass base which stayed behind in India, lost legitimacy. This created a political void, which, in turn, drew the army into the position of leadership. Finally, the unravelling of Pakistan in 1971–72 needs to be understood in terms of the fatal flaw in the basic design of the state in terms of the context where it was ensconced and flawed agency, defective structure and the conjuncture of events that led to it.

Path dependency and unintended consequences

After accounting for the history as it has unfolded over the past 70 years and for its contingent reasons, we need to ask a more fundamental question: was Partition inevitable? What led to the Partition of British India? In this regard, we turn once again to historical analysis in order to identify the sequence of events that led to Partition, and to assess the role that each event played in the occurrence the following ones. There were critical junctures where the leadership chose the 'wrong' turn. Our analysis leads to a *soft determinism*: only the integration of a path-dependent historical pattern with crucial individual choices made in correspondence of critical conjunctures can explain history in the way it has unfolded. We examine this below in terms of the critical nodes on the path to Partition, and at each point, show what the failure to strike a deal on power-sharing led to.

- 1937: Provincial elections were held under the terms of the 1935 Government of India Act. Congress won 716 out of the 1,116 seats it contested. The Muslim League, with the exception of Bengal, fared dismally in the Muslim-majority provinces. The leadership of the Indian National Congress failed to see the importance of sharing power with the Muslim League, and failed to offer any credible guarantees for Muslim rights in India. Failure to create a coalition ministry in United Province sent a signal about the refusal of the Congress to share power.
- 1940: The Lahore Resolution for a Pakistan state passed at the Muslim League's Annual Session got a boost from the Viceroy's assurance that 'power will not be transferred to any government whose authority is denied by important elements in India'.[13]
- 1942: Congress launched the Quit India Movement and was declared an unlawful organization, with most of its leaders sent to prison. The League did not participate in the movement, but supported the war effort.

- 1945: The Simla conference to discuss the formation of a new executive council collapsed owing to Jinnah's insistence that all Muslim members should be Muslim League nominees.
- 1946: Provincial elections in India saw a Muslim League triumph in the majority 'Pakistan' provinces; the League observed a 'Direct Action Day' on 16 August. The 'Great Calcutta Killing' took place from 16–18 August when 4,000 people were killed and 100,000 rendered homeless. Communal killings spread to Noakhali in East Bengal and Bihar.
- 1947: The resignation of the Khizr Tiwana coalition government in Punjab triggered communal killings in Punjab, which had been relatively quiet so far.
- 1947: In June Indian leaders accepted the Partition plan. Lord Mountbatten announced that independence was to be brought forward from June 1948 to 15 August. Pakistan's independence was announced on 14 August. The boundary awards were announced on 17 August.
- 1971: elections in Pakistan resulted in a majority for the Awami League which did not get the opportunity to form a government.

The asymmetric Partition as yet another unintended consequence

The Partition of 1947 was asymmetric in many ways. In the first place, Pakistan was created as a homeland for Muslims of South Asia, whereas the Indian Republic was constituted from the rump and citizenship was conferred on the basis of residence, regardless of religion. Second, once Pakistan came into existence, the leaders of the Muslim League, the main advocates for the creation of the new state, left their political catchment areas in India and migrated to greener pastures, attracted by the allure of high office, security, spiritual affinity and business opportunities in the new state. As for India, the Indian National Congress stayed on, with the leaders continuing to draw on their clientele, leaving the politician-social base linkage intact. Third, the major institutions, including the army, the country's capital cities and its political parties, remained in their historical locations, whereas in the case of Pakistan, practically all of them had to find new homes and in the process became infused with the new Islamic ideology. Fourth, the Partition of British India, which split the two provinces of Punjab and Bengal, affected Pakistan more than India. The parts that went to Pakistan accounted for 80 per cent of the population of the new country, deeply marked by the trauma of Partition. However, the population of Indian Punjab and West Bengal, who were also affected by Partition, constituted barely 10 per cent of the population of India. Indian leaders such as Advani, who were born in what became Pakistan, subsequently carried the scars of Partition for the rest of their careers.[14] However, taken as a whole, they were a small minority among the vast Indian pool of political leaders, most of whom came from the north, south and west of former British India that were not directly affected by Partition. Finally, as a corporate entity, India maintained continuity with the pre-modern state tradition,[15] whereas for Pakistan, it was a relatively blank canvas, to be painted in the ideological complexion that suited the rulers at a particular point of time. The inclusive ethos and unity in diversity which formed the core principle of India's political culture stayed the course. For Pakistan, however, the sheer contingency of having to define its identity in a manner that would be distinctive, generated more exclusion than inclusion, and the progressive identification and exclusion of the social groups considered inimical to Sunni Islam. This was a clear signal to the Hindus, Sikhs,

Christians and Ahmadias, who increasingly failed to meet the criteria for membership of an Islamic political community.

The second Partition of Pakistan in 1971 was path-dependent on the first, although of course the actual creation of Bangladesh was certainly facilitated by the military intervention of India. Partition gave Nehru's Congress, with the continuity of state-party-mass base linkage, the breathing space for the major political institutions of the state to take shape and strike root. In contrast, the absence of similar linkage for the Muslim League whose leadership migrated en bloc from India to Pakistan, leaving behind the social base, did not give the solid political base to the nascent state in Pakistan. As such, if Partition contributed to the resilience of India, the same phenomenon laid the foundations for the unravelling of Pakistan. However, India held together, but at a cost. The violent insurgency in the Indian state of Jammu and Kashmir, and the vulnerability of India's Muslim minority in the face of Hindu 'majoritarianism', are constant reminders of the unresolved issues of Partition.

The unintended consequences of the two-nation theory as the basis of the creation of Pakistan have been fatal for both neighbours, but relatively more so for Pakistan than India. It instilled a sense of insecurity among non-Muslims as well as among those who adhered to forms of Islam that were not considered to be 'pure'. The dominance of the Urdu-speaking Muhajir migrants in the early formative years, and the exclusion of the East Pakistan elite from the high table of power, injected the seeds of Bengali alienation. India's leaders, lacking ethnic cohesion and constantly searching for electoral majorities, had, of necessity, to shop around for partners with whom to build majority coalitions. In the never-ending game of short-term coalition building led by Nehru's Congress party – polyglot, multicultural, plural and secular – Pakistan was born. It still holds, despite the metamorphosis of the country that emerged from Partition in 1947 into 29 states and sub-states within those states.

Partition: the birth and destiny of two nations

Partitions are best thought of as processes and not as 'events'.[16] The process of partition, and the creation of a new political unit, is the manifestation of a collective urge for a homeland which caused disparate and dispersed people to cohere and emerge as 'nations' during the era of the rise of new nations in Europe. Partition and nation-building are two sides of the same coin, laced with blood and wrapped in memory. As such, the process of partition always creates a two-way traffic of the members of the sought-for community moving in, and of those who no longer belong moving out.

The same drive that has urged like-minded people to converge and the opposite impulse to expel those who do not belong to the nation in Europe has had its echo in Asia and Africa where nationalism and anti-colonial movements became complementary forces. However, with fusion also came fission. Such was the case of the Partition of British India and the creation of Pakistan as a homeland for Muslims of South Asia in 1947, coinciding with independence and the transfer of power.

Pakistan and India: contrasting theories of the nation

Partition contributed to the resilience of India, but the same phenomenon laid the foundations for the unravelling of Pakistan. As a consequence, the second Partition of Pakistan in 1971 can be viewed as the logical effect, or repercussion, of the first great

Partition. Partition produced India and Pakistan, two deeply different nations, both of which adopted diametrically opposing forms of nationalism.[17]

The basic divergence started with the very debate on independence: the two-nation theory was contested among Congress leaders[18] and never got legitimacy in post-colonial India; on the other hand, it was the bedrock upon which Pakistan was built.

From the point of view of the theory of nationalism, Pakistan and India came to represent two contrasting concepts of the nation state: ethnic and ethno-civic, respectively.[19] Ethnic nationalism excludes, while ethno-civic includes. In other words, *being Indian* translates into merely belonging to India as a polity; its meaning is reduced to that of common as well as differentiated citizenship. *Being Pakistani* implies belonging not only to Pakistan as a 'political community' defined by territory but also to a specific faith, Sunni Islam, imbued with a specifically Punjabi ethos.

Understanding such discrepancies in the foundational moment of the two nations is critical to examining and interpreting the dynamics of their evolution. In order to create Pakistan, the Partition of British India was carried out based on the principle that religion rather than territory was to be the criterion of exclusion of people from the previous nation and inclusion into the new one. As a consequence, then, once Islam had been achieved, another major criterion of identity differentiation necessarily emerged: this was ethnicity, understood as shared linguistic and ancestral heritage. The dominance of the Urdu-speaking Muhajir elite in the early formative years, and the exclusion of the East Pakistani elite from the high table of power injected, in this way, the seeds of the Bengali exit.

The second Partition, which saw the transformation of East Pakistan into Bangladesh, is rooted in the first one. More specifically, it occurred because South Asian pan-Islamism was eventually unable to neutralize, or at least harmonize, ethnic differences and localism. These factors, following the cultural, political and economic dominance of a specific group of citizens over the others, developed into centrifugal forces which culminated in the Bangladesh Liberation War. While in this way Bengali nationalism found its fulfilment, other would-be nations continue to call for a more complete self-determination today by giving voice to the search for autonomy which has been repressed or not fully worked out, as is the case in Sindh and Balochistan.[20]

The identity India chose for itself, instead, was that of an overtly multireligious, multiethnic and multicultural polity. This represented at the same time both a challenge and an opportunity for the newborn nation. The need to manage such diversity within the boundaries of a single state provided a political system which incorporated an unprecedented degree of flexibility.

Beyond Partition: an agenda for India and Pakistan

The trauma of Partition lingers on in Pakistan and India. The suspicion and distrust it has injected into the relationship between the two countries has stymied any chance of peaceful and prosperous co-evolution.

The way past the present deadlock in India-Pakistan relations entails a probe into the trauma that led to Partition which deeply influences current politics and requires a consequent change in mindsets and the introduction of appropriate institutions for seeking solutions to the enduring conflict.

The conundrum of Kashmir – the bitter residue of Partition – continues to breed hostility and distrust between the two neighbours. In Pakistan, Kashmir continues to be an evocative symbol of unfinished history, a lodestar for militant nationalists, malcontents and a *raison d'être* for the preponderant power of the army, systematically undermining civilian rule. In order to keep up with India, Pakistan's army had to be allocated a large share of the national wealth; invent myths such as the natural superiority of Pakistani soldiers over their Indian counterparts; and admit non-state actors, and nuclear weapons, as force multipliers against a foe that could claim a bigger resource base and a larger, more conventional army.

Thanks to the trauma of Partition, distrust, misperception and distance has grown over the years between Pakistan and India. This has boosted the power of the military over civilian elites and narrowed the scope for diplomacy. Many important opinion-makers in Pakistan hold that possession of the nuclear bomb is the only guarantee of Pakistan's national survival in the face of both persistent brinkmanship by India that cannot be deterred by conventional weapons and external allies who might fail to deliver *in extremis.*

How does one break out of the vicious circle of Pakistani trauma and Indian suspicion? As we have already seen, the traumatic loss of home and roots in India and the much longed-for gain of a secure homeland in Pakistan was the bedrock of the state. Its leaders were determined not just to make Muslims in South Asia safe in their new home, but also to resurrect the lost glory of Islam in South Asia, the ruling power for seven centuries prior to the arrival of the British. The Indian vision was more complex. It consisted of continuing the legacy of European Enlightenment in its Indian avatar and of building a secular, democratic nation within the territorial space bequeathed to the new leaders by the departing British. Acting as the voice of the new nations, the two sets of leaders catered to two different, conflicting visions. Seen from this angle, the clash after independence, independently of Kashmir, appears preordained.

Nehru, who had watched the traumatic events of Partition unfold, had accepted Partition as a necessary price for independence.[21] His evocation of the deeper bond between the two countries, the nostalgia for the pre-Partition days and a subliminal desire to get back together, a sentiment that was widespread among that generation of Indian leaders, made Pakistan unsure about Indian acceptance of its separate identity, its difference and sovereign equality with India. Whether a benign desire for closer ties or a more strident call for a return to *akhandbharat* (undivided India) from the Hindu right wing, these sentiments emanating from within India bred a deep insecurity about India's intentions regarding its territorial integrity from the outset. The loss of Kashmir (more precisely, the Valley) confirmed this fear. The Indian litany about the need for closer relations based on physical proximity and cultural commonalities feeds into it and makes Pakistanis insecure.

The lessons we have learnt from the history of Partition and its poisonous legacies can be boiled down to a single fact. The possibility of a united India had been wrecked on the issue of power-sharing as the only guarantee of the right of peoples. The inability of Congress leaders to agree to a guaranteed power-sharing scheme drove Jinnah away from the brand of secular politics he shared with the Congress leaders, first to the open arms of the colonial rulers and eventually to the support base of communalist violence. There are two important lessons to be learned here. Pakistan can draw a useful lesson from the success of Indian democracy by the way of dispersion of power and iron-clad guarantees of redress to vulnerable social groups. The lesson is for both countries to bury the hatchet of hatred and talk in terms of concrete interests and devise institutions for sharing responsibility for collective goods such as the environment, water, security and joint ventures. The stalemated South Asian Free Trade Area and SAARC can become regional platforms where the two countries can cooperate to mutual benefit.

Conclusion

How does the past affect the present? What can we learn from the past in order to build a better future? The implications of these questions, with reference to the Partition of British India in 1947, have been considered in this chapter. We have argued that an understanding of the trauma of Partition and its lingering effect can help to pave the way towards the normalization of relations between the distant neighbours. The unintended consequences of Partition have been analysed in terms of the basic values that underpinned the concept, and the asymmetry of the consequences of Partition that deeply affected the nature of state and society in Pakistan vis-à-vis India. The path dependency of the sequence of events that led to the Partition has been analysed with a view to questioning its 'inevitability' and to suggest remedial action that might restore normal relations between the two distant neighbours. Path dependency need not amount to path slavery. The creation of appropriate institutions to generate trust, reinforce security, change mindsets, and to commemorate the victims of Partition and to award symbolic compensation to their progeny can help to pave the way towards the normalization of relations between Pakistan and India.

Little realized at the time, the jubilation that followed Partition in the area that came to be known as Pakistan, and the frustration in India and the vivisection of 'Mother India', were both misplaced. Looking back, one can see how Partition helped India to emerge as a relatively more cohesive political entity compared to pre-Partition India, and stymied the chance for a similar development to occur in Pakistan. The 'moth-eaten Pakistan' as Jinnah called it, was allocated less territory than its leaders had expected. India, on the other hand, under the leadership of Ballabhai Patel, swiftly moved on to integrate the princely states. In consequence, India more than made up for the land 'lost' to Pakistan in terms of total territory. Pakistan was less fortunate. Attempts to create a political core by the Muhajir-led, Urdu-speaking elite of Pakistan led to resentment and alienation in the East Wing. Stretched between the East and the West wings, separated by 1,000 miles of hostile Indian territory and ruled by a military-political elite without a mass base comparable to the Indian National Congress, the creation of national cohesion and modern political institutions in Pakistan had severe obstacles to overcome.

For an enduring solution to the conflict between Pakistan and India, one will need to move beyond the tit-for-tat war games of the two respective armies, and to generate solutions for common problems such as water, terrorism, pilgrimage, access to health and educational facilities, and institutions that the stakeholders might find useful. One has to step beyond the analysis of current politics into the deeper trauma that accounts for the mutual hostility and suspicion. The spiral of 'hostility-suspicion-violent retribution-chosen trauma' that deepens over generations through 'chosen trauma' can be broken through institutionalized dialogue, commemoration of victims and symbolic compensation, and effective flow of information, tourists and trade across the border.

The Partition of 1947 is a salutary lesson for students of unanticipated consequences. It shows how a misstep which loosens a stone can launch a landslide. It is for the progeny of Jinnah and Nehru to understand this historical fact, and to pick up the pieces from where they are, so that they can seek the ways and means to revert the current state of animosity between the two countries to normal diplomacy. The cost of reversing the trend of historical path dependency may well be enormous but failure to arrest this trend can only add to the damage already inflicted.

The rewards of reconciliation between the two countries would be substantial. Both countries can learn from one another. India's successful experiment with the three-language formula,[22] federalization, multi-party democracy and popular accountability, could be valuable for Pakistan. Similarly, the costly experience of Pakistan in seeking to build a state on the narrow basis of religion should act as a warning to India against the growth of a majoritarian democracy. This mutual learning could pave the way to a solution to the Kashmir imbroglio – a challenge that has remained unresolved for the past seven decades. That would be a positive 'unintended consequence' of better India-Pakistan relations.

Notes

1 The author alone is responsible for the opinions expressed in this chapter.
2 Jinnah called the state of Pakistan that emerged a 'moth-eaten or a truncated state'. See Mohammed Ayoob, 'Gandhi's Role in the Partition of India: Why He Was Partially Responsible for the Division', *Foreign Affairs*, 19 October 2017. Perhaps the blame should go more to the office-seekers in Congress than the idealists who were keen to keep India together.
3 Casualty figures vary from the low estimate of 200,000 by the British civil servant Penderel Moon, (*Divide and Quit*, New Delhi, Oxford University Press, 1998, p. 293), to those of two million, estimated by the Mohajir Qaumi Mahaz. Ian Talbot and Gurharpal Singh, *The Partition of India*, Cambridge, Cambridge University Press, p. 62. The Indian judge G. D. Khosla puts the total casualties at 500,000, with an equal number of Muslim and non-Muslim casualties. Gopal Das Khosla, *Stern Reckoning: A Survey of Events Leading Up to and Following the Partition of India*, 2nd edn, New Delhi, Oxford University Press, 1999, p. 299.
4 Chosen trauma refers to 'the shared mental representation of a large group's massive trauma experienced by its ancestors at the hands of an enemy group, and the images of heroes, victims, or both connected with it. Of course, large groups do not intend to be victimized, but they *"choose"* to mythologize and psychologize the mental representation of the event. When this occurs the reality of the event no longer matters to societal movements.' Vamik Volkan, 'Chosen Trauma, the Political Ideology of Entitlement and Violence', *Berlin Meeting*, vol. 10, 2004. The psychoanalyst Sudhir Kakar has used this concept to analyse the memories of violence in Kakar, *The Colours of Violence*, Delhi, Viking, 1995. Mitra has analysed two contrasting memories from Kakar in Subrata Mitra, *Puzzle of India's Governance: Culture, Context and Comparative Theory*, London, Routledge, 2005, pp. 213–17.
5 See Subrata Mitra, 'Intimate Enemies: Trauma, Violence and Longing in India-Pakistan Relations', *India Review*, vol. 16, no. 2, 2017, pp. 266–76, for an elaboration of these arguments.
6 Unintended consequences are understood as unanticipated outcomes of interventions in complex systems and processes. Robert K. Merton, *On Social Structure and Science*, Chicago, University of Chicago Press, 1996.
7 Shahid Javed Burki, personal communication, ISAS, 5 January 2018.
8 Paradoxically, the idea of Pakistan as a separate nation-state was not clearly spelt out in the renowned Lahore Resolution of the Muslim League. Perry Anderson argued rightly that the wording of the Lahore Resolution was deliberately ambiguous, and the word Pakistan was not mentioned at all. See *The Indian Ideology*, London, Verso, 2012, pp. 59–60. For further details, see ch. 2, 'Partition', pp. 49–103.
9 'You are free; you are free to go to your temples, you are free to go to your mosques or to any other place or worship in this State of Pakistan. You may belong to any religion or caste or creed that has nothing to do with the business of the State'. Muhammad Ali Jinnah's first Presidential Address to the Constituent Assembly of Pakistan, 11 August 1947.
10 According to Pakistan Bureau of Statistics data, at the time of Partition, Hindus constituted 12.9 per cent of the population of Pakistan, whereas in 2017 they made up only 1.6 per cent of the population.
11 Shah Rukh Khan, Azim Premji and Sania Mirza represent different facets of 'achieving' Muslims of India. There are no legal or constitutional constraints on the upward mobility of Muslims in India, although as one can see from the evidence painstakingly assembled in the Sachar committee report, there are effective social, political and economic conditions that adversely affect the welfare of Muslims in India. See Riaz Hassan (ed.) *Indian Muslims: Struggling for Equality of Citizenship*, Melbourne, Melbourne University Press, 2016.

12 Fear of the 'Balkanization' of India was very much in vogue in the 1950s. See Selig Harrison, *India: The Most Dangerous Decades,* Princeton, NJ, Princeton University Press.

13 Ian Talbot and Gurharpal Singh, *The Partition of India*, Cambridge, Cambridge University Press, 2009, p. xv. That was an indication of the Imperial strategy of Partition in India.

14 See L. K. Advani, *My Country, My Life*, Delhi, Rupa, 2008 for a personal account of the Partition trauma and the origin of Advani's penchant for Hindutva.

15 See Subrata Mitra and Michael Liebig, *Kautilya's Arthashastra. An Intellectual Portrait: Classical Roots of Modern Politics in India*, Baden Baden, Nomos, 2016, for the evolution of India's state tradition from the Gupta dynasty, third century BCE to the present day.

16 For an analysis of the Partition as a long-drawn-out process, see Vazira Fazila-Yacoobali Zamindar, *The Long Partition and the Making of Modern South Asia: Refugees, Boundaries, Histories*, New York, Columbia University Press, 2007.

17 Talbot and Singh, *Partition of India*, p. 179 write: 'Nation and state-building [in Pakistan] after 1947 was to be constructed on the edifice that denied pluralism, regionalism and ethnic diversity with devastating results for relations between the centre and ethnic minorities. The Bengalis were not only geographically distant but had to endure the marginalization of their language and culture in an Urdu-dominated national life. Uneven economic development and the exclusion from the army and the bureaucracy compounded the situation, turning East Pakistan (Bengal) into a colony of West Pakistan. The emergence of Bangladesh in 1971 following civil war and Indian military intervention was thus not the inevitable inheritance of Partition; it was mainly the produce of a flawed nation and state-building enterprise shaped by it.'

18 However, as far as the creation of West Bengal was concerned, the Hindu-dominated Congress leaders of Bengal were desperate for a state for the Hindu Bengalis, and put enormous pressures on the Congress High Command to get it. This was another instance of the application of the 'two-nation theory' which is seldom mentioned in the literature on Partition. See J. Chatterjee, *Bengal Divided Hindu Communalism and Politics 1932–1947*, Cambridge, Cambridge University Press, 1995; see also its sequel, *The Spoils of Partition: Bengal and India 1947–1967*, Cambridge, Cambridge University Press, 2007.

19 H. Bhattacharyya, 'Ethnic and Civic Nationhood in India: Concept, History, Institutional Innovations and Contemporary Challenges', in S. C. Saha (ed.) *Ethnicity and Socio-Political Changes in Africa and Other Developing Countries*, Lanham, MD, Lexington Books, 2008, pp. 169–95.

20 The reference here is to the short-lived Jiye Sindh movement and sub-nationalist stirrings in Balochistan.

21 Talbot and Singh argue that 'Partition was not foisted on reluctant Indian political leaders but in large measure willed into existence by them. As Nehru was to acknowledge in 1969, "The truth is that we were tired men … We saw the fires burning in Punjab … The plan for Partition offered us a way out and we took it"'. See *Partition of India*, p. 178.

22 See Subrata Mitra, *Politics in India: Structure, Process and Policy*, London, Routledge, 2017, pp. 60–61, for a discussion of how India has developed a formula to balance the importance of regional languages with Hindi – the official language – and English, the link language.

4

Evolution of politics

Shirin Tahir-Kheli

First leaders

The circumstances that led to the creation of Pakistan were set in motion by a desire for independence from imperial Britain in August 1947. What transpired thereafter was a combination of decisions made deliberately and events outside state control. In this chapter, we will look at where Pakistan is today and how it got there.

The break-up of colonial empires began in the aftermath of the Second World War. A victorious but exhausted Britain opted out of its 'Crown jewel', the Indian subcontinent, where a movement for independence had taken a firm hold. Concomitantly, the desire for a separate Muslim homeland led by Muhammed Ali Jinnah resulted in the birth of Pakistan on 14 August 1947. Despite the euphoria of independence, it was clear that this was no ordinary beginning. As evocatively detailed by Yasmin Khan,[1] the partition of the Indian subcontinent into India and Pakistan, respectively, was accompanied by the largest and perhaps one of the bloodiest transfers of people across the newly declared international border.

Aspirations for the new state of Pakistan were not matched by performance. Indeed, as Javed Burki and other scholars point out, the new government had to learn to function in the total absence of any set of rules or established order and indeed without the physical facilities that any government requires. The officials of the day recall their sense of being pioneers. Dedication made up for lack of resources. Pakistan's political world of 1947–48 was shaken by the early loss of the nation's founder, Jinnah, who died in September 1948. Thus, the 'movement' for Pakistan, which Jinnah oversaw to a successful conclusion, was not matched by his command over the 'reality' of nation-building.

Much of what became Pakistan lay outside the traditional trappings of governmental institutions under the British Raj. Pakistan was born under what Shahid Javed Burki describes as: 'exceptionally difficult circumstances ... the country had nothing: no capital city, no currency, no central bank, not much of a banking sector, very little industry, and a great deal of poverty'.[2] One of the largest transfers ever of human beings took place within days of independence, when six million Hindus and Sikhs left for India and eight million Muslims crossed over from India into Pakistan.

Today, it is generally acknowledged that one of the key elements of a successful route to building a stable democratic state is the presence of a 'first leader' who serves as a unifying beacon.[3] Jinnah's vision of Pakistan was of a democratic state with important institutions that would safeguard minority interests. The comparison with the stability produced by the long-term leadership of Jawaharlal Nehru as neighbouring India's first Prime Minister offers a stark contrast.

Yet the argument made by the current Indian Prime Minister, Narinder Modi, that India and Pakistan gained independence simultaneously, is simply too facile. So why has there been a discrepancy between the performance of the two countries over these past 70 years?

While the question can legitimately be asked, the qualitative difference might have been less dramatic had the circumstances of independence and the division of assets between India and Pakistan, respectively, had been more equitably managed.

For example, New Delhi refused to pass on to Pakistan its share of the funds allocated by London in recognition of British India's contribution to the British Army during the Second World War. The ostensible excuse was the notable absence of a central bank in Pakistan. It took a visit to New Delhi by Prime Minister Liaquat Ali Khan and his Minister of Finance Ghulam Muhammad as well as Mahatama Gandhi and Lord Louis Mountbatten to persuade the Indian Prime Minister Jawaharlal Nehru to allow the funds to be transferred to Pakistan.[4]

Such challenges, along with the reality that sources of water and electricity remained in India, meant that there was the potential for deprivation and likely sources of future conflict.

The vision of the founders of Pakistan and the commitment of its early leaders carried the new nation across the threshold of survival. However, the promise of Pakistan required much more than that. In that sense, the country was part of the age of decolonization when newly independent states sought prosperity and development in a variety of cultural and social milieus. The 1950s and 1960s demonstrated that it was not simply the Protestant work ethic per Max Weber[5] that spurred modern industrial Europe, but rather crucial decisions by the nascent states to create a political system of power-sharing that led to better arrangements for aligning different objectives and interests.

Pakistan was in particular need of an overarching father figure/first leader to draw together the myriad parts of a tribal or parochial society to help the nation to navigate between the competing interests of regions and to propose the compromises necessary for the establishment of a vibrant and successful state.

Early remarks by the founder, Muhammad Ali Jinnah, gave hope that Pakistan was to be a moderate state with room for all despite its creation as a Muslim nation. Given the difficulties associated with getting a modern state off the ground quickly, the inclusiveness Jinnah spoke of made a great deal of sense.

Linguistic and cultural differences complicated matters. Bengali, a language with its own proud tradition, spoken in what was at the time East Pakistan, meant adherence to rules of the political game put in place in the formative early months after independence in August 1947.

National unity was sought in the search for a common language. Urdu was chosen, but only 8 per cent of the total population of West and East Pakistan combined spoke Urdu as a first language, whereas some 55 per cent spoke Bengali.[6] The language issue and the ensuing struggle is well documented by scholars.[7] Political development and also the establishment of critically needed institutions regulated by a constitution were delayed.

Jinnah died in December 1948 as discussions regarding the choice between Urdu and Bengali as a national language were underway. His passing meant the loss of a great leader and the ideal of collaboration across Pakistan lost its power.

There were other political leaders and they struggled to set up a constitutional government with institutions to govern at the national and provincial level. This was the face of the existing conditions of stress mentioned earlier in this chapter. Then came a second major shock. On 17 October 1951 Liaquat Ali Khan, Jinnah's chief lieutenant and Pakistan's first Prime Minister, who also held the foreign affairs, defence and frontier regions portfolios, was assassinated. Thus, the man who had strived to promote the idea of Pakistan and helped to make it a reality was gone.

The political science literature gives great credibility to the importance of leadership in nation-building. The history of many nations during the post-colonial era demonstrates the need for early agreement on the rules of the game following independence. In Pakistan's political development, the process was made complicated by Liaquat's death.

H. S. Suhrawardy, the last Chief Minister of United Bengal, was the only Muslim League leader of note to have held political power in pre-Partition Bengal. While he went on to become one of the early prime ministers of Pakistan, he was unable to tempt enough East Pakistanis to re-balance the old British-led exclusion of Bengalis from the Pakistan Army and the bureaucracy, which are two rapidly rising power centres.

Pakistan was explicitly created as a separate homeland for the Muslims of the subcontinent. The way in which British India was divided meant that large numbers of Muslims were left in India after independence. Migration continued apace for those who chose to live in Pakistan. Millions did not.[8]

If Pakistan's *raison d'être* was religion, given that Islam did not create or condone a religious priesthood, how would the *ulema* fare? After all, it was the secularist/modernist leaders like Jinnah and Iqbal who had helped to create the very idea of Pakistan and to oversee its birth. Pakistan was situated within the framework of the universal cry for self-determination that sprang up after World War II. As Lawrence Ziring points out:

> The creation of an Islamic state in South Asia therefore was not the work of clerics and religious divines but rather the determined effort by informed, westernized, materially conditioned elements who had the capacity to articulate the desires of a population that could feel but not necessarily express its desires.[9]

Thus, even as leadership was a crucial component of Pakistan's political development, the absence of strong religious involvement sidelined the *ulema*, who were not in favour of establishing a state on the pretext of rescuing Islam. In fact, many prominent *ulema* joined the Indian Congress Party in order to ensure that Muslim fears of Hindu domination were allayed.[10] The *ulema* chafed at being left 'high and dry and were angry at the new leadership mostly out of jealousy because the people listened to it and had no use for the *ulema* who had gradually come to sing a tune that was completely out of harmony with the feelings of the community'.[11]

The diminution of influence by the *ulema* in the body politic of early Pakistan was compensated by the rising importance of two state institutions: the military and the bureaucracy. The distance between them was made even more consequential as the latter two were considered to be modern and the former regressive.

Institutions

Leadership gaps, exacerbated by political wrangling between the two separate wings, diminished early prospects for the development of another critical component for political development, namely institutions.

Condoleezza Rice refers to the critical nature of institutions in her book *Democracy*, calling them the 'scaffolding for democracy'. A more 'ethnically homogeneous population is likely to find it easier to achieve stability. And if civil society – all the private, non-governmental groups, associations, and institutions in the country – is already well developed, the scaffolding for the new democracy is stronger'.[12]

Taking the above criteria into consideration, Pakistan's path is a complicated one. Diversity, uneven growth in the country's political institutions, with the military and bureaucratic portions receiving early support to the detriment of civil society, resulted in weak systems of check and balance.

Pakistan proved a complicated mix hinted at by Rice when she notes that contrary to earlier racist views that only some countries can aspire to democracy, there is a diverse group of countries across the globe who testify to its universal appeal.

Despite periods of martial law and authoritarian control of the political system by military rulers, the Pakistanis grasped democracy whenever they were offered the chance, and even demanded it after the 1960s. From his perch as a federal minister first for Natural Resources and subsequently for Foreign Affairs in the cabinet of General Ayub Khan, Zulfikar Ali Bhutto launched his populist politics aimed at the average Pakistani with the right to vote. Indeed, his early slogan 'roti, kapra, makan' ('food, shelter, clothing') was the cry to enforce the provision of basics (food, clothing and shelter) as the basic right of citizens. The creation of a mindset of expectations, even entitlement, forever changed the relationship between the governors and the governed.

Pakistan's institutional landscape developed during the push and pull of democratic periods interspersed by military rule. Wars with India, over Kashmir and then over Bangladesh's independence from Pakistan, provided watershed moments in Pakistan's political development. Parameters of national politics were set by the absence of peace with India. While political leaders, and even military rulers, sometimes made and accepted overtures with their large neighbour, none of them challenged the commitment of a huge proportion of the national wealth for the purpose of national security, i.e. defence against India.

The Indian mindset of non-negotiation on Kashmir and its sense of superiority in national politics meant mostly cool relations between India and Pakistan at best. Over time, as business and political leaders sensed the importance of normalization and even rapprochement, unofficial attempts at building bridges between people, parliamentarians and even some institutions continued. From time to time, secret channels of communication were opened between the leaders of India and Pakistan seeking a permanent improvement in this state of affairs.[13] However, from the mid-1990s the growth of religious sponsorship of anti-Indian sentiment within Pakistan led to an important role for the very elements who had been sidelined at independence – the *ulema*.

Over the past 70 years political development in Pakistan has been affected by outside influences, often exerted to the detriment of the local institutions. The 'scaffolding for democracy' suffered as short-cuts to national security wove alliances for military collaboration between Pakistan and the United States in the mid-1950s and strengthened them after the invasion of Afghanistan by the former Soviet Union in December 1979. The political game inside the country was sidelined as General Zia ul-Haq made Pakistan the frontline state in expelling the 'Godless Communists' from neighbouring Afghanistan.

The influx of foreign-born *mujahideen* (Islamist fighters) into Pakistan in the 1980s did bring about the expulsion of the Soviets from Afghanistan and helped the United States to win the Cold War following the demise of its Soviet enemy, but it also had profound consequences for Pakistan's political development.

Pakistan no longer had a controlled executive, so essential for lasting political development. A military leader with his own vision for a religious Pakistan changed the power structure with rising religiosity in the severe Wahabi model that arrived with fighters in the 1980s. The military-*mullah* alliance in the Zia period left a legacy of interference in power and resources by uneducated elements in most of the conservative regions.

Pakistan, with its burgeoning population of some 202 million, absorbed these dramatic changes even as civil society developed. Elections meant the right to vote, a critical first step on the road to democracy. However, that right included religious elements with their own vision and agenda for Pakistan's future. They created political parties as platforms and drew on street power to build electoral support and a win via the ballot box. Thus far, the more modernist elements have fared better at the polls.

Militarization of political development

Born in turbulence in a region of strategic consequence, Pakistan at 70 has carved out a niche for politics even as it pays for a robust military to safeguard national security, particularly against India. The upper hand the military establishment holds tends to play out in reduced space for political development, especially during repeated periods of martial law.[14]

Pakistan's experience was no different from that of a host of newly emerging nations where the lopsided development of military authority in the face of weak civilian institutions became a fact of life.[15]

Executive power enabled successive military rulers to seek to consolidate their control over the system, using another type of hybrid political development to transition from strict martial law to a politico-military alliance. This included General Ayub's 'basic democracy' in the 1960s, General Zia's Islamicization and Majlis-i-Shoora in the 1980s, and General Musharraf's 'third way' and support for his leadership of a faction of the Muslim League in the 2002–08 period.

Military leaders searched for political institutionalization through their own brand and sought participation in elections and institutionalization of their preferred models for political development. Each voiced strong belief that their brand would be more inclusive. Some, like General Pervez Musharraf, included strong support for women's participation at the local and national level, provided for a free press, and spoke eloquently of the need for 'enlightened moderation' in the Islamic world in order to combat terrorism following the attacks on the United States on 11 September 2001 (known as 9/11). Pakistan would be a moderate Muslim state but not a supplicant of its richer Muslim neighbours or of its more distant partner, the United States, in the 'war against terror' following 9/11.

While each successive military ruler moved through some form of political legitimization, none aimed political development at the militarization of Pakistan. Even when an increasing number of traditional civilian jobs went to the retired or even serving military officers in bureaucratic, economic or educational realms, the military generally maintained a distance from civil society. Military leaders retained their support for political development, economic progress and eliminating extremism and terrorism.

Governance and justice, respectively, were the two most important things that the Pakistani people hoped would improve when the political order shifted from elected civilians to the military. Corruption, real and perceived, destroyed the credibility of the political leadership and the army leaders stepped in and promised a clear path to political development. Eventually, even they came under scrutiny for underperforming as the rising tide of popular discontent pressed for a 'constrained executive'[16] through elections and a return to legitimate civilian rule. Even as the joke went round that 'there are general elections going on in Pakistan to decide which general will win', in the past elections in Pakistan have been serious affairs with competing visions of political development. A high price has sometimes been paid, for example, the assassination of Benazir Bhutto in December 2007 as she campaigned for the upcoming election.

Building a nation and building its defences

As this chapter shows, the absence of a political architecture at independence ensured a long and complicated path to political development in Pakistan. Limited resources meant institution-building across a diverse polity, separated into two wings with 1,000 miles of hostile India in between.

The often-bloody transfer of citizens both ways across international boundaries at independence added to the chaos as noted earlier. However, the preponderant allocation for defence in Pakistan's annual budget, estimated at 30–55 per cent was a deliberate choice that slowed down political development owing to its impact on scarce resources.

In another conflict taking place half a continent away, the Arabs and the Palestinians were locked in a bitter struggle with Israel over what once were Palestinian lands. With the active help of the United States and other Western powers, Israel fought to keep its then newly independent state intact. Successive wars only served to expand the borders of Israel as the boundaries of neighbouring Arab states shrank.

Israel's defence establishment grew rapidly and the assistance it received in this regard from the United States underwrote robust national capabilities. As for the Palestinians, while Arab and Muslim regimes paid for refugee and other assistance, the support was in the form of diplomatic isolation of Israel in all international arenas. Although Israel chafed at this 'cordon sanitaire', its establishment and prosperity were enshrined in its special relationship with the United States.

Pakistan, however, found itself with an issue it began early to define as critical: inclusion of self-determination for the people of Kashmir whose Muslim majority opted for Pakistan in 1947 even as its Hindu ruler chose India under the British formula for partition. The 1948 Indo–Pakistan war over Kashmir did not substantially change the status quo even as it gave Pakistan some parts of the divided state.

The wider world of Islam paid even less serious attention to Kashmir than it did to the Israeli–Palestinian conflict. Indian diplomacy and Pakistani military action in 1948, 1965 and 1999 to change the status quo led to general wariness despite UN Security Council resolutions supporting a plebiscite for the Kashmiris to decide whether they wanted to be part of India or of Pakistan.

Thus, Kashmir extracted an early and very high price in the political development of Pakistan. War remains an option in the face of Indian incorporation of Kashmir as a state. New Delhi has turned ever more belligerent against its own Kashmiri population with a strong army presence and paramilitary forces that are ready to inflict damage and casualties on Kashmiris even now.

As foreign fighters entered Pakistan in the early 1980s to fight alongside the US-backed war to expel the Soviets from Afghanistan, Pakistan's military ruler cultivated Washington. Large-scale military and economic assistance for Pakistan helped the United States to achieve its goal to expel the Soviet forces and bring about the demise of the Soviet Union. The cost for Pakistan was the preponderantly heavy hand its intelligence and security services received as future arbiters of national security.

The legendary *mujahideen* who had succeeded in defeating a superpower became overconfident in conjuring up ways to help Pakistani security services as an option in Kashmir. Foreign policy, once the sole responsibility of civilian political leaders, never recovered from the shadowy manipulation of these pseudo-religious elements by the system. Despite the heavy price paid by Pakistan in terms of the number of deaths incurred as a result of terrorism over the past decade, right-wing religious elements backed by elements of the security forces supported or at least tolerated their existence in order to keep all options open.

Pakistan's reputation as a nation intent on modernization suffered hugely as a result of terrorism, such as when a handful of members of a militant Pakistani organization, the Lashkar-e-Taiba, carried out a series of co-ordinated attacks that lasted four days in Mumbai, India, in November 2008. The terror they unleashed resulted in 164 dead and over 300 injured.

The event left hopes for a permanent rapprochement between India and Pakistan in tatters. Furthermore, the resulting insecurity in the subcontinent meant that sizeable resources had to be earmarked for the future military needs of Pakistan. Meanwhile, the Kashmir dispute became ever more impossible to resolve. Resources for other key components including education, health, technology development, infrastructure became scarcer.

Assistance from former key allies such as the United States dried up. Then came offer from the People's Republic of China of some US $46 billion via its development of the One Belt, One Road initiative. Under the auspices of the China–Pakistan Economic Corridor (CPEC) the development of infrastructure will aid Pakistan's economic progress and tie it into a transport network with other nations to the north and west of the country. Security concerns to deal with threats to the various planned projects have led to the deployment of some 15,000 Pakistani security personnel to protect the effort.

Besides the scale of the China's commitment of resources in Pakistan, the CPEC will also strengthen ties between these two countries who have over the decades managed their relationship particularly well. China is an important country. Its outreach to Pakistan even at this time while the other traditional ally, the United States, has grave concerns, makes Pakistan a key player in the region and beyond.

Growth of civil society

In the immediate aftermath of independence, the prevailing conditions ensured the chaotic development of participatory government. Control over the state was the business of the political leadership, the bureaucracy and the military.

What is the relationship between nation and state? Taking the subcontinent's experiences into consideration, scholars point to a state of nationhood that implied that more than the geographical boundaries existed even prior to the arrival of the British and the subsequent creation of the state under British rule.[17] As Britain exited its former colony following the creation of India and Pakistan as independent and separate entities, did the sense of a Muslim nation translate into the building and development of a modern Pakistani state?

One can argue that the political development of Pakistan proceeded on two parallel tracks. The first track was the development of the 'state' which in this case meant not only the institutionalization of political parties and the creation of national and provincial legislatures but also the concomitant development of defence institutions and structures.

Meanwhile, the development of the 'nation' involved resolving tensions between the Bengali nationalism of East Pakistan with the Punjabi dominance of West Pakistan. After 1971 Pakistan's national focus involved cementing a broader Muslim identity following the military defeat which gave Bangladesh its independence. As Prime Minister, Zulfikar Ali Bhutto was instrumental in the outreach to the Islamic world and the presence of some 39 Islamic heads of state at the February 1974 Islamic Summit in Lahore was a visual demonstration of Pakistan's Muslim identity.

As the decades unfolded, civil society in Pakistan became active in charting a parallel path to development. Despite economic and social constraints, the people demanded participatory roles in the development of political and economic life of the state. Rising access to education meant a new class of educated youth looking for employment. The rural and urban divide meant varying rates of development. Political parties with access to development funds offered a channel for assistance for the development of constituencies.

Large-scale labour migration to the oil-rich kingdoms of Saudi Arabia and the Gulf states brought some relief from population pressure and assisted in the development of the rural areas from whence these workers hailed. Annual remittances to Pakistan exceeded US $19 billion, with some 63 per cent coming from Arab Gulf states in 2015–16.[18] The links also made the need for greater co-operation with the Muslim world a necessity.

A burgeoning population put stress on domestic resources and services. Combined with political ineptitude, patronage and failing services, Pakistanis learnt to step in for simple and sometimes complicated roles to provide services, particularly in the rural areas.

The rise of female participation in Pakistan is one of its greatest success stories. That women have helped to spearhead services at the village level as well as at the national level is an important indicator of opportunities made and seized. Despite the rise of more religious orthodox elements in the north of Pakistan after 1979, Pakistani women have been trailblazers at all the levels they are able to access.

Over the years, political leaders, including some military chiefs such as General Pervez Musharraf during his period in office as President, offered special quotas and protections for increasing political participation of women in Pakistan at the national, provincial and local level. Their involvement in media showcased talent as media freedom meant exponential growth of print and electronic media sources.

Women led in educational success in schools and universities even as state funding for female literacy as a percentage of overall spending dropped. Women entrepreneurs augmented and sometimes surpassed governmental creativity in expanding educational opportunities.

Non-governmental organizations (NGOs) are today an important part of the political development of Pakistan. Organized by civil society and funded through partnerships, they supplement state-sponsored development. Often, these NGOs are at the forefront demanding good governance and accountability. From private urgings to street demonstrations, civil society shows its muscle and is often hard to ignore.

NGOs cover a range of political development activity. They educate the electorate, help to garner votes, and participate in development schemes in all areas of Pakistan. They are today critical to institution-building. And, as in the case of protection of human rights, unmatched in delivering accountability, especially for women despite great odds. As noted by Rice, 'Because democracy is built for disruption, people are going to challenge the institutions'.[19] Of course she is talking of a 'constrained executive' that is the United States. Yet even in Pakistan, civil society now serves as one of the few constraints that ultimately presses for accountability.

Above all, the work of civil society in Pakistan over the past 70 decades has created ties across the country based on shared work. One can make the case that the values and work have also helped to create and sustain a sense of the 'nation' that is Pakistan.

Conclusion

Amartya Sen, Nobel Laureate in Economics, argues that 'Development can be seen as a process of expanding the real freedoms that people enjoy'.[20] He notes that democratic participatory government is now the pre-eminent model of political organization. The goal of political as well as economic and social development then becomes the advancement of freedom.

For Pakistan, the process of political development was jump-started on 14 August 1947 with freedom having been achieved. It can be argued that, in fact, through the very creation of a Muslim state the founders offered the goal they had espoused for decades in a Hindu-dominated India.

There followed the hard task of political development to promote opportunity, participation, inclusiveness and political and civil liberties.

The record of these past 70 years is a mixed one. Periods of participatory government were followed by more limited alternate models of governance aimed or justified by the promise of a less corrupt, more accountable system of decision making. Traditional centres of power, such as the landed class or the military, play their ongoing roles as arbiters in the political system.

Incentives and constraints in the political development of Pakistan were handled over time with varying degrees of success. Expectations of progress alternated with periods of disappointment. There was no magic formula such as a unifying long-term leader, a given constitution, relative homogeneity of the population, rising rates of literacy, all of which would make the political development aspects a great deal easier.

Compared to several of the countries studied in the *Why Nations Fail* report, Pakistan fares reasonably well. The conflict over institutions and the accompanying distribution of resources was complicated, yet was managed successfully up until 1971 despite the initial division of the country into two separate wings.

The resource pool for political and other development was constrained by the large chunk of funds that went on defence, regardless of who was in power. The desire for a nuclear weapons programme as the ultimate guarantor of national existence against a hostile and increasingly less secular India further enhanced security over political development.

Pluralism is important in accountability despite the fact that it does not guarantee it. Pakistan's political development offers a mixed record even as expectations and even demands for accountability have bubbled up from time to time with important consequences for the political system. The growing role of the judiciary and that of civil society and a free press helps to restrain the traditional political pillars of the state.

Growth of a multi-party system broadened the Pakistan base even if key institutions of power were headed by the elite. As argued by Acemoglu and Robinson, in order to understand why some nations get it right while others get it wrong, you have to 'study how decisions actually get made, who gets to make them, and why those people decide to do what they do'.[21] That is, the politics and political process of Pakistan.

Finally, one has to recognize that despite its difficulties, Pakistan's political development today is much further advanced than that which it inherited in 1947. One need only ask 'as compared to what?' The large population of today's Pakistan is unlikely to have fared better in present-day India. The problems which Muslims face of access to the best education or jobs, and the killing of villagers for eating beef or even for transporting cows is a sharp reminder of the current Indian leadership's position.

However, that does not excuse Pakistan's leadership from working to create a more coherent and accountable state. Pakistan's history of federal-provincial relations is thus far a complicated one with limited decentralization. While institution-building has occurred over the past 70 years, the state record of periods of military rule interspersed with political civilian governments makes for an atypical democratic model of governance.

Change of government through successful national elections is a path that seems to be taking hold. Tensions between main political parties and the desire for democratic rule runs up against pressures of national security. The ever-present military shadow over the government gives a sense of democracy at the sufferance of the military.

Pakistan remains largely outside the circle of countries in the Islamic world under pressure for the creation of 'democracy promotion' by the United States. In the past, economic and military assistance has been suspended when democracy has been overthrown by military rulers. An interesting study points out that the juxtaposition of linkages and leverage accompanied the US push for democracy. While the linkages ensured economic, military and communication ties with the West, leverage exerted in the form of conditionality of assistance, state-to-state pressure and diplomacy, is insufficient to establish democracies as it fails to establish the necessary foundations such as civil liberties, level playing fields, etc. Linkages with the United States fostered the development of the military in Pakistan, thus making Pakistan 'a unique case in which linkages might be fostering authoritarianism rather than democracy'.[22]

The future pace of Pakistan's political development is likely to depend on the growth of its institutional capacity for governance and transparency. While democratization has occurred over the past 70 years, its pace is uneven. Future political development is likely to occur if the trend for the empowerment of citizens, competitive political parties, a growing private sector, a vibrant press and responsible military behaviour become the model. Management of terrorism, both as a critical need for internal development and as a response to outside pressure for regional stability will continue to put stress on resources for political development through civil-military tensions and restrictions on economic and infrastructure development.

Governance, namely 'the mechanism, processes and institutions through which citizens and their groups articulate their interests, exercise their legal right, meet their obligations, and mediate their differences' will be a critical component for future political development.[23] Managing corruption, dealing with exemptions for the landed elite from taxes and a timely access to justice will go a long way to creating a better sense of a more inclusive political system with a rule of law and an independent judiciary. Civil-military relations remain a key factor for sustained political development.

The 28 July 2017 dismissal of Nawaz Sharif as Prime Minister by the Supreme Court on charges of corruption was not expected to end Pakistan's continuation of parliamentarianism through to the next general election in May 2018. Dynastic rule coupled with unaccounted for riches made transparent through publicly released documents had already compromised Sharif. Despite the fact that Pakistan's history from 1971 onwards is nearly equally divided between presidential rule and parliamentary democracy, the current situation – characterized by an independent judiciary, free press, civil society and chastened military – favours the continuation of parliamentarianism regardless of Sharif's dismissal.[24] One has to assume here that political vendettas between personalities of various political parties all see a common good in keeping friction below levels that threaten the entire system.

There is no denying the 'Muslimness' of Pakistan. Both the nation and the state acknowledge that. The narrative of belonging distinguishes Pakistan from the so-called Hindu majoritarian 'communalism' in India.[25] Pakistan at 70 is more than the sum of the Muslim parts of pre-Partition India.

Notes

1 *The Great Partition: The Making of India and Pakistan*, New Haven, CT, Yale University Press, 2008.
2 Shahid Javed Burki and Shirin Tahir-Kheli, *Pakistan Today: The Case for U.S.-Pakistan Relations,* Johns Hopkins University School of Advanced International Studies, Foreign Policy Institute, 2017, p. 33.
3 Francis Fukuyama, *Political Order and Political Decay: From the Industrial Revolution to the Globalization of Democracy*, New York: Macmillan, 2014; Condoleezza Rice, *Democracy: Stories from the Long Road to Freedom*, New York: Twelve, 2017.
4 Stanley Wolpert, *Gandhi*, London, Oxford University Press, 1974.
5 Max Weber, *The Protestant Ethic and the Spirit of Capitalism*, New York, Penguin, 2002.
6 S. M. Ikram and Percival Spear, *The Cultural Heritage of Pakistan*, London, Oxford University Press, 1955.
7 See Wayne A. Wilcox Wilcox, *Pakistan: The Consolidation of a Nation*, New York, Columbia University Press, 1963; Khalid B. Sayeed, *The Political System of Pakistan*, Boston, Houghton Mifflin Company, 1967.
8 See Shahid Javed Burki for a discussion of what would have happened if Britain had not decided to partition India on the basis of religion and left India with a large Indian Muslim community. '*Pakistan Is 70: What If?*', Institute of South Asian Studies, National University of Singapore, 14 August 2017.
9 Lawrence Ziring, *Pakistan: The Enigma of Political Development*, Boulder, CO, 1980, p. 24.
10 Ibid., pp. 23–24.
11 Ishtiaq Husain Qureshi, *Ulema in Politics*, 2nd edn, Karachi, Ma'aref, 1974, p. 384.
12 Rice, *Democracy*, p. 11.
13 See www.fpri.org/article/2017/08/track-ii-indo-pakistani-diplomacy-1995-2003-balusa-group/.
14 For detailed study of politico-military relations in the early years, see Keith Callard, *Pakistan: A Political study*, London, George Allen & Unwin, 1957; Wayne A. Wilcox, *Pakistan: The Consolidation of a Nation*, New York, Columbia University Press, 1963.
15 Samuel P. Huntington, *Political Order in Changing Societies*, New York, Yale University Press, 1968; Henry Bienen (ed.), *The Military and Modernization*, Chicago, Aldine Atherton, 1971.
16 Rice, *Democracy*, p. 10.
17 Sugata Bose and Ayesha Jalal (eds) *Nationalism, Democracy and Development*, New Delhi, Oxford University Press, 1997, p. 71.
18 *Dawn,* 16 July 2017.
19 Rice, *Democracy*, p. 16.
20 Amartya Sen, *Development as* Freedom, Anchor Books, New York, 1999, p. 3.
21 Ibid.
22 Aamer Taj, Muhammad Nouman, and Saleem Gul, 'The dynamics of international political economy relationships and its influence on the process of democratisation, institution building and national governance structure in Pakistan', *South Asian Studies*, vol. 30, no. 1, 2015, p. 203. Available at http://search.proquest.com/docview/1696718546.
23 Abu Rashid Jafri and Farida Faisal, 'Problems and Prospects of Good Governance in Pakistan', *New Horizons*, vol, 8, no. 2, 2014, p. 81. Available at http://search.proquest.com/docview/1558356245.
24 Shahid Javed Burki, 'Pakistan's Democracy Will Survive', *Project Syndicate*, 7 August 2017.
25 Bose and Jalal, 'Exploding Communalism', in *Nationalism, Democracy and Development*, p. 103.

5

Islam, society and politics in Pakistan

Riaz Hassan

Islam has had a profound influence on Pakistani society and the country's political culture. In order to fully appreciate these linkages we need to acquaint ourselves with the history of how Islam came to put down roots in the South Asian subcontinent, as well as understanding why, unlike in Spain for example, Islam succeeded in finding a permanent home in the socio-cultural milieu of the subcontinent. Much of the earlier writings on these aspects highlight the exploits of the Muslim invaders of India and the role of coercion in converting the conquered population to Islam. Over the past 100 years or so historical evidence has been systematically chronicled which shows that missionary work by Muslim Sufi saints in the Indian subcontinent played a critical role in Islamization. This historical evidence has provided valuable insights into the role of missionary Islam in the evolution of Muslim society in the Indian subcontinent and how profoundly the social structure of contemporary Pakistani society has been influenced by the religious and social institutions of missionary Islam.[1]

The Muslim mysticism reached India almost simultaneously with the foundation of the Delhi Sultanate through the mystic orders of Chistiyya and Suhrawardiyya. In the 14th century these orders were all established in their respective zones with extensive networks of Sufi shrines *(khanqahs)*. According to one account, there were around 2,000 *khanqahs* in Delhi and the surrounding areas.[2] The numerous and extensive *khanqahs* were soon assimilated into the complex cultural pattern of India and helped to remove the spirit of mistrust and isolation which permeated relations among the various cultural groups.

The *khanqahs* became an important institution of Muslim and non-Muslim community life in medieval India. Their importance arose from the spiritual and social welfare, educational and cultural functions they performed for the local population. The congenial, unstructured social environment and the unassuming ways of the mystics stood in sharp contrast to the highly stratified and rigid social structure of Hindu society. Within the Muslim community, the social organization of the *khanqahs* was characterized by the Islamic ideals of equality and fraternity, notwithstanding the discriminatory practices of the Muslim ruling classes. The *khanqahs* introduced a new form of religious organization in India that was not bound to the caste system.

The social and cultural impact of the *khanqahs*

Hindu society in the 12th and 13th centuries, especially in North India, was structured along caste lines. The low-caste workers and artisans were outcasts in the deeply hierarchal caste system. They were deprived of all the amenities of civic life and were not allowed to be present in urban areas after sunset. They could not recite the Hindu holy texts and were denied access to the temples. In contrast, the *khanqahs* were egalitarian and non-discriminatory organizations. It was perhaps for this reason that many early *khanqahs* were situated outside caste cities amid the lower-caste Indian population. The unassuming ways of the mystics, their broad human sympathies and the classless atmosphere of *khanqahs* attracted low-caste people and 'untouchables' to their fold. Within the *khanqahs* they found a social and religious organization free from discrimination and the distinctions of Hindu society. All visitors to and residents of the *khanqahs* lived, slept and ate together. The Islamic texts were accessible to all. The *Khanqahs* thus became the spearheads of Muslim culture and the Islamic ideal of *tauhid* (the Oneness of God) as a working principle in social life.

With the passage of time the *khanqahs* as a socio-religious organization evolved and changed. The spirituality of the mystic and knowledge of mysticism shifted from being a learned process to an hereditary one. The spiritual power of the founder of the *khanqah* came to be transmitted through his descendants, who became the centre of the devotion of followers of the Sufi saints who, after their death, were usually buried within the *khanqah*. This was an important change and eventually led to the development of the master-disciple, or what is known as the *pir-murid* paradigm, in which the *pir* (or master) is the leader and the *murid* (disciple) is a faithful follower obliged to surrender themselves completely to the *pir*. [3] The *pir-murid* paradigm was instrumental in the evolution of the devotional saint cults, and these eventually became the cult associations called *ta'ifa*. The charisma of the *pir* was routinized as headship of the cult association based on heredity rather than on merit, and became an accepted practice. This gave rise to a whole new class of people who, by virtue of being blood descendants of a Sufi saint, could claim spiritual status. They are now commonly known as *sajjada-nishins, gaddinashins* or *walis*. The establishment and evolution of the *khanqahs* not only generally correspond to the establishment of Islamic political rule in medieval India, but also to the spread of Islam in the Indian subcontinent.

Khanqahs, Sufi Islam and the social structure of South Asian Muslim society

Besides their central role in the spread of Islam, the *khanqahs* had a profound impact on the evolution of the growth of Muslim culture and the social structure of South Asian Muslim societies. The considerable cultural and social influence that the *khanqahs* and their *sajjada-nishins* (spiritual leaders) exerted on their disciples attracted the attention of the ruling class which, for spiritual as well as for political reasons, sought cooperation from the *khanqah* organizations in maintaining political stability in the country. The dominant, but by no means sole, mechanism through which the *khanqahs* were coopted by the state was the issuing of substantial land grants (*jagirs*) to maintain the *khanqah* shrines and their permanent residents. By the time the Sufi cult associations, led by descendants of the Sufi saints, had evolved from the early *khanqahs*, their spiritual leaders (i.e. the *sajjada-nishins*) were granted substantial *jagirs* by the state not only to obtain their cooperation in maintaining political and social stability, but also to use their influence and power over their disciples to provide military recruits for the state at short notice. These land grants, known as *Ma'adad-e-Ma'ash* (given as *waqf* to the Sufi shrines or *jagirs* to the *pirs, walis* and *sajada-nishins*), were awarded first by the sultans of Delhi and then by the Moghul emperors of India, and later by the British colonial rulers. In fact, under Moghul rule the Sufis and their descendants became known as the *Laskar-e-Du'au* (Army of Prayers) and were considered as important as the regular army during periods of political upheaval and warfare in the country.[4]

Ownership and proprietorship of large estates and their political alliance with the state made the spiritual leaders of popular Islam an important economic and political force within society, and given the extended kinship and *biradari* (brotherhood) system that characterized Muslim social organization, their kin became beneficiaries of this economic and political status. Through intermarriage and social alliances with other Muslim *zamindars* (landholders) they came to constitute the core of Muslim society, occupying a dominant position in its social structure. This structural position made them a formidable force wielding enormous political, economic and spiritual influence over large numbers of their disciples who resided primarily in the villages. The central state could not ignore their political constituency and in due course these spiritual leaders became an integral part of the state's power structure, with primary responsibility for maintaining political stability and ensuring the law and order in the vast countryside. Their political authority varied according to the power of the central state. When the centre was militarily and politically strong they concentrated mainly on their spiritual role, but at times when the political centre was weak they generally played a powerful and important political role in maintaining stability.

Under British rule in India, the *khanqahs* and the hereditary *pirs* and *sajada-nishins* continued to receive state patronage through land allocations and state honours in return for their support. Their economic and political position was strongly reinforced when the government of the Punjab recognized them as 'landed gentry' in the administration of the Punjab Alienation of Land Bill of 1900.[5] The reason for designating *pirs* as landed gentry, as stated by the lieutenant-Governor of the Punjab, Sir Michael O'Dwyer, was because they were venerated by many of the leading chiefs, and such influence had to be taken into account because this influence might be put to political purposes. 'If a man has political influence and uses it well the fact that he is connected with a religious institution and even to a certain extent derives his influence from that connection should not in my opinion stand in the way of obtaining a grant', O'Dwyer argued.[6] As a result, many *sajada-nishins* were thenceforth recognized as landed gentry, and it was this recognition that provided the basis of support by many *pirs* and *sajada-nishins* for the Unionist Party, which represented the common interests of the landed class in Punjab and became the dominant ruling political party there between 1923 and 1946.[7] Only after the Muslim League succeeded in obtaining the support of the *pirs* in 1946 did it succeed for the first time in obtaining the majority of Muslim seats in Punjab – the area which was to become the heart of Pakistani society and government after 1947.

In summary, the *khanqahs* of the Muslim Sufi saints were instrumental in the spread of Islam as well as in the development of popular Sufi Islam in the Indian subcontinent. These *khanqahs* subsequently evolved into Sufi cult associations led by hereditary descendants of the Sufi saints. Owing to their spiritual and social influence over millions of followers (*murids*), the *pirs* were coopted by the state which granted large *jagirs* both to the *khanqahs* and to the *pirs*. This extended their influence within the economic and political sphere, coincided with the interests of the other Muslim landed classes (*zamindars*) and evolved over a period of time into a *pir-zamindar* alliance. This alliance was further reinforced by intermarriage among these groups. Consequently, the *pir-zamindar* elite became the core social stratum of Muslim society as well as an integral part of the 'historical state' in the subcontinent, and after 1947 the *pir-zamindar* alliance became one of the dominant political forces in Pakistani government and society. According to recent estimates, 64 per cent of Pakistan's farmland is owned by 5 per cent of the wealthiest landlords, while 51 per cent of rural households are landless. Pakistan's major political parties are said to be 'feudal oriented'. In 2007 more than two-thirds of the seats in the National Assembly were held by members of the *pir-zamindar* alliance.[8]

Islam and politics in Pakistani society

Muslim society in Pakistan has two major spatial divisions– rural and urban. The city is the centre of government and the home of the professional and business elite, merchants and the urban working class. These groups are responsible for the production of the economic goods and professional services that constitute an important component of the national gross domestic product. In addition to these groups, the city is also the home of the *ulema* of Islamic jurisprudence (*Sharia*) and scripture (Quran).[9] Historically, the *ulema* have been at the heart of various Islamic reform movements in the Indian subcontinent as well as in contemporary Pakistan. Perhaps one of the best examples of *ulema*-led reform movements in recent history is the Deobandi movement.[10] The central concern of movements like Deobandi is to expunge the Islamic culture of extravagant customs such as lavish weddings, dowries and other ritual celebrations, which they regard as un-Islamic. These movements, which are also anti-*pir* and against the cult of the saints, downplay these institutions in favour of individual responsibility for upholding scriptural norms. They ask their followers to be guided by a high degree of internal discipline and to forego immediate material pleasures. They deny the importance of carefully graded social ranking, advocating instead a broad definition of respectability as a basis for marriage and other social relations, based in part on shared religious styles. The *ulema* see themselves as teaching Muslims to be good by following the teachings of great past reformers, including the Prophet himself, for whom the ending of false customs and the creation of religiously responsible individuals was central. In short, the *ulema*, and the movements with which they have been associated, have been engaged in a renewal of the teachings of the Quran and the Prophet. They are the ideologues of Scripturalist Islam from which contemporary Islamic fundamentalist movements derive their ideological inspiration.

Most of these movements are distinctly modern in their orientation. They seek to achieve the renaissance of Muslim society by emphasizing the values of equality, asceticism, individual responsibility, education and economic change. This ideological orientation paradoxically brought the *ulema*-led movements into sharp conflict with the British colonial rulers, and subsequently with the rulers of Pakistan, as well as with the traditional *pirs* because they were perceived as socially and politically destabilising forces. The Jamaat-i-Islami of Pakistan is essentially an *ulema*-led political movement. The Jamaat, like its founder Maulana Abu Ala Maududi, is committed to the establishment of an Islamic state in Pakistan based on an Islamic constitution. It is a tightly organized cadre party with a membership estimated at between 4,000 and 10,000, which sees itself as the vanguard of the Islamic revolution.[11]

Emerging tensions between the two strands of Islam

The *ulema* represent the Gellenrian high, or Scripturalist, Islamic tradition of Islam. They perceive popular Islam based on the *pir-murid* paradigm as misleading, superstitious and vulgar, and they believe that it needs to be replaced by a scripturalist Islam based on the Quran and *Sharia*, and for which they are the principal spokesmen. However, historically, popular Islam has been the dominant religious tradition in Pakistani society and as such it permeates the social and cultural life of ordinary Muslims. As discussed above, the evolution of the state in Pakistan has been profoundly affected by the predominance of popular Islam.

In the past, a relatively weak central state has been able to extend its political jurisdiction over a vast countryside with the help of leaders adhering to the popular Islamic tradition and the traditional *zamindars*. Popular Islam, therefore, has been an integral part of the state, whereas the Scripturalist Islamic tradition existed only at its periphery. The Unionist state in the Punjab as it existed until 1946 provides a good empirical example of this.[12] During the post-independence period the alliance between the central rulers (military and bureaucracy) and the *pirs-zamindars* – the traditional rural elite – has remained essentially intact. The emergence of a military bureaucratic state in Pakistan from 1959 onwards has, in significant ways, sought to strengthen the state by bringing shrine management under state bureaucratic control. During the regime of General Muhammad Ayub Khan the control and management of shrines was institutionalized in the West Pakistan Waqf Properties Ordinance of 1959 (superseded by 1961 and 1976 ordinances). Through these ordinances, an attempt was made to change the religious significance of the *pir*, but not their religious strength, by invoking a new ideology of the *pir* that emphasized their piety and spirituality in the eyes of the common people. The *waqf* ordinances sought to create a sense of unanimity between government policy direction, religious values and the reformist ideals of the *pirs*. Under the government of Zulfikar Ali Bhutto (1972–77), some of the traditional functions of shrine management, such as the celebration of *urs* (death anniversaries) of the major saints, were taken over by the new Auqf bureaucracy. In keeping with the ancient function of *khanqahs* and the *tariqa* phases of Sufism, the Khan and Bhutto governments revived the idea of shrines as welfare centres.[13] However, under the regime of General Zia ul-Haq (1977–88), the affinity between the shrine and government values and purposes diminished, in that shrine celebrations did not occur with government backing. Nevertheless, shrines were not disavowed, and relatives of Sufi saints continued to enjoy government support.

In short, the social structure of Muslim society in Pakistan has been profoundly influenced and shaped by popular Sufi Islam, which has played a pivotal role in the evolution of the rural elite – the *pirs* and the *zamindars* – who together have formed the pillars of the Pakistani state. The emergence of a military bureaucratic state tended to further reinforce its position by bringing some aspects of popular Islam under state bureaucratic control, ostensibly for the benefit of the larger community and so as not to end its spiritual links with popular Islam's traditional leaders. This state intervention, to some extent, is also indicative of the reformist tendencies within the popular Islamic tradition. As a group, however, the *pirs* have remained symbols of this dominant religious and cultural tradition, and the Pakistani state has relied on their political support and it has reflected and served their class interest. On the other hand, the Scripturalist Islamic tradition and its *ulema* leaders have remained at the periphery of the state. The *ulema* are committed to breaking the nexus between the state and popular Islam and replacing it with Scriptualist

Islam. They have made several attempts to do this but until the 1980s they were unsuccessful because the ruling elite was able to exercise its power to contain their agitation and struggle for political power.[14]

However, the social changes that Pakistani society has undergone over the past seven decades have created social and political conditions conducive to mass mobilization in support of the *ulema*-led Scripturalist Islamic tradition, which elsewhere I have called Islamization.[15] Urbanization, increasing literacy and industrialization have created an environment which is sufficiently socially differentiated to provide the *ulema* with an important constituency. Pakistan is becoming an increasingly urbanized society. In 1950 only 6 per cent of the Pakistani population lived in urban areas, compared with almost 40 per cent in 2017. The belief in *pirs* and folk/popular religion is significantly more prevalent among rural and less educated inhabitants, whereas among urban dwellers and educated, significantly fewer people believe in the *pirs*. Urban residence and an increasing level of education have expanded the constituency that is supportive of *ulema*-led Scripturalist Islam and the reformist movements.

Islamization and the rise of Orthodox Islam and sectarianism

These religious trends have contributed to the success of Jamaat-i-Islami in mobilizing its support in urban areas through the tightly organized and carefully recruited cadre membership. As a result, it has made significant inroads into the main civil and state institutions. Its ideological reach received a boost in 1977 following the military coup that ousted the elected government of Prime Minister Bhutto and brought General Zia ul-Haq to power. Lacking political support from the country's main political parties, Gen. Zia turned to the Islamic parties, mainly the Jamaat-i-Islami, to legitimize his martial law administration. In return, he adopted Jamaat's Islamization programme of institutional reform and the introduction of *Sharia* in the country.[16] The declared aim of this programme was to enhance the role of the state in giving direction to the religious discourse in the country. Zia was attracted to the Islamization programme owing to his personal background and inclinations. He and some of his fellow generals believed that Pakistan was created as an ideologically Islamic state and it was the government's duty to ensure that it remained so. The Islamization programme was regarded as a means to instil norms of Islamic life and of Islam into society.

The centrepiece of Zia's Islamization programme was the introduction of *Hudood* laws concerning offences against property, the consumption of intoxicants, *zina* (fornication and adultry) and *qazf* (bearing false witness). According to Islamic jurisprudence, *hudd* (plural *hudood*) refers to punishments prescribed by the Quran or Sunnah, the traditions set by the Prophet Muhammad. These laws were later supplemented by amendments to the Pakistani penal code relating to blasphemy, which made insulting the Prophet or the Quran a capital crime. The express purpose of the *Hudood* laws was to make existing laws regarding these crimes conform with the injunctions of Islam as set out in the Quran and the Sunnah, which it is obligatory for Muslims to follow. The policy was presented as a fundamental necessity for creating a just and equal society. Behind these platitudes, however, the real reason was to bolster the regime's legitimacy among the Pakistani masses, and it was widely seen as a cynical attempt to exploit the common people's devotion to Islam.[17]

The Islamization programme claimed to manifest a universal Islamic vision, but in reality it was based on a narrow interpretation of Islamic theology and law propounded by the orthodox Sunni Deobandi-Hanafi school, and, consequently, was vehemently opposed by the Shias, who comprise around 20 per cent of the population. The Shias were deeply suspicious of the Islamization programme and perceived it as threat to their social position and religious status in the country. In the face of their ardent opposition, the Zia regime capitulated to their demands and granted them exemption from laws that contravened Shia law. This capitulation was deeply resented by General Zia ul-Haq's Sunni political allies, including the Jamaat-i-Islami; it exacerbated the latent sectarian divisions within Pakistani society and paved the way for the rise of militant sectarian organizations. Today, the activities of these sectarian organizations pose an existential threat to the territorial unity of the country.

One of the most significant developments arising from the Islamization polices was the privileging of the orthodox and puritanical sects Deobandi and Ahle Hadees. These sects had a close theological affinity to Wahabism and its political parties, Jamaat-i-Islami and Jamiat-i ulema-i-Islam, and received funding and government patronage at the expense of the moderate Sufi sect, the Bralevi, which represented the dominant popular tradition of Islam in the country. The government's patronage strengthened the orthodox Sunni institutions by providing government funds to their existing religious seminaries (*madrassas*), and by establishing new ones. General Zia ul-Haq's government saw the expansion of the orthodox seminaries sector as an instrument of entrenching Sunni identity of orthodox beliefs.

These developments coincided with the Soviet occupation of Afghanistan, which attracted a huge amount of foreign money, mainly American and Saudi, to mobilize thousands of *mujahidin* (Islamic fighters) to oppose the Soviet occupation of Afghanistan and to contain the influence of the new Islamic revolutionary government of Iran. This development led to the establishment of thousands of new seminaries to train the *mujahidin* ideologically and militarily. According to one estimate, in 1980 there were 700 seminaries in Pakistan, and by the end of 1990s they numbered 7,000, with enrolments possibly running into the millions. An increasing number of seminaries are now funded by private local and foreign donations. They play a significant role in fanning sectarian conflicts in Pakistan and are becoming a major factor behind the militarization of Pakistani society.[18]

The above account shows that the scourge of religious extremism was a product of General Zia ul-Haq's Islamization policy, which privileged the orthodox strand of Islam in the 1980s. By the 1990s the Islamization policies were well institutionalized, receiving the support of the succeeding civilian governments and then of the military government of General Pervez Musharraf from 2001 to 2008. The geostrategic developments relating to the Soviet occupation of Afghanistan played an important part in forging and strengthening them. The United States and Pakistan, along with neighbouring Arab countries, colluded with orthodox radical Islamic groups to fight a proxy war in Afghanistan and Kashmir. However, following the terrorist attacks perpetrated against the United States on 11 September 2001 attacks and the US/NATO-led war in Afghanistan, the strategic shift in US policy has demanded that Pakistan rein in its Islamic militants.

The religious developments outlined above have eroded the political domination of popular Islam in the Pakistani state institution as well as within society at large. However, popular Islam remains a pervasive religious tradition among the masses. There have been periods when the pendulum of political power has swung in favour of Scripturalist Islam only to galvanize opposition to it among the masses. The religious, political and geostrategic developments have strengthened Scripturalist Islam's position in Pakistani society and in the state. As a result, Pakistan is entering a new phase during which it is likely that the two traditions of Islam will jostle for political hegemony. This will manifest itself in the increasingly violent sectarian conflicts as well as in ethnic-based insurgencies in parts of Pakistan, which are posing a serious threat to the social and political stability of the country.

The success of the Scripturalist Islamic tradition largely depends on its ability to mobilize the rural population. This will only be possible if it can enforce and bring about drastic and revolutionary economic and political reforms. However, this would be almost impossible without effective and complete control of the state, especially of its bureaucratic and coercive institutions. So far, there is no evidence that this is happening. It is likely that this conflict will continue until such time when the supporters of both strands of Islam recognize that their future existence depends on the survival of Pakistan and that the ongoing violent religious conflict is posing an existential threat to the country. That realization may lead to a compact for peaceful co-existence which would be to the mutual benefit of the followers of the two traditions. This has happened in Indonesia, where the two traditions of Islam co-exist peacefully, and this has played a pivotal role in Indonesia's political stability and rapid economic development.

Portraits of religiosity in Pakistan

The developments discussed above have contributed to the creation of a general perception that Pakistan is a very religious country and that the Pakistani people are very observant orthodox Muslims. But what do such perceptions mean? Can we offer a comparative perspective on the religiosity of Pakistanis? From a sociological perspective the core of religiosity is religious commitment. It consists of two main dimensions, namely knowledge and ritual. The knowledge dimension refers to the fundamental religious beliefs to which a religious person is expected and often required to adhere, while the ritual dimension refers to the observance of religious rituals which include the specific acts of worship which express a person's religious commitment. Table 5.1 and Table 5.2 provide a comparative perspective of the religiosity of Pakistanis with that of Muslims from nine other countries.

These tables are evidence that the Pakistani people are among the most orthodox in their beliefs, but not when it comes to practice. Based on these indices they can be regarded as very religious. What are the political ramifications of their religiosity? Does their religiosity influence their political affiliations to and support of Islamic parties? Table 5.3 shows the voting patterns of the Pakistani people in the last five national parliamentary elections. The voting trends for Islamic and other parties clearly show that an overwhelming majority of Pakistani do not vote for Islamic parties. They mainly vote for

Table 5.1 Index of orthodox religious beliefs (figures are displayed as percentages)

Score	Indonesia	Pakistan	Kazakhstan	Egypt	Malaysia	Turkey	Iran	Singapore	India
High									
5	49	76	1	39	55	33	14	36	12
4	34	20	3	50	35	26	46	22	14
3	11	2	6	7	7	13	16	18	39
2	5	1	14	3	3	11	10	16	22
Low									
1	1	-	75	1	1	18	14	8	12

Source: Riaz Hassan, *Faithlines: Muslim Conceptions of Islam and Society*, New York, Oxford University Press, 2003; the data on India is from the unpublished Survey of Indian Muslim Religiosity, 2016.

Table 5.2 Index of religious practice: ritual (figures are displayed as percentages)

Score	Indonesia	Pakistan	Kazakhstan	Egypt	Malaysia	Turkey	Iran	Singapore	India
High									
4	44	24	1	45	34	7	7	15	12
3	49	31	3	40	47	18	28	33	34
2	7	28	12	10	16	43	35	34	46
Low									
1	1	17	84	4	3	32	31	17	8

Source: Source: Hassan, Islam and Society, 2013.

Table 5.3 Voting trends in previous elections

Percentage of votes won by major political parties in Pakistan (1993–2013)

Total votes	45,388,404	35,678,035	29,572,712	19,516,716	20,293,307
Political party	*2013*	*2008*	*2002*	*1997*	*1993*
Muttahida Qaumi Movement (MQM)	5.4	7.2	3.1	–	–
Awami National Party (ANP)	1.0	2.0	–	1.8	1.7
Balochistan National Party (BNP)	0.1	–	–	0.6	–
Pakistan People's Party (PPP)	15.2	29.9	25.8	21.3	37.3
Pakistan Tehreek-e-Insaaf (PTI)	16.9	–	–	1.6	–
Pakistan Muslim League (PML–Q)	3.1	22.4	25.7	–	–
Awami Muslim League (AML)	0.2	–	–	–	–
Pakistan Muslim League (PML–N)	32.8	19.1	9.4	44.8	39.3
Pakistan Mulsim League (PML–F)	2.4	1.9	1.1	–	–
Jamiat Ulema-e-Islam (JUI–F)	3.2	–	–	1.7	–
Jamaat-e-Islami (JI)	2.1	–	–	–	–
Muttahida Majlis-e-Amal (MMA)	–	2.1	11.3	–	–
Mutahida Deeni Mahaz	0.8	–	–	–	–
Jamiat Ulama-e-Islam Nazryati (JUI–N)	0.2	–	–	–	–
Jamiat Ulema-e-Pakistan (JUP)	0.1	–	–	–	–
Sunni Ittehad Council	0.1	–	–	–	–
Sunni Tehreek	0.1	–	–	–	–

centre-left, centrist and centre-right parties. Most importantly, their voting behaviour demonstrates commitment to a pluralistic political culture and this has significant implications for the nature and causes of Islamic militancy and terrorism. I would like to suggest that overall this is clear evidence of popular support for a democratic and tolerant society and political culture. Furthermore, a large majority of Pakistanis do not belong to any of the radical militant groupings. These political conditions and declining support for radical and militant movements paradoxically tend to further radicalize militant movements, transforming them into increasingly unpredictable, secretive and violent organizations. The ruthlessness of their violence reflects a desire and strategy to gain public attention and is symptomatic of their desperation. Their militancy is not motivated by struggles to win the hearts and minds of fellow Muslims. It is fuelled by a sense of powerlessness, revenge and religious fanaticism far removed from ordinary citizens. More open and stronger political structures are required to oppose such militancy. It also needs a recognition that increasing religiosity does not increase support for Islamic militancy but in fact does the opposite: it diminishes support for it.

Another common conception of Pakistan that appears to be very popular in the Indian and Western media is that Pakistani state organs are complicit in sponsoring and/or supporting terrorism and terrorist organizations. This was implied in a joint declaration made by the leaders of BRICS (the combined economies of Brazil, the Russian Federation, India, the People's Republic of China and South Africa) following the ninth BRICS summit meeting held in China in September 2017 that militant groups allegedly based in Pakistan posed a regional security threat and called for their patrons to be held to account.

Conclusion

The weight of contemporary historical evidence shows that it was not the coercion of Muslim invaders but the *khanqahs* that played a pivotal role in spreading Islam in the subcontinent. They wove themselves into the complex cultural patterns of India and helped to remove mistrust and isolation among various groups. They were also important in the development of Sufi Islam. The *khanqah* shrines gradually evolved into a Sufi cult led by hereditary descendants of the Sufi saints with millions of followers. Owing to their spiritual and social influence they were co-opted by the state and received large *jagirs* which extended their influence within the economic and political sphere and over a period of time evolved into a *pir-zamindar* alliance. This alliance became the core of Muslim society as well as part of the 'historical state' in the subcontinent and after 1947 became one of dominant forces in Pakistani state and society. Their main opponents were the *ulemas* of the Scripturalist Islam who were committed to expunging Islamic culture of the extravagant customs of Sufi Islam that they regard as un-Islamic. Their aim was to establish a state governed by Islamic principles. Two examples of Scripturalist Islam are the Deobandis and Jamaat-Islami. The *ulema* were committed to breaking the nexus between the state and the elite of the popular Sufi Islam replacing it with Scripturalist Islam. Until recently their attempts to achieve this goal have been largely unsuccessful. However, increasing urbanization, literacy and modernization is increasing their influence among the urban population. General Zia ul-Haq's Islamization programme with its blueprint drawn from orthodox and puritanical sects including Deobandis and Ahle Hadees, boosted the role of Scripturalist Islam. Notwithstanding these developments, Sufi Islam remains a pervasive religious tradition among the Pakistani masses. The religious, political and geostrategic developments have strengthened Scripturalist Islam's position in the Pakistani state and society, ushering in a new phase that is likely to witness increasing conflict as the two traditions of Islam jostle for political hegemony. Today, it can be seen in the increasingly violent sectarian conflicts as well as in ethnic-based insurgencies in Pakistan, thus posing a serious threat to the social and political stability of the country. The evidence shows that Pakistani Muslims are strongly attached to their faith. Does this affinity affect their politics and their political choices? The voting evidence shows a clear preference for a pluralistic political culture signifying support for a democratic and tolerant society and political culture. This has significant implications for radical Islamist movements. Paradoxically, lack of support for such movements tend to radicalize them further, transforming them into increasingly secretive and violent organizations. Their ruthlessness reflects a desire and strategy to gain pubic attention and is symptomatic of their desperation not popularity. It is fuelled by a sense of lack of support, powerlessness, revenge and religious fanaticism far removed from ordinary citizens. Using terrorism-related fatalities this chapter examines the complicity of Pakistani state organs in sponsoring terrorism. The evidence strongly counters it.

Notes

1 See T. W. Arnold, The Preaching of Islam: A History of the Propagation of the Muslim Faith, Lahore, Sh. Muhammad Ashraf [1896] 1961; Burton Stein, '"Nizami": Some Aspects of Religion and Politics in India during the Thirteenth Century (Book Review)', *Journal of Asian Studies*, vol. 25, no. 2, 1966, p. 353; S. A. A. Rizvi, *Religious and Intellectual History of the Muslim in Akbar's Reign*, New Delhi, Munshiram Manoharlal, 1975; A. Schimmel, *Islam in the Indian Subcontinent* Cologne, Brill, 1980; R. M. Eaton, *Sufis of Bijapur, 1300–1700*, Princeton, NJ, Princeton University Press, 1978; K. A. Nizami, 'Early Indo-Muslim Mystics and their Attitudes toward the State', *Islamic Culture*, 23 vol. (1949) and vol. 24 (1950); K. A. Nizami, *The Life and Times of Shaikh Farid ud Din Gunj-i-Shukar*, Aligarh, 1955; A. C. Mayer, 'Pir and Murshid: An Aspect of Religious Leadership in West Pakistan', *Middle Eastern Studies*, vol. 3, no. 2, 1967; F. Barth, 'The System of Social Stratification in Swat, North Pakistan', in E. R. Leach (ed.) *Aspects of Caste in South India, Ceylon and North-West Pakistan*, New York, Cambridge University Press, 1971; K. B. Sayeed, *Politics in Pakistan*, New York: Praeger, 1980.
2 Masalik al-Absar, quoted in Khaliq Ahmad Nizami, 'Some Aspects of Khānqah Life in Medieval India', *Studia Islamica*, 1957, pp. 51–69.
3 In the *pir-murid* paradigm, all *murids* are expected to participate in a formal initiation ceremony during which the *murid* makes a solemn oath, known as *bait* (the swearing of spiritual obedience and allegiance) to the *pir*.
4 The analysis of the evolution of *khanqah* to cult association is based on Trimingham's conceptual framework for analysing Sufism. He suggests that in its organizational aspect, Sufism has passed through three stages: the *khanqah* stage, the *traiqa* stage and the *ta'ifa* stage. The *khanqah* stage was characterized by a relatively unstructured and undifferentiated religious and social life centred around the khanqah; the *tariqa* stage refers to development of mystical schools and gradual systemization of mystical techniques and Sufi learning, leading to the development of *pir-mursid* paradigm and its development of saint cults; and finally, the *ta'afi* stage describes cults associations. See J. S. Trimingham, *Sufi Orders in Islam*, New York, Oxford University Press, 1971.
5 N. G. Barrier, *The Punjab Alienation of Land Bill of 1890*, Duke University Program in Comparative Studies on Southern Asia, Monograph and occasional paper series, no. 2, 1966; D. Gilmartin, 'Religious Leadership and the Pakistan Movement in the Punjab', *Modern Asian Studies*, vol. 13, no. 3, 1979.
6 Gilmartin, 'Religious Leadership and the Pakistan Movement in the Punjab'.
7 Ibid.; Ian A. Talbot, 'Deserted Collaborators: The Political Background to the Rise and Fall of the Punjab Unionist Party, 1923–1947', *Journal of Imperial and Commonwealth History* vol. 11, no. 1, 1982: 73-93.
8 Sharif Shuja, 'Sources of Pakistan's Insecurity', *Contemporary Review*, June 2007.

9 I. A. Qureshi, *Ulema in Politics: A Study Relating to the Political Activities of the Ulema in the South Asian Sub Continent*, Karachi, Ma'aref, 1972.

10 B. Metcalf, *Islamic Revival in India, Deoband 1860–1900*, Princeton, NJ: Princeton University Press, 1982.

11 R. Hassan, 'Islamization: An Analysis of Religious, Political, and Social Change in Pakistan', *Middle Eastern Studies*, vol. 21, no. 1, 1985; R. Ahmad, 'Redefining Muslim Identity in South Asia:, The Transformation of the Jammat-i-Islami', in Martin E. Marty and R. Scott Appleby (eds) *Accounting for Fundamentalism*, Chicago, University of Chicago Press 1994; S. V. R. Nasr, *The Vanguard of the Islamic Revolution: The Jamaat-i-Islami of Pakistan*, London, I. B. Tauris, 1994.

12 Until 1946 it was the Unionist Party, founded in 1923, that formally expressed both Muslim political aspirations and drew most Muslim support, from a limited franchise, under the British Raj. This was despite the formation and development of the Muslim League, which was seen as a predominantly urban-intellectual ideological group. In contrast, the Unionist Party drew its support from influential *pir* families, particularly in Western Punjab. Close family ties, an emphasis on agro-economic matters, and a downplaying of religious concerns all agreed with *pir* interests and outlooks. The Unionist Party managed its rural Muslim support both by way of the rural elite and through local languages, both conforming to cultural norms. The Unionists cooperated with the British Raj and this too suited most *pirs*, though not all. The Muslim League, which shunned *pir* support until the 1940s, was forced to seek their patronage at the expense of its allies – the reformist *ulema* of Jamaat-i-ulema-i-Hind – in order to win the 1946 elections from the Unionist Party and consequently the political leadership in the Punjab Legislative Assembly (see Gilmartin, 'Religious Leadership and the Pakistan Movement in the Punjab').

13 K. Ewing, 'The Politics of Sufism: Redefining the Saints of Pakistan', *Journal of Asian Studies*, vol. 42, no. 2, 1983.

14 See Government of the Punjab, *Report of the Court of Inquiry Constituted Under Punjab Act 11 of 1954*; Rahman, *Public Opinion and the Political Development in Pakistan*, Lahore Government Printer, 1954.

15 Hassan, 'Islamization'.

16 S. A. Maududi, *The Islamic Law and Constitution*, Lahore: Islamic Publication, 1954; Hassan, 'Islamization'.

17 R. Hassan, *Inside Muslim Minds*, Melbourne: Melbourne University Press, 2008.

18 A. Mir, *The True Face of Jihadis*, Lahore: Mashal Books, 2004; H. Abbas, *Pakistan's Drift into Extremism: Allah, the Army and America's War on Terror*, New York, S. E. Sharpe, 2005; R. Hassan, *Life as A Weapon: The Global Rise of Suicide Terrorism*, London, Routledge, 2010.

6

Sustained political progress
The supportive role of the military

Jehangir Karamat

The making of today's Pakistan Army

> In all this turmoil, the Pakistan Army remained a key actor. Perforce, it had to transform itself, from being a largely static and conventional fighting body designed to protect the nation's borders against India and any other external foe, to an army that would fight an asymmetrical war inside its own border ... that war continues today as does the hostility between India and Pakistan.[1]

Various factors and a multitude of circumstances are responsible for Pakistan's military having remained a critical element throughout its 70-year history. The military's evolutionary process has made it a true reflection of Pakistani society. From its inherited legacy of selective recruitment based on the lore of the 'martial tribes' during the British colonial era the military now recruits from across the country and from all segments of the population and without discrimination. The strength of the military system lies in its transparency, with merit being the sole criterion for professional advancement. It may seem that upward progression is simply a matter of reaching certain milestones, but actually it is much more than that; it is based on multiple evaluations and performance indicators over a wide spectrum of situations. The military is therefore seen as the best avenue for upward social mobility within Pakistani society and competition is intense – a change from the carefree days of the 1950s and 1960s when the search for adventure rather than socio-economic consideration was the principal motivation for joining the army.

In response to the demands of a complex environment the military has created a training and education system that incorporates the latest technology and the most modern concepts of leadership and professional skills. The soldier is not only imbued with the warrior spirit but is also motivated by the spirt of a social and religious culture that he fully comprehends. The leadership has a total grasp of the meaning of national power and its orchestration through all the elements that constitute it – especially the significance of economic security, political stability and internal harmony, and security. There has been steady progression and improvement in all the institutions responsible for military training as well as in higher education. This is also the result of a long learning process that has included lapses and ill-considered policies as well as having been in the ruling seat for a little less than half of the country's existence. This involvement has resulted from weak political institutions that have always been, and remain, oriented towards individual personal and party interests rather than national interests. This in no way absolves the military from responsibility for its prolonged periods of military rule nor the judiciary from giving such rule legal sanction and even granting permission to amend the Constitution.

Unlike other institutions the military has not brooked any interference from outside interests. This has enabled it to ensure that institutional interests are second only to national interests and that its culture is not personality-oriented. It is to the credit of the military that no leader has ever demanded that the institution subordinate its own or the national interest to that leader's survival. It is, however, noteworthy that the United States has wielded considerable influence in the evolution of the Pakistan military ever since the alliances formed during the 1950s and 1960s, to the joint action taken by both US and Pakistani troops against the Soviet occupation of Afghanistan, and right up to the present day. Although the United States has not been averse to supporting military dictators and military-backed governments in Pakistan, it has sought to encourage its democratic trends. However, US influence has never been a decisive factor in the military's decision-making processes.

As the demand for resources increased amid growing criticism of the inordinate share of national funds going to the military there was a need for the military to develop a corporate structure and interests in order to supplement its budget. This has led to real estate ventures that provide housing and serve as models for other copycat developers. The military has also ventured into various business enterprises[2] that are controlled by of its welfare organization; all such activities are regulated by the excellent civil professional managers and are within the country's tax regime. Two organizations responsible for construction work in hazardous areas are manned by military personnel, but salaries, allowances and facilities are paid for through the profits generated by projects for which these organizations compete. During wartime this trained manpower would be available to augment troops specializing in engineering. Injured personnel requiring rehabilitation and the families of soldiers who have died in combat benefit from special projects designed to help them. Retired personnel have access to hospitals dedicated to veterans and their families. Such ventures also open up job opportunities for retired personnel with vocation training facilities available not only to the military but also to civilians. The military facilities in remote areas are the only ones available to the population there and these include educational and health care facilities. This entire structure, and the regimental system that creates strong bonds, is truly a cradle to grave commitment by the military to its men and their families. The military is therefore highly motivated and has an enormous *esprit de corps*.

Nearly two decades after it was first proposed Pakistan finally has a National Security Adviser, a National Security Secretariat and a National Security Council. This enables the military to put its organizational and structural strength behind the government in the form of input into a forum where it can be considered and discussed. The military assists the government with custodial control of strategic assets as well as in development and employment concepts within the National Command and Control Authority under the Prime Minister. The evolving and fluid environment in which Pakistan is strategically located makes the Pakistan military a powerful player not only on the basis of its successful defence of the country's boundaries but also through the conduct of determined operations to ensure internal security. The military also supports the country's foreign policy goals through military diplomacy using its international contacts and linkages. It has a very strong presence and an excellent reputation within United Nations peace-keeping operations around the world. The military is fully aware of the fact that security is no longer an exclusively military power-centric concept and that it now includes economic security and political stability. This figures prominently in the military's higher education and leadership training programmes and its overall contribution to national development.

During the period 2008–18 the military has deliberately distanced itself from politics with interaction only at the highest level and for specific purposes. The political institution and the elected government now have full responsibility for establishing their credibility through governance and sound policies. Unfortunately, political stability continues to be elusive and speculation abounds about the military calling the shots in security and foreign policy from behind the scenes. Despite recent media speculation the military has come out strongly to dispel rumours about its political ambitions.

The fact that there are a number of unresolved issues regarding Pakistan's asymmetric balance of power with India and that the possession of nuclear weapons has become a balancing deterrent makes the military the key institution for the provision of external security, and because of the weakness of its law enforcement capacity, also for internal security. The conflict in Afghanistan with all its implications adds to the environment in which the military plays not just a role to ensure security but also has to undertake consolidation and development work for the population in the western border areas. The military response has been to enhance its capacity by integrating paramilitary forces into its combat structure and augmenting its intelligence and surveillance assets to carry out intelligence-driven rapid response operations whenever and wherever required. An assertive and powerful media with a vibrant social media network has led to the military developing expertise in media management and in projecting its image and role. The military has also been given responsibility for the security of the strategically important China–Pakistan Economic Corridor (CPEC) initiative and for this reason the military has had to create special task-oriented assets. This wide-ranging involvement does not mean that the military should also be involved in bringing about political stability. In fact, the opposite is the case. Pakistan's development has not been helped but hindered by past military interventions. These prevented the country from developing the institutional infrastructure necessary for political progress.[3]

Today, Pakistan's military is a highly trained and combat-experienced force capable of a variety of responses. It responds to coercive provocations and has a demonstrated capacity for carrying out defensive and offensive operations as well as counter-insurgency and counter-terror operations. Its cohesiveness and command articulation are outstanding and it is well-known that in combat, sustained over years in extremely hazardous conditions, there has never been a problem with insider dissent. This is because the military is very sensitive to the development of any type of sub-culture within its ranks and does not discriminate on any basis. The higher direction capacity is geared to the scale and dimension of operations across two land frontiers, the coast and at sea which are controlled by integrated land, sea and air capabilities with strategic weapons acting as a strong deterrent. Its response includes the consideration of an internal and external threat that has morphed into a single threat warranting hybrid warfare. The military has a strong support base in the country and is looked up to as a bulwark against all kinds of threats. The fact that while no one wants the military to assume a political role there is some sort of latent unspoken expectation of the military remaining in a protective role to prevent an economic or political catastrophe. This situation can, at times, create tensions between the military and civil polity that, if not handled correctly, could lead to undesirable consequences. Fortunately, as democracy evolves, strengthens and sustains itself with greater capacity the military should recede into the background and its activities would then become restricted to its main role – but this will take time and much hard work on the part of the political institution.

Political developments and civil-military relations

[H]ope for the future is that this delayed development of democracy supporting institutions may have finally begun to happen. Various components of a working and durable democracy are now asserting themselves.[4]

Pakistan has traversed a long and convoluted road to its present state in which its third democratically elected government began its five-year tenure in mid-2018. This is a great achievement considering the fact that since independence there have been four military interventions with three leading to military or martial rule for up to a decade in each case. The fourth, shorter military dictatorship led to a free and fair election but a bungled political aftermath resulted in the 1971 war with India and the break-up of the country. It is interesting to note that during each period of military rule economic growth was greater than during periods of democratic government. With little or no political activity and strong centralized control there was stability and progress. On the negative side the disastrous 1965 and 1971 wars with India were fought under military rule as was the Kargil conflict in 1999. The near-war situation that emerged following the confrontation of 2001 was during military rule. The closest that Pakistan and India came to resolving the Kashmir issue was also during military rule.[5]

The period immediately after independence was marked by the battle over Kashmir in 1948 and political difficulty and instability. The new nation lost its founder and first prime minister leading to a succession of political leaders and unsuccessful attempts to formulate a constitution. The fluid political situation led to the Commander-in-Chief being asked to step in as the Minister of Defence in the government of Pakistan. This marked the first occasion when the military intervened in the political domain. In 1958 the head of the armed services imposed martial law before assuming the presidency for a decade. On being removed from office he handed over the government of Pakistan to his appointed Army Chief who took the country to the events of 1971. The verdict of history is that this catastrophe was the result of a political situation being resolved militarily.[6] The political government under a popular national party and a brilliant, charismatic leader, Zulfiqar Ali Bhutto, led in 1973 to the promulgation of the country's first Constitution that endures to this day. Unfortunately, over-reach, an increasingly autocratic attitude, an attempt to have 'his own man' as the head of the armed services by reaching down the seniority chain and attempts to rig the elections in 1977 led to military intervention and a decade of military rule. The lesson, that once appointed an army chief is no one's man and is answerable only to the institution he commands, was not learnt by all. Bhutto was executed for the alleged murder of a political opponent following a hugely controversial trial that was later acknowledged as being flawed by one of the trial judges.[7]

The decade of 1977–88 under General Zia ul-Haq had profound consequences for the country, its military, its political institutions, its internal security environment and its bilateral relations. This decade marked the disastrous Indian intervention and withdrawal from Sri Lanka, the Sikh insurgency in Indian Punjab and an indigenous uprising in Indian-administered Kashmir after rigged elections. This decade also witnessed the revolution in Iran, the Soviet intervention in Afghanistan, and the US-sponsored successful *jihad* against the Soviet forces in Afghanistan and the subsequent implosion of the USSR. Pakistan's military government sided with the United States and Pakistan's Inter-Services Intelligence with the US Central Intelligence Agency, which funded and directed the Afghan resistance that drew fighters from all over the Muslim world. The sectarian overtones of the Iranian revolution led to reactions from the Sunni Muslim world in the form of funds to Pakistan that spawned the *madrasas* [8] for religious education with many taking on the task of motivating and training fighters for the *jihad* in Afghanistan. These developments coincided with General Zia's own agenda for Islamization in Pakistan that succeeded beyond his wildest dreams owing to his centralized direction, the conducive regional and extra-regional environment and willing collaborators within the country. General Zia was killed in a mysterious air crash in 1988 but his legacy endures, although much of what he ordered has been reversed especially within the military. Pakistan's nuclear programme that was begun following the events of 1971 made great strides as US pressure was lifted during the anti-Soviet joint *jihad*. This enabled Pakistan to respond to India's nuclear tests in 1998 with its own tests and then go on to develop a full spectrum nuclear deterrent much like India's. This has given Pakistan a range of response options to threats that an asymmetrical power relationship with a hostile neighbour could generate – conventional as well as nuclear.

A decade of democracy followed the period of military rule that ended in 1988. The United States withdrew following the collapse of the Soviet Union, and Afghanistan underwent a civil war, resulting in the rise of Afghan Taliban. There followed a violent struggle for power within Afghanistan, with Pakistan supporting the Taliban. The terrorist attacks perpetrated against the United States on 11 September 2001 (known as 9/11) brought the United States and NATO into Afghanistan to wage war against the Taliban, which had given sanctuary to the militant terrorist grouping, Al-Qaeda. The ensuing prolonged violence led to the emergence of the Tehreek Taliban Pakistan and other anti-Pakistan groups that created an insurgency in Pakistan's western border areas with external support. Democracy in Pakistan remained unstable, with four democratically elected governments coming to power but none could complete their terms. Twice the Pakistan People's Party came to power and each time were dismissed by the President exercising his powers under a constitutional amendment brought in under Zia's military rule. The Muslim League (Nawaz) won the national elections twice. The League's first government was dismissed by the President, but the second time around it managed to amend the Constitution so that the power of dismissal by the President was countermanded. The second government was ousted in the military take-over of 1999 – and once again by a handpicked army chief following a botched attempt to replace him. This time the ousted leaders went into a decade-long exile. The period of military rule ended in 2008 following a popular uprising; political pressure forced the military leader out of office. None of the elected governments could establish a rapport with the President and the military. Nor could they deliver the kind of governance that could have given them credibility and popular support. Each of the four democratically elected governments were dismissed owing to alleged poor governance and personal differences between the party leaders and either the President or the army chief, or both. The first three dismissals led to elections after an interim government had been installed with military support, while the fourth was ousted following a military coup. It is incompetence that fails to address disagreements between military and civilian authorities robustly and privately. During the last decade of the last military-backed government three developments were significant for their impact. First, an alliance of religious political parties was formed that was sympathetic towards the Taliban; its seat of governance as in Pakistan's north-western province bordering the Federally Administered Tribal Areas (FATA). Second, towards the end of the decade Pakistan's charismatic, brilliant and internationally renowned leader, Benazir Bhutto, was assassinated. Karachi, Pakistan's port city and financial hub, began to descend into violence and crime. Finally, an attempt to subvert and control the judiciary brought the country's lawyers and their supporters onto the streets, thereby forcing a change of government with no interference by the military.

An elected government led the country for five years after military rule ended in 1999. The chairman of the political party in power, Asif Zardari (the husband of Benazir Bhutto), became President of the country and the de facto decision maker. Two Prime Ministers were changed because of judicial proceedings against them. With the office of the President politicized the office of provincial governors also went the same way. The bureaucracy that had been traumatized during military rule by a hastily structured local government system was also politicized as their appointments, promotions and tenures all came under political control. Civil-military relations remained tense. The elections in 2013 brought in the majority government of the Muslim League under a third-time Prime Minister, Nawaz Sharif. This time hopes and expectations were high but once again tensions with the military began to surface, although the military was careful to remain out of politics. Horrendous acts of violence by terrorists in the western border areas dashed the government's hopes of resolving issues through dialogue. The military began deliberate and determined military operations to clear all anti-state elements from the country and to establish the writ of the government in all ungoverned or marginally governed spaces. The military also helped to formulate a National Action Plan that has the support of all the political parties but so far has only been partially implemented because of capacity shortfalls in the civilian domain. The military also formed 'apex committees' at the provincial level to ensure high-level coordination and followed this up with a wide-ranging internal security and clean-up operation to free the port city of Karachi from the stranglehold of a nexus between the governing body and criminals. This was expanded to the rest of the country and in 2018 was ongoing with political support and in coordination with civil agencies. These military operations have brought to an end the cycle of violence that has become the norm and have created space for the political government to consolidate gains, for the establishment of political stability and a viable economic environment. The military has avoided any involvement in the political domain and its response to provocations has been muted and mature. Pakistan is one of the very few countries to have retaken space lost to extremists and terrorists, re-established governance in ungoverned areas and sidelined the terrorist and insurgent threat through determined and costly military operations that the world has acknowledged.

Owing to an inherent institutional imbalance and the military's past role there is an obsession with the military and all things military in Pakistan. Routine postings, transfers, retirements and promotions within the military are subjected to all manner of analyses and speculations. Any high-level military conferences are expected to result in the publication of a press release or communiqué and, if not, the silence is regarded as ominous. The military (also known as the Establishment) is seen by some to be responsible for judicial and political developments as well being the real power behind security and foreign policy formulation. In the charged atmosphere following the judicial disqualification of Nawaz Sharif, who was ousted in a 1999 military coup, but who then became Prime Minister for a record third term after staging a comeback in parliamentary elections in 2013, the military's remarks about the economy in the context of economic security and national security led to speculations about the army's intentions. This in turn led to clarifications from the military and a strong declaration that it did not seek to usurp democracy. The fact that the situation calmed down is indicative of the maturity that is creeping into civil-military relations and the restraint that the military institution is deliberately exercising. The consensus is that there are prospects for a stable civil-military relationship in the future especially if there is politically stability and the government feels secure.

> The military under the last three Chiefs has stayed on the sidelines ... only and rightfully, interjecting their views in areas of national security policy ... Power follows, like most things in life, a gradient ... in this case it a competency gradient, power in the hands of incompetent teams with no checks and balances would be disastrous if not fatal.[9]

The military's role in national development

> Do not forget that the Armed Forces are the servants of the people ... and it is your duty to carry out the tasks with which you are entrusted.[10]

The military has achieved a great deal in its efforts to act in the national interest and support democracy as part of its contribution to national development. It goes without saying that the military contributes positively to national integration because it ensures representation from all provinces according to the population ratio. It lends significant support to capacity-building in the police and other law-enforcing agencies and it has consistently contributed to civil-military stability operations that include infrastructure construction. The military has delivered with remarkable success in terms of logistics support during natural disasters, and in the health and education sectors. Operations in aid of civil power, agriculture projects and communications are ongoing. In order to ensure the security and success of the game-changing CPEC initiative the army created a Special Security Division besides ramping up the defence of the country's land and sea borders through a series of organizational and structural measures to ward off the external threat that could jeopardize national development. The military has succeeded because of the extent of its influence across the country and its response-oriented capacity.[11]

The military is tasked with providing aid to the civil power under Section 245(1) of the 1973 Constitution of Pakistan. The military has been frequently called upon to undertake rescue and relief operations during floods, famines, earthquakes, avalanches and other disaster and emergency situations. In this context the massive floods in 2010 provide a striking example: the military delivered 68,000 metric tons of emergency supplies of which almost 50 per cent came from its own resources; it used 68 helicopters including 17 from friendly nations; it set up more than 100 relief camps; and it rescued over 800,000 people. During the post-flood period it led efforts to stave off epidemics and disease.[12] The military significantly augments the national education effort through its involvement in primary, secondary and tertiary education through its chain of Public Schools, Model Schools, Cadet Colleges, Technical and Vocational Training Centres, and also provides support and facilities to all the Federal Government Schools and Colleges located within the military cantonments. All of these institutions are open to civilians. At the higher education level, the military runs Garrison Universities, the prestigious National Defense University, the National University for Science and Technology, the Air University, and the Bahria University, in addition to several other degree-awarding institutions.

The military has contributed massively to infrastructure development and logistics support –two key areas for the overall national development effort. Two highly successful organizations – the Frontier Works Organization and the National Logistics Cell) – contribute enormously to the economic development of the nation by undertaking multipurpose national projects such as power projects, road and dam construction, construction of runways and airfields, water supply, telecommunication projects and above all stepping in to resolve logistic crises as was the case following the 2005 massive earthquake, the 2010 floods, the 1995 wheat crisis, the 2010 Attabad Lake event in Gilgit-Baltistan, and the movement of petroleum products in 1983, 1991 and 1995. Particularly significant is the work undertaken under hazardous conditions, in remote areas and in extreme climates, the earthquake relief in the Awaran District of Balochistan and the construction of dams in Balochistan and water supply schemes in the Thar Desert area.[13]

The military works in collaboration with the federal and provincial governments to provide free medical treatment to all the inhabitants of the Kashmir, Gilgit-Baltistan and tribal areas. Free medical camps are frequently set up in remote areas. The Fauji Foundation, the army's welfare organization, runs more than 13 hospitals, 24 day health care centres, 67 mobile and static dispensaries and health units, and operates two state of the art artificial limb centres and rehabilitation facilities. Since 1999 the military has assisted the civil administration in its massive de-silting operations among the canals and waterways of Pakistan, thereby contributing significantly to increasing the land area available for cultivation. The Special Communications Organization works under the Federal Ministry of Information Technology (FMIT) and since 1976 it has developed a massive IT and communications infrastructure, which includes laying thousands of kilometres of a fibre optics network. It is particularly active in the Kashmir and Gilgit-Baltistan areas and stands out as the largest communication network and service provider. The army has undertaken surveys of over 56,000 government schools in Punjab, and according to the 2017 population census across the country over 200,000 troops were deployed to work with civil agencies.

Perhaps the most spectacular example of the military's contribution to national development is the work undertaken in the FATA that border Afghanistan. Determined military operations created the environment for the establishment of law and order. In tandem with these operations the military evolved a strategy of 'winning hearts and minds' through peace, security and stabilization. A border management system has been put in place and this includes technical surveillance measures, manned posts at all crossing places, a mutually coordinated border-crossing control mechanism with Afghanistan, and the erection of a 2,600-km fence to ensure that border crossings take place at designated points only. Military engineers have constructed over 728 km of roads. There are now 27 permanent medical camps which have treated over 300,000 patients. Two military-operated eye care camps provide surgical and other specialist eye treatments. Seven cadet colleges have been established in the FATA area and an Army Public School for boys and girls is located at Shakai, in Wana. One of the most significant developments has been the opening of a Central Corridor that will connect Indus Highway in Pakistan to the Afghan Ring Road. The existing North and South Corridors with Afghanistan have been vastly improved. These developments are having an enormous socio-economic impact within the region. Of special significance is the 'marble city' that became partially functional at the end of 2017 in the Mohmand Agency area of the FATA that is famous for its marble deposits. This road incorporates a tunnel and not only will it facilitate the transportation of mineral deposits through the FATA but it has the potential to link with other areas within the FATA. Upon completion, the massive Gomal Zam Dam, with its huge reservoir and a network of lined canals, will irrigate vast areas in the FATA and generate electricity for thousands of households. The overall impact of the military's development work in the FATA has helped to improve the security and economic situation there, open up business and trade prospects, create employment opportunities and enhance standards of living.

As has been the case in the FATA, the military has undertaken massive development projects in Balochistan in the south-west of the country. Over the past decade more than 10,000 youth from Balochistan have been recruited into the military. Major institutions have been established for the uplift of the province that is the largest in terms of area but with only 5 per cent of Pakistan's population. The Army Institute of Mineralogy, the Balochistan Institute of Marine Sciences and the Balochistan Institute of Technical Education are functional as are a number of Army Public Schools, a vocational training centre, a degree-awarding college, a military college, the Gwadar Institute of Technology and the Quetta Institute of Medical Sciences. Five major hospitals have been set up and eight area development projects have been undertaken by the military across Balochistan. In addition, at least eight infrastructure projects have been completed, thereby vastly increasing connectivity. These include roads, tunnels, airfields, a major new international airport at Gwadar Port, a coastal highway and a dam. The army has been involved in water supply, sanitation and irrigation projects as well as a hydro-power station and two windmill-operated electricity generating projects. The military has worked to provide sports facilities and encourage local cultural and sports activities.[14] It is encouraging and supporting steps to bring international sports to Pakistan and organizes jeep and car rallies and other events around the country in order to promote integration and domestic tourism.

Taking all this into consideration, the military has done a remarkable job in terms of making a significant contribution to national development. Its military operations in the north-western and south-western border areas and its follow-up consolidation and development activities have helped to reduce the threat of terrorism and the possible exploitation of previously marginally controlled areas and dissident segments of the population. The counter-terrorism operations with civilian agencies and supported by intelligence assets across the country have brought internal security and the space for economic viability if political stability is established. By opting to remain out of the political sphere for the present the military has signalled its support for democracy and has followed this up with tangible actions to prove its support.

Conclusion

> The question is what would it take to set a shared long-term vision, much beyond the political cycles, for sustained growth, development and stability in Pakistan?[15]

The military understands that Pakistan's geographical position could be transformed into a major asset were it able to normalize relations with its neighbours. Military diplomacy has been active to bring this about. According to estimates, the confrontation and conflict situation with India has had a negative effect on the growth of gross domestic product, but this could be much improved if India and Pakistan were to agree to holding a sustained dialogue leading to renewed trade relations. Contrary to speculation the military has given its full backing to the Strategic Restraint Regime[16] proposed by Pakistan to India, as well as to a joint mechanism for the investigation of incidents[17] and unconditional sustained dialogue to resolve issues and normalize relations. There is full realization that the military and the government have to work together on these issues and attempts to malign the military and create divides for shallow agendas are not in the country's interest.

As is apparent from the massive infrastructure development work undertaken by the military, the emphasis is on increasing connectivity both within the country and across its borders, especially those to the west. The military is clearly looking beyond the present situation to a future in which there is stability in Afghanistan and outreach and trade opportunities extend beyond Afghanistan into the resource-rich Central Asian states.

The military is frequently blamed for undermining democracy, for not allowing political institutions to develop and mature, for impeding institutional development by involving the judiciary and the bureaucracy during their prolonged periods in office, for its patronage of certain politicians, for interfering in elections, and for never allowing civil-military relations to conform to democratic norms. This placing of blame may not be entirely without substance, however, these perceptions are based on past events and not on the record of the last decade. Nevertheless, they are regularly dredged up to obfuscate the military's current support for democracy and its full understanding of the link between security, the economy, political stability and balanced civil-military relations.

The fact that during the three periods of prolonged military rule the country registered high economic growth is often cited as a virtue of a dispensation that ensures centralized control. The more realistic view would be that during military rule there is no political turmoil, in fact no political activity except that orchestrated by the military. Voices of dissent and criticism are also muted. It is this stability that leads to economic activity and growth and this also indicates how things could change if Pakistan were able to achieve political stability. It is up to Pakistan's economists and planners to bring to fruition the enormous benefits of political stability leading to economic growth and the broader socio-economic impact on the people of Pakistan.

By placing its organizational and structural strength in support of democracy the military has helped to develop structures of governance that will enhance the state's capacity to address future challenges and opportunities. Together the Cabinet Security Committee, the National Security Committee, the National Security Adviser, the National Security Secretariat and the Apex Committees give the political government the tools to assert control, to induct competent teams, to ensure the most capable representation abroad and strengthen its own institutions especially the bureaucracy that should be the backbone of the governance structure. The military continues to defend against external and internal threats and maintains a physical presence in newly pacified areas giving the best possible opportunity for the government to fully establish its writ.

> No amount of window dressing or self-serving arguments will change the basic reality that military rule is incompatible with the democratic principles on which the country was founded, the Constitution and the political ethos of the Pakistani people. The country's destiny was and will remain democratic … a slow burning political crisis

over the last eighteen months has plunged the entire system into a state of uncertainty … trust in democratic institutions weakens when democrats are seen as trying to manipulate the rule of law to their advantage.[18]

The military knows that military rule, in fact any rule, fails when control over the state apparatus is lost and that the environment becomes far too complex and no longer as manageable as it was in 1958 or 1977[19] or even 1999. It is in this context that the military through its official spokesman has categorically stated that democracy faces no threat in Pakistan – if any threat to democracy exists it will be through the conduct of democracy.

The military is aware of the major global and regional trends that will influence the political arena. A multipolar world is emerging as India and the People's Republic of China rise and the United States looks for alliances to contain China. Global climate change will have a huge impact especially on Pakistan as it is already water-stressed with an estimated population growth rate of 2.5%. Technological innovations will have a huge impact on productivity, trade, economy and security. The middle class is expanding and urbanization is showing phenomenal growth. For Pakistan, this translates into a reset in its foreign and security policies, a normalization of relations with its neighbours, steps to ensure a growth rate of above 6%, and urgent measures to bring about political stability and population control in order to halve the present growth rate. It is with this vision of the future that the military will continue its support for democracy.

In addition to the structural economic, financial, electoral and other institutional reforms that need to be implemented there is a need for the judiciary to develop procedures that facilitate the quick dispensation of justice. There is also a need to avoid recourse to military courts or other arrangements. A periodic review of the qualitative aspects of judicial decisions and the need to increase capacity for investigation and prosecution is also required. Above all, it is for the judiciary to ensure that it never condones or attempts to legalize extra constitutional actions.

Finally, as violence surges across its border in Afghanistan, and new actors enter the scene with agendas that stretch beyond the conflict in Afghanistan, and as radical religious nationalism grows in India, Pakistan has to address the forces of extremism and radicalization on a long-term sustainable basis. The military has endeavoured to contain this threat and to ensure internal security but it must continue to support the government because some threats have become latent in order to survive, but cannot be allowed to surface again. The military recognizes the danger that the progress it has made can be reversed and that it has to work with the government to give Pakistan an international image and an internal environment that will support its thrust towards economic and political stability. The military also understands that it does not have to get involved to bring about political stability – in fact its best role lies in continuing to support democracy. 'The challenges of militancy, weak governance and economic insecurity are feeding each other in a dangerous cycle that must be broken'.[20] This is the challenge that the military faces as it supports a democracy in Pakistan that has been making slow and steady progress since 2008.

Notes

1 Shuja Nawaz, *Crossed Swords: Pakistan, its Army, and the Wars Within*, Lahore, Oxford University Press, 2017.
2 Ayesha Siddiqa, *Military Inc: Inside Pakistan's Military Economy*, London, Pluto Press, 2007.

3 Shahid Javed Burki, 'Stability and Growth: What Could Have Been the Case', *Dawn*, Sept. 2017.
4 Ibid.
5 Khurshid Mahmud Kasuri, *Neither a Hawk nor a Dove*, Oxford University Press, 2015.
6 A. R. Siddiqi, *East Pakistan. The End Game: An Onlooker's Journal*, Karachi, Karachi University Press, 2004.
7 'Ex CJP Nasim Hasan Shah Passes Away', *The Nation*, 4 February 2015.
8 'Terror Wave in Pakistan', *Dawn*, 21 February 2015.
9 Personal communication via e-mail between the author and Dilsher Nawaz, 13 October 2017.
10 From a speech by Muhammed Ali Jinnah on 14 August 1947.
11 Inter-Services Public Relations Directorate of the Pakistan Armed Forces, briefing note in possession of the author, 2014.
12 Ibid.
13 Ibid.
14 Ibid.
15 From the brainstorming session for a World Bank-funded ongoing study on 'Pakistan at 100: Shaping the Future.'
16 The Strategic Restraint Regime first proposed by Pakistan in the 1990s envisaged a broad discussion to reduce threat levels by redeployments and limits on weapon system numbers and capabilities as well as advance warnings of impending events that could lead to miscalculations. The proposal was never taken seriously by India because of its perceptions of a threat by China though a trilateral consideration was also suggested. The proposal has been overtaken by events though the concept remains relevant. Some good confidence-building measures negotiated bilaterally remain in place.
17 Ibid.
18 Editorial, *Dawn*, 12 October 2017.
19 I. A. Rehman, 'No Shortcut to Salvation', *Dawn*, 12 October 2017.
20 Hassan Abbas, Pakistan Can Defy the Odds: How to Rescue a Failing State, Institute for Social Policy and Understanding, Clinton Township, MI, ISPU, May 2009.

7

The media in Pakistan

Idiom, ideology and the army

Khaled Ahmed

Any observer of Pakistan will concede that the media is 'relatively' free, a fact that stands out in contrast to Muslim-majority states in general where the state controls the content that appears in the media. It must be noted, however, that in Pakistan erosion of the state owing to asymmetrical war called *jihad* through non-state actors has, to a degree, sapped the capacity of the media to tell the truth as it really is.

Yet even before the state became unstable, media freedom evolved gradually. During the 1960s General Ayub Khan promulgated the Press and Publications Ordinance in order to control the freedom of the press, a policy pursued by the succeeding Bhutto government in the 1970s and then enforced more stringently by General Zia ul-Huq. It was scrapped in 1988 when, after Zia's death in office, media freedom was finally proclaimed through the abolition of the ordinance.

Since the end of Zia era (1978–88) the print media has been reinforced by television, transforming the information environment in the country from the written word to the more sensational heard-and-seen communication. This change in the media, especially after the abolition of anti-press laws, has had an impact on the number of direct consumers. From the condition of literacy imposed by the written word, the freedom to consume information by watching TV has spread to the entire population, with Urdu dominating the field as no English channel was able to make headway in the vernacular-dominated market. With it came the reinforcement of the state-induced ideology and nationalism which English tended to puncture for those who with access to the 'alternative facts' published by the global media.

In 2017 television dominated the information market and the medium of communication was predominantly Urdu although the peripheral channels used regional languages like Punjabi, Sindhi, Balochi and Pashto. There were 124 TV channels in Pakistan out of which 36 were general news channels and 17 regional news channels. The publication of English-language newspapers is minuscule as the Urdu-language newspapers dominate the market. Urdu has replaced the rational-sequential discourse of the English language and has become the medium through which knowledge about ideology and nationalism is transmitted.

Journalism should serve as a spokesman of civil society. However, in the event that journalism is subordinated to state ideology its advocacy becomes limited. In fact, it can become a part of the oppressive mechanism of the state aimed at forcibly moulding society according to the 'mission statement' of the state. Pakistani journalism plays a positive role vis-à-vis Pakistan's civil society when it publishes revelations about the conduct of the national political parties. It plays a negative role when it avoids holding the religious parties and their leaders to account to the same extent. In so far as the religious parties do act against civil society the media thus abets such a challenge to civil society's ability to respond. This negative role is played by the national 'free' media within the parameters of state governance.

Idiom and ideology

Ideology curtails freedom of expression and suppresses the variant point of view. As an 'incomplete' ideological state – the 'complete' ideological state remains part of the unfulfilled charter of all religious parties – Pakistan allows some expression of opinion against ideology. The Urdu press is not included in this ideological exception. The English press has a liberal expression and frequently clashes with the Urdu press, the assault being mostly led by the latter. Pakistan's 'incompleteness' has been frequently highlighted as a rebuke following the rise of Iran and Taliban-ruled Afghanistan as two 'completely' ideological states.

If the English press predominantly scrutinizes the state and its institutions, the Urdu press predominantly scrutinizes the state of the nation. Pakistani nationalism is more effectively expressed in Urdu than in English. Urdu journalism holds firmly to the Pakistan Movement and its foundational doctrine, the two-nation theory, and chastises those who are seen to abandon it in favour of secular moral yardsticks. While it is true that languages are moulded by national experience, once they attain an orientation they begin to command a discourse of their own. Emotive topics under the rubric of nationalism are most appropriately expressed in Urdu. The same exercise often does not succeed in English because of the latter's origin in another culture with whom Pakistan's nexus is still not broken.

Urdu is still struggling with the fast-changing specialized vocabulary of economics. It resists the discourse of philosophy and psychology because that would require new, unfamiliar coinage. The Urdu press in Pakistan is fighting against complexities of expression that threaten the reader with 'difficult' words. At the same time it is struggling to include specialized discussion of the annual budget without expanding the fund of specialized terms. Urdu comment is mostly 'popular' and non-expert, which means that it will condemn inflation even if it occurs as a result of low interest rates aimed at accelerating growth. Most readers take *ifrat-e-zar* literally to mean 'lots of money' instead of 'inflation'. An Urdu-speaking journalist will not dive deep into modern economic terminology for fear of losing his audience.

The English press in Pakistan is 'liberal'. It criticizes quite openly the ideological excesses of the state, the lack of humanism in the state's application of Islamization, and sides with the rest of the world in criticizing laws curtailing the rights of the non-Muslims and women in the country. It also opposes draconian legislations such as the blasphemy law. However, it remains defensive about ideology and will draw a line on how much ideology it will reject. Its expansion in the 1990s has been in excess of the country's English-language readership. As a result, trained manpower is not available to it in the departments of reporting and the newsroom.

Proficiency in English makes a young man eligible for jobs in the global market and the corporate world of Pakistan. However, despite the relatively high wages on offer, only a few good journalists work for the English-language newspapers. These papers' focus is on the big cities in terms of coverage. Owing to the lack of reporters the smaller cities receive virtually no coverage and the districts not at all. This is the biggest drawback for English-language journalism in Pakistan. Owing to the fact that its coverage is restricted to the big cities it is unable to establish links with civil society and respond to the requirements of the masses. Pakistan has at least four major English-language newspapers, but coverage extends only to Lahore, Karachi and Islamabad. In other big cities, such as like Faisalabad and Gujranwala, English-language newspapers have a scanty readership.

The *Dawn* leaks affair

An article filed by Senior Assistant Editor Cyril Almeida for the daily newspaper, *Dawn*, on 6 October 2016 resulted in the federal government putting Almeida on the exit control list (ECL) preparatory to opening proceedings against him for planting a 'fabricated', and 'speculative' report about a highly secret meeting between the government of Prime Minister Nawaz Sharif and the military top brass.

The report described how the government had complained that army-protected non-state actors such as Hafiz Saeed, the head of Jamat-ud-Dawa, Masud Azhar, the founder leader of Jaish-e-Mohammad and the Afghan Haqqani Network had defeated Pakistan's international campaign against India's recent action against Indian-administered Kashmir. The government complained that these elements attacked other states across national borders and had been declared terrorists at the global level. It was also alleged that any preventive action by the government against these non-state actors was intercepted by the military agencies, meaning that the army still used them against India and Afghanistan.

The army also disclaimed the content of the report and denied any role in putting Almeida on the ECL. It asked the government to find out who had briefed the *Dawn* sources behind the report. Meanwhile, *Dawn* stood behind its report and Almeida in his subsequent columns continued to write what appeared to be criticism of the army.

The media rallied behind the *Dawn* report. Discussions on TV in Urdu did not fail to note the negative effect of letting the non-state actors operate. English-language newspapers were more assertive of the right to report while adhering to professional standards. Some newspapers such as *The Nation* in Lahore were more outspoken:

> How dare the government and military top brass lecture the press on how to do their job? How dare they treat a feted reporter [Almeida] like a criminal? And how dare they imply that they have either the right or the ability or the monopoly to declare what Pakistan's 'national interest' is? Or even more laughably, what universally acknowledged principles of reporting are?[1]

Hafiz Saeed, who was caught again in 2017 running his private 'Sharia' courts was keeping quiet, which meant that the army was no longer encouraging him. The army was keeping the clerically dominated Defence of Pakistan Council out of loop. That body had been used in the past to flex intimidatory muscle against the Sharif government. Saeed's latest gem was: 'Fear America more than India and, if you have to choose, then befriending India is safer'. Clearly, he feared that the United States might be able to lift him out of Pakistan with or without the consent of the army top brass.

The Islamabad lockdown

What follows is a description of the new mode of protest in Pakistan that may be decisive in setting the tone of politics for years to come. Throughout this phenomenon known as *dharna* ('protest') the media was on the wrong side of the moral divide. Most of the TV channels and newspapers were reporting against the incumbent government even when it was apparent that the protest was illegal and backed by 'unknown forces'.

The biggest lockdown in the history of Pakistan, which took place from 5–26 November 2017, ended when Major General Azhar Naveed Hayat, the director-general of the paramilitary organization, the Pakistan Rangers of Punjab, parleyed with the agitation leaders of Tehreek Labaik Ya Rasool Allah (TLYR) in Islamabad and was able to get them to bring to an end what appeared to be a popular uprising. Earlier, the army chief, General Bajwa, had met Prime Minister Abbasi and had refused to deploy more troops to combat the lockdown. He advised Abbasi not to use force.

All the major cities of Pakistan were brought to a standstill by a sit-in organized by the Barelvi sect. This amounted to an unprecedented show of force by a sect understood to be quietist and apolitical. The protest was sparked by the introduction by parliament of a change to the 2017 Election Act which now contained an oath which the Barelvi clerics thought was insulting to the Holy Prophet. Just one word caused the country to become paralysed: The phrase 'I solemnly swear' had been inadvertently replaced with 'I solemnly believe – and the culprit for the change was found to be the Minister of Law, Zahid Hamid, despite the fact that all the parties in parliament had passed the amendment. Most of the country's dozen top TV channels turned against the government which was already under siege from the opposition as well as from the army, offended by the *Dawn* leak affair (see above).

When the government finally sent in troops to disperse the Rawalpindi-Islamabad sit-in on the orders of the Islamabad High Court, it was quickly defeated as the *dharna* was more organized than most people had realized. The agitators had been provided with generous quantities of food by anonymous donors, as well as with tents and bedding. They carried firearms and grenades while the state intelligence agencies turned a blind eye. With all the main cities paralysed, the Prime Minister knew that his government was finally defeated. He asked Hamid to resign – which he duly did.

Army as arbite

The great countrywide *dharna* of the Barelvi sect came to an end on 27 November 2017, barring a few straggling groups who liked the power to cause disruptions too much to give up easily. The army swung into action and persuaded the Barelvi leader, Khadim Hussain Rizvi, to call off the siege and to accept Rs 1,000 from the Major-General in charge to be given to those whom the police had arrested and jailed for their part in the protest.

Justice Shaukat Siddiqui at the Islamabad High Court rejected the army's interference in the protest which he thought violated the details of the ruling he had given about how the government should go about removing the mullahs from the roads. This highlighted the innuendo already made by several PMLN spokesmen about how the army was acting behind the scenes, starting with the 2014 *dharna* of Imran Khan and his well-funded Barelvi 'cousin', Allama Tahirul Qadri. Large amounts of money were spent on organizing the *dharna* at the time, and large amounts were being spent on this occasion too. The intelligence agencies kept quiet and turned a blind eye. Furthermore, one source quoted Khadim Rizvi as saying that the army would not harm his great *dharna* 'because we are doing the army's job'.

The Bol TV affair

On 5 December 2017 the dismissed Prime Minister of Pakistan, Nawaz Sharif, decided to take on the forces that had unseated him and hinted broadly at the hand of the army behind the plot to oust him from power. He pointed to the past subversions of democracy by the generals and claimed that he was a victim of the pattern of Pakistan's prime ministers failing to complete their five-year terms in office. As he spoke, his party, which was still in power, was facing an assault from a majority of the TV channels and newspapers for having insulted the Holy Prophet. Of the 40-plus news channels, not one defended him outright and the few that were accused of siding with him tried very hard to balance their coverage of the political aftermath of his ouster.

One glaring example of aggressive partisanship against Sharif was BOL TV, owned by a software and online education company, Axact. Despite the fact that the company was facing criminal charges, it was able to attract a number of well-known, highly paid TV anchors. Just as it was poised to 'revolutionize' the media in Pakistan, a court in New York in May 2015 found it guilty of distributing 370 fake degrees that had awarded through its online correspondence courses.[2] Its representative in America was caught and jailed after his confession. Back in Pakistan, this is not how Axact was treated. BOL TV did not go off the air but started flying high with anti-Nawaz and pro-army agitational propaganda which made it impregnable.

BOL TV's style was aggressive if not abusive. It paid its anchors well for sheer defamation palmed off as patriotism defending the honour of the army which Nawaz Sharif was 'out to smear' through leaking negative reports to 'friendly' newspapers. GEO TV and *The News* came under fire more directly because of their past 'misdemeanors' with the institution of the army. Typically retired senior army officers-turned-interviewees figured on it, blasting the Sharif government for corruption and betrayal of the 'national cause' accusing Sharif of personally cosying up to Indian Prime Minister Narendra Modi.[3]

Then the law in Pakistan caught up with BOL TV. Bogus degrees of various educational qualifications were discovered in the offices of Axact and its CEO Shoaib Ahmad Sheikh was rounded up and a case of fraud was registered against him in 2015. However, just as the TV channel was threatened with closure, counter-moves were made to rescue it. In September 2016 a sessions judge, Pervaizul Qadir Memon, who was hearing its case suddenly decided to acquit the CEO on all charges and allowed him to go back to managing BOL TV. When the decision was challenged by the Islamabad High Court, Memon confessed to having authorized the acquittal after receiving a bribe of Rs 5 million.[4] However, having made his confession, he was rapidly dismissed on corruption charges.

The Federal Investigative Authority (FIA) was probably not aware of the extent of the power behind BOL TV and continued to pursue Axact vigorously. Before the case could be revived, however, Zahid Jamil, the FIA's lead prosecutor, resigned from his position under mysterious circumstances. As reporter Umar Cheema put it in The News on 10 September 2016, 'A top investigator of FIA who collected forensic evidence against alleged frauds of Axact has been chased, intercepted and taken to unmarked locations for counselling on the case several times'. Later, a hand grenade was thrown at his house to firm up his resolve to stay away from the case. Three more prosecutors also mysteriously resigned and BOL TV kept on spewing out its poison.

The unspoken verdict on the direction the media had to take was thus delivered. Most of the TV channels and Urdu newspapers sided with Pakistan's institutions – namely the army – and this strengthened the position of Imran Khan's party, Pakistan Tehreek-e-Insaf, as the next most popular incumbent after Nawaz Sharif's Pakistan Muslim League.

Threatened by terrorists and/or the army

Much confusion was caused among the media professionals by the provenance of the threats they received after reporting too close to the truth. The threat precedes the attack in the form of a terrorist 'list' of those being targeted for assassination, but the recipient remains confused and takes it to be either from the Taliban or the Inter-Services Intelligence (ISI), Pakistan's intelligence agency in charge of defending the nation against external threats.

Anchoring discussions on Express TV in 2014 Raza Rumi, contributing editor of the *Friday Times*, was shot at in Lahore while travelling in his car with a guard and his driver. He narrowly escaped by ducking below the car window but his driver was hit by the bullets and wounded. Rumi, who targeted 'the Taliban, the state and its attitude to minorities', had to seek protection in the United States. In 2017, he was visiting faculty at the Honors Program, Ithaca College, USA.

He was later to write:

> TTP had supporters in the Punjab province namely Lashkar-e-Jhangvi (LeJ) and that the space for Pakistani media and independent opinion has further shrunk due to the threats they face in reporting on the issue of the Taliban and terrorism. At least three media houses have been attacked and the journalists get little or no protection from any quarter.
>
> Earlier, my work had invoked jihadists' hatred on social media, where they are very comfortable and free. In December 2013, someone with a Taliban or ISIS flag accused me on my Facebook page of 'preaching' a 'secular ideology' and 'defaming mujahideen [jihadis] in every possible manner'. This person warned: 'remember your end will be extremely bitter, the worst fate awaits the *desi* seculars like you'.[5]

In 2014 the International Federation of Journalists ranked Pakistan as the most dangerous country in the world for the news media. As a result, self-censorship prevailed. Journalists did it to save their lives, and in many cases, their jobs, too. That year Amnesty International reported under the rubric 'A bullet has been chosen for you', with interviews of 100 journalists:

> Thirty-four journalists may have been killed as a direct consequence of their work since the restoration of a democratically elected government in Pakistan in March 2008. After Prime Minister Nawaz Sharif formed the government on 5 June 2013, at least eight journalists lost their lives across the country as a direct result of their work since the restoration of a democratically elected government in Pakistan in March 2008. After Prime Minister Nawaz Sharif formed the government on 5 June 2013, at least eight journalists lost their lives across the country as a direct result of their

work, and this included five killed in 2014. Of the 34 killings since 2008, nine took place in north-western Pakistan (the Federally Administered Tribal Areas, or Khyber Pakhtunkhwa), 13 took place in the Balochistan province, and of these, six happened in the province's second town, Khuzdar.[6]

Hamid Mir and the army

Then came the attack on Pakistan's top TV anchor, Hamid Mir, a recipient of the highest civilian award, the Hilal-e-Imtiaz, and popular host of 'Capital Talk' on Geo TV. Mir was being driven from the airport to his office in Karachi in the evening, and was sitting in the back of the car when two motorbike riders shot him through the car window embedding five bullets in his stomach. Showing a good presence of mind his driver saved his life by immediately taking him to hospital. From the hospital, Mir's statement, later read out by his brother, Amir, spoke of threats from both the state and non-state actors. Amir Mir, himself a journalist and the author of books on Pakistan's *jihad* through 'proxy warriors', declared on TV that the ISI chief, Lt-Gen. Zaheer-ul-Islam was behind the attack. (At 2018 Amir had not written for any publication after that statement.) Hamid Mir had been told by intelligence officers that he was on a hit list and that the ISI was unhappy about his support for the Baloch rebels. In November 2012 a bomb was found attached to his car in Islamabad. He appeared before a judicial commission appointed to inquire into the attack in April 2014.

The Commission of Inquiry stated:

> What we have noticed during these proceedings is that, prima facie, there was a tug of war among some members of print and electronic media on the one hand, and a Federal Agency on the other. It was so because according to the members of print and electronic media, who had appeared before the Commission, the said agency was not happy with their reporting.[7]

The Commission found that the allegations made by Hamid Mir about the conduct of the ISI were without foundation.[8] However, Amir Mir stated that, two weeks before the shooting, his brother had sent a videotaped message to the US-based Committee to Protect Journalists (CPJ), saying that 'if there was an attack on him, the ISI chief was to be held responsible. Amir said his brother was under threat from the time of the ISI chief, General Shuja Pasha'.

The CPJ website put out the following deposition by Hamid Mir:

> After the May 2011 U.S. raid on Abbottabad, as the TV anchors pounded the military for being incompetent, Hamid Mir, one of the most popular personalities on GEO TV, got a call from a brigadier that the director-general of intelligence at the time, Shuja Pasha, wanted to see him. Here's how the conversation with Pasha proceeded, according to Mir:
> 'Mr. Mir, this system and Pakistan cannot co-exist.'
> 'What system?' asked Mir.
> 'The parliamentary form of democracy and Pakistan.'
> 'Do you want a presidential form?' asked Mir.
> 'Yes.'
> 'This is not your job. It's the job of Parliament to change the Constitution.'

Pasha then spoke abusively about the son of the Punjab chief minister, the son of the President, and the sons of other chief ministers. 'Do you want your children ruled by these sons?' he asked Mir.

'We had a very bad meeting', Mir told me when we met in Islamabad. 'He is talking politics the whole time.' After that meeting, parliamentary democracy and the sons of different politicians began taking a critical beating from talk show hosts and columnists. Suddenly, they were all promoting Imran Khan, the popular cricketer-turned-populist-politician, who led the Pakistan Tehreek-e-Insaf party, or PTI, in the May 2013 elections. Pasha had decided that Khan was the man to back. 'Politicians called me, "Mir, Mir, I want advice. Should I join Imran Khan? Pasha is putting pressure on us"'.[9]

Sethi's ordeal: a divided media

Hamid Mir's 'encounter' was not the only one to make the headlines.[10] In 1999 the Lahore-based journalist Najam Sethi faced the state's wrath for having gone to India where he made a speech that spurred the Foreign Office into action. Sethi, who wrote the editorials in Lahore's popular weekly the *Friday Times*, was imprisoned illegally as he could not be given a fair trial. However, the three weeks he spent in custody was the time of trial for the Pakistani press. There is nothing more damaging to the freedom of the press than division among the ranks of journalists. Governments can swoop down on the divided community, persuade a section of it to support its draconian actions, isolate the so-called rebels and bring them to heel through coercion. The basic human instinct of tertium gaudens (the rejoicing third party) came into play among the journalists in 1999.

The division exposed a permanent schism – the one which exists between the Urdu and the English press, and fbetween the ideological and the objective. The concept of 'treason' was grasped by the two in diametrically opposed ways. The English-language newspapers immediately focused on the importance of habeas corpus, a 'Western' value that secures an individual against the coercive power of the state. The Urdu-language press saw Sethi as a traitor and decided that he deserved the treatment he was getting. In most cases, it glossed over the illegal manner in which the editor of the *Friday Times* was picked up. The 'trial' of Najam Sethi in the Urdu press revealed another fact: that the government agencies and information bureaucrats worked more closely with the Urdu press than with the English press. On the other hand, the English press seemed to be less amenable to official persuasion. A few writers who took the official line were hard put to write convincing copy. The language itself sounded hollow under the burden of nationalism.

In the Urdu press, however, the picture was different. High emotion and passionate metaphor replaced the need for facts and rational argument. Najam Sethi was declared an Indian agent at worst and a pro-Indian renegade at least who deserved to be punished by the government – and by the patriotic Pakistanis if he somehow escaped conviction under the law. Reporters failed to check their facts before filing copy. One columnist asked: 'Why is Najam Sethi always travelling to India while the well-known patriotic journalists are never invited there?' In fact, of the journalists listed in the column, some had already been invited to visit India. While the said columnist was writing his piece a group of 'patriotic' journalists were actually visiting India.

The persistent refrain was that Najam Sethi was not a journalist but a politician. Ironically, most of the newspapers in which these analyses were being printed had editors or owners who had worked in the past as politicians or who were still politically aligned. Senior right-wing editors presiding over Urdu journalism had been jailed in the past for taking part in 'anti-Pakistan activities'. Columnists who expended so much wisdom on Najam Sethi in May 1999 were all known within the community for their political alignment.

As the CPJ recorded:

> Around 2:30 a.m. on May 8, 1999, dozens of government agents raided Sethi's home. According to Jugnu Mohsin, Sethi's wife and the publisher of the *Friday Times*, the raid was the work of Pakistan's Intelligence Bureau in partnership with the Punjab police. She said that the officers forced their way through the locked gate of the residence, assaulted two security guards who had been hired to protect the family, and broke into house. At least eight armed officers – only two in uniform, the rest in plainclothes – burst into the couple's bedroom to make the arrest. Officers pulled Sethi out of bed, and beat him with billy clubs and steel handcuffs, said Mohsin. She added that when she asked the officers to produce a warrant for the arrest, one of them threatened to shoot Sethi immediately and leave his corpse in place of any warrant.
>
> Just two days before his arrest, Sethi had told CPJ that the government was using the state-controlled media to set the stage for his arrest on charges of high treason and sedition. Sethi said he had been warned by senior government officials that his recent work with the BBC was viewed by some members of the administration as an attempt to destabilise the country and overthrow the government, and that his arrest was imminent.[11]

Conclusion: the darkness ahead

Pakistan's media is in thrall to two dominant identity-markers of the state – tightening grip of religious extremist groups and anti-India nationalism – both backed by the informal power of the army. Over time, the army has become more and more disenchanted with the foreign policy pursued by pragmatic politicians intent on achieving peace with India through trade as a solution after facing the economic collapse of a terror-besieged state. Internally, the army has undergone an overhaul of its social orientation – from mildly right-wing religious to hard Islam – as more and more officers now come from the rising middle class. The neglect of the national economy as the new problematic in governance was pointed out by Ejaz Haider, editor of national security affairs for Capital TV:

> Perhaps there's need for the Army to see two things very clearly: one, security policy that is a sub-set of a national security strategy which must define security far more broadly than the military has ever managed to do. Two, flowing from the first, the emphasis must shift from geopolitics to geo-economics.[12]

However, changes taking place within the region have dimmed the chance of bringing Pakistan and its media to normal, responsible functioning. As India hurtles towards a new aggressively Hindu identity and the United States and the People's Republic of China choose South Asia as the arena for a new Cold War, the current trends are expected to continue. If the new political leaders of Pakistan, such as Imran Khan, fulfil their promise to 'revolutionize' mass education, the trend towards extremism is bound to continue in the media.

Notes

1 Editorial, *The Nation*, 12 October 2016.
2 Declan Walsh, 'Fake Diplomas, Real Cash: Pakistani Company Axact Reaps Millions', *New York Times*, 17 May 2015.
3 On 19 December 2017 Pakistan's Chief of Army Staff, General Qamar Javed Bajwa, faced the Committee of the Whole at the Senate in Islamabad and declared that the senior retired army officers who appeared on TV were not voicing the opinion of the army but their own. The opinions expressed by the officers were, however, too uniform to be individual and too forceful and at times too threatening for the state not to back them.
4 Rizwan Shehzad, 'Axact Fake Degree Case Judge Confesses to Receiving Rs5m Bribe to Acquit Shoaib Shaikh, *Express Tribune*, 16 June 2017.
5 https://aeon.co/essays/pakistan-s-political-islamists-tried-to-kill-me.
6 Amnesty International Report, 2014. See https://tribune.com.pk/story/815075/pakistan-most-dangerous-country-for-journalists-in-2014-report/.
7 Commission of Inquiry Notification (S.R.O.) No.2/125/2014(ops)-8221, 21 April 2014.
8 Hasnaat Malik, 'Attack on Hamid Mir: Charges against ISI Were Based on Assumptions, Says Inquiry', *Express Tribune*, 10 April 2016.
9 http://cpj.org/reports/2013/05/pakistan-roots-impunity-threats-intimidation.php.
10 Another victim of the agency hoods, the reporter Umar Cheema, confirmed in his article in *The New York Times* (14 June 2011) that the people who thrashed him almost to death had made it clear that they were not members of the Taliban or of Al-Qaeda.
11 https://cpj.org/1999/10/veteran-journalist-najam-sethi-arrested.php.
12 Ejaz Haider, *Newsweek Pakistan*, 4 November 2017: 'Through the years, in terms of our threat perceptions, we have been trying to commit suicide for the fear of death, to quote Bismarck. Our foreign policy (as also our trade, commerce, investment et cetera) has become a subset of our security policy, a classic case of the tail wagging the dog. Add to that the military's dominance of security policy and the inevitable problem of bounded rationality that afflicts all large-scale organizations and we have landed, predictably, where we have.'

Part II
Pakistan's dependence on the outside world

8

Pakistan, power-play and a new South Asian paradigm

Iftekhar Ahmed Chowdhury

Introduction

Currently, much interest is focused on Pakistan. This is not just because of the myriad challenges it confronts. It is also because of its immense potential. A nuclear-armed nation, with an overwhelmingly Muslim-majority population, it is often in the news, but, alas, almost always for the wrong reasons. With an area of nearly 800,000 sq km and a population estimated at 208 million, it has a gross domestic product of US $885 billion, and an abundance of natural resources whose extent has not yet been fully ascertained. It straddles the Middle East and South Asia, and is a conduit between two volatile and politically significant regions. It borders India and the People's Republic of China, Asia's two foremost protagonists, as well as Afghanistan, a cauldron of incendiary politics. Pakistan itself has its own political uncertainties to deal with, while being intermittently rocked by civil commotion. Its strategic location, untapped resources and domestic inscrutabilities make it an interesting field for certain activities of the world's most powerful nations, and in return, demands an intricate global role for that country to perform three basic foreign policy roles: first, protection of its sovereignty; second, accessing resources for its own development; and third, ensuring sufficient space for itself for policy manoeuvrability.

Pakistan was to have been a secular nation, modelled on the Western democratic tradition.[1] At least that was how the founder of the nation, Muhammed Ali Jinnah, saw it when it came into being in August 1947. Of Jinnah's life, Professor Stanley Wolpert, with a tinge of hagiography, writes: 'Few individuals significantly alter the course of history. Fewer still modify the map of the world. Hardly anyone can be credited with creating a nation state. Mohammed Ali Jinnah did all three.'[2] Intensely secular in lifestyle, habits and behaviour, and deeply fond of most things English, Jinnah used the Western political idiom of the nation-state, promoted the argument that the Muslims of India should constitute a separate nation, and he did this with incredible fervour and faith, and against great odds. He gave ideological battle to towering personalities like Mahatma Gandhi and Jawaharlal Nehru, shrugged off the unfriendliness of the British Viceroy Lord Louis Mountbatten, often rode roughshod over the opposition in his own camp, and based on the Wilsonian paradigm managed to carve out a new country, Pakistan, for his Muslim co-religionists in British India. His death in 1948, too soon after the country's creation, and the assassination of his mentee Prime Minister Liaquat Ali Khan in 1951 caused a period of instability, with no less than six Prime Ministers serving during the next eight years.[3] Thereafter, military rule alternated with often idiosyncratic civilian control, with massive follies committed by generals and civilians leading to the secession of East Pakistan, politically the more liberal and in religious terms the more syncretic and tolerant part of the nation in 1971. True, the separation might have given Pakistan a more compact 'physical identity'.[4] However, this came at a great political price as it severed those elements of civic politics that could have helped to calm Pakistan's future sectarian passions, the current bane of its domestic politics.

History, geography and ideology appear to combine to pit Pakistan against its perceived principal regional rival, India. But what is most palpable is the territorial dispute over Kashmir, claimed by both, that has led to at least three major wars between the two countries, in 1947, in 1965 and in 1999. In fact, the issue has locked Pakistan and India into a war situation, according to Subrata Mitra, of 'attrition which India cannot manage to win and Pakistan cannot afford to lose'.[5] Over the years there have been numerous skirmishes along the borders, or what is known as the Line of Control (LoC), including many since 1984 over the Siachen Glacier. India currently administers around 43 per cent of the region including Jammu, the Kashmir valley and Ladakh, while Pakistan controls around 37 per cent, namely what it calls Azad Kashmir and the northern areas of Gilgit and Baltistan. India is by far the larger of the two, with a land area of 3.2 million sq km and a population of 1.3 billion. India has a military strength of nearly 1.3 million troops, double that of Pakistan's, which stands at 617,000 troops. But a strategic equivalence is rendered in terms of nuclear deterrence: Pakistan possesses about 100–120 nuclear warheads compared to India's 80–100. This also means that an all-out conflict is scarcely conceivable, although at lower thresholds it is still possible, with the nasty risk of it developing into self-destructive nuclear wars. Unsurprisingly, Kashmir and therefore India are central to the way Pakistan shapes its external behaviour. However, it is noteworthy that Kashmir was not a factor in the war that Pakistan fought with India, i.e. the Bangladesh war of 1971. Even when not involved directly India is nevertheless interested in the way Pakistan organizes its policy vis-à-vis Afghanistan, the Taliban, and foreign and domestic terrorism.

Foreign policy models and Pakistan

There are several options that a weaker neighbour may have in terms of dealing with one that is larger and ostensibly more powerful. One is what the Scandinavian political scientist Erling Bjol has described as 'pilot-fish behaviour', which implies 'keeping close to the shark to avoid being eaten'.[6] Finland's relations with the Soviet Union are an example, based on the early Finnish perception that its 'national interests do not permit ties nor the pursuit of alignment with an anti-Soviet policy'.[7] Sweden, on the other hand, in addition to behaving like a pilot fish, tried to make itself as troublesome as possible for the potentially more powerful adversary to overcome. The Pakistani ethos rejected the 'pilot fish' option altogether. Indeed, while making itself a troublesome adversary, much like Sweden vis-à-vis the Soviet Union, it additionally chose the path of seeking to make up the power gap with its neighbour by enmeshing itself into a web of extraregional linkages. Apart from buttressing its sense of security, the extraregional linkages also sought to satisfy the aspirations of quest for resources and expanding the manoeuverability in policymaking.

The literature on foreign policy analyses tends to be either 'process-oriented', especially with regard to developed countries, or 'function-oriented' with regard to developing ones. The former concentrates on a detailed examination of foreign policymaking processes, with emphasis on institutions like bureaucracies, political parties and pressure groups, and the influence they exert on foreign policy outcomes.[8] Regarding developing countries, the argument has been advanced that their institutions, still being rudimentary, deserve less attention than the functions of foreign policy or the purposes they are put to. In other words, their foreign policies are being seen as a function of functions.[9]

There are other ideas. Migdal has identified four broad conceptual models that help to explain foreign policy. One, the 'geo-political model' whereby physical location assumes prime importance and internal changes in regimes or ideologies have little significant impact; two, the 'organization process model' which sees all foreign policy as organizational output; three, the 'bargaining model' whereby 'players' bargain with one another to produce 'political outcomes'; and, finally, the 'rational policy model' which assumes that policy is a result of actions which are calculated responses to achieve certain ends.[10]

In the case of Pakistan, the socio-political system possesses features of both developed and developing countries that intertwine with complexity, render any single model of analysis difficult and instead calls for a 'model-mix', with empiricism as the dominant factor. As in many other developing countries, there have been charismatic leaders – Bhutto, Zia ul Huq, Pervez Musharraf, Zardari, Nawaz Sharif to name but a few – whom Henry Kissinger would call 'prophets' in the system.[11] While they have been powerful and have often given directions, they have been restrained by both the mosque (i.e. the proponents of religious-oriented social leadership), and the military, which has always been a powerful factor in shaping Pakistan's external behaviour. The mosque and the military have often worked, in the words of Husain Huqqani, a diplomat-cum-analyst, in 'alliance' to this end.[12] Ayesha Jalal, another prolific writer, has argued how the generals have often purchased security (purportedly vis-à-vis India) at the expense of democracy.[13] The excessive role of the military has led some analysts to even call Pakistan a 'garrison state'.[14] Others have termed it 'a bureaucratic polity'.[15] Side by side, there also exists a significant modern elite, who draw their intellectual pabulum from the West. Pakistan also has an effective diaspora, with many of its members playing important governmental and legislative roles in their host countries (as in the United Kingdom and the United States), and impacting on policymaking in their country of origin.[16] The upshot of this diversity is that policy, which very often is a result of the interactions of these elements, ends up being irrational, with one element or the other seeming to exert preponderant influence. Some will say that the military has been able to exert the most amount of influence. However, Pakistan's rather efficient and well-equipped Ministry of Foreign Affairs (Pakistani diplomats have a reputation for sagacity developed over the years) may translate this into a modicum of acceptable set of perceived national self-interest.[17]

The total gamut of Pakistan's external policy, aimed at achieving the three-fold objectives identified earlier of making up the power gap with India, accessing external resources and expanding manoeuvrability, can be said to be resting on four pillars: one, relations the United States and the West; two, ties with China; three, linkages with the Islamic countries; and four, interactions with multilateral bodies, in particular the United Nations (UN).

The United States and the West

In Pakistan's early stages of development, starting from the 1950s and continuing into the late 1960s, the strategy followed in economic development was based on the Harrod Domar model. It was one of promoting rapid industrialization under the ownership and control of the rising capitalist class, with the presumption that the benefits of growth would trickle down to the most depressed sections of the community.[18] The received wisdom among Pakistani policymakers was Paul Rosenstein-Rodan's 'Big Push' theory. It favoured planned large-scale investments in industrialization in countries with a surplus workforce in agriculture in order to take advantage of network effects, namely, economies of scale and scope to escape the low-level 'equilibrium trap'. Hence the need for large injections of funds, including from external sources, such as the United States and the West, as well as the Bretton Woods institutions. Enter America and Europe. In the meantime, in 'a desperate need to find an equalizer against a belligerent India', Pakistan had already joined US-sponsored military pacts, such as the Central Treaty Organization (CENTO) and the Southeast Asian Treaty Organization (SEATO) which also was in consonance with Pakistan's ideological predilections to counter the spread of Communism.[19]

Between 1951 and 2011 the United States provided nearly US $67 billion in aid. The flow waxed and waned from year to year, in consonance with the nature of bilateral relations. Mostly connected to the on-going conflict in Afghanistan, and also to certain bilateral differences that erupted from time to time, there were stoppages. To signal renewed commitment to Pakistan, the US Congress in 2009 approved the Kerry-Lugar-Berman Bill, putting security and development on two separate tracks, and authorizing a development-related support package valued at US $7.5 between 2009 and 2014. A variety of factors severely restricted disbursements. Tapping into alternative sources, the government of Pakistan approached the International Monetary Fund (IMF) for a package amounting to $6.6 billion for the financial years 2013–16 to solve the Bank of Pakistan crisis and to shore up its depleting foreign exchange reserves.

When Nawaz Sharif was elected into office in 2013, the government of Pakistan's mantra was 'trade, not aid', and Pakistani officials hoped to achieve a bilateral trade figure of around US $11 billion over the next five years. In 2013 two-way trade between the United States and Pakistan totalled $5.3 billion. The curve has moved up only slightly since that year. The reason for this is that production of textiles is Pakistan's forte, and therefore US legislators are wary of according any preferential treatment to Pakistan that would hurt American textile manufacturers. Outside of textiles, even in agro-business, Pakistanis are unlikely to be able to meet the high American regulatory standards. So, prospects remain dim even beyond the rim of the saucer. Contemporary Europe, recognizing that it is in its own interest to stabilize Pakistan through what Joseph Nye has called 'soft power', fills in the gap somewhat by offering to spread gentler values such as democracy and human rights. Also, from a more pragmatic perspective, by offering Pakistan from 1 January 2014 onwards the Generalized Scheme of Preferences-Plus status that would enhance Pakistani exports to Europe by US $42 billion per year.

It is often difficult to imagine today that Pakistan was once such a close confidante of the United States, providing, for example, bases for secret U2 flights, including the notorious one of pilot Gary Powers in May 1960 over the Soviet Union.[20] President Richard Nixon asked President Yahya Khan to be a conduit to China.[21] The latter effectively complied with the request. Thereafter, Pakistan, during the period that President Zia ul Huq was in office, was a staunch ally in the war against the Russians in

Afghanistan, and Pervez Musharraf rendered unstinting support to President George W. Bush in his 'war on terror'. But this relationship became strained over time, because the United States, dictated by its own strategic interests, moved closer to India. The strain in the relationship was compounded by Pakistan's dual-purpose use of the Taliban, which was seen by the United States as an 'enemy', as a foe domestically, but to be cultivated, largely by the Pakistani military's Inter-Services Intelligence agency as a tool vis-à-vis India. The US operation eliminating Osama bin Laden in Abbottabad deeply embarrassed the powers-that-be in Islamabad. But since both need each other, the US-Pakistan ties have assumed the form of a 'transactional relationship', based on outcomes of negotiations rather than one that is spontaneous. Borrowing an expression from the philosopher Emmanuel Kant, while complex, it is a 'categorical imperative'. The Pakistanis generally indicate to the Americans that they are committed, but not wedded, to the relationship. However, they sometimes like pointing to other options and closer friends: China, for instance.

China

If, among all the variables that mark contemporary international relations there has been one constant, it is the Pakistan-China relationship, the world's primary 'all-weather' friendship. Verbal grandiloquence and flowery terminologies are rarely in short supply when both sides describe their bilateral links. Examples of such expressions as 'sweeter than honey', 'higher than mountains' and 'stronger than steel' abound. But any serious observer will know that these are not mere hyberboles, but, in consonance with the linguist culture of Eastern politics, are fraught with deep meaning conveying the essence of a unique strategic partnership. The links that began in 1963, with the signing of the border agreement, were initially seen by both sides as a counterpoise against India following the Sino-Indian War of 1962. However, as China re-emerged as a global power, this relationship, at least as far as China and Pakistan were concerned, was put to other uses, such as to push China closer to the United States.

A recent example of cooperation between Pakistan and China is the China–Pakistan Economic Corridor (CPEC), a fruition of President Xi Jinping's visit to Pakistan in April 2015. This was a part of Xi's One Belt One Road initiative that is seen as the centrepiece of his foreign policy. It involves the Old Silk Route connecting China with Central Asia, and then with Europe beyond, and the new Maritime Silk Road, linking up the ports of powers friendly to China, combining to facilitate Beijing's quest for trade and resources. The CPEC is an offshoot of the initiative linking north-west China, far from the Chinese seas, to the Pakistani warm water port of Gwadar. China has committed US $46 billion for projects in infrastructure and energy along the 2,000 mile stretch of the One Belt One Road initiative.

To appease Pakistan's powerful security circles, China has been providing military support to Islamabad for years. Pakistan's nuclear programme has been an enormous beneficiary of this relationship. China has in the past not only provided conventional weaponry but also nuclear-capable platforms. Initially, the idea may have been to shore up Pakistani capabilities vis-à-vis India. Now China, with its burgeoning global role, is seeking to detach its relations with Pakistan from those with India. For instance, China's planned sale to Pakistan of eight submarines capable of carrying nuclear-tipped missiles and of strengthening Pakistan's second-strike capability, could in theoretical strategic terms be argued to be stabilizing.

While Pakistan might still perceive its China links as buttressing its sense of security, mainly vis-à-vis India, the Chinese agenda may be broader. The One Belt One Road Initiative into which Pakistan fits in so neatly can be placed on the backdrop of Xi Jinpjng's 'China Dream' or *Chunguo Meng* (in Mandarin). This mainly entails three things: one, a 'new kind of relationship' with the great powers such as the United States; two, 'win-win' with all countries (including India), and strategic partnership with 'all weather friends' (Pakistan) stimulating benefits for all concerned.

All this is purported to support what China likes to call not just its 'peaceful rise' but its far more nuanced *heping juechi* which can be translated as 'peaceful development'. These differences in perceptions, however slight and subtle as some may assess them to be, have caused Pakistan to look to others as well in terms of security and developmental reinsurances. The Islamic countries are the most obvious candidates.

Islamic countries

That is how and why Pakistan came to look to the Islamic countries. These countries also provide spiritual and material sustenance to the Pakistanis, housing, as Saudi Arabia does, Islam's holiest shrines, pilgrimage to which is mandatory for all Muslims; with its oil wealth Saudi Arabia has also generously supported Pakistan's financial needs. Saudi Arabia has provided solace and succour to Pakistani politicians forced to live abroad, including former Prime Minister Nawaz Sharif. The external Islamic links strengthen Pakistan's own Muslim identity. Out of seven million Pakistanis living overseas, nearly two million reside in the Middle East. Indeed, the severance from former East Pakistan also gave Pakistan a geographical contiguity with the region, in some ways rendering Pakistan as much Middle Eastern as South Asian. Furthermore, if it were not for the issues with India, Pakistan's gaze would have understandably focused westward. Under Zulfikar Ali Bhutto, largely credited with the loss of the eastern wing, this 'non-Indian' identity was emphasized. This, to Stephen Cohen, meant that Pakistan ceased to learn from 'the one country it resembled most', India, including the ability to follow suit when down the years India chose the path of economic reform.[22]

In return for their favours, Pakistan gave the Middle Eastern countries intellectual leadership, by among other things, serving as a 'think-tank and laboratory' in political and economic matters.[23] Pakistan has the strongest air force among the Muslim countries, one of the best-equipped armies, and is the only nuclear-armed country. This fact could also be a source of embarrassment to Pakistan: when Saudi Arabia and the United Arab Emirate sought Pakistan's assistance in fighting the Shiite Houthi rebels in Yemen, Pakistan, with its 20 per cent Shia population and sectarian worries of its own, was obliged to risk Arab ire by having to refuse.[24]

But the biggest fillip to the Islamization of Pakistani domestic and foreign policies came during the presidency of General Zia ul Huq. Confronted with the loss of Bangladesh, and perhaps more humiliatingly for the Pakistanis, the defeat by India in the 1971 war, and unwilling to allow any other ambitious power-seekers from damaging the nation, his call to Pakistan's Islamic heritage attained a resonance hitherto unknown.[25] The Soviet invasion of Afghanistan provided Zia with an opportunity and Pakistan went all out in its support of the Afghan *Mujaheddin* in alliance with the United States and the West. The *Mujaheddin* flocked in droves into Pakistan, and when the Soviets quit Afghanistan, the *Mujaheddin* morphed into the Taliban both in Afghanistan and in Pakistan. The traditional Indian 'Deobandi' idea of an Islamic society forged an alliance with the Arab Wahabi School.[26] This deadly mix proved explosive for Pakistani domestic and regional politics, and haunts it to this day.

When the United States and President Bush launched the 'war on terror', and in its pursuit attacked Afghanistan, Pakistan's Pervez Musharraf was obliged to offer support. But this was to be in a complex fashion. Pakistan apprehended that the Taliban in Afghanistan might return,[27] and Pakistan, at least some of its military, needed Afghanistan for 'strategic depth' vis-à-vis India. Moreover, the all-powerful ISI within the Pakistani army was reluctant to let go of the Taliban as a potential tool against India. Finally, succumbing to pressures, many originating from the Taliban itself, the army decided to launch Operation *Zarb-e-Azab*, aimed at eliminating terrorist hideouts in North Waziristan and the tribal belt.[28] With the US-backed military support in a state of draw-down, and a change of guard in Kabul from President Hamed Karzai to President Ashraf Ghanie, who was far more favourably inclined towards Islamabad, Pakistan would need to retool, refurbish and re-energize its Afghan policy, where Indian understanding and empathy would be helpful, indeed, essential.[29]

The United States

Perhaps the most important watershed date for Pakistan is 21 April 1948 in terms of its relations with the UN. On that day the UN Security Council adopted Resolution 47 instructing the UN Commission to proceed to the region to 'prepare for a plebiscite on Kashmir'.[30] It was adopted under Chapter VI of the UN Charter, and was therefore non-binding. Nonetheless, Pakistan has always held India morally accountable for its non-implementation of the resolution. On 13 August 1948 the UN Commission for India and Pakistan adopted another resolution asking both armies to withdraw and the Kashmiris to be given the right to self-determination. Neither side adhered to it. India did not hold the plebiscite and Pakistan did not withdraw its troops. Consequently, there is always continuing tension around the dividing LoC. Pakistan has since then almost constantly sparred with India at the UN on Kashmir, either formally in the Councils or informally in the corridors. This is also the principal reason why Pakistan seeks to block any Security Council reforms that could provide India with a permanent seat by helping to rally opposition to such expansion through groupings such as the 'Coffee club' or 'Uniting for consensus'.

The UN, of course, provided Pakistan with a strengthened sense of security, a source of material support, a venue for Pakistani leaders to meet others from around the globe (for instance during General Assembly sessions each winter), and also with a forum to air its views on global issues, such as those relating to Palestine, the Organization of Islamic Cooperation, the Non-Aligned Movement and thematic subjects on development and the environment. Pakistan despatched a series of excellent Permanent Representatives (Ambassadors) to the UN (for instance Munir Akram and Maleeha Lodhi) who contributed significantly to UN deliberations, thereby raising the profile of the country in foreign opinion. UN peacekeeping operations are close to the Pakistani military's heart. It obtains for them numerous perks and keeps them well trained and fighting fit. It also helps to deflect their interest somewhat from domestic political interventions lest it sullies the international reputation and questions their political correctness, which could damage their chances of being chosen to serve. This role has also drawn praise from the highest levels at the UN.[31] Interestingly, Bangladesh, Pakistan and India provide an overwhelming majority of global peacekeepers, and service together in distant places like

Africa enhances the camaraderie between the three forces. Actually, at the UN, it has been observed that when the professionals want it, Pakistan and India can cooperate very well with one another, as transpired when both Pakistan and India sat in the Security Council in 2012, with their ambassadors, Abdullah Haroon and Hardeep Singh Puri, closely collaborating.[32]

Conclusion

There are several reasons why a paradigm shift in Pakistan-India relations is called for. One, while Pakistan's foreign policy aims rested on creation of external linkages based on the four pillars (US and the West, China, the Islamic world and the UN), over time each of the pillars ceased to be effective as a direct counter to India, as each developed its own Indian connections. Two, the threat from the spread of the ideas of the newly self-proclaimed caliphate of the Islamic State, which sees the Islamic realm as one global entity without frontiers, and does not recognize states as Pakistan created in the Western Westphalian mould already declared Pakistan a part of its 'Khorasan wilayat' may be greater and more existential than that perceived to be emanating from India. Three, and as a corollary of the last point, Pakistanis would be better off shunning the Salafi/Wahabi influence of the Middle East and turning to South Asia to seek greater identity with their original sufistic culture of subcontinental Islam, where Muslims are taught 'to be good by following the teachings of the great past reformers including the Prophet himself', thus creating 'religiously responsible individuals'.[33] Four, both deter each other with nuclear weapons despite the conventional imbalance, and in the words of two analysts: 'South Asia is said to be the acid test of for deterrence optimists. So far, nuclear deterrence has passed all of the many tests it has faced'.[34] Finally, as Pakistan, whose economy the IMF estimated would grow by 4.7 per cent in 2018, needs to achieve sustained growth of 5–7 per cent per year in order to cut poverty.[35] Shahid Javed Burki has argued that this is exactly the amount by which GDP in Pakistan could rise if there is unimpeded trade with India.

In relaxing intra-mural tensions in South Asia, because of India's size, power, influence and endowments, India might need to bear a disproportionate responsibility, even at times, if it is to be without immediate reciprocation. That for some time there has been a willingness to go along that path, both in Islamabad and New Delhi, was already evident in the past attempt at back-channel diplomacy.[36] Prime Minister Narendra Modi made it explicit by inviting all the South Asian leaders to his inauguration in May 2014. The gesture was very well received in Islamabad.[37] The Gordian knot in terms of India's relations with Bangladesh was also cut by the Modi visit to Dhaka in June this year. While there has been very tardy progress in achieving the South Asian Association for Regional Cooperation (SAARC) goals (largely due to structural issues such as avoidance of sensitive issues and the requirement for unanimity for decision making), is it not possible for the three components of former British India – India, Pakistan and Bangladesh – to come together in a form of trilateralism? The answer is yes.

How would it work? The three countries could work out a matrix detailing the problematic aspects of their relations with a view to solving them. This could involve dividing bilateral relations into categories: those that can be resolved with a bit of effort or 'green box' issues; those that will require some dedicated effort or 'orange box' issues; and those whose resolution for now will be difficult, or 'red box' issues. The 'lower hanging fruit' or the 'green box' issues may be addressed first, graduating thereafter to the 'orange' and 'red' boxes, hoping that the resultant generation of goodwill from the forward movement in one box could have a positive impact on the others. SAARC shied away from contentious issues. Trilateralism would turn the organization on its head, and identify the issues with a view to resolving them. Rather than hold formal meetings, starting with officials, then ministers and finally heads, trilateralism could result in the heads meeting informally, unconstrained by decisions at lower levels. The purpose of trilateralism would not be to supplant the more formal SAARC process, not least because it has its values and other actors are involved, but to enmesh the core of South Asia in a web of intimate linkages that would complement, revitalize and strengthen SAARC. India could thus lead South Asia's rise, with Pakistan and Bangladesh following in a 'flying geese' formation, to the benefit of all their peoples. For now, this may seem unattainable, but the idea is worth a try. As the English poet, the mighty Robert Browning, so much admired in South Asia, said: 'Ah, but a man's reach should exceed his grasp, Or what's a heaven for?'

Notes

1 Marie Louise Becker, *The All-India Muslim League 1906–1947*, Karachi, Oxford University Press, 2013, p. 11.
2 Stanley Wolpert, *Jinnah of Pakistan*, New York, Oxford University Press, 1984, p. vii.
3 M. R. Kazimi, *A Concise History of Pakistan*, Karachi, Oxford University Press, 2009, p. 195.
4 B. L.C. Johnson, *Pakistan*, London and Exeter, Heinemann, 1979, p. 1.
5 Subrata K. Mitra, *Politics in India: Structure, Process and Policy*, New Delhi, Oxford University Press, 2014, p. 297.
6 August Schou and Arne Olav Brundtland (eds) '*Small States in International Relations*', Wiley-Interscience, vol. 17, 1971.
7 Finnish President Urho Kekkonen's speech given at the Swedish Agrarian Union in Stockholm on December 1943. See Thomas Vilkuna (ed.) *Neutrality: The Finnish Position, Speeches by Dr. Urho Kekkonen, President of Finland*, P. Ojansu and L. E. Keyworth (trans.), London, Heinemann, 1970, p. 30.
8 For instance, G. Allison, *Essence of Decision*, Boston, MA, Little Brown, 1971; and M. Halperin, *Bureaucratic Politics and Foreign Policy*, Washington, DC, Brookings Institution, 1974.
9 Examples include B. Korany, 'Foreign Policy Models and their Empirical Relevance to the Third World Actors: A Critique of an Alternative', *International Social Science Journal*, vol . 26, no. 1, 1974, pp. 70–94; and, F. B. Weinstein, 'The Uses of Foreign Policy in Indonesia', *World Politics*, vol. xxiv, no. 3, April 1972, pp. 356–381.
10 Joel Migdal, 'Internal Structures and External Behaviour', *International Relations*, vol. IV, no. 5, May 1974, pp. 510–526.
11 Henry A. Kissinger, 'Domestic Structure and Foreign Policy', in Wolfram A. Handreider (ed.), *Comparative Foreign Policies: Theoretic Essays*, New York, David McKay Co. Inc, 1971, p. 47.
12 See Husain Huqqani, *Pakistan: Between the Mosque and the Military*, Lahore/Karachi/Islamabad, Vanguard Books, 2005, p. 3.
13 See, for instance, Ayesha Jalal, *A Struggle for Pakistan: A Muslim Homeland and Global Politics*, Cambridge, MA, Harvard University Press, 2014.
14 K. L. Kamal, *Pakistan: The Garrison State*, New Delhi, 1982; or more recently Ishtiaq Ahmed, *The Pakistan Garrison State: Origins, Evolution, Consequences (1947–2011)*, Pakistan, Oxford University Press, 2013.
15 S. H. Hashmi, 'Foreword', in C. H. Kennedy, *Bureaucracy in Pakistan*, Karachi, Oxford University Press, 1987.
16 For an elaboration of this point, see Iftekhar Ahmed Chowdhury, *Pakistan: A Diplomat's Insights*, Singapore, Research Asia, 2015, p. 82.
17 Currently this system is being led by two sagacious professionals, Sartaj Aziz, a reputable and well-regarded economist, as Advisor for Security and Foreign Affairs, and Ambassador Syed Tariq Fatmi, Special Assistant to the Prime Minister.

18 For an explanation of what it entails, see Mahbubul Huq, *The Strategy of Economic Planning: A Case Study of Pakistan*, Karachi, Oxford University Press, 1963.

19 Shahid M. Amin, *Pakistan's Foreign Policy: A Reappraisal*, Karachi, Oxford University Press, 2002, p. 43.

20 Ian Talbot, *Pakistan: A Modern History*, Lahore/Karachi/Islamabad, Vanguard Books, 1999, p. 173.

21 Henry Kissinger, *White House Years*, Boston, Little Brown and Co., 1979, pp. 180–181.

22 Stephen Philip Cohen, *The Idea of Pakistan*, Washington, DC, Brookings Institution, 2004, p. 170.

23 Shahid M. Amin, *Pakistan's Foreign Policy*, p. 4.

24 Iftekhar Ahmed Chowdhury, 'Yemen, Pakistan and Arab Monarchies: Widening Gulf?', Singapore, ISAS Brief 365, 17 April 2015.

25 Lawrence Ziring, *Pakistan: At Crossroads of History*, Lahore/Karachi/Islamabad, Vanguard, 2004, pp. 174–175.

26 Ayesha Jalal, *Partisans of Allah: Jihad in South Asia*, Cambridge, MA., Harvard University Press, 2008, p. 278.

27 Bob Woodward, *Obama's Wars*, New York, Simon & Schuster, 2010, p. 164.

28 Shahid Javed Burki, 'Terrorism's Most Devastating Blow in Pakistan', Singapore, ISAS Brief, No. 355, 23 December 2014.

29 For an elaboration of the factors and issues involved, see Shahid Javed Burki, Iftekhar Ahmed Chowdhury and Riaz Hassan, *Afghanistan: The Next Phase*, Melbourne, Melbourne University Press, 2014.

30 Security Council Resolution 47, *Resolution of 21 April 1948*, S/7/26 (21 April 1948), available at www.un.org/en/ga/search/view_doc.asp?symbol=S/RES/47.

31 'UN Chief Hails Pakistan's Leading Role in Peace Keeping Operations', United Nations News Centre, 13 August 2013. Available at www.un.org/apps/news/story.asp?NewsID=45613 (accessed 12 May 2015).

32 Iftekhar Ahmed Chowdhury, *The UN and the WTO: A South Asian Perspective*, Singapore, Research Asia, 2015, pp. 63–65.

33 Riaz Hassan, *Islam and Society: Sociological Explorations*, Melbourne, Melbourne University Press, 2013, p. 33.

34 Scott D. Sagan and Kenneth Waltz, *The Spread of Nuclear Weapons: A Debate Renewed*, London and New York, W. W. Norton, 2003, p. 124.

35 'Pakistan's Economy: Fuel Injection', *The Economist*, 2 May 2015.

36 Steve Coll, 'The Back Channel: India and Pakistan's Secret Kashmir talks', *New Yorker*, March 2 2009.

37 The author's meeting with Foreign and Security Adviser Sartaj Aziz and Special Assistant to Prime Minister Nawaz Sharif at the Ministry of Foreign Affairs in Islamabad, 28 May 2014.

9

The making of foreign policy

Changing parameters

Aziz Ahmad Khan

The principal aim of a country's foreign policy is to safeguard national security and promote economic development through fostering friendly and cooperative relations with other countries.

Muhammad Ali Jinnah, the founder of Pakistan, framed the country's foreign policy. Imbued with progressive ideas, a firm belief in democratic principles and confidence in the human ability to resolve differences through adherence to the law, he declared that:

> Our foreign policy is one of friendliness and goodwill towards all the nations of the world. We do not cherish aggressive designs against any country or nation. We believe in the principle of honesty and fair play in national and international dealings and are prepared to make the utmost contribution to the promotion of peace and prosperity among the nations of the world. Pakistan will never be found lacking in extending its material and moral support to the oppressed and suppressed people of the world and in upholding the principles of the United Nations Charter. [1]

This commitment to supporting Muslim nations and those living in the developing countries became an integral component of Pakistan's Constitution.

Pakistan came into being under very difficult circumstances. The experience of communal violence that caused more than a million deaths and the migration of over ten million people was traumatic for the new nation. Added to this was the burden of starting from scratch, establishing a new capital, new defence forces and a new administrative structure. The problem was complicated by India's reluctance to give Pakistan its share of assets, namely a transfer of cash that was delayed for months and also the non-provision of Pakistan's share of defence stores. Further difficulties were created when India suddenly cut off the water required for irrigation purposes from the headworks on the Ravi and Sutlej rivers. For a country that depended almost entirely on irrigated agriculture this posed a dire threat. Added to these difficulties was Jawaharlal Nehru's move to oblige the Maharaja of Kashmir to accede to India in contravention of the agreed principles for the accession of the princely states wherein Kashmir, with an overwhelming Muslim-majority population, should have acceded to Pakistan in keeping with the wishes of the majority of Kashmir's Muslim population.

While problems were being created by India, Pakistan's neighbour to the east, Afghanistan, its neighbour to the west, adopted a hostile attitude that exacerbated the nascent nation's difficulties. Afghanistan was the only country to oppose Pakistan's entry to the United Nations (UN). It refused to accept the Durand Line as the international border and raised the bogey of Pakhtunistan as an independent homeland for the Pakhtuns in Pakistan's north-west frontier province.

Thus, given the threats from east and west, protection of its sovereignty and territorial integrity became the main thrust of Pakistan' foreign policy.

At the very outset Jinnah had expressed the desire for close and friendly relations with India. In a speech he stated that:

> It is of vital importance to Pakistan and India as independent sovereign states to collaborate in a friendly way to jointly defend their frontiers both on land and sea against any aggression. But this depends entirely on whether India and Pakistan can resolve their own differences. If we can put own house in order internally then we may be able to play a very great part externally in all international affairs. The Indian government should shed their superiority complex and deal with Pakistan on an equal footing and fully appreciate the realities.

These were wise and prophetic words and hold true, if not more so, even today. Both countries need to put their houses in order internally, deal with each other as equal sovereign states and resolve issues through peaceful interaction.

Pakistan, as a new country, had to build every state institution and administrative department from scratch. This also included the foreign policy establishment. The country had to create a Foreign Office as well as a corps of Foreign Service officers to open and man embassies abroad. Pakistan lost no time in establishing resident missions in important countries including the United States, the United Kingdom, the Soviet Union, India, Iran, Turkey, Saudi Arabia and Afghanistan. Pakistan was fortunate that besides political leaders of stature it also had a group of experienced civil servants who were up to this formidable task. They set about the task of formulating the foreign policy and implementing it. The Ministry of Foreign Affairs was initially manned by a Joint Secretary and supported by about 40 officers. Within a short time Ikram Ullah, a distinguished civil servant, was appointed as the first Foreign Secretary. Sir Zaffar Ullah Khan, an eminent jurist, was appointed to the position of Minister of Foreign Affairs a few months after independence. Initially Prime Minister Liaquat Ali Khan had held that portfolio. The government also created a regular Foreign Service and in addition to some ad hoc appointments of officers at various levels, recruitment to the Foreign Service at the basic level was also started in 1947 by inducting those who had taken the civil service examination prior to independence and had opted for Pakistan. Officers from the armed forces were also inducted into the Foreign Service through lateral entry. The emphasis was on competence and quality. Pakistan had the services of a distinguished cadre with diplomats such as Mirza Mohamed Ispahani, Saidulla Khan Dehlavi, Aziz Ahmed, Jamshed Marker, Sahibzada Yaqub Khan, Agha Shahi, and Sardar Shahnawaz whose stature was recognized internationally. The Foreign Service team both at the Foreign Office as well as at the missions abroad became the principal source of foreign policy inputs through their analyses and dispatches. They helped the leaders to formulate policy. A brief survey of foreign policy-making from the Liaquat era until the present day follows.

After the death of Jinnah, Prime Minister Liaquat Ali Khan took over the administration of the country and played a key role in formulating and guiding Pakistan's foreign policy.

Like Jinnah, Liaquat was also steeped in democratic values and wished to pursue an independent foreign policy. In an interview to the *New York Times* he stated that Pakistan would not take sides in the conflict of ideologies between the two world blocs. Pakistan's guiding foreign policy was friendship with all and in keeping with this policy Liaquat reached out to the United States and the Soviet Union and expressed a desire to visit both countries. At the same time, mindful of its Islamic moorings, Pakistan supported the Palestinian cause, opposed the creation of the State of Israel and gave full support to the UN's decolonization efforts. As an expression of the independence of its foreign policy, Pakistan was one of the first countries to recognize communist China and establish diplomatic relations with Beijing.

The principal preoccupation for Pakistan's policy-makers was to look for assistance that would strengthen its body politic and preserve its sovereignty and security. Pakistan needed funds to strengthen the new state's economic development and arms to ensure its security. The British provided some funds as Pakistan's share from the sterling balances of British India. The only country that could provide the assistance that Pakistan needed was the United States. The Soviet Union did not have the economic wherewithal to help and Europe and Britain had been devastated by the Second World War. The United States therefore became a natural choice for Pakistan. America also responded in a warm and friendly manner to Pakistan's overtures of friendship.

These overtures resulted in Prime Minister Liaquat Ali Khan's visit to the United States in May 1950. The three-week long visit provided an opportunity to emphasize to the United States the commonality of values and interests like support for democracy, equality before law, support for fundamental rights, and other social economic political ideas that were valued by the United States. Pakistan's strategic location as a bastion between the communist Soviet Union and the Muslim Middle East was also emphasized. Subsequent to Liaquat Ali Khan's visit, at every opportunity in its various official contacts with the United States Pakistan emphasized this commonality of interests. This was also a time when the US-USSR relations were morphing into a Cold War and Pakistan's pitch to the United States was to project itself as an anti-communist state because of its Muslim ethos.

Following the death of Liaquat Ali Khan, the leaders who played a dominant role in shaping Pakistan's foreign policy were Mohammad Ali Borga, Hussein Shaheed Suhrawardy, Sir Zaffar Ullah Khan and General Ayub Khan, first as Commander in Chief of the Pakistan Army, later as Minister of Defence and finally as the President of Pakistan.

Mohammad Ali Bogra served as ambassador to the United States in 1952 before his elevation to the office of Prime Minister in 1953. After leaving that office in 1955 he again served as Pakistan's ambassador to the United States from 1955 to 1959 and as Minister of Foreign Affairs in 1962–63. His views about relations with the United States had developed during his first tenure as ambassador and were reflected in his strong anti-communist and hence anti-Soviet thinking. In the United States, Bogra actively lobbied for Pakistan to be recognized as a 'frontline state' against the expansion of Soviet influence in South and West Asia. In the words of US Secretary of State, John Foster Dulles, Pakistan was a 'bulwark of freedom in Asia'. During his tenure as Prime Minister

Pakistan signed the Mutual Defence Assistance Agreement with the United States and joined the Southeast Asia Treaty Organization (SEATO) in 1954. Pakistan joined the Baghdad Pact in 1955; later this was known as the Central Treaty Organization (CENTO). Initially Bogra had reservations about joining SEATO, but Foreign Minister Zaffar Ullah Khan who was representing Pakistan at the signing of the pact in Manila forced his hand. Khan was criticized for having exceeded his brief but there was little choice since not doing so would have offended the participating states in SEATO after Pakistan had insisted on being invited to the conference.

Bogra also led Pakistan's delegation to the Bandung Conference in Indonesia in 1955. This conference provided an opportunity for a meeting with China's first premier Zhou Enlai during which Pakistan was able to explain the rationale behind its close relations with the United States, thereby removing some of the Chinese misgivings.

Bogra took the initiative to improve relationships with India, visited New Delhi to meet Prime Minister Nehru and eventually both agreed on a plebiscite for the solution of the Jammu and Kashmir issue. Unfortunately, India later reneged on this commitment.

Hussein Shaheed Suhrawardy became Prime Minister in 1956–57. Pro-West in his leanings he was strongly supportive of close relations with America. During his visit to the United States in July 1957 he informed President Eisenhower of Pakistan's agreement to allow the United States to establish a secret intelligence base at Badaber near Peshawar for which the Americans had been lobbying and from whence they could carry out electronic surveillance of the Soviet territory. Pakistan also gave permission to the United States to use Peshawar airbase for its U2 aircraft to fly spy missions over the Soviet territory. As Commander-in-Chief General Ayub Khan was keen to allow this facility as he expected the United States to reciprocate with the supply of B-57 bombers. US personnel manned the Badaber facility and no Pakistani was allowed inside the operational areas. In return for this base the United States gave military and economic aid to Pakistan. A cantonment was also built in Kharian to accommodate US troops. Suhrawardy was also the first Pakistani Prime Minister to visit China.

The period following Liaquat Ali Khan's death witnessed rapid changes in the government. This gave an opportunity to the security establishment, namely the Pakistan military, to play a dominant role in the formulation of security and foreign policy. For example, as Commander-in-Chief Ayub Khan also assumed the defence portfolio, while a retired Major General, Iskandar Mirza, was appointed Minister of the Interior.

This game of musical chairs played by weak civilian governments finally led to their replacement by the military through martial law leading to a takeover by General Ayub Khan.

On becoming President General Ayub Khan set about correcting the course of the country's foreign relations and reducing its exclusive dependence on the United States. Pakistan was unhappy with the United States for not appreciating its concerns vis-à-vis India. President Ayub Khan had already expressed Pakistan's misgivings during a visit to the United States as Commander-in-Chief when he had cautioned US officials, both civilian and military, that a groundswell of disappointment was discernible in Pakistan owing to the US help afforded to India. He started to expand relations with the USSR and China. Pakistan signed an agreement with the Soviet Union in December 1960 for the exploration of mineral and petroleum resources. In his capacity as Minister for Natural Resources Zulfiqar Ali Bhutto was the motivating force behind this. Gen. Ayub Khan visited China in March 1965 and a month later visited the Soviet Union, the first visit ever by a Pakistani head of state. The visit to China was highly successful and both

Chairman Mao and Premier Zhou Enlai talked of lasting friendship and fruitful cooperation. The American leadership showed visible annoyance at these successful visits.

As relations with China developed, Pakistan took up the issue of settlement of the Pakistan– China border and a border agreement was signed in 1963 in which China in a spirit of accommodation ceded a large chunk of its territory to Pakistan. The concern over the disputed nature of the territory could only be resolved through China's willingness to renegotiate if necessary after the settlement of the Kashmir dispute.

A major achievement of Ayub Khan's tenure was the signing of the Indus Water Treaty with India in 1960. Given that Pakistan is located on a lower riparian zone it was vulnerable to Indian interference as was seen when India stopped the flow of water to Pakistan from the Ravi and Sutlej rivers. The Indus Water Treaty gave Pakistan exclusive use of water from the three western rivers, namely the Indus, the Jhelum and the Chenab, and the three eastern rivers were made over to India for its exclusive use. The treaty was brokered and guaranteed by the World Bank. In the event of a dispute which cannot be solved bilaterally both countries have access to the Bank's dispute resolution mechanism. This would allow for the appointment of a Neutral Expert or a Court of Arbitration to resolve the dispute.

Ayub Khan's tenure as President witnessed an expansion of economic relations with the United States and at the same time a more balanced foreign policy. However, the 1965 war with India that resulted from Pakistan's support of the Kashmiri uprising and spread to a full-scale war was a major setback for Pakistan. The Soviet Union played an important role in ending hostilities when it got Pakistan and India to sign a peace agreement, the Tashkent Declaration, in January 1966.

Zulfiqar Ali Bhutto was Minister of Foreign Affairs at the time and was unhappy with this agreement; he subsequently left the government. He later formed his own political party, the Pakistan People's Party (PPP), which later emerged as an important political player in elections held in 1971.

Ayub Khan was replaced through a military coup in 1969 when General Yahya Khan took over as President. During his time in office Pakistan's relations with China moved rapidly forward. He also helped to establish a communications link between China and the United States that ultimately led to Henry Kissinger, the US Assistant for National Security Affairs, making a secret visit to China in 1971 via Pakistan, which paved the way for the subsequent visit of President Nixon in 1972.

General Yahya Khan's presidency also coincided with the break-up of Pakistan when, following Indian military intervention, East Pakistan seceded to become Bangladesh in 1971 and Yahya Khan was forced to resign. He was replaced by Zulfiqar Ali Bhutto, who was at the UN fighting Pakistan's case when he was appointed President of Pakistan. Before returning to take up office he went to Washington to meet President Nixon to thank him for America's help during the period of crisis. To him fell the task of rebuilding a country demoralized by the political break-up, ostracized by the international community and traumatized by defeat at the hands of India. Bhutto lost no time in showing that he was up to that task. He had a natural flair for foreign affairs that he had demonstrated early in his political career. As Foreign Minister in Ayub Khan's government he had advocated Pakistan's support for China's membership to the UN that paved the way for a steady development of relations with China. He was held in high esteem by the Chinese leadership which was demonstrated during his visit to Beijing in February 1972 when the Chinese agreed to write off some of their earlier loans to Pakistan amounting to US $110 million and gave Pakistan a generous military aid package including 60 MiG-19 fighter jets and 100 T-54 and T-59 tanks. The relationship with China was nurtured and strengthened in a meaningful manner during his tenure.

Soon after assuming the presidency Bhutto went on a whirlwind visit to several countries including key Muslim states to seek support for the nation-building that lay ahead. His immediate task was to discuss a peace settlement with India and to seek the release of 90,000 prisoners of war who had surrendered to the Indian army. Bhutto travelled to Simla for talks with Indira Gandhi. Conscious that he would be negotiating from a weak position he included in his delegation leaders from other political parties in order to strengthen his hand. Despite this difficult situation Bhutto managed to secure an equitable agreement. The Simla Agreement stated, *inter alia*, that

> the representatives from both sides would meet to discuss further the modalities and arrangements for the establishment of durable peace and normalization of relations, including the question of repatriation of prisoners of war and civilian internees, a final settlement of Jammu and Kashmir and resumption of diplomatic relations[2].

This provision led to the release of all the prisoners of war while at the same time safeguarding Pakistan's position on the Kashmir issue.

The Organisation of Islamic Cooperation Summit held in Lahore in 1974 was another of Bhutto's foreign policy successes. The presence at this meeting of King Faisal of Saudi Arabia and the Libyan President Muhammad Gaddafi was greatly appreciated by the Pakistani people. He used the opportunity to dramatically announce the recognition of Bangladesh that paved the way for the Bengali Sheikh Mujibur Rehman to be able to attend the summit.

Bhutto visited the Soviet Union in 1972 and among other things the Soviets agreed to establish a steel mill in Karachi.

Relations with the Muslim world received particular attention during this period and closer ties with Saudi Arabia, Libya and the United Arab Emirates were achieved which led to political support and to far-reaching economic benefits, particularly after the financial boom that these countries witnessed following the rise in oil prices.

In addition to his many foreign policy achievements Bhutto also played a seminal role in Pakistan achieving the status of a nuclear power country with its consequent foreign policy implications. Early on, as Minister of Foreign Affairs, Bhutto had realized the value of nuclear capability and had made a commitment to the nation to acquire it even if 'we have to eat grass'. Soon after his appointment as President, Bhutto convened a meeting of nuclear scientists in January 1972 and appointed Munir Ahmad Khan, a nuclear engineer at the International Atomic Energy Agency as Chairman of Pakistan's Atomic Energy Commission to pursue the acquisition of a nuclear fuel cycle. This was a time when nuclear suppliers were tightening controls on nuclear technology transfer. Following India's nuclear test of 1974 these restrictions were tightened yet further. To Pakistan's dismay, instead of punishing India for the test, controls were placed on Pakistan's nascent nuclear programme and Canada halted its supply of fuel for the nuclear power plant in Karachi. The United States also used its muscle to prevent France from setting up a plutonium reprocessing plant that it had agreed to. Fortunately for Pakistan a young metallurgical engineer, Dr Abdul Qadeer Khan, also known as A. Q. Khan, met Bhutto and recommended a way of manufacturing fissile material using enriched uranium. Bhutto authorized him in 1976 to establish an enrichment plant in Kahuta and Khan, along with a team of young scientists, mastered the capability of uranium enrichment through indigenous technology by 1982. By 1983 Pakistan had developed its first nuclear device and had conducted cold tests successfully. By the mid-1980s Pakistan publicly acknowledged possession of nuclear capability but denied that it had produced a nuclear weapon. Pakistan went overtly nuclear only after India tested its own nuclear device in 1998.

General Zia ul-Huq seized power in a military coup in 1977, taking advantage of the political agitation following the general election in which Bhutto was accused of engineering the massive rigging of votes. Prime Minister Bhutto was arrested on charges of murder of a political opponent; following a controversial trial and a suspect judgment he was hanged in 1979. The international community did not view these developments favourably and ostracized General Zia.

General Zia took a keen interest in foreign affairs. He liked to be briefed regularly by the Foreign Office. In fact, he used to visit the Ministry of Foreign Affairs for briefings so frequently that a separate office room was set up for him. He had a good team of advisers, with Agha Shahi and later Sahibzada Yaqub Khan as Foreign Ministers, ably supported by Sardar Shahnawaz (who served as Foreign Secretary and later Secretary-General) and a team of excellent Foreign Service officers. This was a period of important developments in the international arena. The Soviet invasion of Afghanistan and consequent resistance by the Afghan *mujahedeen* became the focus of international attention. Most of the world condemned the Soviet action and the United States and Saudi Arabia decided to support the *mujahedeen* for which they solicited Pakistan's help. This created an opportunity for General Zia to come out of international isolation and take his place on the centre stage. Pakistan's cooperation also brought benefits in the form of a generous aid package, both economic and military, of US $3.2 billion and 40 F-16 fighter jets. The United States also relaxed its close watch on Pakistan's nuclear ambitions, which gave the experts space to pursue their programme. The Afghan *jihad* ended with the Soviet withdrawal of its forces through the Geneva Accords of 1989 and accelerated the disintegration of the Soviet Union in 1992.

During his tenure General Zia made serious efforts to improve relations with India. Early in period in office, India under Prime Minister Indira Gandhi played hardball. However, the Janata Party soon took over government after the defeat of Congress and warmly reciprocated General Zia's overtures. There were exchanges on many issues and agreements were signed on trade, cultural exchanges and communications. Relations cooled somewhat when Indira Gandhi again came to power in 1980. In 1984 India, in violation of the Simla Accord, moved its forces and occupied the Siachin Glacier area that hitherto was a territory where the line of control had yet to be delineated. When Rajiv Gandhi became Prime Minister following the assassination of Indira Gandhi, General Zia made another gesture to improve relations. He made a brief six-hour stopover in December 1985 on his return from the first South Asian Association for Regional Cooperation (SAARC) meeting in Bangladesh and the two sides agreed to start a four-pronged Secretary of State-level dialogue process to discuss the Siachin and Sir Creek issues, trade relations, matters relating to cross-border activities and cultural relations including people-to-people contact. These initiatives resulted in the expansion of trade, an agreement in 1989 to withdraw forces from the Siachin Glacier area and relaxation of the visa regime in order to promote people-to-people contact. However, India's military exercise, code-named Brass Tack that took place at the end of 1986 involving a large number of troops, tanks, armour and live ammunition alarmed Pakistan and prompted counter-moves by its own forces. This created a tense situation, albeit that the matter was resolved when Rajiv Gandhi ordered an end to the exercises and a resolution of the situation through Foreign Secretary-level talks. Subsequently, General Zia visited India ostensibly to witness a cricket match between Pakistan and India, and took the opportunity to discuss bilateral issues.

Following the death of General Zia in a mysterious plane crash, Ghulam Ishaq Khan who was Chairman of the Senate, took over as President. General elections were held and Benazir Bhutto was appointed as Prime Minister. Rajiv Gandhi attended the South Asian Association for Regional Cooperation (SAARC) Summit that was held in Pakistan in 1988 and in July 1989 he made an official visit to Pakistan. This was the first visit to Pakistan by an Indian Prime Minister since Nehru's visit in 1960 to sign the Indus Water Treaty. The period between 1988 and 1999 saw two short-lived terms each of Benazir Bhutto and Nawaz Sharif as Prime Ministers. Both leaders were keen on improving relations with India and made concerted efforts in this regard. During the government led by the Bharatiya Janata Party (BJP) India conduced nuclear tests in May 1998, with Pakistan testing its own nuclear devices a few days later. The situation warranted that both countries discuss the nuclear dimension to reduce the risk of accidental war. This prompted Indian Prime Minister Vajpayee to visit Pakistan and he travelled by bus to Lahore. Besides making a gesture of peace to Pakistan he was also mindful of the international community's concern about the possibility of a nuclear conflict. The Lahore Declaration signed at the end of the visit envisaged immediate steps for reducing the risk of accidental or unauthorized use of nuclear weapons and discuss concepts and doctrines. A Memorandum of Understanding was also signed that covered the moratorium on nuclear tests and other related issues. The Lahore documents covered the whole range of bilateral issues including Jammu and Kashmir, terrorism in all its forms and manifestations, as well as nuclear risk reduction. These documents acquired a symbolic importance far greater than their actual content warranted.

These foreign policy gains received a severe setback when *mujahedeen* forces from Pakistan crossed the Line of Control and occupied the Indian-controlled area in Kargil. India retaliated heavily and ultimately the *mujahedeen* forces had to withdraw from Kargil. Prime Minister Nawaz Sharif solicited US President Clinton's help in diffusing the crisis. The debacle triggered friction between the Prime Minister and General Musharraf resulting in tensions between the military and civil establishments.

The civilian interlude came to an end when General Musharraf staged a dramatic coup as a counter-move to his dismissal as Chief of Army Staff by Prime Minister Nawaz Sharif while he was on a foreign tour. As with General Zia's take over 22 years previously, General Musharraf's military takeover received the disapproval of the United States and the West.

In the realm of foreign policy General Musharraf's tenure was marked by the events of 11 September 2001 (known as 9/11) and its aftermath as well as his efforts to normalize relations with India. For this he relied almost entirely on the Foreign Office and a small group of military colleagues for policy inputs. President Musharraf pursued an active foreign policy and besides Afghanistan, US and India attention was paid to explore progress on the Turkmenistan-Afghanistan-Pakistan-India gas pipeline, the Iran-Pakistan-India gas pipeline, expansion of already deep relations with China, relations with the Muslim world and the West.

After 9/11 Pakistan decided to give full support to the United States. In any case there was little choice after the UN Security Council resolutions and the international outrage at the terrorist attacks on the US.

In order to strengthen his hand General Musharraf consulted with political and religious leaders before announcing full support and cooperation with the US against Al-Qaeda sponsored terrorism emanating from Afghanistan and breaking ties with the Taliban. He also sent a delegation to Afghanistan led by the director-general of Pakistan's Inter-Services Intelligence and including representation from the Foreign Office to impress upon the Taliban the gravity of the situation and the imminence of US military action against their government for giving refuge to Osama bin Laden and other Al-Qaeda elements. The Taliban leaders rejected the advice, were bombed mercilessly and had to flee the country. Subsequently, reports suggest that they did try to get the Karzai administration to offer them an amnesty and allow them to return to Afghanistan. Karzai rejected this under American pressure.

After the fall of the Taliban and the Bonn Agreement, Pakistan sent a high-level delegation to Kabul led by the Minister of Foreign Affairs and including important political personalities to attend Karzai's installation as interim President. Pakistan gave full support to the Karzai government and announced an initial package of US $100 million of assistance to Afghanistan. To promote bilateral trade Pakistan simplified procedures and made the trade rupee based. This resulted in an increase in bilateral trade from $24 million per annum during the Taliban rule to over $2 billion per annum. Pakistan extended full cooperation to the United States during its 'war on terror' including the use of its air bases. The United States reciprocated through assistance in the form of Coalition Support Funds to offset expenditure incurred by Pakistan for providing this support. Pakistan captured a large number of Al-Qaeda members and handed them over to the United States.

President Musharraf pursued an active policy of engagement with India. He visited Agra at Prime Minister Vajpayee's invitation. The talks ended without an agreed final declaration mainly because of the hardline attitude of some of Vajpayee's cabinet colleagues. Nevertheless, the talks served a useful purpose in understanding each other's point of view. A terrorist attack on the Indian Parliament in December 2002 and the subsequent mobilization of Indian forces resulted in a tense war-like situation, with India withdrawing its High Commissioner from Islamabad and insisting that Pakistan should do the same, thereby downgrading diplomatic representation. However, following the intervention of the international community India realized the futility of this policy and Vajpayee offered a gesture of goodwill by extending the hand of friendship and proposing the restoration of diplomatic relations at ambassadorial level, and the resumption of air links as well as sporting ties. Pakistan responded positively and announced a unilateral ceasefire on the Line of Control in November 2003 and withdrew a ban on overflying that Pakistan had imposed following the Indian mobilization of forces.

Prime Minister Vajpayee visited Islamabad in January 2004 to attend the SAARC Summit and on the sidelines also held talks with President Musharraf as a result of which the two sides agreed to the resumption of the Composite Dialogue to settle all issues including that of Jammu and Kashmir. Pakistan reassured India that it would not allow acts of terrorism from any territory under its control. Thus began a phase of active and positive engagement to expand relations and resolve all outstanding issues through the Composite Dialogue process. His visit to India in 2005 further boosted relations. President Musharraf also proposed an original four-point formula of out of the box thinking for the resolution of the Kashmir issue outside the conventional positions of both sides. For this purpose, a 'back channel' was established for discussing ideas away from the glare of public scrutiny. This back channel process made reasonable progress but it was halted after Musharraf left office following the installation of the PPP government in 2007.

Following the commencement of civilian rule in 2007 no meaningful dialogue with India was possible, mainly owing to the terrorist attacks in Mumbai in 2008 and subsequently in Pathankot and Uri. Following the installation of the BJP government in 2014, Prime Minister Modi took a hard line against Pakistan. This also coincided with a massive indigenous uprising against India in Indian-occupied Kashmir.

A prominent feature of the civilian dispensation that has been in place since 2007 is the active role of parliament in discussing foreign policy. Both the National Assembly and the Senate witness healthy debates on foreign relations and assess their role in the making of policy as was demonstrated during the Yemen crisis when Parliament passed a resolution calling upon the government to remain neutral, a policy recommendation that was duly followed.

During his tenure President Musharraf took the bold step of liberalizing the media. This resulted in the mushrooming of scores of private TV channels and a vibrant print media. The free media started the trend of debates through TV talk shows and Op-ed articles that could boldly discuss and criticize all political, economic, social and foreign policy issues. This frank and open discussion has brought foreign policy-making from being a preserve of a select group of leaders and diplomats to a more participatory and inclusive process.

While political leaders supported by members of the Foreign Service and the security establishment have been the principal players in the making of foreign policy they have also benefited from the support of think tanks and specialized institutions. These institutions provide sophisticated data, in-depth analysis and feedback on current policy. Pakistan started with only one think tank, the Pakistan Institute of International Affairs that was established in 1947 in Karachi. Over a period of time several think tanks and study centres have been established in Pakistan that deal with a variety of disciplines. Notable among those dealing with international relations are the Institute of Strategic Studies, Islamabad, established in 1973, the Institute of Regional Studies, Islamabad (1982) and several centres at different universities for studies on South Asia, Central Asia, the Middle East, North America, Latin America, etc. Several other think tanks specializing in nuclear and other security-related issues have also sprung up in the past decade. These think tanks prepare studies on important developments in different parts of the world that are of great benefit to the foreign policy establishment, parliamentarians, as well as to analysts interested in writing op-eds on foreign affairs. This new trend is likely to grow and become an institutionalized source of inputs for those dealing with foreign policy-making.

A brief mention may also be made of the recent trend of Track II diplomacy in the realm of foreign affairs. Track II dialogues are unofficial and informal efforts to discuss contentious issues between two antagonistic parties usually facilitated by an impartial third party and involving individuals with a close connection in their respective official communities. Track II dialogues focus on cooperative efforts to explore new ways to resolve contentious issues. Such dialogues usually move away from conflict resolution to developing new approaches to solving problems and quietly feed those ideas to the official establishments. The spirit behind such dialogues is to step back from the official positions to jointly explore the underlying causes of the disputes in the hope of developing alternative ideas. Such dialogues are held under Chatham House rules, namely the principle of non-attribution in order to encourage out of the box thinking and come up with bold ideas to be fed to the policy-makers.

In 2018 a number of Track II processes were under way between Pakistan-India and Pakistan-Afghanistan. The oldest Pakistan-India dialogue is the Neemrana Dialogue that was initially supported by the United States and later by the Foreign Offices of the two countries. Currently this process is at a standstill. Another Track II process is the Chao-phraya Dialogue conducted by the Jinnah Institute in Islamabad, and the India-Australia Institute in New Delhi, with the support of the British government. Ottawa University is also engaged in a military-to-military Track II Dialogue, an intelligence-to-intelligence dialogue and a nuclear issue dialogue between India and Pakistan as well as a Pakistan-India-Afghanistan trilateral dialogue. A German think tank, the Friedrich Ebert Stiftung, is also facilitating Pakistan-Afghanistan and Pakistan-India Track II dialogues. Partici-pants in all these dialogues are retired diplomats and army generals, parliamentarians, security analyst and important media personalities. The hope behind all these dialogues is that those attending it having access to high levels in policy-making will be able to plug in the ideas generated at these discussions to help policy-makers with fresh approaches to problem-solving.

Pakistan's foreign policy-making has evolved from being the exclusive preserve of poli-tical leaders and the security establishment to a more inclusive and democratic process. National security remains a principal preoccupation mainly due to hostility from India and the ongoing turmoil in Afghanistan. This has constrained the policy-makers from taking full advantage of Pakistan's geographical location for economic benefit. A shift by all the regional states from geostrategy to geo-economics will go a long way in promoting peace and bringing economic development and prosperity to the entire region. The China–Pakistan Economic Corridor initiative will not only be a game changer for Pakistan, but should provide an opportunity to the neighbouring countries to benefit from it through their participation, thus strengthening regional connectivity and cooperation.

Notes

1 Muhammad Ali Jinnah, speeches while Governor-General 1947–48.
2 See www.mea.gov.in/bilateral-documents.htm?dtl/5541/Simla+Agreement.

10

Living in a rapidly changing world

Shahid Javed Burki

At 2018 Pakistan found itself precariously placed. In order to deal with its geographic location, Islamabad will need to show some deft handling of its external relations in a rapidly changing world.[1] Pakistan has to be mindful of what is happening in Afghanistan, the People's Republic of China, India, Iran, the Russian Federation, Saudi Arabia, the United States, as well as in Europe and the Middle East. It has borders with four of these countries which are in the throes of political change, and it is hard to predict which way they will go. A great deal of this change can be attributed to the election of Donald Trump as President of the United States in 2016. In reviewing Pakistan's place in the world – where it is today and where it might be headed – this chapter will look at how the country will be affected by the changes occurring in these seven countries and the two regions.

Trump won the election by promising to 'make America great again'. Once in office the new President moved quickly to dissolve several parts of the old system without putting anything new in their place. The result has been global chaos, particularly in the area of the world in which Pakistan is located. According to the thinking in the Trump's White House, America would only become great again by focusing exclusively on its own interests. Not given to deep thought or reflection, some of Trump's actions could not be deemed to be in America's long-term interests. Within days of his taking office, the United States had exited the Trans-Pacific Partnership (TPP) agreement negotiated by the previous presidential incumbent, Barack Obama. One guiding principle of Trump's approach to policymaking was to undo all that Obama had done during his eight years in office. The TPP would have created a trading system that would have given enormous advantage to US corporations. Trump also got involved on the wrong side of the Middle East equation and left the Afghan issue in the lap of the generals. He repeatedly threatened to abandon the deal Obama had reached with Tehran on the issue of the latter's suspending its work on developing nuclear weapons. Furthermore, he changed his approach to China. In this chapter, I will discuss briefly how what is happening in these seven countries will affect Pakistan, beginning with the United States.

The United States

Having come across a great deal of resentment among one seemingly neglected segment of the American population – generally defined as the low-income, non-college-educated white people in the country's mid-West – Donald Trump, while campaigning for the presidency, promised that he would ditch the old order in favour of an approach that would 'make America great again'. In his inaugural address the new President promised an 'America first' approach to policymaking that would affect the country's position in the world. This approach led to a number of significant changes in the way Washington dealt with the world.

Some of Trump's first acts upon taking up residence in the White House included the US withdrawal from the TPP; banning of entry into the country of the citizens from seven Muslim majority countries; exertion of pressure on the members of the North Atlantic Treaty Organization (NATO) to increase their defence expenditures thus easing the burden on Washington; attempts to persuade China to have North Korea pull back from the further development of nuclear weapons and missile systems for delivering them; threat to walk out of the nuclear deal President Barack Obama had signed with Iran along with five other large powers; and encouraging Saudi Arabia to be more assertive in the Middle East. All these moves have consequences for Pakistan and its relations with the world beyond its borders. Other chapters in this volume examin Pakistan's relationship with the United States and Saudi Arabia; in this I will focus on the country's immediate neighbourhood. I will use two developments as the context for this analysis. First, the new US policy towards Afghanistan announced by President Trump on 21 August 2017. Second, the release on 18 December 2017 of the Trump Administration's national security policy.

The new policy stance also showed a strong preference for remilitarizing the approach towards Afghanistan. President Trump, unlike his predecessor Barack Obama, has given the Pentagon the responsibility for deciding the level of troops the United States will need to maintain in Afghanistan. There is little doubt that the military leaders will ask for more American boots on the ground and for the assurance that the US involvement will continue into the distant future. The commanders are rightly worried that as Islamic State loses ground in those parts of the Muslim world in which it had been causing disruption, it will turn its attention to the areas where the governments are weak. Afghanistan is a clear candidate for the attention of Islamic State. It is believed that the Islamic extremists have already infiltrated parts of the country. They have a significant presence in Nangarhar, an Afghan province that neighbours Pakistan.

While the military commanders may succeed in increasing the troop strength in Afghanistan, US policy in the country will have to deal with the significant and growing anti-Islam sentiment in the United States.

Afghanistan

Two moves by President Trump – one with respect to Afghanistan and the other relating to the Middle East – will greatly matter for Pakistan. With regard to the former, the decision concerning the number of American troops who will operate in the country has been left to the Secretary of Defense, General (retd) Jim Mattis. In 2017 US military officials expressed growing concern about the war in Afghanistan. Mattis indicated that the course could change. The previous surge by the insurgents took place under Obama when he announced in a speech at the US Military Academy in 2009 that he was sending 30,000 additional troops to the country. At the same time, he provided a timeline for the withdrawal of the US forces. This indication of a withdrawal timetable was controversial. Many experts believed that it emboldened the Taliban who began to map out their long-term strategy.

While the US strategy was still under consideration, the idea appeared to be to provide just enough American presence to help President Ashraf Ghani to keep the Taliban at bay. Soon after Trump assumed office, the insurgents mounted some daring and costly attacks in the middle of Kabul that shook the Ghani government. Would the arrival of more American troops change the balance between the government and the Taliban? One answer to the question was provided by Lt-Gen. (retd) David W. Barno who led the American war effort in Afghanistan for 19 months from late 2003. 'I'm skeptical', he said. 'I know the region and the environment and the sanctuaries they have and the amount of resilience they have. None of these things are amenable to a large number of troops being able to defeat the insurgency.'[2]

Mattis appeared to accept that much more than a military approach to solving the Afghanistan was needed. 'We would have to change the priorities, we would have to factor in a more regional construct.'[3] And when the American authorities speak of a regional construct, they have both Pakistan and China in mind. It was not made clear at the time what Pakistan and China should do to help to bring peace to this land destroyed by decades of war. These two countries as well as Afghanistan's other neighbours will need to confront another reality: the arrival of Islamic State in Afghanistan. Raqqa, the Islamic State stronghold in eastern Syria, was liberated in late 2017 following US-backed air and artillery strikes on the city. Deprived of a physical presence in the region, the Islamists began to turn their attention to other troubled and weakly governed areas such as Afghanistan.

Trump increased pressure on Pakistan to aid the American effort in Afghanistan. In August 2017 he accused Pakistan of playing a double game with Washington. Islamabad, he said, had received billions of dollars from the United States but had allowed the Taliban to maintain sanctuaries in its territory. From there they had repeatedly attacked the US troops fighting in Afghanistan as well as the Afghan troops being trained by the United States. In early 2018 the language Trump used about Pakistan hardened further. Washington had 'foolishly' provided Pakistan with US $33 billion over the past 15 years to fight terror, but 'they have given us nothing but lies and deceit, thinking of our leaders as fools', he tweeted on 1 January 2018. 'They gave safe havens to the terrorists we hunt in Afghanistan with little help. No more!'

China

However, Afghanistan was not the only one of Pakistan's neighbours that was changing. The country's four neighbours were engaged in making adjustments to their rapidly changing external environment. Some of the changes Pakistan needed to make are the consequence of China's impressive economic rise. It is now the world's second largest economy, and is expected to become the largest. In 2017 the largest, of course, was the United States but since its rate of economic expansion is less than one-half that of China, it is likely to lose its place in the next decade or two. The other reason for change is the necessary reaction to Donald Trump's view of the world. The 45th President of the United States, sworn in on 20 January 2017, has moved away from the position his country carved out for itself in the global order it helped to create after the ending of the Second World War and the Cold War. 'Globalization' was the most important building block of this order. It implied the relatively free flow of goods, capital and information. It had also reduced some of the most egregious obstacles to the movement of people across international borders. And it left most of the important policymaking that affected the world at large to the formulation of consensus within international institutions that Washington dominated.

Changes in Pakistan's external environment has pushed it towards seeking a closer alliance with China. This is in part a response to the hardening of Washington's position towards Islamabad in the context of Donald Trump's evolving approach towards Afghanistan. The White House believes that America's position in Afghanistan is due to Pakistan's tolerance of extremists who are operating out of the sanctuaries they have established in the country's tribal areas. As America fails in Afghanistan, it shifts the blame on to Pakistan.

A study prepared for a Washington-based think tank concluded that Islamabad should give a clear message to Washington that while in the past it might have relied heavily on America's financial assistance, that is no longer the case.[4] Now, in China, Pakistan has a more reliable source for the capital it needs. In the three periods when Washington was deeply engaged with Pakistan, capital inflows helped the country to achieve high rates of economic growth. But Washington came into the country for its own reasons and left, often abruptly, when it no longer needed Pakistan. However, China has long-term interests in the geographic region of which Pakistan is a part. The Chinese approach to the outside is sometimes referred to as 'geo-economics.' This implies the use of economic instruments to achieve geopolitical goals. According to Robert Blackwill and Jennifer Harris, China is 'the world's leading practitioner of geo-economics, but it has also been perhaps the major factor in returning regional and global power projection back to an importantly economic (as opposed to political-military) exercise'.[5]

Shunned and often scolded by the United States and shunted aside by Narendra Modi's India, Pakistan has moved firmly into the Chinese orbit. This move will have positive consequences for both Pakistan and China. Given this dramatic shift in Pakistan's external orientation, policymakers in Islamabad should keep a careful watch on how the Chinese are developing their approach to the world outside their borders. Three developments are influencing the way Beijing is looking at the world: the rise of Donald Trump in the United States; the consolidation of power in the hands of President Xi Jinping; and the adoption of Beijing of a new economic growth model.

In a tweet followed by a television interview, President Trump said some might call Xi the 'king of China'.[6] While the description is exaggerated it does raise the question as to how Xi was vaulted into a Chinese pantheon occupied only by Mao Zedong and Deng Xiaoping. 'Xi Jinping thought' is now celebrated as the guide to a 'new era' for China. Xi planned his rise carefully, using the Chinese citizenry's disgust with pervasive corruption in the country's political and economic systems. An anti-corruption campaign by the government led to the prosecution of 278,000 members of the Communist Party, including 440 ministerial or provincial officials, and 43 Central Committee members. The military was not spared, either. Under the campaign, 13,000 officers were dismissed from their posts and more than 50 generals were imprisoned for corruption. Having thus cleared the decks, Xi brought in his own people. Of the 25 members of the Politburo elected by the 19th session of the Chinese Communist Party held in Beijing in October 2017, 17 were Xi's allies while four of the seven members of the Standing

Committee – the highest policymaking body in the country – were closely aligned with the President.

Having consolidated his hold over the Chinese system, Xi has begun to focus on the world at large. Five years ago, when he was appointed as President and as Secretary-General of the Communist Party, Xi spoke of China's ambitions to become a regional power. At the October 2017 Congress, Xi presented an agenda for China's growth to 2050 that would transform the nation into a modernized, strong country that would dominate technology, finance and security and develop strong connections with the world. China's political model can be sold to the rest of the world as an alternative to America's promotion of democracy. In this respect, Beijing is being helped by the way Trump is governing in America. China is also increasingly confident that it can combine tight political control with continued rapid economic growth and technological innovation. China is now a leading presence in a range of fields including robotics, drones, solar technology and artificial intelligence.

It is in geopolitics that China will have the greatest impact. While the United States has the capacity to challenge Beijing on the open seas, it is in land connectivity that the Chinese will rule supreme. According to the *Financial Times*,

> The heavily promoted Belt and Road Initiative (BRI) is aimed at developing new markets for China across Eurasia – with infrastructure links across central and south Asia towards Europe and Africa. Twenty Chinese cities are now connected to Europe by direct rail links and the amount of freight sent this way has quintupled since 2013, as routes such as Chengdu to Prague and Wuhan to Lyon establish themselves.[7]

The Lahore-based Burki Institute of Public Policy focused its 2017 annual report on the China–Pakistan Economic Corridor (CPEC) initiative, and concluded that the CPEC will prove to be a game-changer for Pakistan.[8]

China's increasing global presence is being helped by the posture adopted by Donald Trump in world affairs (see above). The new approach that China is taking will have a direct bearing on Pakistan. Chapter 14 in this volume examines the CPEC in detail, but I will briefly refer here to what this initiative will deliver to the two countries involved.

India

There was a significant deterioration in Pakistan-India relations after Narendra Modi, the hardline Hindu nationalist, won the 2014 national elections at the head of the Bharatiya Janata Party. The worsening relationship between the countries was manifested in several ways, including cricket. On 18 June 2017 Pakistan won the International Cricket Council Champions Trophy by beating India in the final match played at the Oval in London. Pakistan surprised the cricketing world having begun the eight-country contest ranked at the bottom of the pack. The victory was not only unexpected but was convincing. The Indians were bowled out after scoring 176 runs against the 338 runs put on the board by the Pakistani side. While there were celebrations in Pakistan at the country's unexpected win, the Indians mourned. However, some of the Indian Muslims also celebrated, upset with the way they were being treated by the Modi government and its affiliates in the states. 'The police in India have arrested at least 19 people on charges of sedition for jubilantly celebrating Pakistan's victory over India in the final of cricket tournament played in Britain this week', reported the *New York Times*. 'The arrests took place in the central Indian state of Madhya Pradesh and the southern state of Karnataka. It involved students, laborers and shopkeepers, all Muslims aged 20 to 35, the police said. The arrests came as some Muslims in India say they feel a sense of rising alienation. There have been episodes of violence, including by vigilante groups that have staged attacks on Muslims and low-caste Hindus suspected of slaughtering cows.' Those arrested were 'charged for sedition and criminal conspiracy'.[9]

Russia

Russia was largely factored out of the global equation after the occupying Soviet Union troops left Afghanistan having suffered an unexpected defeat at the hands of seven groups of *mujahideen*. This army of resistance was trained by Pakistan's Inter-Services Intelligence agency which received funding from the United States. Saudi Arabia was also involved, using its personnel to motivate the fighters who were mostly students at the string of schools established all along the long Pakistan–Afghanistan border. The Russian withdrawal was completed in early 1989. Unable to absorb the shock of this defeat, the Soviet Union collapsed in 1991. European communism withered away along with the Soviet Union. Russia became the successor state. It was assumed that following the collapse of communism, Russia would join the ranks of the liberal states of the West. It was admitted into a number of Western institutions such as the International Monetary Fund, the World Bank Group and the G7. With the accession of Russia the G7 group of industrialized nations became the G8.

Once Vladimir Putin, the successor to Boris Yeltsin, the first popularly elected President of the new Russian Federation, had consolidated his hold over the country he set about establishing his country as a prominent global player. In this he has been helped by the rise of Donald Trump in the United States. Russia, which has an active role in Syria, has increased its presence in the Middle East. With the United States shunning Pakistan, Islamabad has turned towards Moscow to enlist Russian assistance in meeting its military needs.

Iran

Soon after Pakistan came into existence on 14 August 1947, the new country's leadership reached out to Iran and expressed a wish to develop close relations. Iran is one of Pakistan's four neighbours. The country had difficult relations with two of these. India adopted a hostile attitude towards its sister state from the moment the two countries came into existence. The rulers of Afghanistan were also not pleased with the fact that Pakistan had inherited a boundary the British had forced on Kabul when they ruled over India. This was the Durand Line, drawn by a British diplomat after the British fought two 'Afghan wars' but failed to bring the country under their control. While China was a distant presence, Iran was close and Pakistan made a real effort to draw close to that neighbour. Muhammad Reza Pahlavi, the Shah of Iran, was the first head of state to visit Pakistan and was warmly received.

The election of an Islamic government in Iran in 1979 complicated relations between the two countries. While Iran was Shiite, Pakistan was a majority Sunni country. However, some 20 per cent of its population was Shiite which made it the second largest Shiite country in the world. However, what really made relations between the two nations difficult to manage was the extreme hostility displayed by the Saudi Arabian Crown Prince.

Muhammad bin Salman adopted an aggressive stance towards Iran as he prepared to ascend the Saudi Arabian throne. The Kingdom severed diplomatic relations with Iran in January 2016 following an attack on its embassy in Tehran following the execution of a prominent Shiite cleric and three other members of the sect. There are, however, common interests that should compel the two countries to work together. Following a sharp decline in the price of oil, both countries were failing to cover their domestic expenditure, let alone finance foreign adventures. According to the IMF, Iran's government needs oil at US $55 per barrel to break even; Saudi Arabia needs $80. 'The oil producers can't sustain the external and proxy wars they once could when oil was $120 a barrel', stated a former World Bank economist.[10]

One of the prince's many moves was the resignation that he forced on Saad Hariri, the Lebanese Prime Minister by taking him as a virtual prisoner while the latter was making a visit to Riyadh, the Saudi Arabian capital. 'As bizarre as the episode was, it was just one chapter in the story of Prince Mohammed, the ambitious young heir apparent determined to shake up the power structure not just of his own country but of the entire region', wrote the *New York Times* in assessing the developing situation in the Middle East. This assessment was based on conversations with numerous officials from Saudi Arabia, Lebanon and Western capitals. 'At home, he has jailed hundreds of fellow princes and businessmen in what he casts as an anti-corruption drive. Abroad, he has waged war in Yemen and confronted Qatar.'[11] It appears that the heavy-handed treatment meted out to the Lebanese Prime Minister was intended to reduce the increasing power of the Iran-backed Hezbollah, a Shiite militant grouping that was now included in the cabinet headed by Hariri. The Saudis, it appears, were thinking of preparing the Palestinians refugees living in the camps in Lebanon to take on the Shiite militia. Hariri was not prepared to go down that route which is the reason why the Crown Prince forced him to resign. If these machinations were to bring Iran and the Kingdom closer to open conflict, it would put Pakistan in a difficult position. The Hariri affair was a long step back from the overtures made earlier to forge a working relationship with Iran. 'Some observers foresee a rapprochement between Saudi Arabia and Iran, talking of a grand bargain whereby the Saudis might recognize Iran's preeminence in the north of the Middle East, including Syria , in exchange for a Saudi free hand in the Gulf states and the Arabian peninsula', speculated *The Economist.*[12]

As discussed in Chapter 13, there has been a long-standing defence collaboration between Islamabad and Riyadh. General Raheel Sharif who served as the Chief of Army Staff in Pakistan until 2016 assumed the position of Commander of the multi-national security force to which dozens of Sunni states have committed themselves. It is a Saudi Arabian initiative; the force headquarters are located in Riyadh.

The Middle East and the world of Islam

As discussed in Chapter 13 on Pakistan's relations with Saudi Arabia, ever since Pakistan became a state it has sought to develop close relations with the Muslim world. Two countries figured prominently in this effort: Saudi Arabia and Iran. Increasingly, the form of Islam practised in Saudi Arabia influenced the religious beliefs and practices in Pakistan. However, the developing conflict between Iran and Saudi Arabia meant that Islamabad had to walk a thin line between the two protagonists.

A number of developments have occurred in and around the Middle East that have made the region even more volatile than in the past. These events will have consequences for Pakistan for reasons that need to be understood by the policymakers working in Islamabad. Some of can be attributed to the policies adopted by President Donald Trump. Others can be attributed to the path followed by Mohammad bin Salman, the son of King Salman bin Abd ul-Aziz Al Sa'ud on his way to the Saudi throne. In late 2018 the King was reported to be in poor health, and it was suggested that he might abdicate the throne in favour of the Crown Prince.

Donald Trump's approach to the Middle East is part of his ambition to unwind what he and some of close associates call 'Obamaism', the stance taken by Barack Obama during his eight-year presidency. Obama dealt with the Middle East by choosing not to involve his country in the many disputes that had resulted in the region becoming volatile and unpredictable. At the same time, he made a point of sending a message to the Muslim world that he and his country had great respect for Islam while recognizing that, on several occasions in the past, Islam and the West had been in conflict. In a powerful speech given at Al-Azhar University in Cairo, Egypt, on 4 June 2009, before an audience largely made up of students, Obama promised to work with the followers of the Islamic faith to produce a more stable world which would provide greater opportunities for the young.

The most significant step taken by Trump and his Administration was to draw closer to Kingdom of Saudi Arabia and the ruling royal family. During the Obama years the United States had distance itself from Saudi Arabia while initiating a programme to bring Iran out of isolation. Riyadh had long regarded Tehran as a rival not only because the Iranians were mostly followers of the Shiite sect of Islam, but also because it did not wish to see Iran expand its influence in the Muslim Middle East. The 1979 revolution that brought the Shiite clerics to power had done so by removing the king who had ruled over the country for decades. The overthrow of the monarchy and the introduction of a more representative political system were perceived as threats by the rulers of Saudi Arabia.

There was no subtlety in the way the newly inaugurated US Administration tilted Washington towards Riyadh. Trump chose Saudi Arabia as the first country to visit as President. In a public speech to some 50 heads of Muslim countries, including Nawaz Sharif, Pakistan's Prime Minister, the US President focused on his commitment to destroy Islamist radicalism. He was advised not to use the terms 'Islamic terrorism', 'Islamic radicalism', 'Islamic extremism', since to Muslim ears they might sound as though these were the attributes of their religion. Instead, he was to use 'Islamist' as the defining element since that referred to political Islam. In his speech he implied that Islamist terrorism had gained a foothold in some areas of the Muslim world owing to the support given to it by Iran. The Saudi response to these words was ecstatic.

There are three interests that guide Saudi Arabian policymaking: to preserve the house of Saud; to beat back any possible challenge from Iran for leadership in the Middle East and West Asia; and to diversify the country's economy. All three have consequences for Pakistan.

Riyadh is now engaged in the delicate task of passing the reins of power from the second generation of the Saudi dynasty to the third. Until recently, King Salman bin Abd al-Aziz Al Sa'ud, the founder of the state of Saudi Arabia, was succeeded by six of his sons. Soon after Trump's visit to Riyadh, the King appointed his son, Muhammad bin Salman, as the Crown Prince. This move reversed appointments made upon Salman's accession to the throne, when initially he named Muhammad bin Nayef, his nephew, as Crown Prince. Meanwhile, Muhammad bin Salman was appointed Deputy Prime Minister and was given significant responsibilities including the defence and energy portfolios.

Riyadh is nervous about the 'Arab Spring' movements. In 2011 they succeeded in deposing several authoritarian governments, in particular in Egypt, Libya, Tunisia and Yemen. What made the Saudi rulers nervous was the merging of interests of the restive Arab youth and political Islam. The two forces worked together to push the long-serving Hosni Mubarak from office. In the elections that followed, the Muslim Brotherhood came to power, a development of great concern to those who were wedded to the old order. The military struck in Cairo and removed the Brotherhood-led government and established an administration under General Fatah al-Sisi that was even more authoritarian than the one over which Hosni Mubarak had presided. Egypt joined Saudi Arabia, Bahrain and the United Arab Emirates in severing all relations with the tiny but oil- and gas-rich nation of Qatar. This move won the support of President Trump who claimed that it was the outcome of his visit to Riyadh.

Pakistan has an important place in the Islamic world. It is the only Muslim country to be founded on the basis of religion. Israel is the only other state that came into existence to serve a particular religious group. Both countries were created at about the same time. But there are differences, of course. Israel could accommodate the entire Jewish population in the world within its borders. It is committed to do precisely that. On the other hand the world's Muslim population is now estimated at 1.6 billion.

Pakistan has about 195 million Muslims in a population of 210 million. In other words, about 12 per cent of the world's total Muslim population lives in the country. What these numbers mean is that Pakistan's policymakers have to be concerned about developments in the parts of the world where Muslims are living under some kind of stress. That is why developments in the Middle East are of great concern to the people in Pakistan.

The Muslim world was concerned by a speech made in December 2017 by the US President Trump, who announced that he had decided to recognize Jerusalem as the capital of the Jewish State of Israel. He claimed that in 1995 the US Congress had passed a resolution that the United States should relocate the Jewish capital from Tel Aviv to Jerusalem. However, for almost a quarter of a century US presidents continued to issue waivers for not implementing the decision. Nonetheless, the current incumbent justified his move by saying that the facts on the ground supported his decision. Since the establishment of the State of Israel, Jerusalem had been its capital; it is where the government is located and from where it works; the houses of the country's President and Prime Minister are located in the city; and it is also the seat of the country's Supreme Court.

There were other facts. The Muslim world regards Jerusalem as its religion's third holiest place, after Mecca and Medina. Even though in the 1967 Six-Day War Israel had defeated the Jordanian forces that defended East Jerusalem, its occupation of that part of the city and the West Bank were not recognized by the world community. It is against international law to hold a territory won through warfare. It was always recognized that the status of Jerusalem would be part of the agreement between the Israelis and the Palestinians whenever the final settlement was reached. By moving the US embassy to Jerusalem, thereby recognizing the city as the capital of Israel and ignoring its major significance to Muslims, Donald Trump put himself and his country squarely on the side of the Jewish state. America can no longer be an honest broker, a role it has played ever since the 1967 war.

What would be the reaction of the Muslim world to this move by the US president? Would it, paradoxically, split the Muslims into two parts: those who would show only mild unhappiness and those who were likely to be highly agitated? The paradox is that most of the Arabs – the people as well as their governments – were likely to shrug their shoulders and move on. On the other hand, in countries such as Turkey, Pakistan, Malaysia and Indonesia, the reaction would be more negative. According to the *New York Times*,

> While Arab leaders have continued to pay lip service to the Palestinian cause, it has slipped in importance, displaced by the Arab Spring, the wars in Iraq, Syria and Yemen, the threat of the Islamic State, and the contest between Saudi Arabia and Iran for regional dominance. Persian Gulf states like Saudi Arabia, more concerned about their rivalry with Iran, have found their interests increasingly overlapping with those of Israel.

What we are seeing, therefore, is the move of the Sunni part of the Arab world attempting to counter the Shiite bid to dominate in the Middle East. The Asians in the Muslim world will move further away from both the United States and Saudi Arabia and will be more inclined to join forces with Iran and China. Iran, having invested massively in developing its human resources, can be predicted to have a better economic future than the Sunni Arabs. Meanwhile, China's One Belt, One Road initiative will help to bring the countries of Muslim Asia into its orbit. It would appear that Trump has taken sides in the Sunni–Shia confrontation.

US national security goals

How should the policymakers in Islamabad prepare for the world that President Trump has begun to shape? In December 2017 he introduced in person his Administration's national security strategy (NSS). This was the first time that a US president had spoken while the Administration announced the NSS. The document that pronounced the new American world strategy will be consequential for Pakistan. It was designed to reshape the world in which countries such as Pakistan must function. It was envisaged that there would be a strong reaction to the NSS and that South Asian nations would be divided in their opinions of it. According to the NSS, China will attract Pakistan and bring it more firmly into its orbit while India will be recruited as a partner in Washington's 'contain China' policy.

A document announcing the US Administration's approach to the world order is required by law. It guides Congress for the Administration's view of the world. The NSS echoed the 'America first' approach laid out by Trump is his inaugural speech. Much of the focus of the NSS was on China and Russia, the two countries that it claimed were 'determined to make economies less free and less fair, to grow their militaries, and control information and data to repress their societies and expand their influence'. This was unfortunate 'since after being dismissed as a phenomenon of an earlier century, great power competition has returned'. This statement is ironic since it is Trump's America that is set to challenge the world order that brought all countries into a framework based on international laws, rules and regulations.

Those who wrote the new policy must be aware of the work of the Greek historian, Thucydides, who, centuries ago, predicted that one great power replacing another in leadership role inevitably leads to conflict and open war. He presented his thesis when Athens had begun to challenge the dominance of Sparta. The result was war. The United States now faces a rising China, already the world's second largest economy. It is bound to translate its economic power into military strength. How should China be prevented from dominating the world in the way the that United States had done in the more than 70 years since the end of the Second World War?

'China and Russia challenge American power, influence, and interests attempting to erode American security and prosperity', the security statement said. 'They are determined to make economies less free and less fair, to grow their militaries and to control information and data to repress their societies and expand their influence'. In his preamble Trump stated that intellectual and property theft would be targeted. This was a clear warning to China about whose behaviour American companies have complained for years. 'We will no longer tolerate trading abuse', said the President.

Washington hopes to contain Beijing on several fronts. Xi Jinping, China's powerful President who, at the 19th session of the Communist Party's session was accorded the status enjoyed by Mao Zedong, has outlined what is being called Globalization 2.0. Through the One Belt, One Road initiative China is set to invest US $1 trillion in 60 countries. By building, railways, ports, fibre optic cables, oil and gas pipelines, Beijing plans to dominate international commerce. A new global economy would emerge with China at the centre. The Americans had factored themselves out of the global economic equation by withdrawing from the TPP that was negotiated by Barack Obama, Trump's predecessor in the White House. The TPP was meant to fashion the global trading system in the image of the United States. In fact, Obama had excluded China from the TPP as its economy was not free and was still dominated by the state sector. By rejecting the agreement, Trump gave Beijing an opportunity to put its stamp on global commerce.

As articulated in the NSS, Trump's vision has four components: to protect the US homeland; to protect US prosperity; to preserve peace through military strength; and to advance US influence. But some of these aims were contradictory. Unless the aim was to use its admittedly enormous military strength to establish its dominion over the globe, the only other way was to make the number of global institutions it had helped to establish even more powerful. These institutions could be used to constrain China's global reach. Initiatives such as the One Belt, One Road could be regulated with the help of global institutions pursued within agreed legal frameworks. But Trump had begun to attack the international institutional structure, leaving the ground clear for an assertive power such as China to fashion the world to reflect its increasing economic power.

The thoughts of Thucydides were only half right if applied to the tussle for power between the United States and China. There will not be a war between the two as was the case with Sparta and Athens. But there is likely to be an economic war and the way it is being fought, America will come out the loser. Also on the losing side will be countries such as Pakistan that do not participate fully in the global economy. In order for them to improve their positon, they need a role-based institutional structure and not the one in which issues are settled bilaterally, which is the Trump preference.

Notes

1 Shahid Javed Burki, *Rising Powers and Global Governance: Changes and Challenges for the World's Nations*, London and New York, Palgrave Macmillan, 2017.
2 Thomas Gibbons-Neff and Dan Lamothe, 'Delegating of Afghan troop decisions draws scrutiny,' *New York Times*, 15 June 2017, p. A4.
3 Ibid.
4 Shahid Javed Burki and Shirin Tahir-Kheli, *Pakistan Today: The Case for U.S.-Pakistan Relations*, Foreign Policy Institute Studies in Policy, Johns Hopkins University, Washington, DC, 2017.

5 Robert Blackwill and Jennifer Harris, *War by Other Means: Geoeconomics and Statecraft,* Cambridge, MA, Harvard University Press, 2016, p. 11.

6 See www.independent.co.uk/news/world/americas/us-politics/donald-trump-xi-jingping-king-of-china-president-general-secretary-asia-tour-a8021576.html.

7 Gideon Rachman, 'China's Bold Challenge to the West', *Financial Times*, 24 October 2017, p. 9.

8 Shahid Javed Burki Institute of Public Policy, *The State of the Economy: China Pakistan Economic Corridor,* Lahore, 2018.

9 Hari Kumar and Nida Najar, 'Arrests in India after Pakistan's Cricket Win', *New York Times,* 22 June 2017, p. A6.

10 Quoted in *The Economist*, 'Saudi Arabian Diplomacy: Outpaced by Iran', 10 December 2016, p. 49.

11 Anne Barnard and Mari Abi-Habib, 'How Hariri Fell, then Regained His Balance', *New York Times*, 25 December 2017, pp. A1 and A8.

12 *The Economist*, 'Saudi Arabia's Foreign Policy: Sunnis and Shias: Enemies No More?' 9 September 2017, p. 47.

11

Defenders of the crescent
Pakistan-Saudi Arabia relations

Farah Jan

Introduction

Since its inception Pakistan's foreign policy has been marked by wars and crises, shifting alliances and persistent rivalries. The country has witnessed the collapse of formal alliances, whereas other non-formal alliances (for example the People's Republic of China and Saudi Arabia) maintain vigour and vitality, despite the usual ebb and flow of relations as well as regional and systemic changes. This chapter discusses Pakistan's longstanding relationship with Saudi Arabia. The relationship, as described by the former head of Saudi intelligence, Prince Turki bin Faisal, is 'probably one of the closest relationships in the world between any two countries without any official treaty'.[1] What explains the persistence and endurance of this partnership? As the 19th-century British statesman Lord Palmerston noted, 'states have no permanent friends or permanent enemies, only permanent interests that might cause a state to align with a particular country at some times and against it at others'.[2] This chapter seeks to explore the interests that have converged between these two allies, particularly in the absence of a common enemy or threat.

In order to understand Pakistan's foreign relations, we must explore the factors that influenced Pakistan's decision makers in addition to the regional context that shaped Pakistan's policy orientation as an independent nation-state. History and geostrategic location play a crucial role in shaping any country's foreign policy and alliance patterns. In the case of Pakistan, so too does self-perception. Pakistan was born out of calls of faith by millions of Muslims who sought a sanctuary while witnessing the collapse of the colonial order at the end of the Second Word War. Conceptualizing independence through an identity of faith had an impact on Pakistan's perceptions of friends and foes. Plagued by insecurities as a new nation-state at the dawn of the Cold War, Pakistan could hardly ignore its rival that was larger in size, population and capabilities: India. The core of Pakistan's insecurity was and remains India, and as this chapter explains, any adjustments in Pakistan's alliance formation has India as the main motivating factor. In this sense, Pakistan's relations with Saudi Arabia need to be understood in the context of Pakistan's history, aspirations, geostrategic location and, most importantly, its insecurities.

In the case of Saudi Arabia, the primary goal has been the survival and continuation of the House of Saud, and since the 1979 Islamic Revolution the Kingdom's main foreign policy objective has been the containment of Iran. Like Pakistan, Saudi Arabia has looked for allies on the world stage based on its vital interest in the preservation of its monarchy and territorial integrity. Saudi Arabia's partnership with Pakistan dates back to the early 1960s and since then it has remained exceptionally close on defence, security and economic issues. From the very beginning, the Saudi kings made it a priority to visit Pakistan. Visits by King Saud in 1954, King Faisal in 1966 and 1974, King Khalid in 1976, King Fahd in 1980, King Abdullah in 1984, 1988, 1997, and 2003, and King Salman in 2014 have all served to emphasize the importance of bilateral ties between the two countries.[3] The Pakistan-Saudi Arabia engagement runs deep, and has been valuable for both parties. Pakistan assisted the Kingdom in structuring and maintaining its economy, including its banking and construction sectors, but it has also contributed to the establishment of its armed forces, including the Saudi Arabian royal air force. Similarly, Saudi Arabia has continued to support Pakistan during the economic crises that it has faced, and many scholars believe that Saudi Arabian economic assistance and diplomatic backing were instrumental for the development of Pakistan's nuclear programme. It is not surprising that out of all the Middle Eastern states Pakistani citizens hold the most favourable view of the Kingdom.[4]

This chapter proceeds first with a brief history of Pakistan-Saudi Arabia relations, and elaborates on the defence, security and economic factors of this relationship. It challenges and explores the notion of Sunni Islam as a cohesive bond between the two states from 1947 until the present day. However, scholars have tended to focus on the cultural and religious bonds between the two countries, and the existing literature has ignored or downplayed the deeper defence and economic nature of this relationship.[5] The aim here is not to diminish the role of religion in this relationship; however, it is not the only factor that keeps this alliance moving forward. With the structural liberal reforms unfolding in Saudi Arabia under the leadership of Crown Prince Mohammed bin Salman since 2015, religious motivation for sustaining the alliance has abated in the Kingdom's foreign policy. Thus, the new Saudi Arabian foreign policy position demonstrates that the relationship with Pakistan is not solely due to its Sunni Muslim majority status, but instead is invested in what Pakistan can do for Saudi Arabia, and vice versa. It is the defence and the economic interest of these two nations that converge; the Sunni identity is an added benefit of this alliance.

This chapter concludes with an overview of the shifting regional relations with respect to Iran and India. Along with the evolving security and economic interests of the great powers, namely the United States, the People's Republic of China and the Russian Federation. The conclusion raises and briefly addresses the following issues and questions that might impact this long-standing relationship. Will the great power rivalry impact Pakistan-Saudi Arabian relations, particularly with Pakistan being in the Chinese orbit and Saudi Arabia a traditional ally of the United States? With the domestic changes in Saudi Arabia upending the centrality of the religious dimension of Saudi Arabian foreign policy, how will this impact relations with Pakistan? And most importantly, will Saudi Arabia follow the United States's South Asia strategy and side with India?

Past as prelude

Since independence, Pakistan has been keen on forging support from states with which it has shared religious identity. Saudi Arabia, being the home of the two holy mosques and a leading Sunni state, was a natural partner with which Pakistan could seek closer ties. While Britain attempted to maintain its influence in the Middle East by encouraging membership among its former colonies in the Baghdad Pact formed in 1955 (also known as the Central Treaty Organization – CENTO), Saudi Arabia was by then officially part of an oil-for-security pact with the United States. Saudi Arabia initially had identified India as a potential partner because Prime Minister Jawaharlal Nehru had declared a non-alignment policy and remained neutral. On the other hand, Pakistan, due to its security needs, had aligned itself with the West, first with the United Kingdom and then with the United States. At the time of Pakistan's founding, the UK was a declining power and the United States had emerged as the strongest state in the system, both economically and militarily.

From the very beginning Mohammad Ali Jinnah understood the importance of good relations with the Middle Eastern states and sought strong economic ties with the Muslim world. By October 1947 Jinnah had appointed Malik Firoz Khan Noon as a special envoy to Iraq, Iran, Lebanon, Syria, Turkey, Saudi Arabia and Egypt. The main goal of the special envoy was to amplify trade and economic ties with these states. In addition to developing economic relations, Jinnah wanted to form an organization that would serve as a league for Muslim countries. His aim was to emulate President Franklin Roosevelt's achievement in forming the United Nations (UN). The influence of the then recent independence of Pakistan and Indonesia, two major Muslim states, cannot be overstated. Jinnah saw the importance of capturing the momentum of Muslim triumph and nationalism as a way to strengthen Pakistan. Jinnah envisioned a league that would consist of 400 million Muslims from Pakistan, Indonesia, Turkey, Iran and the Middle East, as well as North Africa. The Egyptians welcomed the initiative, as it did not clash with the League of Arab States, and requested that its establishment be postponed until the creation of Pakistan and Indonesia. Mohammad Ali Jinnah died in the first year of Pakistan's formation, and the idea withered away after a few years. We will see that the events of the late 1960s and early 1970s (the 1967 Six-Day War, Nasser's death in 1970, and the Al-Aqsa attack in 1969) would once again bring the discussion of Muslim unity to the fore, and would result in the formation of the Organisation of Islamic Cooperation in 1969 – in which Saudi Arabia and Pakistan played a crucial and leading role.

At independence, Saudi Arabia's King Abdel Aziz sent a cable to Mohammed Ali Jinnah expressing his great satisfaction and offering him his best wishes. Early interactions between Saudi Arabia and Pakistan were based only on their religious affinities. Saudi Arabia, at this point in history, was interested in expanding its ties with India and did not consider Pakistan as a feasible partner. As a result, Saudi Arabia's relationship with India flourished in the 1950s, despite the India-Pakistan rivalry and Pakistan's efforts to win the Kingdom's explicit support during the Kashmir dispute. Pakistan joined the Baghdad Pact in 1955 at which point relations with the Kingdom were at their lowest. Saudi Arabia had strongly condemned Pakistan's decision to join the Pact and the Saudi Arabian embassy in Karachi issued a statement that Pakistan's signing of the Pact was 'a stab in the heart of the Arab and Muslim states'. Furthermore, the Saudi Arabian embassy distributed the press handout of the text in which Radio Mecca emphatically asked Pakistan to withdraw from the Baghdad Pact and 'return to the right path'.[6] The Saudis were vehemently against Pakistan's stance, and at that time they found in India a partner with similar interests. Towards the end of his visit to India, King Saud issued a joint statement with Jawaharlal Nehru. King Saud declared, 'I desire to say to my Muslim brethren all over the world with satisfaction that the fate of Indian Muslims is in safe hands'. The *raison d'être* for the 1947 Partition was to create a safe political space for the Muslims of India, and King Saud's statement discredited the very ideological grounding for Pakistan's existence.

In 1956 Jawaharlal Nehru, the Indian Prime Minister, reciprocated with a visit to Riyadh and reaffirmed the earlier joint statement. During his visit to Saudi Arabia he was hailed as a *marhaba rasul-e-salam* (messenger of peace).[7] This generated such immense controversy in Pakistan that the Saudi Arabian embassy in Karachi had to issue a statement that the phrase had been uttered merely to welcome a 'messenger of peace' and did not refer to the prophet of peace. In response, an editorial in the *Dawn* newspaper of Pakistan communicated the national disappointment and stated that readers should 'calmly and dispassionately take all these bitter truths into consideration and restrain to some extent their vain expectations from the so-called Muslim world'.[8] The events that followed made the formative days of this relationship turbulent, and it was not until 1961 that the Pakistan-Saudi Arabian relationship improved and the partnership between them strengthened. Simultaneously, Pakistan replaced India in the Saudis' strategic calculations. It would take the next Indian Prime Minister to visit Saudi Arabia's capital city, Riyadh, 26 years later when Indira Gandhi visited the Kingdom in 1982.

What led to the friction in the 1950s and why did events turn around after Ayub Khan's visit to the Kingdom in 1960? The initial unsteady ties between Pakistan and Saudi Arabia was the result of a political calculus of Saudi Arabia that aimed at gaining powerful allies on the world stage. India's anti-colonial stance and Nehru's support for Palestine were highlighted by the Saudi decision makers to justify their counter-intuitive outreach to India and not Pakistan at the time. It was during Ayub Khan's era that Pakistan-Saudi Arabian relations turned positive. However, the turning point of their relationship correlates with Saudi Arabia's increased security and defence needs in the 1960s starting with the civil war in Yemen. In 1962 a *coup d'état* by the revolutionary officers in Yemen dethroned Imam Muhammad al-Badr and a civil war ensued. Yemen from the very beginning has been critical for Saudi Arabian national security. Thus, in response to the 1962 coup, Saudi Arabia supported the Yemeni royalists who fought against the revolutionary corps backed by Egyptian President Jamal Abdul Nasser. It is important to emphasize that both Iran and Saudi Arabia helped the Yemeni royalists back in 1962 because their strategic interests were aligned despite of the Shia–Sunni divide.[9] Riyadh and Tehran were both determined to contain Nasser's influence and the communist forces in the Arabian peninsula. Riyadh never viewed the Shah of Iran as the representative of Shia Islam; instead, he was regarded as a feudal element of the Persian empire. Pakistan's role was important at that time, as it became the arms supplier (like Iran) to the royalist forces in Yemen that further strengthened the Saudi position. India on the other hand sided with the anti-monarchical and pro-Arab nationalist cause championed by Nasser and supported the revolutionary officers in Yemen. Egypt under Nasser became a direct threat to the Saudi Kingdom as Nasser was recognized by India as the progressive leader of Arab nationalism. Thus, Nehru's endorsement of Nasser as the sole and undisputed leader of a resurgent Arab nationalism affected Saudi Arabian-Indian relations negatively. Pakistan, on the other hand, proved to be supportive of the Saudi Arabian foreign position and leadership in the region.

Following the Yemen war, relations between Saudi Arabia and Pakistan became warmer. In August 1967 the Saudi Arabian Minister of Defence visited Pakistan and this led to the signing of the first official defence agreement between Islamabad and Riyadh. Under the 1967 agreement, Pakistan trained and advised Saudi Arabian armed forces and

Saudi Arabia extended economic assistance to Pakistan. This landmark agreement not only established bilateral defence and security relations, but it also positioned Pakistan to reach the zenith of its faith-based identity. Pakistani soldiers began protecting the two holy mosques in Saudi Arabia, and the state of Pakistan could thus rightfully claim credibility and national pride as it served and protected the land of the two Holy Mosques. For Pakistani soldiers, deployment to the Kingdom was not just a fulfilment of a work contract but an honour, and the Saudis understood the emotional depth of their security cooperation.

In the 1970s Saudi Arabia supported Pakistan during its multiple crises with India. This was the time when Pakistan lost its Eastern Wing and Zulfiqar Ali Bhutto came to power. The Saudi Arabian leaders were apprehensive of Bhutto, particularly given his role in removing President Ayub Khan, with whom the King and the Crown Prince had established a personal relationship of trust.[10] Under Bhutto, Pakistan-Saudi Arabian ties were further strained when he appointed an ambassador to the Kingdom who was rejected by King Faisal on the grounds that he belonged to the Ahmadi sect.[11] Bhutto understood the importance of Saudi Arabia for Pakistan, and he made it his primary objective to assure the Kingdom of his support. Bhutto extended strong support during the oil embargo of 1973 and the Arab–Israeli War in 1974. In return, Saudi Arabia exempted Pakistan from the 1973 oil embargo. India, on the other hand, was not on the list of countries that were exempted.

Following the 1971 war, Pakistan and Saudi Arabia cooperated closely and the second session of the Islamic Summit conference was held in Lahore, Pakistan, in February 1974. The Islamic Conference was a masterful display of Bhutto's regional diplomacy. In his opening remarks, he declared that the conference symbolized the rebirth of Muslim unity and an attempt to stimulate questions of identity for Muslim majority states. The conference accordingly focused on two vital political issues: Kashmir and Palestine. King Faisal represented the Saudi Arabian delegation and led the Friday prayers at the Grand (Badshahi) Mosque in Lahore. Prior to the opening of the conference Bhutto said,

> The object of the conference is to find a common approach in principle for a clearer thinking and outlook. All of us [Muslim leaders] would like to see the evacuation of territories conquered by force. All of us want a settlement of the dispute and all of us subscribe to the previous UN resolution on the subject.

The conference was also used as a platform to improve ties between Pakistan and Bangladesh. It was on this occasion that Bhutto invited the Prime Minister of Bangladesh to attend the conference at the request of Egypt, Algeria and Saudi Arabia.

The year 1979 marked a turning point in history, not just for South Asia but the world at large. The Islamic revolution in Iran, the Soviet invasion of Afghanistan, and the siege of Mecca occurred in the same year. Thus, it represented a watershed moment that cemented the Pakistan-Saudi Arabian strategic alliance. For Saudi Arabia, the new revolutionary Islamist Iranian regime posed an unequivocal and direct threat to the House of Saud and the other Gulf monarchies, as well as the US interests in the region. Furthermore, the Soviet invasion of Afghanistan threatened the stability of Pakistan and a threat to the US interests in the region. Saudi Arabia's insecurities peaked after the takeover of the Grand Mosque in Mecca. King Khalid requested additional troops from Pakistan in 1980 after the siege of Holy Haram in Mecca. These events strengthened the defence and security cooperation for decades to come and led to expanded intelligence-sharing between Islamabad and Riyadh.

The centerpiece of the Saudi-Pakistan alliance in the 1980s was strictly security-related. The Pakistan Army, whose general Headquarters were located at Rawalpindi, was entrusted with providing military training and support to the Kingdom under the pretext of protecting the Holy Land. In return, Saudi Arabia provided economic assistance in two ways: oil concessions and funding for Pakistan's arms purchases from the United States. During this period the two countries engaged in an alliance of convenience cloaked in religious affinity and governed by an unmistakable pro-US regional context.

With the collapse of the Soviet Union and the emergence of the United States as the sole global superpower, Afghanistan remained as one of the focal points for intelligence-sharing and security cooperation between Pakistan and the Gulf states. Pakistan and Saudi Arabia continued to support the Afghan *mujahideen* and were the first to recognize the Taliban government. During the 1990s Afghanistan became the de facto proxy battleground between Iran and Pakistan/Saudi Arabia, with Tehran supporting the Northern Alliances and Pakistan backing the *mujahideen* that had by that time become the Taliban. The Saudi Arabian government utilized Pakistan's influence over the Afghan Taliban to keep Iran diverted and occupied on its border with Afghanistan, instead of meddling in the affairs of the Gulf states.[12] The late 1990s was also the period when the Saudi Arabian government became concerned about Pakistan's stability following its nuclear test and the US sanctions. A declassified US intelligence report noted Saudi Arabia's concern for Pakistan after the US sanctions in 1998. The report claimed that 'the Saudis were interested in Pakistan's missile and nuclear weapons program'.[13] For Riyadh, the Pakistan-US crisis was another example of the reliability (or lack thereof) of the United States towards an old ally, and it 'reflected the Saudi leaders' own fears that someday the United States will leave them in the lurch'.[14] The Saudi Arabian government demonstrated its commitment to Pakistan by suppling it with 50,000 barrels per day of oil to help it to cope with economic sanctions as a result of the atomic test it carried out in 1998.[15]

Strategic or transactional allies

Alliances in interstate relations are a 'means to security against adversaries'.[16] Hence, the core component of an alliance is the convergence of interests, and the value of any alliance is contingent upon the degree and credibility of the allies' commitment to advancing those mutual interests. Glenn Snyder notes that there are two types of alliances: formal and non-formal. A formal alliance explicitly reiterates commitments through verbal or non-verbal promises that are usually followed by a contractual type of agreement. However, Snyder notes that the political reality manifests not necessarily as a result of a formal agreement, but because of the expectations created by the contract. Non-formal alliances are formed due to common interests and mutual expectations in aiding an ally that exists apart from any official agreement. Snyder maintains that 'non-formal alliances can range from "special relationships" to ententes, to merely good relations'.[17] Pakistan-Saudi Arabia relations have the components of both a formal and a non-formal alliance. They have maintained security, defence and economic commitments to each other since the 1960s, which continue to the present day. However, there is a transactional dimension to this alliance that has conclusively transformed this partnership into an interdependent alliance in which Pakistan's economic and diplomatic needs are fulfilled by Saudi Arabia. Likewise, Saudi Arabia is provided with a continuous supply of manpower for its economy and security. It is this interdependence and mutual aid that keeps the alliance moving forward.

Economic engagement

From Mohammed Ali Jinnah to Ayub Khan, from Zulfiqar Ali Bhutto to General Zia, and more recently to Imran Khan, all the Pakistani leaders have stressed the importance of closer economic cooperation with the Gulf states. Likewise, since the rule of King Faisal, successive Saudi leaders have pushed for and maintained good relations with Pakistan to bolster bilateral economic cooperation. Pakistan-Saudi Arabian bilateral economic relations have three important features: (1) Pakistan's supply of a skilled and unskilled workforce for most economic sectors in Saudi Arabia; (2) Saudi Arabia's aid to Pakistan in the form of oil concessions and lines of credit; and (3) bilateral trade and commercial ties on both sides.

Saudi Arabia's oil-based economy is among the top 20 in the world and its oil reserves are pegged at 260 billion barrels, a capacity that is far greater than any of its competitors.[18] However, like other Gulf economies the Saudi Arabian economy depends on migrant labour. Since the 1970s Saudi Arabia has remained the largest source of remittances for Pakistan. Between 1973 and 2017 Pakistan received more than US $60 billion in remittances from Saudi Arabia. The Pakistan Economic Survey for the fiscal year 2015–16 noted that Saudi Arabia has become the largest market for Pakistani workers in the world.[19] On the trade front, 90 per cent of Pakistan's imports from Saudi Arabia are based on oil and petroleum, with annual bilateral trade figures for 2017–18 totalling approximately $2.5 billion.[20] However, these figures have decreased sharply from 2016–17 when bilateral figures stood at $5.08 billion.[21] The recent drop in trade volume sparked talks on a preferential trade arrangement between Pakistan and Saudi Arabia. In January 2018 a two-day long commission was convened to discuss ways of improving trade by addressing issues of securing business visas and resolving tariff and non-tariff barriers.[22]

Defence ties

Since Ayub Khan's visit to Saudi Arabia in 1962, defence and security cooperation has played a major role in bilateral ties with Pakistan providing training and troops to the Kingdom. The Saudi Crown Prince and Minister of Defence, Prince Sultan, categorically stated that 'Saudi Arabia regards Pakistan as its number one friend in the world. Whenever the Kingdom needs [military] help, Pakistan is the first place that we confidently look to'.[23] Domestically, Pakistani troops have ensured the survival of the monarchy and the continuation of the House of Saud. Pakistan has also defended Saudi Arabia's borders by providing armoured brigades along the Jordanian and Yemeni borders to fend off any threats to the territorial sovereignty of Saudi Arabia.[24] Most importantly, Pakistani forces have demonstrated their willingness to fight Israel. As one diplomat noted, 'Pakistan's involvement in providing security support to Saudi Arabia developed on a scale unmatched by any other country. A portion of the Pakistan military will be made available for the Kingdom, if the need arises. No country will make a greater commitment than that for Saudi Arabia.'[25] In return, Saudi Arabia has extended support to Pakistan during its wars with India and, most importantly, during the Kashmir dispute. Defence and security cooperation have become an enduring feature of Saudi Arabian-Pakistani relations, at least within the defence ministries and intelligence agencies. As noted by one senior official, 'the military bond with Saudi Arabia is stronger than the political relationship with the Kingdom'.[26]

One of the earliest defence interactions recorded between the two states was the 1950 visit of Pakistan's naval warship, the *Sindh*, to Saudi Arabia. The aim of the ship's voyage was to enhance good relations between the two Muslim countries.[27] Likewise, one of the first formal defence agreements signed between the two states was the 1967 agreement and as a consequence Pakistani military advisors were sent to Saudi Arabia to help 'expand and modernize the Saudi Armed Forces'. Saudi military personnel were also trained in Pakistan.[28] The support extended by Pakistan was not limited to military training but also to light combat. For example, in 1969 the Pakistani air force flew Saudi-owned jets to push back South Yemeni border incursions into Saudi Arabia.[29] From 1970 onwards, an estimated 15,000 troops were stationed on the Iraqi, Jordanian, and Yemen borders in order to protect Saudi Arabia. The numbers remained consistent through the 1980s, and during the Iran–Iraq War the number of Pakistani troops increased with the presence of army, navy and air force personnel. Furthermore, a US diplomatic source reported that Pakistan and Saudi Arabia were holding secret negotiations in the early 1980s, according to which Pakistan would station one-third of its defence forces in Saudi Arabia in order to deter external aggressors or domestic threats and in return Saudi Arabia would pay US \$1 billion per annum to Pakistan for this service. Pakistani officials made the point that Pakistani forces could reach Saudi Arabia faster than American forces. The fact that the troops were Muslims made harbouring them more acceptable than hosting American GIs.[30]

Following the Iran–Iraq War during the late 1980s, the relationship hit a low point when King Fahd requested Pakistan's General Zia ul-Haq to send only Sunni soldiers to Saudi Arabia. The King also called for the removal or reduction of Shia troops from Pakistan's armed forces. This request amounted to sectarian discrimination and put General Zia in a difficult position; ultimately, he rejected it. This led to a reduction in the number of Pakistani troops sent to Saudi Arabia.[31] One year later, Pakistani troops were requested back when Saudi Arabia perceived an external threat to its sovereignty from Iran. Despite the close understanding, Riyadh has not grasped the intricate sectarian balance within Pakistan. In Saudi Arabia, excluding the Shia minority from military service is a standard security precaution; however, in Pakistan, it could potentially destabilize the country. General Zia was aware that a professional army could not tolerate discrimination based on sect because it would fracture and weaken the armed forces. However, when it came to the Ahmedis/Qadyianis, both Zulfiqar Ali Bhutto and General Zia declared them non-Muslims in a move that was appreciated by Saudi Arabia. General Zia took it a step further by passing the ordinance in 1984 that called for the persecution of Ahmedis for praying in public spaces.[32]

Saudi Arabia's response to Pakistan's wars and crises

By the mid-1960s relations between Pakistan and Saudi Arabia had improved markedly, whereas Indo-Saudi Arabian relations were at their lowest point due to Nehru's support for Egypt's Nasser and the Soviet Union. During the 1965 India–Pakistan War, Saudi Arabia gave material, diplomatic and moral support to Pakistan. The Saudi embassy in Karachi issued a strong statement of support on the eve of the 1965 war and called on 'India to not take undue advantage of its friendship with the Arabs by committing aggression against Pakistan'.[33] Similarly, with regard to the Kashmir dispute, King Faisal extended Saudi support for the Pakistani position. At the UN, the Saudi Arabian Permanent Representative Omar Sakkaf pressed India to resolve the Kashmir issue and to improve ties with Pakistan. In response, the *Times of India* noted that the Arab states appeared to have sided with Pakistan and reported that the UN speeches of some of these states were 'so patently partial that it could have been drafted by a Pakistani'.[34] It further noted that the Muslim community in India had appealed to the governments of Arab countries to support India on Kashmir. Much to India's chagrin, after the war, the government of Saudi Arabia offered Pakistan an economic assistance package to which India responded by expressing its concerns. India's ambassador in Jeddah was instructed to meet with the King and deliver the message that 'any arms [and economic] help to Pakistan would be considered an unfriendly act by India'.[35] The Saudi government initially denied that the financial assistance rendered to Pakistan was for the purpose of purchasing military equipment.[36] It was later reported and confirmed that the loan was intended and used for defence purposes.[37]

Following the 1965 war, King Faisal visited Pakistan in 1966 for a six-day state visit. During his stay he stated:

> If we have shown brotherly feelings and cooperation for this Islamic country it is because this is the least of what our religion and belief demands from us ... In the face of international upsets and undercurrents, the Muslims are more than ever in need of solidarity and unity of purpose.[38]

Additionally, it was during this trip that the idea of holding an Islamic summit to create a unifying platform for the Muslim countries was discussed. This idea was also supported by the Shah of Iran, who, together with King Faisal, signed the joint communiqué.[39] The King's visit was followed by the Saudi defence delegation that led to the signing of the Pakistan-Saudi Arabia Defence Agreement of 1967. This was a significant step in strengthening Pakistani-Saudi Arabian bilateral military ties, and the agreement called for technical cooperation in the civil and the defence aviation sectors.[40] This was also the time when the Kingdom was under significant threat from the short-lived United Arab Republic, a sovereign entity formed between Egypt and Syria to demonstrate Arab nationalism and unity. Saudi Arabia was in critical need of allies in the region and found Pakistan to be a reliable and trustworthy partner who was also in need of a patron and ally.

During the 1971 Indo–Pakistan War and the Bangladesh crisis, Saudi Arabia once again provided full cooperation and support to Pakistan. It warned other neighbouring countries that no one had the right to interfere in Pakistan's internal politics. At the UN General Assembly, the Saudi ambassador Sakkaf said, 'We believe what is happening in Pakistan is strictly and without any doubt the affair of the Pakistanis themselves, and therefore any outside interference in the internal affairs of Pakistan will surely constitute a violation of our Charter.'[41] On the establishment of Bangladesh, Saudi Arabia refused to recognize its statehood officially until Pakistan had accepted it. Indo-Saudi Arabian relations further deteriorated on the issue of Pakistani prisoners of war (POWs) after the 1971 war. The Saudi Arabian Ministry of Foreign Affairs considered India's refusal to resolve the POW issue to be a 'flagrant violation of the Geneva Convention'. Saudi Arabia played an important role behind the scenes prior to the signing of the Simla Agreement in 1974 between Pakistan and India.

Similarly, during the other multiple India-Pakistan crises the Kingdom played an important role on Pakistan's behalf. During the Kargil crisis, Saudi Arabia and the United States played an important role in diffusing tensions between the two rivals.[42] However, it was the Saudis who used their leverage to encourage the Pakistani military leadership to retreat. Saudi Arabia, along with Iran and Egypt, was not pleased about Pakistan's military adventurism in Kargil.[43] However, Saudi Arabia continued its support for Pakistan's position on Kashmir and urged India to seek a peaceful resolution to the Kashmir dispute.[44] During the crisis Saudi Prince Bandar bin Sultan, who was also Saudi Arabia's ambassador to the United States at that time, played a crucial part in getting the Americans engaged diplomatically. Bruce Riedel notes that 'Bandar asked for a briefing on what the President [Clinton] needed from [Pakistan Prime Minister] Sharif'.[45] Over the years and throughout numerous crises between India and Pakistan, Saudi Arabia has maintain its support for Pakistan and its struggle over Kashmir.

Yemen and the Qatar crisis tests of alliance resilience?

Although the defence and security relationship between Saudi Arabia and Pakistan is defined as the long-term transactional engagement that is interdependent, more recently, the shift in regional politics and power relations created difficulties in their alliance. The power dynamics in the region shifted radically following the nuclear pact (the Joint Comprehensive Plan of Action – JCPOA) that was signed between Iran, the United States and European states. The lifting of the economic sanctions allowed Iran to restore its oil production levels to the pre-sanction era.[46] Although the Trump Administration withdrew the United States from the JCPOA in May 2018 amid the threat to reinstate sanctions, the impact of these measures are yet unrealized. However, the lifting of the sanctions during the Obama Administration strengthened Iran's influence in the Middle East and emboldened its allies Russia and China. Beijing had already increased its economic and defence footprint in Asia with its One Belt, One Road initiative, an ambitious transnational infrastructure investment project. Pakistan plays a crucial part in China's infrastructure and maritime routes project and Iran is eager to join it. For Pakistan, strengthening economic ties with Iran has the potential to affect its historic bonds with Saudi Arabia, and for the time being relations with Iran are on hold, especially keeping the deep strategic ties between Tehran and New Delhi.

Faced with an emboldened Iran, Saudi Arabia under King Salman and Crown Prince Mohammad bin Salman opted for an aggressive foreign policy to contain Iran's influence in the region. In 2015 Saudi Arabia initiated a military intervention in Yemen against the Houthi rebels backed by Iran. During the 1962 Yemen war, Saudi Arabia, Pakistan and Iran fought together against the revolutionary forces backed by Egypt's Nasser. However, in the Yemen conflict that was ongoing in 2018, Saudi Arabia was fighting the Houthi forces that had been armed and supported by Iran. This has placed Pakistan in a difficult position. At the start of the military intervention in Yemen, Saudi Arabia had asked Pakistan to provide troops, ships and aircrafts for the military campaign against the Houthis.[47] Islamabad was confronted with the possibility of a third enemy front with Iran, and troops were already stationed on the border with India and Afghanistan as well as ongoing military operations against al-Qaeda and Taliban elements conducted in its tribal areas. For Riyadh, Pakistani troops were a key part of their Yemen strategy. For the first time in this long-standing partnership, Pakistan had to turn down Saudi Arabia's request, and the Pakistani parliament voted not to join the Saudi-led military intervention in Yemen. The decision to remain neutral in the Yemen conflict marked a crisis point in their relationship.[48] Parliament also issued a statement of assurance to the Kingdom that emphasized Pakistan's commitment to Saudi territorial integrity and the two holy mosques. In response, Saudi Arabia publicly downplayed the decision. However, three years after the parliamentary decision, Pakistan decided to deploy its troops in Saudi Arabia to take part in the Yemen conflict. The exact role and number of Pakistani troops in the

Kingdom in 2018 was unclear, but the initial statements highlighted the advisory and training role of the soldiers.

The Saudi Arabian strategy since the 1979 Islamic Revolution has been to contain Iran and its influence in the region. To achieve this, it has relied on two foreign policy objectives: to keep Iran's influence completely out of its neighbouring states in the Gulf Cooperation Council (GCC) and to place a restraint on Iranian activity within the Middle East through the promotion of US sanctions. Following the Iran nuclear deal in 2015, the easing of economic sanctions on Iran threatened Saudi interests in the region. In reaction to this, Saudi Arabia is determined to defend its national interests in the region and has vigorously pushed back with an anti-Iran strategy. Within this context, Qatar, a GCC member state, pursued an ambitious foreign policy that was independent of Riyadh. Doha was reluctant to accommodate Saudi Arabian policy and position regarding counter-terrorism measures in the region, Qatar's position on the Muslim Brotherhood, and most alarming for Riyadh was Doha's cordial overtures to Iran. As a result, Saudi Arabia and other GCC states and Egypt severed ties with Qatar on 5 June 2017 by closing off the land border and airspace and docking ports. Pakistan once again adopted a neutral position and a parliamentary resolution was passed by the National Assembly that read 'the house calls upon all countries to show restraint and resolve all differences through dialogue'.[49]

The cornerstone of the Saudi Arabia-Pakistan alliance has always been security. However, recent events have strained ties between them. The question is: where does the Saudi Arabia-Pakistan alliance stand today? Starting in 2018, both states have worked hard to strengthen and formalize the alliance and have recovered from the setbacks created by the Yemen war and the Qatar crisis. In addition, Pakistan joined the Saudi Arabia-led Islamic Military Alliance to fight terrorism headed up by the former Army Chief of Pakistan, General Raheel Shareef. The continuation of the Pakistan-Saudi Arabia alliance confirms what Winston Churchill said about allies and alliances, 'There is only one thing worse than fighting with allies, and that is fighting without them'.[50] In the current shifting power structures and unpredictable alliances, the long-term interests and goals of both states continue to be aligned. The patron-client transactional partnership will persist as long as both states maintain their traditional roles, whereby Pakistan provides manpower and Saudi Arabia assists Pakistan in improving its economic woes. The concluding section analyses the recent domestic changes that are helping to shape Saudi Arabian society and offers a prognosis for the future of relations between Pakistan and Saudi Arabia.

The future of the Pakistan-Saudi Arabian alliance in the new Saudi Arabia of Mohammed bin Salman

The Kingdom is currently going through a major social, economic and political transformation. Crown Prince Mohammed bin Salman implemented major social reforms in 2017, including lifting the ban on female drivers and opening up public entertainment centres such as cinemas and theatres to both sexes. These domestic social changes were coupled with economic reforms and a shift from an oil-based economy to a production- and manufacturing-based sector. The sweeping reforms introduced by bin Salman were aimed at reducing corruption and unemployment in the Kingdom. In order to enable Saudi Arabian nationals to participate in the economy, it was expected that the number of expatriates would be reduced. In 2017 Saudi Arabia hosted around 11 million foreign workers in the Kingdom.[51] The new measures will impact both Pakistani and Indian migrant labour working in the Kingdom. The question is, will these major domestic reforms impact the economic dimension of Pakistan-Saudi Arabia relations? Will Saudi Arabia shift towards India as a more reliable economic partner? In recent years, Indo-Saudi Arabian relations have drastically improved. Saudi Arabia is India's third largest trading partner and the Kingdom remains its main supplier of crude oil. In addition, there are about 3.2 million Indian workers in Saudi Arabia. How will the warming of Indo-Saudi Arabian ties impact the Kingdom's relationship with Pakistan? One of the biggest hurdles for the improvement of Indo-Saudi Arabian relations is New Delhi's historic and strategic ties with Tehran. India has invested heavily in Iran's Chabahar Port and gasfields. Iran, on the other hand, is expanding and enhancing its economic links with India by pursuing a gas and oil pipeline through the deep waters in the sea of Oman and the Indian Ocean.[52] Hence, a shift in India-Iran ties is not expected, and in fact New Delhi appears to be ignoring the Trump Administration's warnings with regards to Iranian sanctions and moving forward with its investments in Iran.

Given the balance of forces in the region, the alliance between Pakistan and Saudi Arabia will continue at least for the foreseeable future, and will embrace a formal approach, which until now has remained on a personal basis. This chapter has offered a historically grounded analysis of the unique alliance between Pakistan and Saudi Arabia. The strength of this alliance was contingent and determined by common defence and economic interests born out of the regional security context that took shape between 1960 and 2018. While the Pakistan-China alliance has the common foe factor that keeps the alliance consistent and moving forward, the Pakistan-Saudi Arabia alliance lacks the common enemy factor. This makes the alliance unique and interesting to follow, as transactional and strategic relations are subject to change. What is remarkable about this relationship is that each country has sought to persuade the other that its enemies should become their common enemies. Over time, both states have indeed stood firmly together when their interests have converged. Foreign policy, as Henry Kissinger argued, is 'the art of establishing priorities',[53] and when the priorities of the allies are aligned an equilibrium is attained in an alliance. As Kissinger surmised, the test of an alliance is not about absolute satisfaction but a balanced dissatisfaction. After five decades of partnership, Pakistan and Saudi Arabia have attained an equilibrium that is maintained by their aligned interests and religious homogeneity, as well as their balanced dissatisfactions.

Going back to Lord Palmerston's statement that states have no permanent friends or permanent enemies, only permanent interests that might cause a state to align with a particular country at some times and against it at others, this chapter ends with a question based on Palmerston's statement: can Pakistan and Saudi Arabia prove to be permanent friends in times when the states' interests are shifting? The US President Lyndon Johnson quoted Lord Palmerston at a formal state dinner when he said, 'with due respect to that illustrious British statesman [Palmerston] I must disagree. For Americans, Britain is a permanent friend, and the unbreakable link between our two nations is our permanent interest.'[54] In the case of Pakistan and Saudi Arabia, this chapter holds that only time will tell, but for the foreseeable future the alliance between the heartland of Sunni Islam and the only Muslim nuclear power remains strong.

Notes

1 Arif Rafiq, 'The Dangerous, Delicate Saudi-Pakistan Alliance', *Foreign Policy*, 1 April 2015. Available at http://foreignpolicy.com/2015/04/01/the-dangerous-delicate-saudi-pakistan-alliance-yemen-iran/.

2 Richard Haass, *Foreign Policy Begins at Home: The Case of Putting America's House in Order*, New York, Basic Books, 2013, p. 80.
3 Aftab Alam *et al.*, 'An Economic Analysis of Pak-Saudi Trade Relations between 2000 and 2011', *American Journal of Research and Communication*, 2013, pp. 210.
4 See www.pewglobal.org/2013/10/17/saudi-arabias-image-falters-among-middle-east-neighbors/.
5 Samuel Martin Burke and Lawrence Ziring, *Pakistan's Foreign Policy: An Historical Analysis*, New York, Oxford University Press, 1990.
6 Burke, *Pakistan's Foreign Policy*, p. 204.
7 Ibid., p. 205.
8 Ibid.
9 John K. Cooley, 'Saudi Arabian Diplomacy Scores: Complicated Politics', *Christian Science Monitor*, 22 December 1965.
10 Amin, p. 133.
11 Ibid.
12 United States Department of State, *Secretary's Morning Summary for 7/10/99 Current Intelligence: 1, Saudi Arabia, Concern for Pakistan*, 1999.
13 Ibid.
14 Ibid.
15 http://journals.sagepub.com/doi/pdf/10.1177/2347798916632325.
16 Glenn H. Snyder, 'Alliance Theory: A Neorealist First Cut', *Journal of International Affairs*, vol. 44, no. 1, 1990, pp. 106.
17 Ibid., pp. 105–06.
18 Stanley Reed, 'An Oil Giant Is Taking Big Steps: Saudi Arabia Can't Afford for It to Slip', *New York Times*, 16 June 2018. Available at www.nytimes.com/2018/06/16/business/energy-environment/saudi-arabia-aramco.html.
19 Government of Pakistan, *Economic Survey of Pakistan, 2015–16*, 2016.
20 'Saudi-Pakistan Joint Ministerial Commission Meets', *Arab News*, 16 January 2018. Available at www.arabnews.com/node/1227131/world.
21 'Preferential Trade Deal with Saudi Arabia', *Dawn*, 16 January 2018. Available at www.dawn.com/news/1382883.
22 Ibid.
23 Author's interview with a senior diplomat in Pakistan.
24 Author's interview with senior military official.
25 Shahid Amin, pp. 133.
26 Interview with a senior military official.
27 Foreign Broadcast Information Service Daily Reports (FBIS) Document Type Government Document 14 September 1950. Published in *Daily Report*. Foreign Radio Broadcasts, FBIS-FRB-50–179.
28 Abdullah Sindi, 'King Faisal and Pan-Islamism', in Willard A. Beling (ed.) *King Faisal and the Modernization of Saudi Arabia*, London, Croom Helm, 1980, pp. 185.
29 Bruce Reidel, 'Saudi Arabia: Nervously Watching Pakistan', Washington , DC, Brookings Institution, 28 January 2008.
30 William Beecher, 'Talks Held on Use of Pakistan Units', *Boston Globe*, 25 September 1981, pp. 1.
31 Interview with a Pakistani diplomat.
32 'The Ahmedis of Pakistan', *Daily Times*, 15 September 2014.
33 Naveed Ahmad, 'Pakistan-Saudi Relations', *Pakistan Horizon* vol. 35, no. 4, 1982, pp. 51–67.
34 R. Azer, 'Arab Friendship', *Times of India*, 12 November 1965.
35 'Saudi Arabian Loan to Pindi', *Times of India*, 24 October, 1965.
36 'Purchase of Arms', *Times of India*, 11 May 1966.
37 'Pakistan to Get Loan', *Washington Post*, 20 April 1966.
38 'President Ayub, Faysal Begin Formal Talks', Karachi Domestic Service, FBIS-FRB-66–077, 20 April 1966.
39 S. Bhat, 'UAR Disappointed by Pakistan's Stand', *Times of India*, 22 April 1966.
40 Mujtaba Razvi, *Pak-Saudi Arabian Relations: An Example of Entente Cordiale*, pp. 84.
41 Krishan Gopal and Kokila Krishan Gopal, *West Asia and North Africa*, vol. 1, Publications, New Delhi, 1981, pp. 394

42 'Saudi Role in Kargil Endgame', *The Hindu*, 9 July 1999.
43 'The Hindu Editorial: Pakistan's Isolation', *The Hindu*, 23 June 1999.
44 Pakistan: Premier Holds Talks with Saudi Crown Prince', *BBC Monitoring South Asia – Political*, 19 July 1999.
45 Bruce Riedel, 'American Diplomacy and the 1999 Kargil Summit at Blair House', Policy Paper Series 1, 2002, pp. 10–14.
46 https://oilprice.com/Energy/Crude-Oil/Iran-Looks-To-Ramp-Up-Production.html.
47 Mohammad Mukashaf, 'Pakistan Declines Saudi Call for Armed Support in Yemen Fight', Reuters, 10 April 2015. Available at www.reuters.com/article/us-yemen-security-idUSKBN0N10LO20150410.
48 www.bbc.com/news/world-asia-32246547.
49 National Assembly of Pakistan, Resolution, 8 June 2017. Available at http://na.gov.pk/en/resolution_detail.php?id=296.
50 Quoted in Hal Brands and Peter Feaver, 'What are America's Alliances Good For? *Parameters*, vol. 47, no. 2, 2017.
51 'Saudi Arabia has 11 Million Foreign Workers from More than 100 Countries', *Arab News*, 1 December 2017. Available at www.arabnews.com/node/1201861/saudi-arabia.
52 I was informed about the pipeline project in an interview with an Iranian serving diplomat. 'Oman, Iran, India Discuss Gas Pipeline at Trilateral Meeting in New York', *Times of Oman*, 24 September 2017. Available at http://timesofoman.com/article/117889.
53 Henry Kissinger, *Diplomacy*, New York, Simon and Schuster, 1994.
54 John T. Woolley and Gerhard Peters, 'The American Presidency Project', University of California, Santa Barbara, 2008. Available at www.presidency.ucsb.edu/ws/?pid=27747.

12

Adversarial peace

India–Pakistan nuclear rivalry

Farah Jan

Introduction

The partition of British India in 1947 gave birth to one of the longest and most enduring rivalries in South Asia. The India–Pakistan rivalry has dominated regional politics for the last 70 years, resulting in four wars, multiple crises, and an arms race that nuclearized South Asia. As a result of the rivalry with India, Pakistan's foreign policy from the very beginning has been shaped and guided by the threat from India. Furthermore, India's conventional superiority along with the loss of East Pakistan in 1971 played a major role in Pakistan's decision to acquire nuclear weapons. On 28 and 30 May 1998 Pakistan tested six nuclear devices in the mountains of Balochistan, thereby officially becoming a nuclear weapons state.

This chapter takes the rivalry approach to unravel the factors and events that led to Pakistan's decision to acquire the nuclear bomb, and scrutinizes the impact of nuclear weapons on the India–Pakistan rivalry. The scholarship on nuclear weapons and their implications has argued that nuclear weapons have altered statecraft from war-fighting to a war deterrence strategy.[1] As one of the early nuclear security scholars, Bernard Brodie, cautioned, 'in the nuclear age the aim of states is not to win wars, but to be able to deter wars'.[2] Other scholars hold the same line of rationality and contend that 'when you introduce nuclear weapons in a dyadic interaction the outcome is the elimination of total war between nuclear rivals'.[3] This chapter supports the argument that nuclear weapons have acted as a stabilizer in South Asia.[4] Furthermore, McGeorge Bundy's concept of existential deterrence is an apt description of the India–Pakistan rivalry, which suggests that nuclear weapons deter aggression based on the fact that they exist, and not because of strategic theories, or for that matter, international commitments.[5] Nuclear weapons have intensified the mutual vulnerability dilemma, whereby both states have the capability of destroying what the other values, marked by heightened threat perception and distrust on both sides. In the case of Pakistan and India, the mutual vulnerability dilemma can best be understood by the two scorpions metaphor: each can kill the other but in doing so the killer guarantees his own death. This raises the question: did the addition of nuclear weapons change the India–Pakistan rivalry? What impact did nuclear weapons have on the Kashmir issue that is crucial for both states? One way to address the first question is to compare the scale and occurrence of conflict between the two rivals. Both states have been able to prevent the use of outright military force, but neither has been successful in compelling the other to do what they want them to do. As Thomas Schelling pointed out, 'compellance is harder to achieve and certainly more dangerous'.[6] To answer the second question: Kashmir is of intrinsic value to both states, and thus as predicted by the nuclear revolution theory, the consequence of war is worse than maintaining the status quo, therefore the status quo is preserved.

This chapter proceeds with a detailed history of the India-Pakistan rivalry, highlighting the events and factors that have shaped this rivalry. The chapter then examines the role of nuclear weapons on that rivalry and the Kashmir conflict. For Pakistan, nuclear weapons are the ultimate equalizer against India. Over the past 70 years the relationship between India and Pakistan has been unceasingly conflictual, and a nuclear deterrence is a way of denying India future victory in a large-scale war. That said, nuclear weapons have preserved the status quo in Kashmir, which works in India's favour as a non-military victory, but at the same time Pakistan's nuclear programme has prevented India from achieving its goal of becoming a regional hegemon.

History of the rivalry

The first question that arises when analysing any rivalry is: what is the starting point of the rivalry? And, what were the factors responsible for these adversarial relations? In the case of Pakistan and India, the rivalry started before the birth of the two nations. The independence of Pakistan and India was supposed to be a jubilant celebration marking the end of the 200-year British rule, but instead it was stained by communal riots on both sides of the border, turning it into a bloodbath. Hostilities existed before the birth of the two nations. British India was polarized, before Partition, insofar as the Congress and the Muslim League could not agree on any agenda. The country was on the verge of a civil war, and violence erupted before the assigned date of independence. As British General Sir Frank Messervy observed, 'having served for 34 years ... I would never have believed that agitation could have aroused the normally chivalrous and decent Punjabi ... to such frenzied savagery as was widely prevalent'.[7] The two countries harboured deep animosity and hostility towards each other, and following the partition of India this erupted into violence when caravans and trains were attacked on both sides.

The massive exodus of people that followed independence in August 1947, moving in both directions, was completed within a year. It is estimated that around 7.226 million Muslims migrated from India to East and West Pakistan, and about 7.249 million Hindus and Sikhs moved from Pakistan to India.[8] To resettle seven million people can be viewed as a daunting challenge for any state, but as Dilip Hero noted, 'these challenges ... paled before the steep hurdles Jinnah and his government had to surmount at the birth of Pakistan'.[9] Adding to this was the position of some Congress party leaders who passionately believed that 'the division is only of the map of the country and not in the hearts of the people, and [surely] it is going to be a short-lived partition'.[10] Furthermore, the British and the Congress party could not see the viability of Pakistan and believed the Partition to have been a short-term solution to prevent a civil war in India. Thus, Pakistan's initial existential insecurities were rooted in the anti-Pakistan position of Congress leaders and other powerful actors in the region. One of the best examples of other actors questioning the viability of Pakistan resides in China's position towards the newly formed states. China was the first country to appoint an envoy to India with the rank of ambassador and to exchange diplomatic representatives. However, China hesitated in appointing an ambassador to Pakistan and toyed with the idea that one ambassador should be appointed for both dominions.[11] It was not until one year later in August 1948, on the insistence of the government of Pakistan, that the Chinese government agreed to establish separate diplomatic outposts for the two states and allowed Pakistan to open an embassy in Nangking and a consulate in Kashgar, the part of China that is linked to Pakistan by trade and land border.[12]

In addition to the insecurities concerning whether the state would endure, at independence the government of Pakistan faced a shortage of funds and supplies at the institutional level. Although Pakistan did inherit a major share of the cash crops (cotton and jute), on the industrial front it practically had to start from the beginning. Pakistan's share was around 18.75 per cent of the cash balance of India and at the time of independence the treasury held around 200 million rupees.[13] The supplies that were dispatched from India via train were looted en route from Delhi. Muhammad Ali Jinnah had to use his personal connections to keep the state solvent, but his appeal to the British Commonwealth was dismissed. In one of his missives to British Prime Minister Attlee, Jinnah complained, 'every effort is being made to put difficulties in our way by our enemies to paralyze or cripple our state and bring forth its collapse. It is amazing that top-most Hindu leaders repeatedly say that Pakistan will have to submit to the union of India. Pakistan will never surrender.'[14]

The strained relationship between India and Pakistan kept the two states from improving trade. Prior to Partition the economy in the subcontinent was interdependent in nature, in the sense that Pakistan provided raw materials (cotton and jute) for industry in India. Following Partition, the two states pursued policies of economic autarky, and their rivalry reduced trade and, in turn, decreased economic interdependence. Pakistan's exports to India in 1948–49 accounted for 53.4 per cent of its total exports, but these dropped to 4.7 per cent in 1951.[15] This sharp drop was also the result of poor monetary policy and strategy by the government of Pakistan. The two states signed a bilateral trade agreement in 1951 with the aim of improving trade relations. However, economic relations remained competitive, and the two sides could not reach an agreement on the export of jute from Pakistan and coal from India. Both states imposed a discriminating license fee on their respective exports to each other. The Economist Intelligence Unit's India review noted that 'trade relations between the two countries remain dangerously poised falling just short of open hostilities – in much the same way as do their political relations'.[16]

Political relations between the two remained strained, and on the Indian government's side Dilip Hero noted that some members of Nehru's government 'were determined to strangle the nascent Muslim homeland at birth'.[17] However, Nehru understood the complexity of the ties between the two states, the close border, and the historical and cultural similarities. For Nehru, war was to be avoided at all costs because both sides would lose, as he said, 'we may do a great deal of injury to Pakistan and might defeat it in war. But both countries will in effect be ruined if that extreme step had to be taken'.[18] Nehru's perspective was based on conventional war, but his viewpoint in today's nuclear South Asia is pertinent, as it would be the extreme step that would devastate both states.

The intractable issue of Kashmir

In July 1947 Jinnah held a press conference and hoped that the 'relations between Pakistan and India would be friendly and cordial'. Since the partition of India, relations between the two neighbours have never been 'friendly or cordial'. The division of funds and of the princely states proved to be critical issues that further exacerbated tensions. At the time of Partition India had around 565 princely states under different rulers. Lord Louis Mountbatten had advised them to accede either to Pakistan or India, and the choice was to be determined on geographical position, as well as the predominance of their populations. This accession choice had to be made before the final transfer of power in August 1947, and all but three states – Kashmir, Hyderabad and Junagadh – had delayed their decision.[19] The Muslim-majority states were expected to accede to Pakistan, and the Hindu majority were to join India. However, the choice was also dependent upon the geographical contiguity. The princely state of Jammu and Kashmir was ruled by a Hindu maharaja and had a Muslim-majority population. Junagadh and Hyderabad acceded to Pakistan, and although both were surrounded by India, they were forcefully taken as a part of India. Kashmir, on the other hand, was ruled by a Hindu maharaja and had a predominantly Muslim population; it was also the source of the three rivers that provided water to West Pakistan. Following the partition of India, Maharaja Hari Singh had signed a standstill agreement with Pakistan that allowed supplies to be delivered and extended the existing arrangements until the 'pending settlement of details and formal execution of fresh arrangements'.[20] The Maharaja delayed the accession decision, and at the end of September the Muslim peasants in the southern part of Kashmir revolted. By mid-October had Pakistan stopped all shipments of petrol and supplies to Kashmir.[21] Before any formal arrangements could be made, a group of tribal rebels, around 5,000 armed Pashtuns, crossed the border into the western part of the state to join forces with the Muslims of Kashmir against the Hindu Maharaja. In his panic, the Maharaja signed the accession papers with India and requested military assistance from New Delhi. Thus, in the early hours of 27 October 1947 Indian troops landed in Srinagar to push back the tribals that had infiltrated from Pakistan.[22]

When Jinnah found out about the presence of Indian troops in Srinagar, he ordered General Douglas Gracey who was serving as the acting Commander-in-Chief 'to move two brigades of the Pak army into Kashmir … one from Rawalpindi and another from Sialkot. The Sialkot army was to march to Jammu, take the city and make the Maharaja a prisoner. The Rawalpindi column was to advance to Srinagar and capture the city.'[23] Wolpert notes that General Gracey refused to accept Jinnah's orders and issued orders to stand down that meant the withdrawal of all British officers from the Pakistan army.[24] The question is: had General Gracey carried out Jinnah's orders on the eve of 27 October 1947 and had the army succeeded in capturing the cities, would a rivalry have developed between India and Pakistan, once that has endured since the events of 1947? We will never know the answers to these questions, but we do know how events unfolded following the Kashmir invasion and the multiple wars and crises that ensued between the two states. We also know that the rivalry became nuclear 50 years later.

We must also not negate the importance of Kashmir for India's first Prime Minister, Jawaharlal Nehru, who once said to a British army officer, 'in the same way that Calais was written on Mary's heart, Kashmir is written on mine'.[25] Nehru belonged to the Hindu Pandit population of Kashmir, and the loss of Kashmir to Pakistan was a personal loss to him. Henry Kissinger once opined, 'history … is made by men who cannot always distinguish their emotions from their analysis'. Nehru's decision to send troops in pursuit of the Maharaja as he fled Kashmir was based not on upholding the legality of the accession document but also on preserving a part of his identity and his family heritage and keeping it a part of India.

Crises, conflicts, wars before nuclearization

Conflicts, crises and wars have characterized the relationship between India and Pakistan since the creation of the two states. Communal violence at the time of independence and the deficit of trust that existed before 1947 created an adversarial narrative on both sides from the very beginning, and it remains high and consistent even today. Pakistan and India have fought four wars (1947–48, 1965, 1971 and 1999) and multiple crises and conflicts, and the public perception of each other has remained consistently negative, with mutual suspicions and imputations on both sides. Initially, the rivalry between the two states was based on territorial and resource-based issues, namely the Kashmir dispute and the Indus water basin. The Indus water basin issue was resolved, and the Indus Agreement was signed in 1960 between President Ayub and Prime Minister Nehru on 19 September 1960.[26] The Kashmir issue remains unresolved to the present day and violence on the subcontinent has oscillated, but adversarial relations have been a permanent feature of the subcontinent.

India–Pakistan rivalry in the 1960s

When tracing the trajectory of a rivalry it is crucial to explore the role of decision-makers, domestic politics and regional or system-level factors. In the case of India and Pakistan, there have been moments when the rivalry could have been terminated, yet it has persisted. Feldman notes that Ayub Khan had hoped for 'the possibility of a rapprochement between the two states, but discovered that the prospects were slender and politically undesirable'.[27] The Indo–China war of 1962 resulted in the United States and the United Kingdom providing arms and supplies to India; for Pakistan, this was a setback as it had hoped for a weaker India after the war with China. The Ayub administration was also disappointed on the Western front as India had remained non-aligned, and Pakistan had aligned with the West, and the Soviet Union continued to side with India on the Kashmir issue at the United Nations by employing its veto power at the Security Council.

Indo-Pakistan relations during the 1960s remained consistently adversarial and the sense of hostility remained high on both sides. Pakistan perceived the arms assistance by Western powers to India as a threat to its interest in Kashmir.[28] By April 1965 the two states faced a crisis over a desolate area known as the Rann of Kutch. The border of this area was based on an agreement made many years before Partition.[29] By mid-April both sides blamed the other for employing artillery, and casualties were reported. The crisis ended when India and Pakistan signed a ceasefire agreement on 30 June 1965. The agreement was facilitated by the UK and the dispute was to be settled according to binding arbitration by International Court of Justice (ICJ). The tribunal reached its decision in February 1968 and awarded 10 per cent of the disputed territory to Pakistan that included the area of the fighting.[30] The government of India reluctantly accepted the decision as it claimed sovereignty over the entire Rann of Kutch. Pakistan benefited from the ICJ decision as it was 'awarded the larger portion of the usable land … and much of it has been the principal bone of contention between the two countries in the 1965 conflict'.[31] In the Rann of Kutch crisis Pakistan aimed to calculate India's response. Russell Brines agrees that 'Pakistan's strategy was to use a low-cost conflict to assess India's resolve and to a certain degree her capabilities'.[32] The Rann of Kutch episode emboldened Pakistan to take a more aggressive stance on Kashmir and it thus initiated the war of 1965 by sending armed guerrillas to Indian-controlled Kashmir. This is evident in the communications between the key decision makers in Pakistan. In a letter to Ayub Khan after Kutch, Zulfikar Ali Bhutto pushed for 'a bold and courageous' stance on Kashmir and argued that 'India is not in the position to risk a long unlimited war with Pakistan', while particularly keeping in mind Pakistan's 'relative superiority of the military forces' in terms of its equipment.[33]

The 1965 war

The Rann of Kutch episode was followed by the war of 1965 between India and Pakistan. This was initiated by Pakistan to contain India's military rise and aimed to further internationalize the Kashmir dispute.[34] Following the Kutch conflict, in August 1965 around 7,000 armed and trained guerrillas entered Kashmir to target Indian military installations and incite a rebellion in Kashmir.[35] After failing to stir up a revolt or 'war of liberation', Pakistan escalated the level of aggression in Kashmir 'by throwing in regulars, because they can't cope with Indian retaliation across the cease-fire line'.[36]

The origins of this war can be traced back to both domestic and external factors involving the unresolved issue of Kashmir. External factors can be directly linked to the 1962 Indo–China War and the Western arms assistance to India. The Indo–China war emboldened Pakistan to attempt to resolve the Kashmir issue. The US arms supply to India after the 1962 war had stimulated insecurities within Pakistan, and Rawalpindi viewed this step as strengthening India's military capabilities. Thus, according to Pakistan's calculations, a stronger India would not negotiate on Kashmir. During the Indo–China war of 1962 Pakistan aligned with China. The question is: had Pakistan sided with India, would that have marked the turning point for the rivalry? Instead, Pakistan's decision to side with China set its relationship with China on the course of an all-weather friendship, and its rivalry with India on a perpetual adversarial trajectory.

I argue that 1962 provided a missed opportunity for Pakistan to improve its relationship with India and by continuing to push for a resolution of the Kashmir issue under a bilateral framework. Would India have negotiated with Pakistan at that time? Selig Harrison points to the lost opportunity which is not likely to recur, 'when India showed a fleeting awareness of its stake in friendship with Pakistan following the Chinese border incursions ... however, Pakistan had started on its intensified diplomacy in Peking'.[37] We do not know the answer for that, but Nehru's speech in 1963 certainly highlighted the damage it did to the relationship. As he said, 'in the history of the world you will find very few examples of such deceit and duplicity as Pakistan has shown in siding with China in the dispute between India and China ... Pakistan is mistaken if it thinks that it can intimidate us because we are facing this threat from China'.[38] Pakistan's calculations paid off in the form of Chinese unconditional support for its position on Kashmir, and further agitated India. Before large-scale war broke out in 1965, President Ayub visited China for an eight-day state visit, and during it the emphasis was on the peaceful aspirations of China in its friendship with Pakistan. A crucial accomplishment of the trip was Peking's support for a plebiscite in Kashmir. In a joint communiqué, the Chinese Minister of Foreign Affairs, Marshal Che'en Yi, 'made the first of several equivocal statements implying Chinese military support for Pakistan without pledging it. The evident purpose was to intimidate India'.[39]

Starting in 1963, 'the Indian government adopted certain policy measures to fully integrate Kashmir, the Home Minister and Prime Minister Nehru announced that Kashmir's special status has gradually eroded and it is now a fully integrated part of India'.[40]

These policy directives further aggravated relations between the two states, and Pakistan raised the issue of the violation of the UN Security Council resolutions. India responded that the UN resolution was based on the condition of Pakistan withdrawing fully from Kashmir and that this condition had not been met. Thus, India was not bound by the 1948–49 UN resolutions.[41] This was also the period when Nehru died unexpectedly and with his death any hope of rapprochement between the two countries disappeared as well. Selig Harrison argued that

> the Kashmir settlement envisaged by Nehru presupposed a larger Indo-Pakistan accommodation based on confederal relations between the two countries. This was rejected by Ayub out of fear that even a limited confederation with adequate safeguards would imply separate status for east Pakistan.[42]

Both newly independent states were concerned about separatist movements.

The war ended on 23 September 1965 after a military standstill and intense pressure from the international community. In the aftermath of the war both states rushed to expand and maintain their territorial holdings and military positions.[43] Russell Brines notes that

> Pakistan was compelled by the military situation to accept India's insistence upon restoring the status quo ante, with only minimum face-saving provisions in the UN resolution for some future consideration of the problems for which the country had embarked on war ... Pakistan had lost the conflict.[44]

The 1965 war could not achieve what President Ayub had hoped to archive, namely a final solution on Kashmir. Instead, Pakistan realized that India would respond with full force when it came to Kashmir.

The Soviets played a crucial role in the ceasefire and called for the convening of the Tashkent conference in January 1966 to settle the outstanding disputes between India and Pakistan. Both sides had publicly maintained rigid positions. From the beginning of the Indo–Pakistan conflict, the Soviets adopted a policy of neutrality. Premier Alexei Kosygin told Lal Bahadur Shastri to 'avoid any actions that would lead to major conflict with Pakistan'.[45] During the 1965 war the Soviets avoided taking sides and continuously pushed for a resolution on Kashmir. This was a drastic change from the 1955 Soviet position, when Nikita Khrushchev stated 'Kashmir is an integral part of India'.[46] The Russians carefully measured their steps by publicly calling for peace, avoiding the UN veto and refusing to join the Americans in the arms embargo. The cautious strategic line adopted by Moscow was to prevent an adverse reaction from India and gain Pakistan's confidence.

At the Tashkent conference, India maintained its position that Kashmir was not to be discussed at all but later softened up. Shastri initially insisted on not negotiating on Kashmir. However, in the end the Indian Prime Minister made concessions both by giving up outposts like those at Haji Pir and Tithwal and abandoning the demand that Pakistan should acknowledge its responsibility for being the aggressive party and sending infiltrators to Kashmir.[47] Shastri also agreed to withdraw Indian troops from Azad Kashmir, and in return Pakistan agreed to withdraw from territory it held on the Indian side. Ayub, on the other hand, pushed for a political settlement on Kashmir. Brines notes that 'India's hope from the meeting was to clean up the aftermath of the war, by agreeing on matter as withdrawal of forces, without touching the central problem. Pakistan's purpose was the unchanged desire to keep the Kashmir question alive.' In the end the two sides agreed and the Tashkent Declaration read as follows:

> both sides will exert all efforts to create good neighbourly relations ... not to have recourse to force and to settle their disputes through peaceful means ... considered that the interest of peace in their region [is in] the interests of the peoples of India and Pakistan were not served by the continuance of tensions between the two countries. It was against this background that Jammu and Kashmir was discussed, and each of the sides set forth its respective position.[48]

The United States was convinced that a lasting political solution could only be achieved between the disputant parties themselves and adopted that policy. At the outbreak of the war President Johnson urged both India and Pakistan to call for a ceasefire. When Johnson's call to peace produced no results, he was sufficiently upset to order Rusk to halt military aid to both countries. The Johnson Administration warned both sides about the continuation of hostilities and played the China card for both Pakistan and India. Pakistan was alerted not to invite the Chinese into this conflict and that if they did it would impact future military or economic aid to the country. India was told to consider restraint because of what would happen if China came to Pakistan's defence. The United States told India, 'Continuation of the conflict is likely to plunge India more deeply into the cross currents of the Cold War and internal Communist bloc conflicts ... [the] Chinese ... will be certain winners. It is difficult to see how either India or Pakistan could benefit regardless of the outcome'. And if the call for a ceasefire and troop withdrawal is ignored that can lead to 'sheer disaster'.[49]

India came out of the 1965 war confident and determined to keep Kashmir. Pakistan demonstrated heightened patriotic zeal, and Ayub Khan's government claimed that it had won the war, despite not gaining Kashmir or finding a solution for Kashmir. However, the lessons that both sides learnt from the war were the lack of reliance on the great powers in the region. Yet both states failed to improve their relationship with each other, and continued with their rivalry that would turn nuclear in the decades to come. The 1965 war also pushed Pakistan closer to China and away from the United States due to the arms embargo. Pakistan felt betrayed by the United States for not supporting it in its position on Kashmir. China not only assisted Pakistan militarily, but also provided a countervailing threat to India. China's support for Pakistan further cemented the regional rivalries. The 1965 war left Pakistan's President Ayub Khan weak and deeply unpopular. He handed over power to another military dictator General Yahya Khan on 25 March 1969.

The 1970s and India–Pakistan rivalry

The internal political crisis of the previous decade continued into the 1970s. East Pakistan transformed into Bangladesh, and Pakistan and India were once again at war on December 1971. The crisis ensued after the December 1970 elections where the East Pakistan leader Sheikh Mujibur Rahman had won by a landslide. Zulfiqar Ali Bhutto, who had succeeded in West Pakistan, did not accept the results and persuaded Gen. Yahya Khan to hold the transfer of power. By March 1971 Sheikh Mujibur had assumed de facto power in East Pakistan. In response, the West Pakistani army moved into East Pakistan and started killing civilians indiscriminately. As a result, a large number of people began to pour into India. On 3 December 1971 Indian troops entered East Pakistan, and after a short war with India, the Pakistan army surrendered. On 20 December Gen. Yahya Khan resigned, and Zulfiqar Ali Bhutto was sworn in as President while Sheikh Mujibur Rahman became the leader of Bangladesh.

After the defeat in the 1971 war, President Bhutto and Prime Minister Indira Gandhi met in Simla for peace talks in July 1972. During the Simla talks Bhutto told Gandhi that 'his political enemies at home ... would denounce him for surrendering what many in Pakistan considered their vital interest'.[50] Bhutto agreed to the following points: the Kashmir issue should be resolved; the Line of Control (LoC) could be converted into a *de jure* border between India and Pakistan; and the release of Pakistani prisoners of war. According to P. N. Dhar, Gandhi asked Bhutto, 'Is this the understanding on which we proceed?' He replied: 'Absolutely, *Aap mujh par bharosa keejiye* (trust me).' At his specific request there is no written record of these agreements between Bhutto and Indira Gandhi. But Gandhi was sufficiently convinced, not so much because of Bhutto's sincerity but because of his compulsions and limitations, to go ahead with the Simla Agreement. It was signed late at night on 2 July 1972.[51]

The 1971 war and the dismemberment of Pakistan had a lasting impact on regional diplomacy and security. India's insecurities with regard to the stance taken by the United States, the Soviet Union and China during the 1965 war were further confirmed. By 1974 had India tested its first nuclear bomb, and by the end of the decade the country had doubled its naval capacity. Following the 1971 war and the Simla talks, Pakistan's internal crises and the critical decision to draft and adopt a constitution had kept Bhutto occupied. During this period a small group of military officers had conspired to seize power, and their conspiracy was crushed before it could take place. Ironically, it was General Zia ul-Haq who oversaw the trial of the conspiring officers. It would be Gen. Zia who would once again intervene in 1977 and impose martial law and remove Bhutto.

Following Bhutto's removal in 1977, Gen. Zia stayed in power for almost 11 years. Zia remains the longest serving head of state in Pakistan. He owed his survival in power to a combination of factors: his ruthlessness and political astuteness; the shift in focus from India to Afghanistan after the Russian invasion; the easing of economic pressures due to remittances from the Middle East, and most importantly Western aid and its massive arms package. By September 1981 the United States had assured Zia of a US $3.2 billion arms and aid package, despite American concern over Pakistan's nuclear intentions. By 1982 peace talks had once again resumed on a no-war pact, and an agreement was reached on the establishment of joint commissions to consider questions of trade, cultural and economic cooperation.[52]

President Zia faced tremendous domestic pressure, and the campaign for the restoration of democracy gained momentum, with increased incidences of violence. By November 1984 both countries were once again holding a series of military exercises near the border that violated the ceasefire line in Kashmir. Tensions continued near the Kashmir border over the Siachen Glacier. This was the second major border clash, and it took place on the world's highest battlefield. The conflict over Siachen had its roots in the UN-supervised Karachi agreement of 1949, when the states parties agreed to extend the ceasefire line north of the map grid. Due to the assumption that human habitation was not feasible there, this large stretch between the Chinese border and the LoC and was thus left undemarcated.[53] On 13 April 1984 India launched Operation Meghdoot, prompting Pakistan to deploy troops as well. Both armies were unable to advance their positions and maintain a military presence in that region.[54]

By the end of 1985 the relationship with India remained delicate and adversarial. On the nuclear issue, India rejected the possibility of signing the non-proliferation treaty and refused international inspections of nuclear facilities or the establishment of a nuclear-free zone in South Asia. When Zia and Rajiv Gandhi met at the UN in 1985, India rejected Zia's proposal of technical-level meetings between experts.[55] However, the shift was on the United States' side. The United States once again tilted towards India, despite India's nuclear plans. This set provoked a sense of insecurity in Pakistan, which was afraid of a pre-emptive Indian strike on its nuclear facilities at Kahuta.

From 1984 to 1986 Pakistan's insecurity was heightened as it continuously perceived an attack on its nuclear facilities. Pakistan strongly believed, based on intelligence reports from Canada and Europe, that Israel along with India was planning an attack on Kahuta.[56] The Soviet forces in Afghanistan and the hawkish and aggressive posture adopted by Indian Prime Minister Gandhi further added to Pakistan's insecurities. Pakistani officials approached the United States, and Washington confirmed that Israel was not planning an attack on Pakistan, but concluded that war between India and Pakistan was possible, based on India's military posture; the position of her fighter bombers; as well as the Indian-Soviet connection of a joint attack on Pakistan.[57] Operation Brasstacks, the code-name given to an Indian military exercise carried out by the Indian defence forces in November 1986, was set in motion by Pakistan's fear of the imminence of an attack on its nuclear facilities.

Brasstacks was planned as a series of large-scale military readiness exercises by the Indian Army Chief Sundarji supported by the young Prime Minister Rajiv Gandhi. Pakistan assessed that a quarter of million Indian troops and 1,300 tanks and about quarter of a billion dollars were spent on the Brasstacks exercises. The political context of Brasstacks, according to a civilian strategic analyst Ravi Rikhye, was to lure Pakistan into a first move via deception and thus unleash a massive attack in response. The analysis of Chari *et al.* agrees with Rikhye's analysis and notes that, 'conversations with key Indian participants tend to support this interpretation of Brasstacks'.[58] The Brasstacks crisis ended when Indian and Pakistani officials agreed to hold talks in January 1987. On 26 January Pakistan's Minister of Foreign Affairs Abdul Sattar met with his Indian counterpart and began negotiations to de-escalate the tensions between the two rivals. Many questions surfaced after the crisis ended, starting from the nuclear dimension. In an interview with Indian journalist Kuldip Nayar, the central figure in Pakistan's nuclear programme, Dr Abdul Qadeer Khan, hinted at the weaponization of Pakistan's nuclear programme. The question remains: did this nuclear activity signal the peak of a crisis? After the interview, General Sundarji, the architect of Brasstacks, remarked that this was India's last chance to defeat Pakistan through the use of conventional arms, as nuclear weapons would make an all-out war impossible and extremely dangerous. Up until December 1986 US assessment of Brasstacks was that it consisted of military exercises, but should it go beyond those, Washington's concerns would be raised. Its assessment noted that, if India were to advance across the international border, there would be little warning and Pakistan would not last more than a month. US officials believed that Rajiv Gandhi was facing domestic pressure and that his aim was to demonstrate anger towards Pakistan for their support of the Sikh and Kashmiri separatist elements.

The India–Pakistan rivalry in the 1980s was a roller coaster of the wars that never happened or the crises that had the potential to result in large-scale war. Leaders in both the countries were engaged in domestic political struggles and the cardinal sin on either side was to appear weak with regard to each other.

Crises in the shadow of the bomb

On 11 and 13 May 1998 tensions between India and Pakistan escalated drastically when India conducted a series of five nuclear tests, with Pakistan following on 28 and 30 May with six tests of its own, thereby officially transforming the India–Pakistan rivalry into a nuclear rivalry. During the 1990s Pakistan was engulfed in political turmoil, with a new prime minister taking office every few years. Pakistan's economy suffered and its annual rate of growth declined to just 1 per cent between 1990–1998. In July 1998 this instability resulted in the total collapse of the Karachi stock exchange, which lost more than 60 per cent of its value in one year.[59] The nuclear tests further aggravated the economic outlook of Pakistan, as the United States imposed sanctions after May 1998.

Relations between India and Pakistan remained delicate and the Kashmir issue was as passionate as ever. With the collapse of the Soviet Union and Afghanistan swallowed up in a civil war, Pakistan and India once again could focus on their rivalry and the unresolved issue of Kashmir was at the forefront. From 1947 to 1971 India and Pakistan had fought three wars and two out of the three were on Kashmir with a non-nuclear dimension. The Kargil conflict was the first crisis they faced as nuclear weapons states. Although Kargil was a small-scale war, its importance and significance was due to the fear of a higher level of violence and the potential of a nuclear exchange between the two rivals.

The Kargil crisis started when both relations between the two countries were improving diplomatically, and came at the heel of India's Prime Minister Vajpayee's bus diplomacy tour that took him to Lahore in February 1999, where he and his counterpart Nawaz Sharif signed the Lahore Declaration. The Declaration stated that India fully acknowledged the existence of Pakistan and means it no harm and the two countries would forge a new bilateral relationship based on atomic peace in the subcontinent.[60] Visa restrictions between the two states were also eased.[61]

In October 1998 India claimed that Pakistan had carried out attacks on the Siachen area. The clashes continued till May 1999. By the end of May 1999 India had deployed a large number of ground troops and had started using its air force to evict the intruders on its Siachen posts. During the Kargil crisis diplomacy initially proved ineffective, but later a diplomatic hotline was established between Nawaz Sharif and Vajpayee to reduce tensions. The Kargil crisis is significant due to its nuclear dimension. Pakistan's foreign secretary issued a nuclear warning when he said, 'Pakistan would not hesitate to use any weapon in our arsenal to defend out territorial integrity'. In response India placed its nuclear weapons on 'readiness state 3' level – in other words, its assembled warheads were prepared to be loaded onto the delivery vehicle.[62] However, it is important to highlight India's restraint in not expanding the conflict to other parts of the region. The Indian air force was given strict orders to avoid targets in Pakistani-administered Kashmir. Pakistan's air force avoided escalating an already dangerous situation. Thus, nuclear deterrence prevented the crisis from escalating or spreading.

After Kargil, the LoC was deemed to be the international border between the two states. The Kargil episode was a major miscalculation on the part of Pakistan; however, the question remains: was it a step to assess India's resolve on a territory that was not necessarily of intrinsic value (like the Rann of Kutch episode of 1965 before the war)? Did nuclear status embolden Pakistan to test India in Kargil first and later in Kashmir? The answer can be found in the steps that followed. Since India demonstrated its resolve on Kargil, Pakistan avoided a push on Kashmir. Or perhaps India was concerned that if it did not act on Kargil, then Pakistan would try to wrestle Kashmir from India based on its emboldened position due to its possession of nuclear weapons. At 15,000 ft Siachen Glacier is extremely remote and inhospitable, but it is of great strategic importance owing to the access it affords to the Karakorum mountain ranges. For India, the lessons learnt from the Rann of Kutch episode was that if India failed to show resolve, Pakistan would take a more hawkish position the second time around, as it did in the 1965 war. In the case of Kargil, both states demonstrated restraint. Nevertheless, India went one step further and demonstrated both resolve and restraint. Pakistan and India were aware that a 'crisis can lead to limited uses of force which in turn, through a variety of mechanisms, could produce an all-out war. Even if neither side initially wanted this result, there is a significant, although impossible to quantify, possibility of quick and deadly escalation'.[63]

Cold start or hot air?

In April 2004 India's Chief of Army Staff introduced and adopted the 'Cold Start' doctrine, which gives India the ability to 'shift from defensive to offensive operations at the very outset of a conflict, relying on the element of surprise and not giving Pakistan any time to bring diplomatic leverages into play vis-à-vis India'.[64] Although the operational details of Cold Start remain classified, its main objective is to 'leverage India's modest superiority in conventional forces to respond to Pakistan's continued provocation'. The offensive elements of Cold Start involve a swift and decisive attack on Pakistan, as one analyst have argued, 'to bring about a favorable war termination, a favorite scenario being to cut Pakistan into two at its midriff'.[65] Pakistan responded to India's Cold Start doctrine by stating that 'proponents of conventional application of military forces, in a nuclear overhang, are chartering an adventurous and dangerous path, the consequences of which could be both unintended and uncontrollable'.[66]

It is true that geographically Pakistan lacks strategic depth, but as Walter Ladwig notes, 'even a small incursion employing the Cold Start could pressure Pakistan to escalate the conflict'.[67] India's Cold Start doctrine fails to pay proper attention to the notion of existential deterrence, which holds that

> the mere existence of nuclear forces means that whatever we say or do, there is a certain irreducible risk that an armed conflict might escalate into a nuclear war. The fear of escalation is thus factored in political calculations: faced with this risk, states are more cautious and more prudent than they would otherwise be.[68]

Additionally, the Cold Start doctrine disregards the threat of unintentional escalation that could lead to the failure of restraint and thus a nuclear catastrophe. During the Kargil crisis Bruce Riedel reported that the Pakistani political leadership was unaware that the army had begun to activate plans for a nuclear strike. Similarly, on the Indian side, during Operation Parakram, a rogue commander ordered troops to advance into assault position near the LoC without approval from the authorities.[69] These are just a few examples of how unintentional escalation can bring about a nuclear catastrophe. The evidence from Kargil to Mumbai, the bombing in 2007 of the Samjhauta Express, heavy exchanges on the border, and surgical strikes suggests that nuclear weapons have kept the two rivals from escalating any crisis.

Pakistan's quest for nuclear weapons is directly linked to its rivalry with India and the need to protect its sovereignty, and indirectly due to the lack of trust in great powers. As

President Ayub noted, 'from the day of independence Pakistan was involved in a bitter and prolonged struggle for her very existence and survival. The cause of our major problem is India's inability to reconcile herself to our existence as a sovereign independent State'.[70] The history of the rivalry presented in this chapter suggests that for Pakistan nuclear weapons are the ultimate equalizer against India. The relationship between India and Pakistan over the past 70 years has consistently been one of conflictual coexistence, and for the Pakistani side it was the nuclear deterrent that would deny future victories in wars between them. Leaders on both sides have stayed away from major concessions at the risk of appearing weak. In the case of Pakistan, as George Perkovich noted, the decision makers had hoped that 'nuclear weapons would rebuild Pakistan's strength, heal its wounds, buttress its pride, and ensure better results in a future war'.[71] Kargil, and the events that followed, proved otherwise, but nuclear weapons have helped to keep the peace in the region in the sense that the two states have avoided large-scale war. However, nuclear weapons proved to be inadequate with regards to solving the Kashmir conflict; instead, the preservation of the status quo has been a beneficial outcome for India.

Conclusion

On 15 August 1947 Prime Minister Jawaharlal Nehru delivered the stirring speech on India's independence from the British. In it he said, 'Long years ago we made a tryst with destiny, and now the time comes when we shall redeem our pledge … At the stroke of midnight hour … India will awake to life and freedom'.[72] The tryst with destiny that Nehru romanticized in his speech resulted in a splintered subcontinent and a region that since independence has witnessed wars in 1947, 1965, 1971, and a limited war in 1998 under the nuclear umbrella. The issue of Kashmir remains the unresolved element of the partition that continues to haunt both sides of the border, and now under the shadow of nuclear weapons.

This chapter offered a historically grounded analysis to understand the factors and events that have shaped the India–Pakistan rivalry and the impact of nuclear weapons on this adversarial relationship. In all crises, conflicts and wars between India and Pakistan, external and internal factors have had an impact on the rivalry. This chapter argued that nuclear weapons have played a role in the India–Pakistan rivalry. Nuclear weapons have made an all-out war difficult if not impossible. Furthermore, their close geographical proximity makes it irrational for either state to use nuclear weapons, or as John Mueller would say, expect to profit from it.[73] Unimaginable devastation would unfold if an all-out war were to break out between Pakistan and India, and neither state can emerge victorious. The outcome of nuclear weapons in a strategic rivalry is always the absence of large-scale war and thus results in an adversarial peace.

After independence, Prime Minister Nehru raised the question, 'can newborn nations escape the cycle of wars which plagued old nations?' The answer is simple. New nations, like old nations, have similar conflicts over territory, resources and influence, along with the role of great powers in the region. New nations have competing power structures, just like old nations, and leaders in new nations must answer to their populace like they did in old nations. Why must they escape the cycle of wars? Since independence India and Pakistan have been embroiled in a rivalry based on unresolved issues engendered by Partition. Kashmir remains the principal cause of the rivalry, along with Pakistan's existential fear of India and its aspirations of parity with India. However, it seems reasonable to assume that nuclear peace in South Asia will prevail as long as India and Pakistan continue to possess their nuclear arsenals. I will conclude this chapter on a line from Jinnah's speech on 14 August 1979 to the Constituent Assembly of Pakistan:

> the whole world is wondering at this unprecedented cyclonic revolution which has brought about the plan of creating and establishing two independent Sovereign Dominions in this sub-continent. As it is, it has been unprecedented; there is no parallel in the history of the world. This mighty sub-continent with all kinds of inhabitants has been brought under a plan which is titanic, unknown, unparalleled. And what is very important with regard to it is that we have achieved it peacefully and by means of an evolution of the greatest possible character.

Notes

1 Robert Jervis, *The Meaning of the Nuclear Revolution: Statecraft and the Prospect of Armageddon*, Ithaca, NY, Cornell University Press, 1989.
2 Bernard Brodie, *War and Politics*, New York, Macmillan, 1973.
3 Kenneth Neal Waltz, *Man, the State, and War: A Theoretical Analysis*, New York City, Columbia University Press, 2001, p. 232.
4 The broader literature on nuclear weapons is characterized by the debate between nuclear optimists and pessimists. The optimists (Waltz and Ganguly) argue that nuclear weapons are stabilizing because of the mutual vulnerability dilemma. The pessimists (Sagan and Kapur) have noted that nuclear weapons are destabilizing as anything can go wrong from accidents to mistakes and rouge leaders.
5 Bundy McGeorge, 'Existential Deterrence and Its Consequences', in Douglas Maclean (ed.) *The Security Gamble: Deterrence Dilemmas in the Nuclear Age*, Totowa, NJ, Rowman and Allanheld, 1984, pp. 3–13.
6 Thomas C. Schelling, *Arms and Influence*, With a New Preface and Afterword, New Haven, CT, Yale University Press, 2008, pp. 96–114. The concept of compellance was introduced by Schelling and is defined as a direct action that persuades an opponent to give up something that is desired.
7 Dilip Hiro, The Longest August: The Unflinching Rivalry between India and Pakistan, New York, Nation Books, 2015, p. 233.
8 Ibid., based on the 1951 Government of India census.
9 Ibid.
10 In Maulana Abul Kalam Azad's autobiography he noted Lord Pathick Lawrence and Sir Stafford Cripps statements that they could not see how a state like Pakistan could be viable and stable. *See India Wins Freedom: The Complete Version*, Hyderabad, Orient Longman, 1998, p. 150.
11 National Documentation Centre, Islamabad. Accession No. 7517, Diplomatic Representation in China, 22 June 1948–49. Document title: Reuters India Service, China plans Exchange of Envoys with Pakistan, Nanking, 2 August 1947.
12 National Documentation Centre, Islamabad. Accession No. 7517, Diplomatic Representation in China, 22 June 1948–49. Memo. No. 2317. From Pakistan to Nangking on 20 June 1948.
13 Economic Review of Pakistan, Economist Intelligence Unit, no. 1, April 1952.
14 Hiro, 'The Longest August', p. 276.
15 Economic Review of Pakistan, Economist Intelligence Unit, p. 11.
16 Economic Review of India, Economist Intelligence Unit, No. 3, October 1952, p. 8.
17 Hiro, 'The Longest August', p. 276.
18 Ibid.
19 Hector Bolitho, *Jinnah: The Creator of Pakistan*, London, John Murray, 1954, p. 206.
20 K. Sarwar Hasan (ed.) *Documents of the Foreign Relations of Pakistan: The Kashmir Question*, Pakistan Institute of International Affairs, 1966, p. 43.
21 Stanley A. Wolpert, *Jinnah of Pakistan*, New York: Oxford University Press, 1984, p. 348.

22 Ibid.

23 Ibid., p. 350.

24 Ibid., pp. 350–51.

25 Bolitho, *Jinnah*, p. 206.

26 'Country Report: Pakistan', Economist Intelligence Unit, 8 November 1960, p. 1 .

27 Ibid., p. 126.

28 On 15 August 1962 Prime Minister Nehru issued a statement that India did not want to fight Pakistan. President Ayub in his reply questioned the intentions of India and said that the facts belied Nehru's statement as India was spending around 375 crore rupees on its defence budget.

29 Office of the Historian, Bureau of Public Affairs, United States Department of State. 'South Asia (Foreign Relations of the United States, 1964–1968, Volume XXV).' p. 1085.

30 Mukund G. Untawale, 'The Kutch-Sind Dispute: A Case Study in International Arbitration'. *International and Comparative Law Quarterly*, vol. 23, no. 4, 1974, pp. 818–39.

31 Ibid.

32 Russell Brines, *The Indo-Pakistani Conflict*, London, Pall Mall Press, 1968, p. 288.

33 Shivaji Ganguly, US Policy toward South Asia, Boulder, CO, Westview Press, 1990, p. 122.

34 Padmanabha Ranganatha Chari, Pervaiz Iqbal Cheema and Stephen P. Cohen, *Four Crises and a Peace Process: American Engagement in South Asia*, Washington, DC, Brookings Institution Press, 2009, p. 16.

35 General K. M. Arif, *Khaki Shadows: Pakistan, 1947–1997*, Karachi, Oxford University Press, 2004, p. 47–49.

36 Office of the Historian, Bureau of Public Affairs, United States Department of State. Memorandum from Komer to President Johnson, 31 August 1965. 'South Asia (Foreign Relations of the United States, 1964–1968, Volume XXV),' p. 1020.

37 Selig S. Harrison, 'Troubled India and Her Neighbors', *Foreign Affairs*, vol. 43, no. 2, 1965, p. 321.

38 Ganguly, US Policy toward South Asia, p. 117.

39 Brines, *The Indo-Pakistani Conflict*, p. 252.

40 Ibid., p. 236.

41 Ibid.

42 Harrison, 'Troubled India and Her Neighbors', pp. 321–22.

43 Brines, p. 400.

44 Ibid., p. 375.

45 Ibid., p. 363.

46 Ibid.

47 Ibid., p. 405.

48 Ibid., pp. 404–05.

49 Ibid., p. 145.

50 P. N. Dhar, *Indira Gandhi, the 'Emergency,' and Indian Democracy*, New Delhi, Oxford University Press, 2000, p. 190.

51 Jyotindra Nath Dixit, *India-Pakistan in War and Peace*, London and New York, Routledge, 2003, p. 223.

52 Economist Intelligence Unit, quarterly report, 1982, 3, p. 8.

53 Chari *et al., Four Crises and a Peace Process*, p. 21.

54 Ibid.

55 Economist Intelligence Unit, quarterly report, 1984, 4, pp. 8–9.

56 Chari *et al.*, p. 24.

57 Ibid., p. 25.

58 Ibid., p. 47.

59 Zahid Hussain, 'Panic Grips Pakistan as Sanctions Bite', *The Times*, 13 July 1998.

60 Chari *et al.*, p. 120.

61 Economist Intelligence Unit, quarterly report, 1999, 1, p. 9.

62 Chari *et al.*, p. 139.

63 Robert Jervis, 'The Political Effects of Nuclear Weapons', *International Security*, vol. 13, no. 2, 1988, p. 84.

64 Harsh V. Pant, 'India's Nuclear Doctrine and Command Structure: Implications for Civil-Military Relations in India', *Armed Forces & Society* vol. 33, no. 2, 2007, pp. 238–64.

65 Firdaus Ahmed, 'The Calculus of Cold Start', *India Together*, May 2004.

66 General Parvez Kayani's statement in Zia Mian and M. V. Ramana, 'Imbricated Regional Rivalries and Global Order: South Asia, China and the United States', *South Asia* vol. 1, 2010, p. 2
67 Unintentional escalation could lead to the failure of restraint and thus a nuclear catastrophe. W. C. Ladwig, III, 'A Cold Start for Hot Wars? The Indian Army's New Limited War Doctrine', *International Security*, vol. 32, no. 3, 2007, p. 174.
68 Marc Trachtenberg, 'The Influence of Nuclear Weapons in the Cuban Missile Crisis', *International Security*, vol. 10, no. 1, 1985, p. 139.
69 Ladwig, 'A Cold Start for Hot Wars?' p. 174.
70 Mohammad Ayub Khan, *Friends Not Masters: A Political Autobiography*, London, Oxford University Press, 1976, pp. 115–16.
71 George Perkovich, Could Anything Be Done to Stop Them?: Lessons from Pakistan. Available at www.npolicy.org/article.php?aid=285&rid=6.
72 Jawaharlal Nehru, Speech given at midnight on 15 August 1947.
73 John Mueller, 'The Essential Irrelevance of Nuclear Weapons: Stability in the Postwar World', *International Security*, vol. 13, no. 2, 1988, pp. 55–79.

13

A potential game changer

The China–Pakistan Economic Corridor

Daud Ahmad

Introduction

The China–Pakistan Economic Corridor (CPEC) is part of China's new global initiative, known as the Belt and Road Initiative (BRI); it is also often called the One Belt, One Road initiative. In this chapter, the term BRI is adopted. The BRI reflects China's grand vision of connectivity extending from the People's Republic of China to the Baltics in Europe, the Middle East, Africa and South-East Asia. Under the BRI, announced in 2013, China is planning to invest US $ 1–3 trillion, over the next 30 years or so, in 60 countries all over the world to establish possibly six different economic corridors. The CPEC is a key part of and the 'front runner' in this grand scheme. It could prove to be a game changer for Pakistan and usher it in a new era of economic development. Unlike the old Silk Road, the BRI is a framework of regional connectivity. The CPEC will not only benefit China and Pakistan but should have, in due course, a positive impact on Iran, Afghanistan, India, and the Central Asian Republic.

The CPEC is a part of China's efforts to deliver security through economic development. It is partly a broad development scheme and partly a strategic gambit. Pakistan and China formalized plans[1] for the CPEC in April 2015, when they signed 51 agreements and Memoranda of Understanding (MOU) on Chinese investments totalling US $46 billion over the next 10–15 years, in three phases. Now even larger amounts are being talked about. Some projects are already underway, including highways and energy projects that have been partially completed.

Although Beijing and Islamabad have been close partners for decades, the CPEC is a reflection of intensified and expanded bilateral cooperation at a time of rising Chinese geopolitical ambition and persistent concerns about Pakistan's security and development.

The CPEC is intended to promote connectivity across Pakistan with a network of highways, railways and pipelines accompanied by energy, industrial and other infrastructure development projects to address critical energy shortages needed to boost Pakistan's economic growth. Eventually, the CPEC will also facilitate trade along an overland route that connects China to the Indian Ocean, linking the Chinese city of Kashgar in Xinjiang Province to the Pakistani port of Gwadar, in Pakistan's Balochistan Province.

The concept of a 'corridor' inevitably evokes images of a transit route and geopolitical speculation about Chinese access to the warm waters of the Indian Ocean. The cross-border dimensions of the CPEC plans, were, at the end of 2018, very modest. There are some ongoing energy and road upgrade projects, but fibre optics, pipelines and railways to Xinjiang are only at the planning stage. The rugged physical conditions pose serious capacity constraints; is entirely conceivable that the land route to China may only assume limited commercial significance. The bulk of the projects in each proposed phase are largely intra-Pakistan in nature. Achieving long-term benefits from the CPEC will require transit linkages to the other neighbouring countries as well.

Pakistan's economy continues to grow, and with economic expansion come new opportunities for international cooperation as well as geopolitical developments. Simultaneously, China is seeking to increase its regional influence both economically and politically. China's BRI strategy seeks to increase its economic and political ties in Asia, the Middle East and beyond. The CPEC is one project under the broader BRI umbrella. The billions of dollars that will be invested in projects related to the CPEC in Pakistan pose a number of opportunities and challenges for the nation.

The main components of the CPEC

The CPEC is an evolving package of competitive economic initiatives intended to enhance trade and economic development. The ambitious CPEC programme has two main components: a new trade and transport route extending from Kashgar in China to Gwadar Port in Balochistan; and the development of special economic zones (SEZs) along the route, including power projects and other auxiliary facilities. The first-phase projects will receive about US $46 billion in concessionary and commercial loans, for which financial facilitation to the Chinese companies involved is being arranged from different Chinese sources. The CPEC projects can broadly be listed in four categories: infrastructure, energy, industry/trade and others.

At the moment, the criteria for inclusion of a project/investment proposal for CPEC financing is quite fuzzy. On the Pakistan side, the Ministry of Planning, Development and Reform has set up a website[2] which provides basic information about the CPEC, including projects included in the scheme so far. Table 13.1 provides an overview of all the CPEC infrastructure projects under way at 2018. A 2017 report by the US Institute of Peace[3] provides the most comprehensive overview and analysis of the CPEC. Beside the official list of projects, there are numerous media reports containing 'wish lists' of projects from all over the country. With respect to Chinese financing, the feeling one gets in Pakistan is that whatever one wants, one gets. At 2018 the total CPEC financing is now reported to be in excess of US $60 billion. As the composition of CPEC investments is still evolving, it is too early to envisage how these fit together as a comprehensive development package.

A safe and efficient transit corridor between Gwadar and Kashgar is a critical prerequisite of the overall scheme. Currently, there are three possible existing land routes, all part of the national road network, which have been developed to different standards. Each would require new construction and upgrading to serve CPEC needs. The northern section (Karakoram Highway, Kashgar–Burhan, near Islamabad, 850 km) is common to the three routes. It was developed in the 1960s, with Chinese help, and traverses a rugged and crumbling mountain terrain. Sections of this highway are now being upgraded.

From Islamabad onwards to Gwadar there are three possible routes:

Table 13.1 Overview of the CPEC infrastructure projects

No.	Project name/ description	Location	Size/capacity	Cost ($ million/finance)	Executing agencies[5]	Status/ remarks
1	KKH Phase II (Thakot-Havelian section)	Gilgit/Balochistan	118 km	1,305 m GoC loan, terms n.a.	RA: MoC SA: MoC EA: NHA	Construction started in September 2016; completion date: December 2019
2	Peshawar Karachi Motorway (Multan–Sukhar section)	Punjab/Sindh	392 km, 6 lanes	2.980 million	RA: MoC SA: MoC EA: NHA	Construction started in August 2016; completion date: April 2018
3	Khuzdar– Basima Road N30	Balochistan	110 km	80 million	RA: MoC SA: MoC EA: NHA	Feasibility study completed; Letter of Intent forwarded to Chinese
4	DI Khan (Yarik)–Zhob N50 Upgrade	KPK/Balochistan	210 km	195 million	RA: MoC SA: MoC EA: NHA	Early preparation stages; PC approved; land acquisition underway; framework agreement under consideration
5	KKH Thakot- Raikot N35 136 km	KPK	136 km	720 million	RA: MoC SA: MoC EA: NHA	Preparation underway
6	KHI-LHE Peshawar rail line, Rehabilitation/upgrade of existing ML1 line.	KPK/Punjab/Sind	1872 km	8,172 million GoC concession loans	RA: MoR SA: MoC EA: MoR	Feasibility completed, framework agreement signed

- Western alignment (2,520 km, Kashgar–Gwadar), via Quetta, comprising the existing section of highways N50, N85 and M8.
- Central alignment (2,190 km), via Dera Ghazi Khan, N55 and M8.
- Eastern alignment (3,050 km), mostly existing motorways via Lahore, Multan and Karachi.

The CPEC alignment has been a controversial issue from the outset, given the provincial interests. Pakistan, in consultation with China, has now prepared a plan to develop the all three corridors over time. The current official position is that all three alignments will be developed, but the longest Eastern alignment has reportedly been selected for development during the first phase. Article 3 of the July 2013 MoU on the CPEC Long-Term Plan explains the rationale behind favouring the Eastern corridor. 'The routes should be developed under the principle of scientific planning and steady development by taking the easiest first,' it states. Security concerns along other alignments are also cited as a factor for giving the eastern route a higher priority.

China envisages the CPEC more as an investment package than a set of transport connections. The sectoral breakdown of the US $46 billion package is: infrastructure 28 per cent, energy 70 per cent, industrial estate and others 2 per cent.

Transport infrastructure

The original US $46 billion plan included roughly $14.82 billion for transport infrastructure – $4.65 billion for five roads and $8.57 billion for railways.[4] Another $0.79 billion has been allocated for 12 Gwadar Port development projects. The infrastructure projects, particularly roads, are labelled as the 'early harvest projects'. Two critical bottlenecks of the selected route – Thakot-Havelian (Northern section) and Multan-Sukhar motorway (Eastern alignment) were already under construction in 2018, at a total estimated cost of $3.65 billion. The huge railway investments aim to upgrade the existing Peshawar to Karachi main line; the proposal is still at the feasibility stage.

Development of the Gwadar Port is a critical link of the CPEC. Gwadar is a natural warm water deep port facility in western Balochistan, purchased by Pakistan from Oman in 1958 for US $8.4 million. The port's potential was identified in the 1950s, but efforts to seek financing for its development did not succeed for couple of decades. A small wharf was completed in 1992, and formal proposals for a deep-sea port at Gwadar were unveiled one year later. China finally agreed to finance development of Gwadar Port during the Musharraf era. Phase I covered the construction of three multipurpose berths and related port infrastructure, and port handling equipment, and was completed in December 2007 at a cost of $248 million. Its operations were initially handed over to the Port of Singapore Authority. This port is now being operated by a Chinese company. The second phase of construction, consisting of four container berth terminals, a bulk cargo terminal, oil and grain terminals and related facilities, is currently underway as part of planned improvements under the CPEC and other ancillary projects. The total project is expected to cost $1.02 billion. A build, operate, transfer agreement is currently being worked out. It should be mentioned that India is actively supporting the development of Chabahar Port in Iran, only 170 km away. India is investing $500 million in this deep-sea port in order to compete with Gwadar. Timely completion of the Gwadar Port projects will be crucial for the success of the CPEC.

Energy projects

The lion's share of China's investment – roughly US $32 billion (70 per cent) – is expected to go to energy projects, including coal, solar, hydroelectricity, liquefied natural gas (LNG), and power transmission. If all goes according to plan, by 2020 some 20 projects will generate nearly 17,000 MW of additional energy, nearly double Pakistan's installed capacity. This is an ambitious target; already a number of projects are facing delays and the target date is slipping to 2023. A number of ongoing China-financed power projects[5] are included in the CPEC list; only a few of which have since been completed. The CPEC will significantly impact Pakistan's energy mix. According to the US Institute of Peace report, during the period 2015–20 reliance on coal will increase from a negligible amount to about 24 per cent, LNG share will increase from 4 per cent to 13 per cent, solar and wind 1 per cent to 6 per cent. The share of hydroelectricity will fall from 31 per cent to 26 per cent. The successful implementation of the ambitious energy generation programme will depend on other activities as well, such as transport improvements to move coal and gas, and the power transmission/distribution networks. Already a number of proposed power projects are being put on hold owing to a lack of feasibility.

Industry/trade

Nine SEZs are being proposed. One will be located in each in the four provinces and in various special areas – Fata, Gilgit, Azad Jammu and Kashmir, Qasim Port and the Capital regions. Most of these SEZs are at planning stage. Each one will need to have a special focus based on how they compare for location, material inputs and market linkage advantages. An ongoing controversy surrounding these SEZs concerns their ownership.

Other components

This includes fibre optic networks and various educational facilities, the share of which amounts to 13 per cent, rail 8 per cent, and others 4 per cent.

Financing arrangements

CPEC financing falls under the umbrella of the BRI. China has accumulated over US $3 trillion in foreign exchange reserves. These funds can be used both for investment purposes and to buy influence around the world. The bulk of the investments would be made through commercial contracts between corporate entities on both sides with commercial loans from Chinese sources. China has so far identified the following three financial institutions for this purpose:

The Silk Road Infrastructure Fund: launched in February 2014, the China-led US $40 billion Silk Road Infrastructure Fund will directly support the BRI mission.
Asian Infrastructure Investment Bank (AIIB): Founded in October 2014, the AIIB aspires to be a global development institution serving 21 Asian member countries, with a registered capital of US $100 billion. Pakistan was one of the first to join this institution. The AIIB will focus on medium- and long-term equity investment in infrastructure, energy development, industry cooperation, and financial cooperation.

New Development Bank (NDB): BRICS refers to an association of five major emerging national economies: Brazil, Russia, India, China and South Africa. The NDB, located in Shanghai, is a multilateral development bank established by the BRICS in July 2014. The bank began with an initial capital of US $50 billion, which was expected to increase to $100 billion.

CPEC projects are being negotiated on a government-to-government basis, with Chinese firms selected by Beijing. The infrastructure projects are covered by low or zero interest concessional loans that include financing from China's Export-Import Bank and the Silk Road Fund. All the Chinese loans will be insured by the China Export and Credit Insurance Corporation (Sinosure) against non-payment risks, and the security of the loans is guaranteed by the state. The details of the financing, primarily in the form of loans, but also a small number of outright grants, have not been publicly released, and the terms vary considerably. A good analysis of the way in which the CPEC is being financed appeared in *Dawn*. [6] The bulk of CPEC financing is for energy projects, which will be executed in the Independent Private Power mode. Foreign investors are guaranteed a 17 per cent rate of return in dollars on their equity investments. The loans will be taken by the Chinese companies, mainly from the Chinese banks, against their own balance sheets. These borrowings would not impose any liabilities on the Pakistani government. The infrastructure components of the CPEC are to be financed though government-to-government loans on concessionary terms; debt servicing would be the government of Pakistan's responsibility. Several reports in the media paint a different and unfavourable picture of the financing arrangements and resulting debt burden. According to the US Institute of Peace report, the current financing for the CPEC can be broken down thus: foreign direct investments 64 per cent; concessional loans 24 per cent, commercial loans 6 per cent and grants 1 per cent. The financing arrangements, will no doubt, have a major impact on the success of the project.

Implementation arrangement

Information about the CPEC implementation arrangements remains scarce. A joint cooperation committee has been established co-chaired by Pakistan's Minister of Planning, Development and Reform and the Chinese Vice-Chairman of the National Development and Reform Commission. Under this umbrella, five 'working groups' have been established to cover planning, transport infrastructure, energy, Gwadar Port, and industrial parks/economic zones. For each project a responsible agency, a supervising agency and executing agency have been designated, but few details are available on the due diligence process, namely the feasibility, design and construction details. The provinces will, no doubt, play a key role as they will provide land for development projects and allied facilities. The Pakistan army is responsible for project security.

Current status

In 2018 there were over 40 projects to be undertaken by the CPEC. It has been reported that China has committed to 30 early harvest projects, of which 16 are under construction; these have been valued at between US $10–14 billion.[7] The CPEC should be seen as a 'work-in-progress' rather than a single mega-package. At 2018 construction work is underway on a number of road projects while several power generation projects (including

Sahiwal coal and Bahawalpur wind) are at the completion stage. Gwadar Port projects are regarded as being high priority. The remainder of the CPEC projects are at the feasibility/preparation stage. It should be recognized that the CPEC will face serious financing and implementation capacity issues. It is a huge undertaking for both Pakistan and China. Pakistan has not undertaken foreign investment projects of this scale before. Just to put things in perspective, between 2001 and 2011 the sum of $66 billion in financial assistance was pledged by China, but only 6 per cent of it ever materialized. It is easy to reach 'Banquette Deals', but extremely difficult to convert those into real projects/investments. On a positive note, the CPEC has been accorded the status of a 'flagship project'/ 'front runner' for the BRI, because arguably it presents the most developed set of plans to date among the various proposed corridors. In February 2015 Wang Yi, the Chinese Minister of Foreign Affairs, stated in that 'If "One Belt, One Road" is like a symphony involving and benefiting every country, then construction of the China–Pakistan Economic Corridor is the sweet melody of the symphony's first movement'.[8]

There is no reliable information available on the actual implementation status and disbursement of funds under the CPEC projects. The CPEC projects of about US $18 billion are currently in the implementation phase while another $17 billion worth of projects are in the active pipeline[9]. In the original plan, the CPEC completion target was 2030. Early-harvest energy projects were to be completed by 2020. This is unlikely to be achieved. Already delays of three to five years are anticipated for the completion of the energy and infrastructure projects. According to the World Bank,[10] delays were evident from the first year's performance. The biannual report considered the lack of consensus on the CPEC projects as posing one of the risks to the high-growth potential of the country's economy. China has also started raising concerns over the delay, notably in the energy sector transmission and generation projects. The latest State Bank of Pakistan report[11] on foreign direct investments (FDI) showed a surge of 65 per cent in the third quarter of 2017 (July–September) compared to the same period in the previous year. China's contribution to FDI was reported at $430 million out of $662 million for the reported quarter. The annual disbursement under the CPEC umbrella will need to amount to $ 3–4 billion on a sustained basis.

Regional implications of the CPEC

The success of the CPEC, in the long term, will depend on greater regional cooperation with neighbouring countries: Afghanistan, Iran, India and the Central Asian Republic. India, which enjoys the support of the United States, has objected to the scheme on political grounds. The United States will also have its own long-term concerns about the CPEC, as it represents the leading edge of China's expanding access to neighbouring regions and Eurasia. Afghanistan will be a critical link in the future development of the CPEC, even though at this stage it is not clear how Afghanistan fits into the vision for the BRI. The October 2015 International Monetary Fund (IMF) Regional Economic Outlook report on the Middle East and Central Asia estimated that China is committed to investments valued at US $100 million for One Belt, One Road projects in Afghanistan – a fraction of the total planned investment valued at $890 billion. China is gradually increasing its presence in Afghanistan, mostly through economic investment. Whereas China's foreign aid to Afghanistan in past decade was miniscule, compared to global foreign aid of nearly $25 billion, China is rapidly emerging as a major foreign investor in Afghanistan. It is reported[12] that during 2005–13 China's share of net foreign investment in Afghanistan was 79 per cent of the country's total. A Chinese joint venture won a large $3.5 billion contract to develop the Mes Aynak copper mine, reported to be the largest undeveloped copper resource in the world. China is fast seizing a substantial share of Afghanistan's natural resources.

Potential benefits

Much has been said and written about the potential benefits of the CPEC on Pakistan's economy, security, regional development and linkages with neighbouring countries. China can also gain in terms of its long-term global political and economic objectives. The BRI is a key element of China's national 'reaching out' strategy and is expected to be a critical driver for the country's long-term ambitions. The proposal aims to redirect the country's domestic overcapacity and capital for regional infrastructure development to improve trade relations with Asian, Central Asian and European countries. China's key objectives in promoting the BRI include secure shipping lanes; developing Western China; utilization of China's surplus construction and materials capacity; creation of new export markets; and generating goodwill with neighbouring countries. It is too early to estimate the impact/outcome of CPEC projects, although some efforts to do so are underway.

The CPEC, a part of the BRI, offers great strategic advantage to China as it gains physical access to the Indian Ocean and closer proximity to Middle Eastern oil resources. Other BRI projects around the world do not offer such early advantages to China. As Pakistan has the potential to serve as a nexus for the BRI, Beijing labels the CPEC as a 'flagship project'. Although Beijing is quick to downplay geostrategic motivation behind the CPEC, many commentators have noted that in the long term an overland link across Pakistan to the Arabian Sea could help to alleviate the 'Malacca dilemma'. This refers to China's vulnerability given that roughly 60 per cent of its international trade and 85 per cent of its oil imports travel through the single chokepoint of the Strait of Malacca.

The CPEC projects and related developments pose numerous economic opportunities for Pakistan and neighbouring countries. These projects, *if implemented in an efficient and timely manner*, will boost Pakistan's role in global trading networks and augment Pakistan's gross domestic product (GDP) growth rate. The infrastructure development is a first step in linking China to the Arabian Sea via an efficient route, enhancing connections between numerous South Asian states, and streamlining transshipment projects through Pakistan. Simultaneously, the expected substantial increases in regional trade and transshipment require an understanding of the trade security implications of the CPEC. For trade purposes, Gwadar Port will be designated as a free trade zone, providing the area with economic benefits for foreign traders and manufacturers.

The total amount of investment that Pakistan is expected to receive will amount to 20 per cent of its annual GDP. According to the World Bank, Pakistan's economy is projected to grow comfortably at a modest 5 per cent for the next few fiscal years, buttressed by increasing domestic demand and an improving service sector. If CPEC investments are factored in, the GDP rate is expected to rise to 5.5 per cent by 2018 and to 5.8 per cent in 2019.[13] This will, if successful, contribute to an already steady GDP growth rate in the country. This includes growth of 4 per cent in 2014 and 4.2 per cent in 2015. Pakistan continues to investigate ways to increase its competitiveness and ability to connect with foreign trading partners, and the CPEC is increasingly viewed as an important part of that growth strategy by many Pakistani government officials. The CPEC will have the best chance of transforming Pakistan's economic outlook if it sparks a wave of foreign investment from other countries, boosts industrial export and creates jobs.

At present, the CPEC is mainly being seen as a series of project investments along the selected corridors. In order to achieve the maximum benefit, Pakistan has to look at a comprehensive package to maximize internal and external linkages as well as development benefits. This will require national consensus as well as supportive policy and institutional environments. The investments alone will not yield the required results unless supporting policy changes are made to facilitate export growth, investments in manufacturing and skills development. Since the bulk of investments are in the energy sector, supporting power sector reforms and improvement of the transmission and distribution system will be essential. CPEC planners need to focus on the potential long-term regional benefits as well, involving Afghanistan, the Central Asian countries, Iran and India.

Potential risks

The CPEC project is huge and complex. Naturally there are risks associated with it which need to be recognized and mitigated. These risks can be summarized below:

Political

There are both internal and external political risks. Pakistan's politics is highly polarized by competing provinces and regional, tribal and religious divisions. Building national consensus on an undertaking like this is a huge challenge. On the other hand, the success of the scheme will depend on building national consensus. The debate on the alignment of the CPEC corridor is a pertinent example. The selection of CPEC projects/investment would pose further challenges. The fact that India is openly opposing the scheme and a number of other countries, including the United States, have apprehensions about it, presents another set of political risks.

The CPEC also faces domestic political opposition in Pakistan, with in-fighting between the provinces and the central government over the allocation of investments. Opposition parties have levelled accusations of preferential treatment along the eastern route, claiming that the government's proposals for the distribution of services, industrial parks and SEZs deny some provinces access to investment opportunities and only benefit Punjab. The lack of transparency surrounding the negotiated deals has heightened concerns that only a select few, if any, in Pakistan will benefit from the investments. *The best way to mitigate the political risks is to introduce transparency in the system and ensure sustained implementation progress.*

Security risks

The CPEC routes, especially the highway infrastructure, must pass through increasingly difficult territory and some areas where insurgency is rife. The Pakistan Army has taken over the responsibility for securing the project areas and are working diligently on this. A special security division (of at least 13,000 troops) comprising army battalions and Civil Armed Forces (CAF) wings has been deployed as a dedicated force for Pakistan-China economic projects. Security risks are, in a way, linked to political risks. To overcome these, the local population in the concerned areas have to see and be convinced of the potential economic benefits of the scheme.

Financial risks

These include the overall size of foreign investments having implication on the future debt burden. This is an important topic in Pakistan with different views and analysis fuelled by the lack of transparency financing arrangements. Suitability/competitiveness of financing terms of individual projects will have implications on their future success. Inflation and foreign exchange risks will have additional implications on debt repayments. In the past, Pakistan's annual FDI was well below US $1 billion. Pakistan's economy could struggle to absorb $3–4 billion per year of FDI, projected under the CPEC. At this stage, it is very difficult to project the future debt servicing burden with reasonable accuracy, given that the composition of the projects is uncertain and that the implementation schedule is already slipping. Ishrat Hussain has attempted to make preliminary projections on the CPEC's disbursements and debt liabilities.[14] He estimates that the debt burden from energy and infrastructure projects would be of the order of $ 3.5 billion per year (about 7 per cent of current total foreign exchange earnings) for a 15–20 year repayment period. Energy projects are likely to save about $1 billion per year in foreign exchange from imported fuel costs.

Operational risks

The implementation capacity of Pakistan, and for that matter of China, for a huge under-taking of this kind is a key factor. Special implementation arrangements will have to be devised and put in place. Currently there is perceived lack of transparency in the selection, design and contracting of the projects. The normal due diligence process is essential for the success of any scheme. The situation is complicated by the fact that BRI investments are different from the conventional regional economic cooperation programmes, as these do not prioritize investments and trade concessions. Instead, the emphasis is on regional infrastructure connectivity. The bulk of the investments would be through commercial contracts between corporate entities on both sides with commercial loans from Chinese sources. This approach in itself poses few risks. Mitigation of the operational risks would require a comprehensive implementation framework along the following lines:

- The overall ownership of the CPEC should rest with the Ministry of Planning, Development and Reform and its focus should be on articulating national objectives and benefits from the project. It should not be involved as a 'line agency' in project implementation.
- The ownership of individual projects should rest with the relevant provincial and local agencies. They should be responsible for project design, implementation and financial obligations.
- The Ministry of Planning, Development and Reform should set up a special task group of professionals/specialists to review and vet the scope and design of the individual projects. They would need to make sure that each proposal is technically sound; economically feasible; financially viable; environmentally sustainable; and organizationally implementable. Such a task group could be set up with a fixed life of five years, for example.
- An independent monitoring agency, in an academic setting, should be put in place to serve as an 'information warehouse' for the overall scheme. This group should also monitor broad implementation progress and impact /benefits of the programme.

Summary and recommendations

The CPEC has been widely welcomed in Pakistan. It has been recognized as a unique opportunity and a game changer for which Pakistan has waited for quite some time, If successful it could have long-term positive effects on Pakistan's economy, security and regional trade. The main challenge is going to be ensuring the effective and efficient implementation of the scheme. The recent US-Afghan policy shifts make it essential for Pakistan to align its interests with China and other neighbours. The timely and successful implementation of the CPEC will become even more important. To this end, the following recommendations can be made:

1   Pakistan needs to recognize China's interests/objectives in promoting this initiative and define its own objectives in the best interests of the country. China's main interest is in developing an efficient and safe transit corridor from Kashgar to Gwadar for its long-term geopolitical and economic interests. Pakistan must facilitate this. The CPEC, in return, provides opportunities for large Chinese investments in Pakistan that will facilitate its economic growth and security. Pakistan needs to develop a clear strategy on how best to achieve this at the national level.

2   The CPEC has to be depoliticized. It must be seen as a 'national undertaking'. Keeping politicians out of the micro decision-making process will be a big challenge that has to be faced. The role of the politicians should be to define the broad framework and strategy for the scheme. The responsibility for project selection and design should be left to the professionals and other stakeholders.

3   Essential due diligence processes for vetting the selection and design of projects must be put in place. This should be the key role of the Planning Commission (now the Ministry of Planning, Development and Reform). This will be critical for ensuring the success of the individual projects and for curbing possible corruption.

4   The CPEC projects need to be made transparent. The public needs to know what is being financed under the scheme, at what cost and on what terms and by whom? It might be a good idea to set up an independent CPEC information centre in an academic setting, which could act as a comprehensive warehouse for all the information on this huge and long-term scheme.

Notes

1   'Long-Term Plan on China Pakistan Economic Corridor', National Development and Reform Commission, December 2015.
2   The Ministry of Planning, Development and Reform website provides basic information on the status of various projects under the CPEC. It is also a good source of up-to-date information on current CPEC projects. See www.cpec.gov.pk.
3   Arif Rafiq, *The China–Pakistan Economic Corridor, Barriers and Impact*, US Institute Peace (USIP), 2017.
4   The latest reports suggest that the Lahore Mass Transit (Orange line, US $1.6 billion) has already been included in the CPEC list and the Karachi Circular Railway ($3.5 billion) has also been added.
5   Sahiwal Thermal Plant; Port Qasim Power Plant; solar and wind projects in Sindh, etc.
6   Ishrat Husain, 'Financing Burden of CPEC', *Dawn*, 11 February 2017.
7   Ministry of Planning, Development and Reform, Government of Pakistan.
8   Andrew Small, 'First Movement: Pakistan and the Belt and Road Initiative', *Asia Policy* vol 24, no. 1, 2017, pp. 80–87.

9 Statement by the Minister of Planning, Development and Reform, *Dawn*, 30 September 2016.
10 'Fading Tailwinds', South Asia Economic Focus, World Bank, Spring 2016.
11 Directors of the State Bank of Pakistan, 'The State of Pakistan's Economy', 3rd quarterly report, 2016–17', State Bank of Pakistan, 2017.
12 'The World According to China', *New York Times*, 24 July 2015.
13 World Bank, 'Growth: A Shared Responsibility', Pakistan Development Update, Washington, DC, World Bank, May 2017.
14 Husain, Financing Burden of CPEC.
15 Key: RA: responsible agency; SA: supervising agency; EA: executing agency; GoC: Government of China; MoC: Ministry of Communications; NHA: National Highway Authority; MoR: Ministry of Railways.

Part III

Economic development and the importance of good governance

14

Macroeconomic achievements and challenges

Masood Ahmed

A brief history of macroeconomic management

Over the past 50 years, Pakistan's record on macroeconomic management has been mixed. In the face of a variety of internal and external shocks, the country has managed to avoid excessive macroeconomic instability in the form of hyperinflation or severe exchange rate volatility. While its internal and external public debt has grown as a share of gross domestic product (GDP), and is now approaching levels that warrant attention, Pakistan has so far managed this growth without resorting to sovereign defaults, which leave a long shadow on a country's ability to access capital markets. Finally, Pakistan has also avoided the kind of large-scale banking crises that many other developing countries have experienced with lasting impact on credit availability and private sector development.

Alongside these positive features, however, Pakistan has demonstrated an almost unique proclivity to allow fiscal and balance of payments pressures to build up into a near crisis situation every few years, which then must be dealt with through orthodox economic stabilization tools, often with the help of the International Monetary Fund (IMF). In general, these stresses have been contained before they could become a full-blown economic crisis, but the cumulative cost of these periodic crisis aversion programmes has been to slow down economic and social development, resulting in the mediocre – and in some cases, poor –comparative development indicators that we see today. And, because each episode was addressed with short-term actions that stabilized the economy without adequate follow-through on structural reforms, the underlying weaknesses simply manifested themselves again with the next external shock or period of internal economic mismanagement. Moreover, this preoccupation with managing short-term macroeconomic vulnerabilities has limited the attention that leading policymakers can devote to more fundamental issues of economic development and structural transformation.

One consequence of this pattern has been Pakistan's frequent and repeated recourse to stabilization assistance from the international community, led by the IMF. Since the late 1950s Pakistan has resorted to IMF assistance on 18 occasions, more than almost any other of the IMF's 188 member countries. Apart from the sheer frequency, what is striking about Pakistan's resort to IMF assistance is that the majority of these IMF-supported programmes were abandoned before completion, a feature that has become even more prevalent in recent programmes (Table 14.1).

Why has Pakistan abandoned so many IMF assistance programmes? Although each episode and each programme is unique, there is a common pattern. In most cases, the initial year of the programmes went well, with the government taking the urgent fiscal, monetary and exchange rate measures necessary to stabilize the economy and restore a degree of confidence. However, in the latter years, when the programmes moved on to tackling some of the underlying structural weaknesses that had given rise to the macroeconomic stress, the government's ability and political will to follow through waned and, as the crisis-related pressures were also abating at the time, the programmes were left to wither.

The principal factors leading to periodic episodes of macroeconomic stress are chronic and uncorrected structural weaknesses in Pakistan's economy. While – as in most

Table 14.1 Pakistan's history of lending arrangements with the IMF as of 30 June 2018 (millions of Special Drawing Rights – SDRs)

#	Facility	Date of arrangement	Date of expiration or cancellation	Amount approved	Amount drawn	% undrawn
1	EFF[2]	9/4/2013	9/30/2016	4393.0	4393.0	0
2	Stand-by	11/24/2008	9/30/2011	7235.9	4936.0	32
3	PRGF[3]	12/6/2001	12/5/2004	1033.7	861.4	17
4	Stand-by	11/29/2000	9/30/2001	465.0	465.0	0
5	EFF[1]	10/20/1997	10/19/2000	454.9	113.7	75
5	ESAF[1,4]	10/20/1997	10/19/2000	682.4	265.4	61
6	Stand-by	12/13/1995	9/30/1997	562.6	294.7	48
7	ECF[1]	2/22/1994	12/13/1995	606.6	172.2	72
7	ESAF[1]	2/22/1994	12/4/1995	379.1	123.2	68
8	Stand-by	9/16/1993	2/22/1994	265.4	88.0	67
9	Structural Adjustment Facility Commitment[1]	12/28/1988	12/27/1991	382.4	382.4	0
9	Stand-by[1]	12/29/1988	11/30/1990	273.2	194.5	29
10	EFF	12/2/1981	11/23/1983	919.0	730.0	21
11	EFF	11/24/1980	12/1/1981	1268.0	349.0	72
12	Stand-by	3/9/1977	3/8/1978	80.0	80.0	0
13	Stand-by	11/11/1974	11/10/1975	75.0	75.0	0
14	Stand-by	8/11/1973	8/10/1974	75.0	75.0	0
15	Stand-by	5/18/1972	5/11/1973	100.0	84.0	16
16	Stand-by	9/17/1968	10/16/1969	75.0	75.0	0
17	Stand-by	3/16/1965	3/15/1966	37.5	37.5	0
18	Stand-by	12/8/1958	9/22/1959	25.0	0.0	100

Source: IMF Financial Data, Pakistan Lending Arrangements. Available at www.imf.org/external/np/fin/tad/extarr1.aspx.
[1] Blended Arrangement.
[2] EFF stands for Extended Fund Facility.
[3] PRGF stands for Poverty Reduction and Growth Facility.
[4] ESAF stands for Enhanced Structural Adjustment Facility.

developing countries – there are many areas of economic management that can be improved in Pakistan, the two principal causes of macroeconomic problems have been the imbalance between public sector spending and income, and Pakistan's underdeveloped export base, which makes the country highly vulnerable in the international trade arena.

Income and expenditure of the public sector

There has been a chronic imbalance between the income and expenditure of the public sector. This is not because Pakistan's public budget is much larger, in relative terms, than that of other emerging markets. Rather, it is because the government's income from taxes, fees and other sources is strikingly low compared with other countries.

This is not to say that there is no wastage in public spending or that it could not be better allocated. There are well-documented studies that show how both current and capital spending by the federal and provincial governments, and their associated bodies, could be dramatically improved to get far better value for money. Similarly, the persistent losses made by some public sector enterprises,[1] and the even larger losses made in the energy sector,[2] provide additional scope for improving public finances. The case is all the more compelling given the comparatively low level of public spending on health and education (Table 14.2), which explains, at least in part, why Pakistan lags woefully behind on social indicators of development. Finally, inadequate public investment in infrastructure constrains the potential for sustained high growth. There is, therefore, a clear need to rationalize and improve the effectiveness of public expenditure.

It is important to note that low levels of public expenditure do not necessarily imply a limited public sector footprint in the economy. Public enterprises have a large presence in many economic sectors, large tracts of prized land are owned by the government, and the use of regulations, subsidies, administered pricing of key inputs and outputs, and discretionary regulations ensure that the heavy hand of government is felt across much of the economy. Reforming these dimensions is important not only for their fiscal impact, but also to improve the efficiency of the economy and to address problems of corruption and governance.

Moving on to the revenue side, Pakistan is among the weakest performing countries in the developing world in terms of mobilizing public revenues efficiently from taxation and other fees. Despite 40 years of efforts to improve both tax policy and tax administration, the ratio of taxes to GDP remains stuck in the low teens,[3] below the middle-income countries average of 18.5 per cent.[4] Table 14.3 shows how the levels and composition of taxes in Pakistan compare with selected emerging market countries.

Table 14.2 Public spending on health and education

Country or group	*Public spending on health*		*Public spending on education*	
	Year	% of GDP	Year	% of GDP
Pakistan	2014	0.92	2013	2.50
Bangladesh	2014	0.78	2013	1.97
India	2014	1.40	2013	3.84
Thailand	2014	3.20	2013	4.12
Low- and middle-income[1]	2014	3.03	2013	4.09

Source: World Bank, available at https://data.worldbank.org/.
[1] Definition and list of countries, available at https://data.worldbank.org/indicator/SE.XPD.TOTL.GD.ZS?locations=XO.

Two features of the tax structure are worth noting in particular: the high proportion of taxes collected through indirect taxes (around 55 per cent of total tax revenue) and the small number of individuals who file income tax returns. Indirect taxes – essentially excise taxes, import duties and fees of various sorts – are generally more regressive than direct taxes; in other words, their burden falls disproportionately on the poor and less well-off households. This is not to say that higher-income households pay less in indirect taxes; rather, the indirect taxes that they do pay are likely to be a smaller share of their income than the less well-off households. A further problem is that the system of withholding and presumptive taxes has grown very complex, adding to the negative perceptions of the overall tax system. Attempts to introduce a value-added tax (VAT), a more efficient indirect tax, have failed in the face of political opposition.

The low number of people filing income tax returns (just over one million out of an estimated working population of 116 million[5]), and the prevalent underreporting of income by those who do file, has important consequences. First, it limits total tax revenue for the government. Indeed, it is hard to envisage how the tax-to-GDP ratio could be increased by 50 per cent (to reach the norm for developing countries) without a substantial increase in the number of those filing their tax returns.

Second, tax avoidance or underpayment undermines public confidence in the fairness of the tax system. The perception (and reality) that people who are known to have very high incomes pay little or no income tax fosters a sense that the system is rigged to protect the rich and powerful. The annual publication of tax payments by parliamentarians, demonstrating in many cases a clear disconnect between their declared tax payments and their visible standard of living, has been a great advance in transparency but, so far, it has not altered the underlying pattern of behaviour. Those who claim to derive their income from agriculture (on which no income taxes are paid), and those engaged in trading or professional services who are either unregistered as taxpayers or who pay small amounts in relation to their perceived incomes, are also often viewed as benefiting from an inequitable system. Property is mostly undervalued for tax purposes, so the revenue from this potentially important source is also very low by international comparison. Tax avoidance is also found in the corporate sector. Of the 72,500 firms registered with the Security and Exchange Commission of Pakistan in 2016, less than half filed a tax return and half of those who did filed a 'zero return'.[6]

A related problem in the tax system is the distribution of revenues between the federation and the provinces. Under the 18th amendment to the Constitution and the last National Finance Commission (NFC) Award,[7] the devolution of responsibilities and resources to the provinces generated an imbalance at the aggregate level. The plans to manage the overall fiscal deficit implicitly relied on the expectation that the provinces would generate a surplus

Table 14.3 Composition of tax revenues for select countries (percentage of GDP, 2014)

	Direct tax revenue[1]	*Indirect tax revenue[2]*	*Total tax revenue[3]*
Pakistan	3.6	5.6	10.5
Philippines	6.2	6.7	14.8
India	–	–	16.6
Malaysia	10.5	3.4	14.8
Thailand	6.8	10.2	17.2
Egypt	6.1	6.2	13.0

Source: IMF World Revenue Longitudinal Dataset.
[3] Sum of direct taxes, indirect taxes, property taxes and other taxes.

that would partly offset the larger deficit at the federation level. This worked for a couple of years, but the provinces have now started to build up their spending capacity while the federation has not yet cut back on some expenditures that it should no longer undertake because the associated responsibilities have been allocated to the provinces. Thus, it has become harder to control the aggregate budget deficit and this will remain the case unless the allocation mechanism or the pattern of federal expenditure is revised. Another problem with the current allocation formula is that about two-thirds of all new tax revenue mobilized at the federal level is passed on to the provinces as their share. This reduces the incentive for the federation to raise revenue – which in effect faces a 60 per cent tax rate on all additional revenue it raises – as well as for the provinces to undertake stronger tax mobilization efforts of their own since they can rely on the share of additional revenue they will receive from the federation's efforts. It is commendable that, despite these constraints, some provinces have made marked progression in enhancing their revenue creation efforts.

Many studies have considered the problems of tax policy and tax administration. On the policy side, the recommendations range from proposals to address specific anomalies or missed opportunities all the way to plans for a complete revamp, with a new simplified and efficient approach to setting up a tax system. Similarly, there are incremental as well as radical proposals to reform tax administration, which is generally seen as inefficient and plagued by corruption. There have also been a variety of projects over the years, many supported by international agencies with technical assistance and policy conditionality, to promote these recommendations.

Why have past programmes failed to generate a substantial and lasting improvement in Pakistan's tax outcomes? Many blame corruption and incompetence in the tax administration, and this is certainly part of the explanation. Others point to the large share of the informal sector in Pakistan's economy, which makes it harder to track individual and small business incomes. Yet others will point to the fact that a large share of the working population would fall below any reasonable income threshold for paying taxes. Finally, there is the problem of lack of trust in the quality and integrity of government spending. Many observers point to the generous levels of private charity by people who pay little in taxes as demonstrating that people are willing to contribute to the larger social good if they can be confident that the money will be put to good use. These observers maintain that lower levels of tax avoidance would naturally follow a demonstrated improvement in the coherence and effectiveness of government spending. All these points have some truth in them, but they also apply to other countries that have, nevertheless, succeeded in drawing a higher proportion of their working population into the tax net.

The wider and more important explanation for Pakistan's failure to improve its tax outcomes, in my view, is one of political economy. Pakistan simply lacks a sufficiently powerful coalition of interests to raise more taxes and to push for real improvements in the quality of government spending. Normally, this would come from a combination of those in government who want to spend money without raising the deficit and private taxpayers who are increasingly resentful of the high tax rates they pay while their peers remain outside the tax net. While both groups exist in the country, they have not been able to come together and overcome the powerful interests on the other side. In particular, governments have often backtracked on their efforts to widen the tax net when faced with opposition from their political constituencies or linked interests. As a result, in times of fiscal stress it has proved easier to cut back on the already low level of public investment spending, with damaging – but lagged – consequences. Many donor agencies and international partners – including the World Bank, the IMF and bilateral aid agencies – have tried to influence this process through a combination of 'carrots and sticks', but they too have not succeeded.

Until Pakistan can substantially raise tax revenue by broadening the base of direct taxpayers, it will remain constrained in its ability to expand the delivery of much needed public services and infrastructure without building up unsustainable fiscal deficits. And without that extra infrastructure and improved human development, growth will remain elusive and the country's place in an ever more competitive world economy will remain fragile. Which events or forces will bring about the political consensus to overcome long-standing constraints in this regard remains a subject of discussion.

The external sector

The second source of macroeconomic vulnerability for Pakistan has been its external sector. Most successful emerging markets followed a strategy of promoting both the quantity and quality of their exports. Starting from low export levels comprised mainly of relatively unprocessed commodities or low value-added manufactures, these countries have dramatically expanded the volume, diversity and sophistication of their exports. The most often cited examples are the People's Republic of China and the so-called East Asian tigers (the Republic of Korea, Thailand, Vietnam and Malaysia), but countries in other regions also provide good case studies.

In contrast, exports have remained a much smaller share of the economy in Pakistan since independence. Furthermore, during the period 2015–17 a combination of factors – security and energy supply problems, lower commodity prices and an appreciating real exchange rate –brought exports down to well below 10 per cent of GDP. As Table 14.4 implies, exports from Pakistan would have to increase by more than three times their current level to match the average for middle-income countries. Pakistan's exports have also been remarkably concentrated in a few low-value-added products. Cotton and cotton products, rice and leather still account for over 70 per cent of the country's exports and the bulk of exports in each of these categories is in primary or little processed form. Service exports, which have been a rapidly growing source of high-value-added export revenue in many countries, remain a small fraction of Pakistan's exports.

Given its low level of exports, Pakistan has relied in recent years on a large and growing volume of remittances and on official and private financing to cover its import bill. It is worth noting, however, that these international flows, especially private flows, can be volatile because they are subject to external and internal shocks. Pakistan has had a consistent rising trend of remittance flows for many years, but recent macroeconomic developments suggest that this is unlikely to persist. Remittances from the Gulf countries, which have been a large and growing

Table 14.4 Exports of goods in 2017

Country or group	US $ billion	% of GDP
Pakistan	23.1	7.62
Turkey	166.6	19.56
Malaysia	188.0	59.76
Thailand	235.1	51.63
India	304.1	11.65
Bangladesh	35.30	13.51
Middle-income countries' average[1]	76.65	24.47

Source: IMF balance of payments statistics.

[1] Data missing for numerous middle-income countries. For a list of middle-income countries, see fn. 4.

share of the total, are likely to plateau as these countries adjust their spending to the new lower price of oil. Pakistan will need to adjust to lower growth in remittances going forward.

In good years, these international inflows have been sufficient not only to meet the demands for foreign exchange – even with an appreciating real exchange rate – but to lead to an increase in the country's foreign exchange reserves. However, when there was an external shock – such as the increase in oil prices in the years leading up to 2014 – or when an excessively loose fiscal stance or a misguided exchange rate policy translated into an increased demand for foreign exchange, as has been the case more recently, these reserves were drawn down, sometimes to a level that threatened a macroeconomic crisis and led to recourse to the IMF. In 2018, after a few years of being on a positive trajectory, these reserves were again on a downward trend and were hovering around US $10 billion, below the three months of imports mark that is used by many institutions as a minimum for certain kinds of financial operations.

There are many factors that underpin Pakistan's long-term export performance. Security problems, energy shortages, poor infrastructure and other shortcomings in the business environment provide a good part of the explanation. Pakistan is ranked 136th out of 190 countries in the World Bank's *Doing Business* report[8] – an indication of its less-than-favourable business climate. A lack of investment in the export sector, or in updating technology and research and development that would raise the value added of exports, or in the educational system to generate enough trained technicians, workers and managers are another group of reasons.

Also contributing to the small share of exports in Pakistan's economy is the protected environment for the domestic market, which has made import substitution a profitable and less risky endeavour for many businesses. It is noteworthy that the largest corporations in Pakistan are either in manufacturing for the domestic market or in the service sector. A few rely on explicit or implicit protection in the form of import barriers or administered prices for inputs and outputs.

Finally, over the years a misguided adherence to an overvalued exchange rate has made it harder for Pakistani exporters to compete in international markets (while also resulting in the loss of a substantial share of foreign exchange reserves in an attempt to prevent necessary

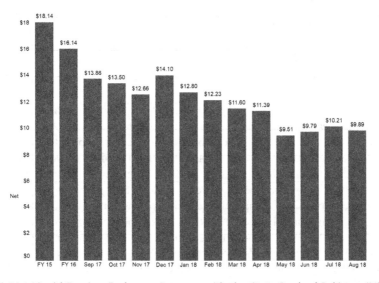

Figure 14.1 Net Liquid Foreign Exchange Reserves with the State Bank of Pakistan (Billion Us $; end period)
Source: State Bank of Pakistan.

exchange rate depreciation). In contrast, some of the more successful emerging market exporters have seen the exchange rate as a tool to preserve their competitiveness and to build foreign exchange reserves to enhance their resilience and economic independence.

Behind these specific factors is the political economy of reforming the anti-export bias. Under the current regime, consumers have benefited from cheaper imports and entrepreneurs have moved into producing for the domestic market with some degree of protection or in other non-tradeable activities. Exporters have voiced their concerns about the exchange rate and other factors affecting their competitiveness but have sought government financial support rather than effectively lobbying for a more export-friendly regime.

Can Pakistan's economy be made more export-oriented? The entrepreneurial capacity and business acumen are certainly available. The performance of the small and medium-sized enterprise sector in Sialkot is a striking example of success despite the weaknesses in the business environment and in infrastructure. However, to generalize this type of success requires a combination of public policy and supportive infrastructure investments. In this context, recent improvements in the security situation are welcome as are the investments being made to increase the capacity for electricity generation and – less so – distribution.

These efforts will need to be supplemented by a much more fundamental revisiting of the public policy and business environment to better align incentives towards exporting. Exchange rate policy will need to prioritize economic fundamentals overseeing a 'strong' exchange rate as a mark of national pride. Incremental schemes to provide limited subsidies or special incentives to exporters will only have a limited effect. If Pakistani policymakers truly want to quadruple the volume of exports, this will take nothing short of a national drive sustained over at least a decade. And it will need the political will to resist the calls of vested interests that gain from the current protectionism and anti-export bias.

The role of the IMF

These two main structural weaknesses – fiscal imbalance and weak export performance – have been present for many decades, and their role in generating macroeconomic vulnerability is well understood. It is legitimate then to ask why they were not addressed under the numerous IMF-supported programmes. Of course, the IMF is only one external agency engaged with Pakistan on economic policy questions. Still, the IMF's focus on macroeconomic stability and its unique access to senior policymakers make the question more directly relevant to it. To be sure, many IMF programmes did attempt to address these structural issues but, in the end, they were only partially successful. Why wasn't a better and more sustainable improvement achieved despite repeated recourse to IMF financing and the associated policy conditionality?

The answer is that while IMF policy conditionality can reinforce that which national governments are committed to doing, it cannot by itself achieve sustained policy change where there is no national commitment to the underlying reforms. Moreover, by its nature IMF engagement is more effective at addressing short-term problems of macroeconomic instability and can play only a limited role in promoting longer-term actions to address underlying structural issues. In some countries, governments have used the presence (and conditionality) of the IMF to undertake difficult structural reforms, but these were reforms that the government wanted to carry out. Where the IMF has been less successful is in pushing reforms that the host country government itself does not support. In these cases, good intentions generally remained just that.

In Pakistan, as in many other countries needing IMF support, the decision to ask the IMF for help is typically deferred until a crisis appears imminent. At that point, both the authorities and the IMF staff agree that the immediate focus of the IMF programme should be, first and foremost, on arresting the deterioration in macroeconomic imbalances and restoring macroeconomic stability. And in most instances, the programmes have been quite successful in doing that. Fiscal and current account imbalances were contained, reserves started to be rebuilt, and confidence in the economy was strengthened leading to a pick-up in domestic investment and external financing. In parallel to these stabilization measures, the authorities and the staff of the IMF also agreed on a set of plans to address the underlying structural weaknesses. On the fiscal side, this has often comprised targets for increased tax revenues backed up by plans to enhance tax administration or to draw more people into the tax net. This has sometimes been accompanied by plans to reduce losses in public enterprises through tariff policy, better management or privatization. On the external front, the structural agenda has mainly focused on improvements to the business environment or tariff policy to encourage increased exports.

The difficulty arises when these plans are not fully implemented either because of opposition from the affected interests or because of a lack of follow-through by the administration itself. And the difficulty is compounded when, despite this lack of implementation on the structural agenda, the macroeconomic aggregates – such as the reduction of the fiscal deficit or the build-up of reserves – continue to show the anticipated progress. At this point, the IMF finds itself in a dilemma. Either it must continue to support the programme (sometimes with 'waivers' on conditionality) while encouraging the authorities to make better progress on the structural agenda, or it must call a halt to its support even though the macroeconomic performance is showing the agreed level of improvement. In these situations, the IMF staff and board have generally adopted an accommodative posture and given the benefit of the doubt to the country authorities.

This accommodative approach has not always worked. Since the structural weaknesses affect the macro outlook, in a few cases failure to follow through on the structural agenda has led to slower than agreed progress on macro indicators. In this case, the IMF has sometimes insisted that a particular tax or other structural measure be implemented as a condition of continuing its support for the programme. And this has resulted in an impasse and the abandonment of the programme before completion. A recent example of this is the 2008 Stand-By Agreement, which ended prematurely amid fiscal slippage and lack of progress on introducing the VAT and energy sector reforms. A related trade-off is when tax administration is not improving while the fiscal situation remains difficult. In this case, the authorities sometimes opt for low-quality tax measures that increasingly over-tax an already narrow tax base or further complicate the tax system.

It is sometimes asked whether the availability of IMF financing is itself a disincentive to fundamental reforms. Since policymakers know that the IMF will be there with a bail-out if they run into a macro crisis, the argument goes, there is less incentive for them to undertake difficult reforms that would counter the interests of powerful stakeholders. Economists refer to this as the 'moral hazard' problem. This is a serious argument with a foundation in both economic theory and empirical evidence.

The question becomes whether, given the history of past programmes, the IMF should refuse to finance a new programme when approached by Pakistan in the hope that the ensuing crisis would trigger reforms that would obviate the need for subsequent support. This is theoretically a possibility, but it faces intellectual, moral and practical difficulties.

Intellectually, it is true that deep crises can lead to deep reforms, but this is not inevitable in any given episode. Reforms are generated by a variety of factors and conditions, and each country context is different. It is equally possible that a deep crisis will simply result in a prolonged period of chaos and stagnation. On a moral plane, the cost of crisis is borne disproportionately by the poor and vulnerable. Millions would fall below the poverty line and some would suffer permanent damage to their welfare and living conditions. It is not evident that any policymaker or international institution has the right to willingly bring about a crisis with such severe consequences for the poor in the uncertain expectation that it will lead to a change in national behaviour. On a purely practical level, the IMF was created to help its members facing an imminent financial and economic crisis, and it would not be realistic to expect its staff or board to refuse assistance to a member to teach it a lesson and change its behaviour.

Another issue is whether the design of IMF programmes is flawed in promoting stabilization over growth or structural change. This is a complex topic on which much has been written both by the IMF and by independent observers. However, at the end of the day, the fundamental problem is that a country facing an imminent balance of payments or economic crisis must make (often painful) adjustments to reduce fiscal or external account imbalances. While the pace and scope of these adjustments can be moderated by the additional funding that comes from the IMF, some adjustment remains necessary. The relevant question becomes how to design the adjustment to minimize the negative impact on growth or on the welfare of the more vulnerable sections of society. This requires the active engagement of a broader set of policymakers – at both the federal and provincial level – than has sometimes been charged with managing the discussions with the IMF on macroeconomic issues.

Can the future be different?

How can Pakistan break out of these repeating cycles from near crisis to a merely temporary degree of stabilization, and from partial structural reform which then proves inadequate, and from the build-up of vulnerabilities leading to yet another crisis? One suggestion is for Pakistan to embark on a process to develop and agree upon a national economic agenda. A striking feature of successful emerging market countries is that there is a broad consensus around a core economic agenda. Politicians of different parties, private sector leaders, opinion makers and economic experts all agree on the general direction and content of the economic programme. To be sure, there are differences of emphasis on specific policies or on timing, but much of the content enjoys broad support. This has two advantages: first, when the government in power is trying to undertake a difficult reform – privatization or labour market reforms – there will be debate on the method or the manner in which it is carried out, but not on the basic objectives. And second, this broad consensus provides domestic and international investors with a degree of certainty about the future business environment within which they can operate and make long-term investment decisions.

In Pakistan, there is a broad consensus on a national security agenda and on the direction of foreign policy, but when it comes to economics, such a consensus is lacking. The result is that the party in power manages the day-to-day affairs of the economy, and if a crisis is looming, takes steps to restore macroeconomic stability. But it finds it much harder to implement more fundamental reforms. There is no shortage of visions for the future, but there is a disconnect between these visions and the willingness or ability to take the actions required to make the vision a reality.

Pakistan needs a national discussion on what kind of economy it wants to be in 10 years, and then it must agree on the actions needed to get there. This is a broad topic, but even at a narrow macroeconomic level, Pakistan needs a realistic plan of actions that will generate the growth rates that are often set as aspirations rather than objectives. A non-exhaustive list of questions that a national discussion could seek consensus on includes: What kind of macro-economic policies would support Pakistan's broader growth and distribution objectives? What level of inequality is Pakistan comfortable with as a society and what actions is it willing to take to reduce inequality? Do Pakistani policymakers want the government to have tax revenues that are close to the emerging market norm of 20 per cent of GDP? If so, what would be the composition and structure of those taxes and what kind of revenue administration system would deliver that outcome? What is the appropriate level and composition of public spending and how should it be divided between the federal and provincial administrations? Where should defence spending be most effectively focused in the context of a tightly constrained overall resource envelope? Does the country want to raise exports from under 10 per cent of GDP to 25 per cent of GDP? If so, what actions are needed to change the incentive structure for exporting, and is there broad consensus to implement them? Are policymakers willing to support indefinitely a set of loss-making public enterprises, both in the energy sector and outside? If not, can they agree upon a plan for their restructuring and privatization? Does the government have a role in fixing administered prices for a variety of products, in effect protecting the producers from market forces? If so, which products and at what cost?

An often voiced objection to developing a national economic consensus is that it has not happened in many decades and is unlikely to come about now. Perhaps. But it is also the case that attempting to make major structural reforms without such a consensus has failed so far, and there is enough underlying agreement across the political spectrum on core economic fundamentals that, with a degree of political leadership, forging such a consensus should be possible.

The key challenge for Pakistan is to break through to a high-level equilibrium that would avoid the need for repeated stabilization through reforms that leverage the talent of its youth and the entrepreneurial skills of its private sector, and deliver the economic and social performance that its population demands and deserves.

Notes

1 The cumulative losses of these enterprises stand at around 4 per cent of GDP. See IMF Staff Report, 'Pakistan's First Post-Program Monitoring Discussions', *IMF*, 2018. Available at www.imf.org/en/Publications/CR/Issues/2018/03/14/Pakistan-First-Post-Program-Monitoring-Discussions-Press-Release-Staff-Report-and-Statement-45724.

2 Electric power transmission and distribution losses stand at 17 per cent of output for 2014. See World Bank, https://data.worldbank.org/indicator/EG.ELC.LOSS.ZS?locations=PK.

3 Tax revenue-to-GDP ratio for FY 2017 is 12.4. See Pakistan Economic Survey, 2017–18, Ministry of Finance. Available at www.finance.gov.pk/survey_1718.html.

4 For the year 2014. See IMF World Revenue Longitudinal Dataset. The list of middle-income countries can be found at the World Bank's Lending and Country Groups, available at https://datahelpdesk.worldbank.org/knowledgebase/articles/906519-world-bank-country-and-lending-groups.

5 Serhan Cevik, 'Unlocking Pakistan's Revenue Potential', IMF, August 2016. Available at www.imf.org/external/pubs/ft/wp/2016/wp16182.pdf.

6 www.dawn.com/news/1354151;https://tribune.com.pk/story/1562414/2-40-companies-not-pay-tax-2016.

7 The 7th NFC Award. The federal government is bound to transfer 57.5 per cent of resources to all four provinces from the federal divisible pool. For the FY 2017, net transfers to the provinces were estimated at 1,938 billion rupees. The provinces account for about 35 per cent of total spending.

8 World Bank, *Doing Business*, 2018 pp. 22–32.

15

History of the development discourse in Pakistan

Asad Ejaz Butt

Introduction

The great economist of the Austrian school and author of one of the most popular texts in economics, *The Road to Serfdom* by F. A. Hayek,[1] is reported to have criticized another great economist of the same era and author of another popular economics text, *The General Theory of Employment, Interest and Money* by John Maynard Keynes,[2] for not knowing economic history well enough, especially that of the 19th century. In a popular video interview,[3] Hayek opined that Keynes knew very little of the history of economic thought and that his knowledge was predominantly only Marshallian in nature.

What Hayek refers to is not only an intellectual deficit but a fallible inclination suffered by a majority of Pakistani economic policymakers since the very early days of the country; namely a total neglect of economic history, especially when it comes to its utility as a tool to inform future decision- and policymaking. Not only are the country's policymakers deficient in knowledge of its economic history but also of that which pertains to politics, anthropology and other social sciences, some of which are inextricably linked to economics.

The utility of economic history

Hayek implies that to make inferences about an economy based on its current state while ignoring experience, historical patterns and trends is to flirt with imprudence and irrationality. Economic actors and institutions often behave in harmony or discord with certain historical trends and hence need to be understood against the backdrop of these long-term trajectories. The study of horizons is therefore a vital component in an understanding of economic relationships and any fact-finding or predictive exercise must therefore begin from this.

There is good reason to believe what Hayek espoused. Economic actors and institutions are often dependent upon the past and to make inferences about them without analysing their historic behavioural patterns and interactions with other actors and institutions is often expected to result in inaccurate assessments of the economy. This obviously does not imply that Keynes' assessments of the economy were inaccurate but, being a post-crisis economist, the circumstances available to him were unique and to a large degree disconnected from the past and therefore his neglect of history as an informant for future macroeconomic policy-making is reasonably justified. However, whether such neglect of history can be afforded during normal economic circumstances[4] is questionable and expected to result in misappropriations, misjudgements and inaccurate assessments of the economy.

The high value of history as an enabler of economic understanding is undeniable. That is why economic history, even as a taught science, has gained much popularity among Western scholars and universities and the trend in the developing countries is also advancing in the same direction. There are more taught programmes in history than ever before and economists, despite the visible onslaught of the neo-classical economics which is highly invested in the mathmatics, empirics, statistical models and theoretical underpinnings of economic behaviour, have started to recognize that economics devoid of history is bound to engender assumptions, inferences and value judgements that are often incorrect and present weak and implausible inputs to the policy and programme formulation process.

The literature produced in Pakistan does include some economic history particularly that relating to the dynamics of growth, but the perspectives and opinions of experts that feed into the discourse, and which more often than not enhance its pragmatic value, are either not documented or, if they are, they are not made use of to bring a clearer understanding of the inspirations underlying the various policies and programmes.

Certain ideas, albeit not indigenous, have attracted the attention of local policymakers but their potency to invite rational discourse has remained weak. One such guiding principle for policy concerns human development which involves prioritizing the development of human beings through investment in education, health and standards of living in comparison to other development objectives such as infrastructure. The discourse on human development in Pakistan has remained limited in several ways. And clearly, one overarching limitation is the very lack of knowledge among policymakers regarding economic history in general and the history of human development in particular.

To that end, this chapter traces the roots of the current discourse on human development by analysing the 70-year economic history of the country. This is done through analysis of the policy and structural transformations that have taken place. A secondary focus of the chapter is to delineate and bring to the fore the utility of economic history as a science that can facilitate honest and accurate assessments of the economy, thereby also enabling effective policy design and formulation.

Pakistan's development context

Pakistan's problems, deprivations and insecurities at the time of Partition in 1947 are well documented, although it is conjectured intentional omissions were made to protect the political interests of certain groups and individual stakeholders. Economic historians interested in the initial conditions of Pakistan have pointed to the lack of inheritance, the migration of Hindu and Sikh entrepreneurs and the dishonouring of financial commitments by India as possible clues to Pakistan's initial woes.

In *Pakistan's Economy at the Crossroads,* [5] Parvez Hasan mentions that the departure of the Sikh and Hindu entrepreneurs from the region that ultimately became Pakistan was a huge blow to the country's business, industry and enterprise. Only limited capital was available, growth in investment was low and only a few cities had any road or rail infrastructure installed. Punjab was slightly better endowed with infrastructure, especially that relevant to agriculture; however, its growth too only seems satisfactory when juxtaposed against evidence from within South Asia.

Health and education infrastructure was generally poor in the region. Institutions, both public and private, were predominantly non-existent while schools, hospitals and government service delivery centres, although present, were quite sparse. This was a key deficit considering the antecedents of underdevelopment and low economic performance postulated by Acemoglu and Robinson in *Why Nations Fail* [6] and Douglas North in several of his works including *Institutions, Institutional Change and Economic Performance.* [7]

In the three decades that followed the birth of the nation, there was a power contest between the three key institutions of the state: the military, the bureaucracy and the parliament. The three contested to arrogate more power and constituency as the country swung between various military and civilian regimes, each of which brought a set of totally new economic policies and defined different roles for the bureaucracy. In times when the bureaucracy was allowed a larger role in the decision-making process, economic policies independent of the administrative priorities and formalities could not be produced. And during authoritative military regimes, democratic institutions that emphasized principles of equity, good governance and distributed powers at the local and subnational level could not be developed. Under civilian governments, when on one end, the sovereignty of the parliament was held supreme, a lack of professionalism and scrutiny in the operational and functional dealings of the government held back the growth and progress of the country.

Hence, the East Asian economies, which at one time had experienced slower growth rates than Pakistan, developed at a rapid pace in the 1970s. Clearly, institution building and strengthening had an important role to play in the divergence not just between Pakistan and the selected East Asian states but between the two regions of South and East Asia.

History of economic planning in Pakistan

South Asia's discourse history of human development dates back to the 1970s when Amartya Sen started publishing accounts of the human losses owing to the Bengal famine in the 1940s. Sen's work on savings, investment, welfare economics and social choice theory predated his shift in focus to human development in the 1970s. His works on capabilities and welfare economics are well cited and earned him global recognition culminating in a Nobel Memorial Prize in Economics in 1998. However, apart from Sen, the indigenous discourse on human development was nearly non-existent in the decades prior to the 1990s.

The early discourse was largely centred on budgeting for the operational and functional costs and expenditures of the government and thus, economic planning was relegated to the status of a sub-discipline of accounting and public finance management. In fact, the civil service, bureaucracy and economics were so enmeshed that most civil servants, bureaucrats and people of scholarly eminence, who were often not trained economists, carried out public financial management and local budgeting functions. Planning and policy discourse that could ensure better human development outcomes was a far cry in a country like Pakistan where debate between the public and the private sectors and that between mainstream political parties remains subdued to this day.

The history texts that were published either documented the economic developments and achievements of the various political eras or just managed to do a comparative periodic analysis of growth. The history of economic thought, especially that aimed at drawing lessons for future policymaking, was hardly an interest area in the global south and the inclination seemed to find ample expression in Pakistan.

Thematic inquiries that tended to explore particular economic themes such as human development were largely absent and while data analytical studies that compared Pakistan's health and education numbers with its South Asian counterparts or countries in East Asia were mostly published by foreign authors and international research organizations, a history exercise that traces the roots of the development discourse was a rather unexplored area of inquiry. The policy discourse was incoherent among political eras and was one dimensional, lacking the essential diversity of thought. Even within eras, the focus was too narrow to invoke the generation of fresh ideas for reform.

As the policy discourse entered a new political era, a complete divorce from the previous one was seen and therefore policy transitions in the country were neither smooth nor coherent, causing major shocks and disturbances.

The greatest handicap faced by most Pakistani economists was their lack of econometric and quantitative skills and had it not been for the Harvard Advisory Group in the 1950s and the 1960s, many of the skills acquired by the successful economists of the later era could not have been developed. Even today, the low probability of the Sustainable Development Goals (SDGs) being mainstreamed, accelerated and given policy support (MAPS)[8] depends upon data that the statistical arms of the government do not have the capacity and expertise to collect and report.

The five-year centralized economic plans dominated decision and policymaking in the first two decades and the Planning Commission, Pakistan Institute of Development Economics and the State Bank of Pakistan, three institutions primarily tasked with economic policymaking were all fragmented and worked quite independently of each other. While this was one of the factors that led to the incoherence of the plans, the growth achieved during the second plan was higher than expected. However, the policy incoherence between plans and the decline of foreign aid post-1965 contributed to the low growth results of the third plan.

The Harvard Advisory group's[9] findings and conclusions were the cornerstone of Pakistan's economic policy during the 1960s. Even though human development was not used as a term in the analysis of economists such as Stern, Falcon, Papanek and Ranis, they did well to draw up the health, education and poverty profiles of Pakistan's initial years.

According to ul-Haq et al.,[10]

> A second element in the thinking of the HAG economist was the concern with inequality. Haq and Baqai (1986), two important economists of the HAG era, note with concern that 'early writing on economics in Pakistan surprisingly did not contain much reference to poverty-related themes.' It is very interesting that most of the early econometric or behavioural research is done mainly by the HAG advisor, whereas the work on measuring poverty, productivity (the ratio calculation work) is done by the Pakistani economist. Before anything about the economy was understood, poverty indices, regional inequality indices, and declines in real wages (when hard wage data was hardly available) were the main areas of concern.

The most successful crop of Pakistani economists, including ul-Haq and Moeen Qureshi, were also trained under the supervision and auspices of the Harvard Advisory group and a large part of Pakistan's success during the first three plans could be attributed purely to good planning. However, whether the discourse moved beyond budgeting and the East–West[11] inequality during these years is highly questionable.

It seems that the penchant for public financial management and effective budgeting in a newly formed state aiming for austerity was understandable yet dangerous since it had to happen at the cost of focus driven away from the development and long-term sustainability of the economy. In fact, even the five-year centralized economic plans were divided into medium-term targets and the focus of the planning and policy frameworks was largely to achieve and report on performance within those temporal parameters.

Industrialization did take place during the 1960s and the discourse on industrial economics, if not on institutional development or strengthening, at least on the impact of investment on the gross national product, did develop. However, the subsequent nationalization of industries in the 1970s held back industrial progress in the country and the discourse underwent a paradigm shift from focus on the positive growth impacts of industrialization to the political economy of nationalization and how industries may lack optimal technical and economic performance under nationalized structures.

The only time when the discourse was mainstreamed and hardwired into the economic planning and public-policy formulation process was during the first three planning periods from 1955–70. Not only can one experience the richness of economic history from this era but one can also find perspectives that were instrumental in ascertaining the policy direction of the country. As shown by the figures presented in the section below, the curtailment of public discourse on economic planning under Zulfikar Ali Bhutto in the 1970s and his unpopular nationalization plans brought about the implicit discontinuation of the plans even though they continued to feature in the policy disclosures of the government.

Furthermore, despite the fact that the discourse was neither inclusive nor participatory, the availability of perspectives that can be considered a semblance of the public discourse has reflected quite positively on the development outcomes achieved during the first three five-year plans. The figures presented below provide evidence for this claim.

The first three Five-Year Plans

The first Five-Year Plan (1955–60) proposed an increase of 15 per cent in national income and per caput income of 7 per cent after allowing for a 7 per cent growth in population. This was interesting given the actual reported increase of 18 per cent in the pre-plan period. Ul-Haq's argument suffices any fact-finding exercise that tries to understand the likely causes of this reversal in economic objectives. He believed that

> if the planners accepted a lower target of increase in national output while proposing an increase in real investment of about 80%, the reason might be that they regarded the increase in national income during the pre-plan period as fortuitous rather than related to investment during that period: an understandable caution in a predominantly agricultural economy where the relationship between investment an income may be quite tenuous in view of weather fluctuations.[12]

The chairman of the Planning Commission during the development of the first plan, Zahid Hussain, in his annual address in November 1956, delineated the direction and purpose behind some of the key elements of the plan. Speaking of priorities at such an early phase of economic development, Hussain observed that all countries, democratic or authoritarian, have concentrated in the early stages of development on economic programmes. Social services, that is education, health, housing, etc. are important and some of the main ultimate objectives of national policy. We shall, however, meet with frustration and defeat if we put social services before economic development. Agricultural, industrial, power, water and other developments must receive higher priority for many years.

The second priority, he believed, was to

bring about a substantial improvement in the foreign exchange position of the country in order that we should be able to support a sizeable development pro-gramme year without dependence on foreign sources. This is essential to gain some sort of economic independence and to extricate the country from its present state of helplessness. This objective determines the pattern of agricultural and industrial programmes. We must be self-sufficient in food to prevent large demands for imports to feed starving populations. We must increase the production of cotton.

Ul-Haq's evaluation of the plan understandably differed from that of Hussain's, as the two perspectives could be understood in terms of the positions they assumed during the first plan period. Hussain was the formulator and ul-Haq an ardent critic. He believed that the plan was quite modest as it proposed increase of only a 15 per cent in national income in the face of an actual increase of 12 per cent in population. Investment targets fell short by 30 per cent and the momentum built during the early phase of indus-trialization was lost. The plan gave agriculture the highest priority although it allocated only 11 per cent of the total investment funds to agriculture as opposed to the 28 per cent that was allocated to industry.

Ul-Haq did concur that the plan devoted two-thirds of funds to economic and social overheads and the progress in this field was encouraging. He believed that the first plan succeeded in building some infrastructure and improving the industrial sector but failed to address the basic problems of Pakistan especially in relation to agriculture, education and housing.

While methodologies and priorities of the government were disputed by ul-Haq, an obvious achievement of the first plan was providing a direction to an economy that was proceeding on the whims and experimental tendencies of the ruling class. The transi-tion toward the second plan and onwards involved realistic economic expectations that avoided under or overstatement of objectives.

The second Five-Year Plan (1960–65) envisaged an increase of 20 per cent in the gross national product which would require the injection of 19,000 million rupees of investment from both the private and public sectors. Analysing the plan's objectives, Aziz-ur-Rehman Khan stated that

In an underdeveloped country like Pakistan, where low income accompanied by high propensities to consume yields an inadequate rate of capital formation, financing a plan of such large magnitude is very difficult. Without foreign assistance, financing the second plan would require a high rate of domestic capital formation – 13.4% of GNP. Even if 42% of the total investment programme is financed externally, as is expected, domestic capital formation will have to be 7.8% of GNP.

Interestingly, not only was the plan successfully financed, in fact, according to Griffin and Glassburner in their post-second year analysis,

> GNP grew by 29% instead of by 24%. According to government data, per capita income was expected to increase by 10%, but grew by 13%, foreign exchange earnings were expected to grow by only 15% whereas they grew by 40%, agricultural output increased by 7% during the first plan – after increasing by 19% in the second plan when it was expected to double to 14%.[13]

Aziz felt that the plan was overly optimistic and that its magnitude was disproportionate to the expected inflow of financial resources. Meanwhile, ul-Haq belived that the 24 per cent increase in national output was a target that was well within the reach of Pakistan. In his analysis of 1963, when he had the luxury of having the mid-plan review figures at his disposal, ul-Haq predicted that if the proposed investment took place, the plan's target might even be exceeded.

The third Five-Year Plan (1965–70) period started with satisfactory economic and fiscal conditions that carried forward from the good work done by the social planners during the second plan. By 1964–65 gross domestic savings, an imperative towards achieving an internally financed economic output, as a percentage of gross national product had risen to 9.5 per cent. This was an increase of approximately 70 per cent compared with the 1959–60 plan.

Griffin and Glassburner, in 'Evaluation of the Third Five-Year Plan'[14] enumerate the initial successes and rational fiscal expectations from the plan thus: 'Large-scale industry was saving and reinvesting 75% of its profits. Government's marginal rate of saving from its revenue will be over 40% and that revenues are expected to rise by 70%.'

The marginal savings rate, a key indicator used by ul-Haq and other analysts revealed trends in industrialization and the extent of reliance on foreign assistance – especially in circumstances where balance of payments figures were unfavourable and foreign exchange reserves were depleted to alarmingly low levels. From 24 per cent during the second plan to 5.7 per cent during the third, the marginal savings rate represents the relative effectiveness of the two plans and the glaring economic transition that had taken place within just five years.

Discourse following the first *Human Development Report*

Apart from the first three five-year planning periods, the discourse in Pakistan, especially that facilitated by indigenous means, methods and sources of research production was largely non-existent until 1990 when the first *Human Development Report* was published.[15] Even during the planning periods, the perspectives were available but the discourse in its most refined form, i.e. when it is inclusive and participatory, was not available.

The research around human development only started after the first human development report was published by Haq *et al.* in 1990. Prior to that, Pakistan's human development-related analyses were carried out by external commentators such as the Harvard Advisory Group and usually without making explicit reference to the term 'human development' which at that point had not gained the popularity and coinage that it did post-1990.

A sister concept of human development, the Basic Needs Approach (BNA) that evolved in the work of the World Bank economists Streeten, Haq and Burki in the 1970s, was briefly adopted as the global development agenda and endorsed by the Bank itself and the UN agencies. Subsequently, however, its adoption campaign did muster initial support but it was unable to survive the challenge posed by the modern research in economic theory enabled by data, statistical and econometric tools that could build more proficient and robust models. The BNA was soon to be taken over by other poverty and human welfare measurement techniques such as the Human Development Index (HDI).

The research produced post-1990 lacked in various capacities and is hardly a continuation of the legacy created by the South Asian scholars of the likes of Sen and Haq. It has mainly focused on exploring the causal side of the economic ideas put forward by the leading international scholars of the period. The indigenous human development research, while being absent in the pre-1990 era, has not really gone too far ahead of the proposition put forward by the 1990 *Human Development Report*.

During the 1990s there was too much focus on the consequences for economic growth and human development of foreign aid and fiscal policy liberalization. This inhibited efforts to localize and implement the human development agenda or to engage in discourse that envisaged means, methods and processes to move beyond it.

The human development discourse

Thanks to the Millennium Development Goals (MDGs) formulated by the United Nations (UN) in 2000, the human development paradigm and the HDI approach to human development estimation gained international popularity and significance. This surge in the popularity of human development as an aim of the development process was felt more severely in the global south where the standards and practices pertaining to health, education and poverty bear poorer outcomes compared to the north. Not only did the local policymakers in countries of the south adopt human development as an agenda that could provide an impetus to attain welfare gains and improvement in the living conditions of the people but it could also bring home a level of recognition, respect and amelioration in the international image of countries in the developing world that are often perceived as reckless, irresponsible and oblivious to the needs of their people.

In order to realize its human development objectives and align itself with the UN's international development agenda encapsulated in the MDGs, Pakistan adopted the MDG targets in 2000 but its performance could at best be termed poor. None of its targets were achieved and despite a mid-term evaluation and recommitment expressed in the health and education policies of 2009, the country fell far short of its MDG targets in 2015. Poor planning and implementation frameworks, especially those that could ensure the devolution of powers and resources to the local and provincial level and a lack of resource commitment from the government clearly led to this failure.

Learning from the MDG experience, one obvious transformation that has taken place is the inclusion of human development in the political and governance discourse. The leading political parties of the country and the bureaucracy are now found reiterating their commitment to the SDGs while also expressing dismay over the fact that the country fell short of achieving the MDGs. An increasing number of parliamentarians and civil servants mention human development as an end goal of the development process and exalt their potential achievement as the only solution to a host of economic problems that the country faces today.

A significant contribution of the MDGs and the SDGs is that they have ensured policy coherence and continuity not only in Pakistan but elsewhere in the developing world. By the end of the SDG timeframe in 2030, sustainable development with a focus on human beings would likely become a priority, and in Pakistan where some level of interest towards achieving the goals is found already, any divergence from the agenda seems highly improbable. Hence the anticipated greater coherence and continuity seem assured.

The two leading political parties of the country have started to debate whether human development is a greater imperative than that of infrastructure. In what has been predicted to be a fiercely fought battle between the two right-wing parties, the Pakistan Tehreek-i-Insaf, a centre-right populist party formed in 1996, and the Pakistan Muslim League (Nawaz), an offshoot of the Muslim League that is credited to have won independence for the Muslims of South Asia, both appear to be locking horns on whether human development should precede that of infrastructure, or vice versa.

This is clearly a new direction in a predominantly agrarian country like Pakistan where the debate throughout the 1960s and 1970s, as Parvez Hasan points out, was whether investment in agriculture should be a larger priority of the government or industry. And while both were pursued as part of the first three Five-Year Plans, the discourse could not evolve out of prioritizing one over the other.

In 2016, the government of Punjab, with technical support from UNDP, launched the multi-dimensional poverty index (MPI) methodology to measure deprivations across a range of development indicators. This has been effectively mainstreamed into the government's human development planning for the province of Punjab that took an implementation lead vis-à-vis MPI, and other provinces have also followed suit.

The Ministry of Planning, Development and Reform launched a comprehensive economic plan for 2025, whereas the government of Punjab presented an agenda for 2018 vis-à-vis the 2014 Punjab Growth Strategy. These plans, policies and strategies underscore the government's shift towards a focus on human development from the earlier focus on industrialization and capital accumulation as a means to the economic growth and development process.

Foucauldian discourse analysis

An interesting dimension to the study of discourse is a discourse analysis of human development that not only traces the roots of the present discourse as is the case with a discourse history exercise but also focuses on power relationships as manifested in language, customs, traditions and practices.

Power relationships are often expressed through language and behaviour. This form of analysis developed out of Michel Foucault's genealogical work,[16] where power was linked to the formation of discourse within specific historical periods. Some versions of this method stress the genealogical application of discourse analysis to illustrate how discourse is produced to govern social groups. The method analyses how the social world, expressed through language, is affected by various sources of power and attempts to understand how individuals view the world, and studies categorizations, personal and institutional relationships, ideology and politics.

Given Pakistan's civil-military divide and the manner in which the pendulum of power has swung numerous times between the two, discourse analysis to understand the historic policy formulation process and its relevance to the current political, economic and social landscape has becomes imperative. Not only should the discourse be traced in order to extract lessons for the future but also to discover the extent to which language and behaviour used to delineate and even dictate policy were similar or varied from one regime to the next.

Conclusion

It is critical to note here that one common aspect shared by all developing nations is their disconnect with history in general and that pertaining to their economic policy and structural evolution in particular. And therefore, while the importance of economic history as an informant for future decision- and policymaking has long been recognized in the developed world, it has now become indispensable in the developing world. In such a case, economic planning that does not give requisite attention to historical patterns, trends and trajectories may induce skewed investments and allocations. The discourse in Pakistan, having absorbed a number of external shocks and disturbances, has reached a stage where human development and governance alongside tools that enable their intersection[17] have become large imperatives.

Notes

1 Hayek was a Classical Liberalist British-Austrian economist famed for his magnum opus *The Road to Serfdom*.
2 The father of the Keynesian School of Economics, regarded as one of the most influential economists of the 20th century and author of *The General Theory of Employment, Interest and Money*.
3 See www.youtube.com/watch?v=y8l47ilD0II&t=116s.
4 This refers to a non-crisis economic situation. A large part of Keynes' research focused on the aftermath of the Great Depression of the 1930s and hence is regarded as post-crisis.
5 Parvez Hasan, *Pakistan's Economy at the Crossroads: Past Policies and Present Imperatives*, New York, Oxford University Press, 1998.
6 Daron Acemoglu and James A. Robinson, *Why Nations Fail: The Origins of Power, Prosperity, and Poverty*, Danvers, MA, Broadway Business, 2013.
7 Acemoglu and Robinson define institutions as either inclusive or extractive. Their focus is on the building and strengthening of democratic and inclusive institutions as a key contributor to economic growth. See *Why Nations Fail*. North was a pioneer of institutional economics and a historian who observed the constraints on the development of institutions to see how they reflect on economic performance. See C. Douglass, 'North, Institutions, Institutional Change and Economic Performance', Cambridge, Cambridge University Press, 1990.
8 Mainstreaming, Acceleration and Policy Support (MAPS) is a key tool that originated in the work of the UN Development Group to localize the SDGs.
9 The Harvard Advisory Group that included economists such as Gustav Ranis, Papanek and Falcon frequented Pakistan during the Ayub era and worked closely alongside the Pakistan Institute of Development Economics. In fact, they are credited with the capacity building of PIDE and the training of a number of economists including Haq and Moeen Qureshi who went on to serve in key positions in the government of Pakistan and international institutions.
10 Nadeem ul Haque, Hasan Khan Mahmood and A. R. Kemal, 'The Economics Profession in Pakistan: A Historical Analysis [with Comments]', *Pakistan Development Review*, 1998, pp. 431–52.
11 This refers to the economic inequalities between East and West Pakistan. West Pakistan, which forms the Pakistan of today, was considerably more developed than its Eastern Wing that is now Bangladesh.
12 Mahbub ul-Haq, *The Strategy of Economic Planning: A Case Study of Pakistan*, Lahore, Oxford University Press, 1966.

13 Keith B. Griffin and Bruce Glassburner, 'An Evaluation of Pakistan's Third Five-Year Plan', *Journal of Development Studies* vol. 2, no. 4, 1966, pp. 431–59.

14 Ibid.

15 A team led by Mahbub ul-Haq wrote the first *Human Development Report* for the UN Development Programme. The report was instrumental in putting forth the Human Development Index that is used to rank countries on the basis of their human development status.

16 See Rainer Diaz-Bone, Andrea D. Bührmann, Encarnación Gutiérrez Rodríguez, Werner Schneider, Gavin Kendall and Francisco Tirado, 'The Field of Foucaultian Discourse Analysis: Structures, Developments and Perspectives', *Forum Qualitative Sozialforschung/Forum: Qualitative Social Research* vol. 8, no. 2, Art. 30, 2007. Available at http://nbn-resolving.de/urn:nbn:de:0114-fqs0702305.

17 See the MPI report for Punjab that has become the basis of prioritization of the poorest districts for implementation of the SDGs and the Human Development agenda.

16

Recent economic developments and prospects

Farrukh Iqbal

This chapter is organized in two parts. The first part documents the main features of the macroeconomic recovery in recent years while noting key areas of concern. The second part turns to a discussion of Pakistan's economic prospects in the light of (a) the surge of Chinese investment and loans under the China–Pakistan Economic Corridor (CPEC) initiative and (b) continuing fiscal and external account imbalances.

Recovery and growth

The economy grew by 5.3 per cent in 2017, the highest growth rate during the past decade and capping a four-year run of above 4 per cent growth. All the major sectors grew at decent rates, with industry growing by a healthy 5.3 per cent and agriculture growing by 3.5 per cent. The recovery in agriculture (up from 0.3 per cent in the previous year) was partly due to strong performance in the livestock sector which contributed 2 out of the 3.5 percentage point growth of the sector. The crop sector contributed another one percentage point. This was due to a revival of the cotton crop, which had crashed the previous year from around 14 million bales in 2015 to 9.9 million bales in 2016 before rising to 10.7 million bales in 2017. It was also due to the rise in sugar cane output, up from 65.4 million metric tons in 2016 to 75.6 million tons in 2017, due to generous price supports.

Growth in industry was consistent with bank lending to the private sector, which rose by 16.8 per cent in 2017 compared with 11.2 per cent in 2016. However, despite the fact that about one-third of this credit was meant for fixed investment, the rate of private fixed investment has remained at around 10 per cent of gross domestic product (GDP) (provisional data). The stagnation in the private investment rate at this level for the last 10 years or so suggests that the private sector continues to hang back in making long-term commitments. While improvements have taken place in energy supply and general security over the last few years, these have not made a significant difference to the private sector's confidence in the long-term prospects of the economy.[1] It is possible that, while some aspects of the business environment have eased, others have worsened. The tax burden on formal sector businesses, for example, remains very high.

On a related note, the stock market experienced a significant correction during 2017, with the Pakistan Stock Exchange (KSE 100) declining by about 20 per cent from its peak of around 52000.

Price stability

While inflation, as measured by the growth of the Pakistan Consumer Price Index, picked up somewhat, registering 4.2 per cent in 2017 compared to 2.9 per cent in 2016, it remained at a comfortable level from the point of view of macroeconomic management and was below the originally anticipated level of 6 per cent. The upward tick in inflation was due partly to delayed domestic adjustments to changes in international oil prices and an increase in the prices of some food commodities such as palm oil. The monetary policy stance remained stable, with M2 money supply rising by 13.7 per cent in 2017 and the policy interest rate pegged at 5.75 per cent, the same as in 2016.

Resumption of fiscal pressures

The overall fiscal deficit rose sharply to 5.8 per cent of GDP in 2017, higher than the 4.6 per cent registered in 2016 and much higher than the 3.8 per cent targeted at the beginning of the fiscal year.[2] This was due mostly to an increase in development spending.

The improving trend in the revenue-to-GDP ratio seen in the past three years weakened in 2017. Revenue collections came in at 4.9 trillion rupees, or 15.5 per cent of GDP, much below the target of 5.3 trillion rupees set at the beginning of the fiscal year. Direct tax revenues grew by only 10.3 per cent in 2017 compared to 17.8 per cent in 2016. Indirect tax collection growth fell off even more sharply, from 21.8 per cent in 2016 to only 6.5 per cent in 2017. The most likely causes of the deceleration in collections were (a) lower petroleum sales tax rates introduced to prevent pump prices from rising in line with international oil prices; (b) relief measures and tax breaks provided during the course of the year to support investment and exports; and (c) lower dividends declared by public sector enterprises and lower disbursements under the Coalition Support Fund.

On the expenditure side, current spending was 5.2 trillion rupees as targeted at the beginning of the fiscal year. Development spending, however, was much higher than

Table 16.1 Output and price developments

	2014	*2015*	*2016*	*2017*
Real GDP (annual % change)	4.1	4.1	4.5	5.3
Agriculture	2.5	2.1	0.3	3.5
Industry	4.5	5.2	5.8	5
Services	4.5	4.4	5.5	4.2
Consumer Price Index (period average)	8.6	4.5	2.9	4.2
Fixed investment (as % of GDP)	13	14.1	14	14.2
Public	3.2	3.7	3.8	4.3
Private	9.9	10.4	10.2	9.9

Source: GDP and price data from the State Bank of Pakistan, *The State of Pakistan's Economy*, Annual Report, 2016–17; Fixed investment data from the Ministry of Finance, Pakistan, *Pakistan Economic Survey 2016–17*.

Table 16.2 Fiscal developments (% of GDP)

	2014	2015	2016	2017
Government revenue	14.5	14.3	15.3	15.5
Tax revenue	10.2	11	12.6	12.5
Non-tax revenue	4.3	3.3	2.7	3
Government expenditure	20	19.6	19.9	21.3
Current expenditure	15.9	16.1	16.1	16.3
Development expenditure	4.9	4.2	4.5	5.3
Government overall deficit	−5.5	−5.3	−4.6	−5.8

Source: State Bank of Pakistan, *The State of Pakistan's Economy*, Annual Report, 2016–17.

originally projected, coming in at 1.7 trillion rupees compared to a target of 1.4 trillion rupees due to high outlays by provincial governments, in particular. In relation to GDP, current spending came in at 16.3 per cent and development spending at 5.3 per cent. Developments in 2017 raised concerns about the path of fiscal spending in the year ahead as pressures were likely to rise due to impending elections.[3]

Widening external account imbalances

Three developments in 2017 reflected pressure on the external accounts. First, the current account balance expanded sharply to 4 per cent of GDP as exports continued to decline, although at a decelerating pace. Second, worker remittances declined, in nominal terms, indicating a new phase in this important source of foreign earnings. Third, gross international reserves declined by close to US $2 billion. All three developments suggested near term volatility as the rupee was predicted to come under pressure and investors to worry about the timing and severity of the eventual exchange rate adjustment.[4]

Exports declined in nominal dollar terms from US $25 billion in 2014 to $21.7 billion in 2017. As a share of GDP, Pakistan's exports declined from 10.3 per cent in 2014 to 5.3 per cent in 2017. A move of this magnitude sustained over several years draws attention to structural and policy factors. Among critical policy factors is the exchange rate. The real effective exchange rate has been rising since 2010 and the International Monetary Fund (IMF) considered it overvalued by between 10 and 20 per cent.[5] Among critical structural factors are soft demand in key export markets in recent years as well as low skills and infrastructure and business environment deficiencies that prevent Pakistan from improving export unit values and competitiveness.[6]

At US $19.3 billion worker remittances declined in 2017, in nominal terms, for the first time in many years, continuing the decelerating trend that began in 2015 as the demand for Pakistani workers faltered in the Cooperation Council for the Arab States of the Gulf. Given that oil prices may not rise substantially over the coming years, Pakistan is likely to continue to see declining remittances over the next few years.

International reserves also declined in nominal terms after a four-year period of accumulation. State Bank of Pakistan liquid reserves were reported at US $16.1 billion at the end of June 2017, down from US $18.1 billion a year before, possibly because of repeated attempts to defend the exchange rate during the year. Although import cover was still above 3 per cent, the reversal of trend was yet another signal of growing pressure on the exchange rate.[7]

Table 16.3 External sector developments

	2014	2015	2016	2017
Trade (as % of GDP)				
Exports	10.3	8.9	7.9	5.3
Imports	17	15.2	14.5	11.1
Current account balance	−1.3	−1	−1.7	−4
Foreign investment ($ billion)	1.6	0.9	1.9	2.1
Worker remittances ($ billion)	15.8	18.7	19.9	19.3
International reserves ($ billion)	9.1	13.5	18.1	16.1

Source: State Bank of Pakistan, *The State of Pakistan's Economy*, Annual Report, 2016–17.

One positive development in the external accounts was an increase in foreign direct investment. At US $2.1 billion in 2017, this was similar to the $1.9 billion received in 2016 and a significant increase from the $0.6 billion recorded in 2015. The bulk of this investment was from the People's Republic of China and was related to the CPEC initiative. Of course, the enhanced investment also generated high levels of machinery imports that contributed to a widening current account deficit. The current account deficit reached 4 per cent of GDP, up significantly from 1.2 per cent in 2016.

There were some preliminary indications that the export picture had begun to improve in 2018. Provisional data from the Trade Development Authority of Pakistan for the first quarter of 2018 showed exports increasing by 10.8 per cent over the same period in 2017, up from US $ 4.7 billion to $ 5.2 billion.

Prospects and challenges

Macroeconomic consequences of the CPEC

The CPEC comprises a large package of investments in energy and infrastructure projected to amount to US $55 billion by 2030. This represents about 19 per cent of Pakistan's GDP of $280 billion in 2016 or, very roughly, about 1.5 per cent of GDP per annum over the next 10 years. CPEC investments alone should boost the investment ratio in Pakistan from 15 per cent of GDP to 16.5 per cent over the next decade. The IMF has calculated that first-round effects of CPEC-related investments should add about $13 billion to GDP within the first seven years.[8] CPEC investments may also crowd in other private sector investments in which case the impact on output will be even stronger.[9] This would happen, for example, if CPEC investments eliminate power outages for Pakistan's industrial sector. The extent to which this happens will depend on the extent to which higher power generation is successfully transmitted through Pakistan's distribution networks to industries. There remain concerns about the technical and financial ability of Pakistan's power distribution companies to pass through the increased power supply in an efficient and timely manner.

Over the longer term, CPEC investments will generate outflows of dividends and interest payments that will affect the balance of payments. There are a range of financing modalities associated with CPEC investments. The infrastructure projects (roads, railroads and port expansion) are mostly financed through concessional loans from the Chinese government. Associated loan repayment flows should be moderate in size. The energy projects, however, are financed by foreign investment under contracts that involve sovereign guarantees relating to rates of return to the investors. These will generate outflows in the form of profit repatriation and fuel imports. Some savings are also expected as the input mix for the energy sector will shift from furnace oil to coal, gas and renewables. On balance, the IMF estimates that peak outflows in the order of US $3.5–$4.5 billion will occur by 2025.[10]

Fiscal and external sector pressures

As noted earlier, fiscal and external imbalances widened in 2017. The fiscal deficit was higher than anticipated and above the ceiling set by the Fiscal Responsibility and Debt Limitation Act. Improved revenue performance can reduce fiscal pressures and risks. This will require further reducing tax exemptions, raising withholding taxes and improving tax collection at the provincial level. At present, provincial authorities are responsible for collecting taxes on property, agricultural income and services. All three have low yields. Improving revenue performance will also require strengthening tax administration through such measures as widening the scope and frequency of tax audits, using third party information and monitoring financial transactions through withholding taxes on non-filers. According to the IMF, unless these measures were implemented effectively, additional tax policy and administrative measures of around 1.5 per cent of GDP might be needed to meet 2018 targets.[11]

On the expenditure side, it is necessary to control the losses of public sector enterprises; these average about 0.3 per cent per year and are cumulatively around 3.8 per cent of GDP. It was revealed in 2017 that the airline company, PIA, had been running losses of 4 billion rupees per year and of approximately 40 billion rupees over the past 10 years.

Improving the external position will require policy measures to enhance trade competitiveness. One of these is greater exchange rate flexibility to offset the real appreciation that has occurred in recent years. Others include measures to improve the supporting policy environment for businesses such as introducing e-payment for transactions with government agencies (such as taxes, customs and property-related transactions); establishing more one-stop shop arrangements for business permits; increasing the use of Alternative Dispute Resolution facilities; and setting up a registry for secured transactions. Facilitating greater financial inclusion would also help to develop a more robust small and medium-sized enterprise sector that could become a bigger part of the domestic value chain feeding exports. Finally, enhancing energy security for Pakistani industry through both higher generation and better distribution of electricity and gas would help to make it more competitive. This has already happened to some extent in recent years but more needs to be done. Power sector arrears were reduced in 2014–15 but were then allowed to rebuild in 2016–17. Losses due to theft and inefficiencies remain high at around 30 per cent.

Prospects

The consensus was that growth in 2018 would be above the rate of 5.3 per cent recorded in 2017, possibly touching 6 per cent. This was based on the prevailing economic momentum coming from foreign investment and domestic demand and the improving security and energy supply situation. Moody's Investors Services reconfirmed its B3 rating for Pakistan in July 2017, noting short-term dynamism and the benefits of the CPEC. However, several risks were looming on the horizon that could affect longer-term prospects. In particular, fiscal balances were expected to come under more pressure in the run-up to the national elections in May 2018. Combined with external account imbalances, these could well lead to exchange rate depreciation, higher inflation and lower growth after 2018. Gross public debt stood at 67.2 per cent of GDP. Servicing this debt could become more challenging if the exchange rate were to weaken, interest rates to rise and growth to falter. Debt servicing costs were expected to amount to 7.5 per cent of GDP in 2018 as the Paris Club rescheduled payments due to it. These concerns were feeding repeated stories in the media that the country might approach the IMF for a new stabilization programme within a year.

Notes

1 Business confidence may be turning around after a dip lasting more than a year. The most recent wave (November 2017) of the Overseas Investors Chamber of Commerce and Industry (OICCI) Business Confidence Survey showed confidence at 21 per cent, up from 13 per cent in April 2017. This is still far below the 36 per cent confidence rate observed in April 2016. The recent uptick was strongest in the retail and wholesale sectors, followed by manufacturing. Fluctuations in short-term business confidence appear to co-exist with long-term stagnation in private investment rates. See https://propakistani.pk/2017/11/17/business-confidence-pakista n-increasing-oicci-survey/.

2 During 2014–16 the fiscal deficit was constrained by targets set in consultation with the IMF under the terms of a financing programme. During 2017 and beyond, deficit levels were to be guided by the Fiscal Responsibility and Debt Limitation Act (FRDA). As amended in 2016, this Act set a deficit limit of 4 per cent of GDP for the three-year period 2018–20 and of 3.5 per cent thereafter. The amended Act also constrained the maximum general government debt to stand at no more than 60 per cent of GDP through 2018 and no more than 50 per cent by 2033. Neither the fiscal deficit target nor the public debt target was met in 2017.

3 The budget announced for 2018 contained a large increase in development spending that was to be offset by enhanced tax and non-tax revenues. The projected deficit was 4.2 per cent of GDP; see International Monetary Fund, *Pakistan: 2017 Article IV Consultation Staff Report*, IMF Country Report No. 17/212, 2017, Table 1, p. 28.

4 Signs of exchange rate volatility emerged in early July 2017 when the State Bank of Pakistan withheld intervention over a day-long trading period. The rupee declined by close to 3 per cent on 5 July. Concerned about the implications for debt servicing and price inflation, the Ministry of Finance arranged for intervention over the succeeding days to roll back the depreciation. See https://profit.pakistantoday.com.pk/2017/07/06/our-exchange-rate-policy/.

5 International Monetary Fund, Pakistan: 2017 Article IV Consultation Staff Report, IMF Country Report No. 17/212, 2017, para. 14, Box 2.

6 Several emerging market economies have suffered export declines in recent years as commodity prices have been low and as Western economies and even China have experienced slow growth. During 2016 Turkey, Singapore, Malaysia, Indonesia, Taiwan, the Republic of Korea, and India all experienced export declines. However, all these economies returned to positive export growth in 2017, with the exception of Pakistan.

7 Growing external imbalances have put pressure on the rupee. The State Bank of Pakistan has been managing this pressure for the most part through administrative measures rather than by allowing the value of the rupee to depreciate. Among such measures was the introduction in February 2017 of cash margin requirements on the importation of non-essential consumer goods.

8 International Monetary Fund, *Pakistan*, p. 36.

9 The evidence on this is mixed. The April 2017 OICCI survey noted that investors planned to decrease planned investments in the latter half of 2017. However, the November 2017 OICCI survey reported improving business confidence and rising investment plans.

10 International Monetary Fund, p. 37.

11 Ibid., p. 14.

17

Economic governance

Ishrat Husain

Pakistan was one of the top 10 economic performers among the world's developing countries during the first 40 years of its existence. These 40 years were tumultuous in the history of the nation but its record of achievements was impressive: starting with a very weak economic base at the time of independence in 1947, followed by nation building, and continuing political instability in the aftermath of the death of its founder, Muhammad Ali Jinnah. It successfully absorbed and rehabilitated eight million refugees, or one-fourth of the total population, fought a war with a much larger and powerful neighbour, India, in 1965, and went through a painful and traumatic dismemberment of the country in 1971. The emergence of a populist political regime that indulged in the massive nationalization of private assets in the 1970s accompanied by an external shock of major oil price increases delivered a big blow to business confidence and brought about a dislocation of the economy. Close involvement with the United States in the Afghan war to oust the Soviet Union in the 1980s and the associated fallout, namely the spread of sectarian violence, drugs and armed conflict, shook the social fabric of the country. Despite these many challenges, internal and external, the country was able to achieve average annual growth of 6 per cent during the first 40 years of its existence. Pakistan was ahead of India and Bangladesh in all economic and social indicators.

Since 1990 the country has fallen behind its neighbouring countries, and following a period of boom and bust average annual growth has declined from 6.5 per cent to 4.5 per cent. The booms were short-lived and could not be sustained over extended periods of time. Political instability and frequent changes of government in the 1990s may have created uncertainty for investors, thus slowing down the pace of economic activity. Although there have been two smooth and orderly transitions of power from one elected government to another since 2008, economic and social indicators have failed to show much improvement.

This chapter will examine several hypotheses that can explain this slowdown and the volatile and inequitable growth of the last 25 years, and through a process of elimination it will advance theoretical and empirical evidence to show that the most powerful explanatory hypothesis lies in the decay of institutions of governance. The chapter will also propose a selective and incremental approach towards restructuring some key public institutions that pertain to accountability, transparency, security, economic growth and equity.

A popular image of Pakistan externally is that of a fragile or even a failed state in possession of a large and expanding arsenal of nuclear weapons, encircled by Islamist extremists, and a safe haven for nurturing and training terrorists who pose a threat to other countries. There is considerable unease within the international community about the unceasing rivalry and hostility between nuclear-armed India and Pakistan, which have fought three wars against each other. Kashmir continues to be a highly contentious and volatile powder keg. Relations with Afghanistan remain tense and mutual recriminations and mistrust vitiate the atmosphere. Although Pakistan is a non-NATO ally of the United States, the popular sentiment in both countries about each other is largely unfavourable. The United States considers Pakistan duplicitous in its dealings with the Afghan Taliban and the Haqqani network, while Pakistan is bitter that, despite incurring huge losses and sacrificing hundreds of thousands of lives, its role in the 'war against terror' is not fully appreciated. Pakistan is perceived by outsiders as a source of regional instability, and as an ungovernable country.

Therefore, the popular hypothesis about Pakistan's economic drift is explained by the increasing influence of religious extremists and terrorists who have threatened Pakistan's law and order and disturbed its peace and security. Economic agents are reluctant to undertake new investments in this kind of environment. This hypothesis may be partially valid, but the economic decline started in the 1990s, long before the country became embroiled in the 'war against terror' in the post-2001 period. Average annual growth in the 1990s when the country was relatively peaceful and tranquil had already declined from 6.5 per cent in the 1980s to 4 per cent. Investment ratios, export growth and social indicators all took a dip in the 1990s. Poverty, which had been showing a downward decline up until the 1980s, had worsened by the end of the 1990s. However, from 2002–08 the country was affected by violence and terrorism, including assassination attempts and terrorist attacks on the sitting President and the Prime Minister. Even so, the country recorded a remarkable turnaround. Average annual growth touched 6–7 per cent, the investment-to-GDP ratio peaked at 23 per cent, and foreign direct investment flows reached above US $5 billion.

The recent experience of the 2013–16 period is illuminating. Macroeconomic stability was achieved and economic growth rates had begun to move upwards. The confidence of domestic and international investors (Pakistan has been upgraded to the MSCI Emerging Markets Index from the Frontier Markets Index and its credit ratings by Moody's Investors Services and Standard & Poor's have also improved) has been regained. These developments also negate the view that Pakistan's security situation and particularly its deep involvement in 'war against terror' is responsible for its poor economic and social performance. Therefore, the security deficit hypothesis does not stand up to serious scrutiny.

Another group of analysts argues that the availability of generous foreign assistance has been the main determinant of Pakistan's economic success or failure and the country's fortunes vacillate with the ebb and flow of funding from external donors. It has been argued that the three periods of economic spurts in the history of Pakistan, i.e. the 1960s, 1980s and early 2000s, can be ascribed to the heavy infusion of this money into the country. Pakistan was the recipient of large military and economic assistance and that was the major reason for the turnaround during these three periods of growth spurts. Despite this popular perception, the empirical evidence does not prove this assertion.

Let us examine the data on the foreign capital flows during the periods of slow growth in the 1950s, 1970s, 1990s and the post-2008 era. In the 1950s Pakistan received huge amounts of military, civilian and food aid. It was the imports of food made available through the US Public Law 480 (known as PL–480 or Food for Peace) that helped to prevent a food crisis in Pakistan. In the 1970s Western aid amounted to US $700 million annually but in addition to this, official grants and concessional loans (some of which were subsequently transformed in grants or waivers) from oil-rich Arab countries and workers remittances did not pose major problems and financed the huge imbalances in the current account. From 1973–74 to 977–78 commitments of assistance were made by Iran and countries belonging to the League of Arab States totalling $1.2 billion, mostly on concessional terms. Aid disbursements during the mid-1970s stood at a level far above that reached during the 1965–70 period (on average $600 million was disbursed annually, including flows to East Pakistan) after allowing for international inflation. In the 1990s foreign currency deposits of resident and non-resident Pakistanis in Pakistani banks amounting to $11 billion were utilized to finance external payments. The International Monetary Fund (IMF), the World Bank and the Asian Development Bank continued to make loans amounting to several billion dollars between 1988 and 1998, while Japan was the largest bilateral provider of concessional loans and grants. During the post-2008 period, the Kerry Lugar Act authorized $7.5 billion of economic and military assistance from the United States to Pakistan for a five-year period. Multilateral banks and the IMF increased their support, while Pakistan became the largest recipient of aid from the United Kingdom valued at £1 billion for a five-year period. Thus, despite higher volumes of foreign assistance, average annual growth hovered at around 3 to 4 per cent during this period. It can be seen that there was no significant difference in the availability of foreign capital flows between the periods of high and low growth. Thus, the hypothesis of high foreign assistance resulting in high economic performance is not validated by these facts.

Coterminous with the foreign aid dependence syndrome is the widespread belief that the United States and the West supported Pakistan's military dictators at the expense of democracy. They are able to twist and turn the arms of the strong man running the country to follow their own agenda and interests. Thus, Pakistan's economy has done well only under the autocratic regimes which have received the blessing of the United States. The frequent dismissal of elected regimes in the 1990s, the suspension of US aid under the Pressler Amendment in the early 1990s intended to stifle Pakistan's nuclear ambitions, and following the nuclear tests carried out in 1998, the coup to overthrow Zulfikar Ali Bhutto in 1977, were all engineered under this compact. The drop in economic performance was caused by the consequential political instability. It must be recalled that the United States suspended or curtailed economic and military assistance at crucial times in Pakistan's history when the military dictators were still in power. US aid was suspended soon after the 1965 war with India, after the 1971 separation of East Pakistan, and the early period of General Zia ul-Haq's rule, and sanctions were imposed in 1999 when General Pervez Musharraf took over the reins of the government. Whenever the US interests converged with those of Pakistan (one needs to remember that in the 1950s Pakistan joined both SEATO and CENTO; in the 1980s both countries joined forced to oust the Soviets from Afghanistan, and in 2001–16 they took part in the war in Afghanistan) the United States, despite quibbles on both sides, chose to assist Pakistan irrespective of the nature of the regime in power.

We then examine another factor, namely the global economic conditions that may have played a negative role in Pakistan's poor economic performance. The fact of the matter is that the external environment between 1990 and 2008 was highly favourable. Most emerging and developing countries have made great strides as chronicled by Steve Radelet in his recent book *The Great Surge.* [1] Per head incomes in the emerging and developing countries (EDCs) increased by more than 70 per cent between 1995 and 2013. The number of those living in poverty halved from 2 billion in 1990 to 897 million by 2012 bringing down the proportion of poor people in the total population from 37 to 13 per cent in 2012. The share of EDCs in the world exports rose from 24 to 41 per cent during this period. International capital flows jumped from US $91 billion to $1,145 billion. Bangladesh tripled and India quadrupled their share of the global market during this period, while Pakistan's share declined. All social indicators including life expectancy, maternal mortality, infant mortality, adult literacy, net enrolment ratios, and average years of schooling showed significant improvement for developing countries as a group. Therefore, the external economic environment cannot be blamed for Pakistan's poor performance.

Some analysts have attributed the overall poor performance of Pakistan to the 'garrison state' syndrome. Since its formation Pakistan has sought to contain its larger rival – India – and as a result it has had to allocate a much larger proportion of its resources to defence expenditure and to preserve and expand the corporate interests of the military. Therefore, the neglect of education, health, human development in general and diversion of resources to meet the demands of defence, nuclear capability, and other security-related expenditures has led to the present economic and social outcomes. In fact, the ratio of defence expenditure to gross domestic product (GDP) was consistently high during the country's first 40 years as a nation-state, but in 2016 it stood at 2.9 per cent of GDP, having fallen from an average of 6 to 7 per cent in the 1980s. Most of the country's nuclear-related expenditure was also incurred in the 1970s and 1980s. In FY 2016 the budgetary allocation for education was 2.7 per cent of GDP. In that year the budgetary allocation for the health and education sectors was 3.7 per cent, higher than that of defence and internal security but certainly lower than what is required to fill in the huge gap in patient enrolment and primary health care services. In the education and health sectors it is the governance and management issues that impede the delivery of these services, not budgetary allocations. A popular myth that has now become quite entrenched and even accepted in many circles is that the military holds large corporate interests.

It is true that the armed forces have established foundations and trusts that run enterprises but the proceeds and profits they earn are utilized for the welfare of the army veterans, particularly those soldiers who retire at an early average age ranging from 45 to 50 years. The education and health care of their families are financed by the income generated by these foundations and trusts. To put this in perspective, the total market cap in November 2016 of all the listed companies owned by the Fauji Foundation, the Army Welfare Trust, the Shaheen Foundation and the Bahria Foundation together was only 4.5 per cent of the total market cap of the companies listed on the Pakistan Stock Exchange. Ayesha Siddiqa claimed that 'the military has arrived at the point where its business today control about 23 percent assets of the corporate sector with two foundations – Fauji Foundation and the Army Welfare Trust representing two of the largest conglomerates in the country'.[2] It is true that the listed companies owned by such foundations and trusts are major players in the fertilizer sector, but they are competing with a number of equally large conglomerates such as Engro and the Fatima Group. All of these companies pay full taxes on their income, sales and imports and do not enjoy any exemptions or concessions of a preferential nature. The share of other unlisted companies owned by these foundations and trusts in the total assets of unlisted companies is not known but it would be quite insignificant as the pool of privately owned enterprises and businesses is substantial. Therefore, the 'garrison state' hypothesis, despite its considerable appeal, also does not meet the test of evidentiary confirmation.

Having ruled out factors such as security and terrorism, inflow of foreign assistance, preference for military rule, external economic environment, and diversion of public expenditures towards defence which may have all played some role but were not the main determinant of Pakistan's poor performance, we turn our attention to the institutions of governance.

Numerous studies have demonstrated the linkages between good governance and healthy economic growth. Acemoglu and Robinson in their book *Why Nations Fail* [3] demonstrate that it is the institutions that determine the fate of nations. Success comes when political and economic institutions are 'inclusive' and pluralistic, creating incentives for everyone to invest in the future. Nations fail when institutions are 'extractive', protecting the political and economic power of only a small elite that draws income from everyone else. Institutions that promote good governance and facilitate broad-based and inclusive growth have come to occupy the current consensus on development strategy. According to Acemoglu and Johnson, good institutions ensure two desirable outcomes: relatively equal access to economic opportunity (a level playing field); and the likelihood that those who provide labour or capital are appropriately rewarded and their property rights are protected.

Rashida Haq and Uzma Zia have explored linkages between governance and pro-poor growth in Pakistan for the period 1996–2005. The analysis indicates that governance indicators have low scores and rank at the lowest possible percentile compared with other countries. The results of their study show a strong link between governance indicators and pro-poor growth. Their econometric analysis shows a strong relationship between good governance and a reduction in poverty and income inequality.

The reasons for the poor governance can be explained with the help of the model of an elitist economy that was articulated in 'Pakistan: The Economy of an Elitist State'[4] which sets out the politics of patronage as the main driver of the capture of the state and the rigging of markets in Pakistan. It is postulated that a narrow elite constituting about 1–2 per cent of the population has used state and markets for their political power and self-enrichment to the neglect of the majority of the population, particularly the poor and the less privileged segments of the society. This small minority was thus able to enjoy this unjust accumulation of wealth amid widespread poverty and squalor. In the absence of a neutral umpire, markets are rigged by the elite for its own advantage and thus market outcomes and resource allocation are inefficient. The state, which has to ensure the equitable distribution of gains from economic growth, is also controlled by the same elite that evades taxes and appropriates the public expenditures for its own benefits. Inequities – interpersonal, regional, gender – become commonplace in such an environment. Access to the institutions that deliver public goods and services is mediated by the elite through a patronage-based system.

Thus, both theoretical as well as cross-country empirical evidence and Pakistan's own experience supports the argument that poor governance manifested in weak institutions could be the predominant influence in the unsatisfactory economic and social performance of Pakistan in the last quarter century relative to its own previous four decades and to other countries in the region. The evidence to substantiate this point of view is the gradual decline in Pakistan's ranking and score on the following indices compiled by international and multilateral bodies, independent think tanks, academics, researchers, non-governmental organizations:

The World Bank, World Governance Indicators[5]
The World Economic Forum, Global Competitiveness Report[6]
The United Nations Development Programme (UNDP), Human Development Index[7]

Freedom House, Economic Freedom Index[8]
Transparency International, Corruption Perception Index[9]
International Country Risk Guide[10]
The UN Educational, Scientific and Cultural Organization (UNESCO), Education for All Index[11]
The Legatum Prosperity Index[12]

Sakib Sherani (2017)[13] reviewed the World Governance indicators for the period 1996–2015. His analysis shows that Pakistan has performed poorly in all six sub-components of governance. The average percentile rank for the 16 years, excluding political stability and absence of violence (extremely low), ranges from 18 to 32. He notes that in four out of the six parameters – government effectiveness, control of corruption, regulatory quality, and political stability and absence of violence – the best scores were recorded under President Musharraf (a period during which economic growth averaged 6–7 per cent annually). Again, there was some modest improvement in the World Governance Indicators, Ease of Doing Business and Corruption Perception Index for 2015 and 2016 when the economy was beginning to perform well. The same picture emerges by examining other indicators and indices compared to India and Bangladesh. Pakistan has fallen below these countries in the Human Development Index, the Corruption Perception Index, and the Legatum Prosperity Index, and continues to lag behind India and Bangladesh in Education for All and the Economic Freedom Index. Diagnostic studies, particularly the Conference volumes based on the Annual Conferences on Pakistan organized by the Woodrow Wilson Center in Washington, DC, suggest that every crisis faced by the country – low tax mobilization, energy shortages, the unsatisfactory law and order situation, the loss of public sector enterprises, poor delivery of education and health services, stagnating trade – can be traced back to this governance deficit, institutional weaknesses, exacerbated by the military rule that did nothing to strengthen the institutions. Tax collectors enjoy wide discretionary powers that they use to extort money and enrich themselves rather than raise additional revenue for the exchequer. Power and gas companies find a huge gap between the sales revenues they assess, bill and collect and the purchases of units which they have to pay for. Law and order suffer and the common citizen feels insecure because the police officials are appointed on the recommendations of the elected members of parliament and assemblies in exchange for outright payment rather than on their professional capabilities. Public sector enterprises naturally face losses when, at the behest of the ruling party, they become the dumping ground to accommodate thousands of employees whose services they do not require. In competitive markets they lose market share and in public monopolies they fleece the consumers but still incur losses due to inefficiency, waste and corruption. There is a general consensus in Pakistan endorsed by the international organizations that the civilian institutions have decayed over time.

What can be done to redress this situation? The National Commission for Government Reforms comprising members drawn from both the private and public sectors travelled throughout Pakistan during 2006–08, consulted with different stakeholders, carried out field studies, made on the spot observations about the delivery of public services, reviewed research work and compiled its report. The Commission made exhaustive recommendations concerning the structure, human resource policies, business process, re-engineering of the federal, provincial and local governments, public enterprises and corporations, and autonomous bodies. The recommendations of the Commission were welcomed by the previous and the current governments but have not been formally accepted or implemented. Based on this record, it seems unrealistic to expect that a comprehensive reform of the civil service and of all the civilian institutions of governance is feasible under the current political circumstances.

The dilemma facing academics and technocratic policy reformers is that inefficient policies and institutions exist and the status quo is defended because it suits the politically influential elite, but the constituency and coalitions required to deliver efficient policies and strong institutions do not exist. If the best solution for across the board reform is not feasible, can a second or third best solution be designed for a selective and incremental approach by beginning with a few key institutions of democratic governance in the expectation that it might not meet the same kind of fierce resistance, especially as those affected by these reforms would form a miniscule proportion of the entire corpus of civil servants. The choice of institutions should be driven by consideration of those where powerful spillover effects could gradually spread over a much wider area in the course of time.

This chapter proposes an incremental and selective reform of some of the key institutions that can help in moving towards the goal of restoring the efficacy, efficiency and effectiveness of democratic governance. It is proposed that these institutions get back on the same pathway – merit, integrity, dedicated service and problem solving – that was their main asset historically. There are already many examples of successful institutions working quite well amid this general atmosphere of institutional decay and their success reflects adherence to the same principles. The performance of the Punjab government in many respects is much better than that of the other provinces and it can be attributed to a strong exemplary leadership but its sustainability would be assured were its institutional infrastructure also strengthened.

Key institutions proposed for restructuring and strengthening

Any schema of selection from such a huge administrative machine is bound to meet with scepticism. Therefore, it is important to lay down the criteria against which the screening has been done and selection of these key institutions (listed below) made. The criteria are:

1   Institutions of market governance: whether they would enable the private businesses to operate unhindered and without incurring high costs of transactions in a competitive environment observing standards of corporate governance while protecting the interests of consumers and minority shareholders.
2   Institutions for delivery of services: whether they would be able to improve efficient and non-discriminatory access to basic public goods and services such as education, health, water and sanitation
3   Institutions for the administration of justice: whether they would be able to provide security for the life and property of the country's citizens and ensure expeditious and cheap justice and dispute resolution.
4   Institutions of accountability, transparency and oversight: whether they would be able to take timely action without fear or favour against those indulging in malfeasance, corruption, or misuse of public office for personal gain.
5   Institutions for promoting equity: whether they would be able to strengthen the capacity of those who do not have assets or skills to fully participate in market-based economic activities.

Another dimension that has been taken into account in the choice of these institutions is the relative strength of their knock-on spillover and crossover effects on other sectors and institutions. For example, the reform of the Public Service Commissions would be able to attract and retain talented young men and women into the civil service based on open, merit- based, fair competitive recruitment procedures. The higher quality of the civil servants would, in turn, improve the performance of the institutions that deal with service delivery, market governance and administration of justice.

In the light of their linkages and synergies with the long-term agenda outlined above we can identify about two dozen key state institutions that would help in meeting the development objectives of security, growth and equity for Pakistan. They have been chosen because of their inherent constitutional or legal standing, their possible positive impact on other sectors and spillovers to other institutions. We have relied upon the existing institutions except for a new National Science and Technology Commission to be set up on the lines of the Higher Education Commission. Some of these institutions would require reform in the shape of some adjustments, incentive alignments and business process re-engineering, while others may have to undergo major surgery.

The institutions are grouped together below according to their possible contribution towards achieving the development goals of security, growth and equity. In addition, there are cross-cutting institutions that directly or indirectly impact all the three objectives and are mainly concerned with accountability, transparency and standard setting.

Accountability/transparency/oversight

- Parliamentary committees
- Local governments
- Auditor General of Pakistan, and the Public Accounts Committees
- National Accountability Bureau/Provincial Anti-Corruption departments
- Election Commission of Pakistan
- Public and Provincial Service Commissions
- Information Commissioners under the Freedom of Information Act
- E-Government Directorate-General/Provincial IT boards

Security

- Lower judiciary
- Police including investigation and intelligence agencies
- Federal Investigation Agency
- National Counterterrorism Agency
- Prosecution departments

Growth

- State Bank of Pakistan
- Securities and Exchange Commission of Pakistan
- Higher Education Commission
- National Science and Technology Commission
- Federal Board of Revenue
- Trade Development Authority of Pakistan
- Board of Investment
- Competition Commission of Pakistan

Equity

- Pakistan Agriculture Research Council/Provincial Research Institutes
- Local covernments
- State Bank of Pakistan
- Higher Education Commission needs-based scholarship programme
- Benazir Income Support Programme/Zakat committees/Baitul Maal
- Irrigation authorities
- Urban Development Authorities
- National Vocational and Technical Education Commission

Conclusion

This chapter has examined several alternative hypotheses in an attempt to explain Pakistan's declining economic growth rate and weak social indicators over the past 25 years. The most satisfactory explanation lies in the decay of the institutions of governance that have failed to achieve the interrelated development outcomes of security, growth and equity.

Comprehensive reforms are unlikely to be introduced at the same time because it is neither practicable nor feasible to do so, due to both the absence of political will and capacity constraints. The first best solution – sweeping reform throughout the institutions of governance – is therefore ruled out. This chapter therefore proposes a second or third best solution that targets a subset of key institutions which, if set right, can make a substantial improvement in the governance landscape of Pakistan over time. The spillover and knock-on effects of these institutions over others would enlarge the space for beneficial outcomes over time. What needs to be done to set them on the right course is well known and documented. The challenge of reforming even this subset is formidable as the vested interests wishing to perpetuate the status quo are politically powerful and the coalition and alliances between the political leadership and the beneficiaries of the existing system are so strong that they cannot be easily ruptured. The elected governments with an eye on the short-term electoral cycles are not in a position to incur the pains of these reforms upfront while the gains accrue later on to a different political party. The authoritarian governments are not effective as they do not enjoy legitimacy for sustaining reforms. Changing institutions is a slow and difficult process requiring, in addition to significant political will, fundamental measures to reduce the opportunity and incentives for particular groups to capture economic rents.

The exact steps required for restructuring these institutions have already been developed, some in conjunction with the World Bank, and are fully documented. Lessons learnt from the neighbouring countries mentioned earlier in this chapter, if adapted and applied, can further refine and reinforce this restructuring effort.

It will be impossible to effect these reforms unless all the major political parties agree and reach a consensus so that partisanship and point scoring do not get in the way of the implementation of these reforms. Civil servants who have assumed a passive role can be reactivated, if they know that the risks of retribution and penalties involved in implementing these reforms would be minimal. Politicians of all persuasions have to realize that the growing disaffection for political parties and leaders in the country, the quickening spread of violence and intolerance, the rising popularity and respect for the armed forces, and the widening gap between the expectations of the general populace and delivery by the government are indeed a wake-up call for altering their past conduct, practices and behaviour. A growing educated urban middle class, an information and communication revolution permeating even the rural areas through electronic and social media should act as catalysts for this change. The ultimate beneficiaries of such altered behaviour would be not only the citizens of Pakistan but also the political parties themselves. The cynicism and wide distrust of politicians among society at large would be replaced by improved access and delivery of essential basic services, thus bolstering confidence in the politicians.

Notes

1 Steven Radelet, *The Great Surge: The Ascent of the Developing World*, New York, Simon and Schuster, 2015.
2 Ayesha Siddiqa, *Military Inc.: Inside Pakistan's Military Economy*, Haryana, Penguin Random House India, 2017.
3 Daron Acemoglu and James A. Robinson, *Why Nations Fail: The Origins of Power, Prosperity, and Poverty*, New York, Broadway Business, 2013.
4 Ishrat Husain, 'Pakistan: The Economy of an Elitist State, Oxford, Oxford University Press, 2000.
5 http://info.worldbank.org/governance/WGI/#home.
6 www.weforum.org/reports/the-global-competitveness-report-2018.
7 http://hdr.undp.org/en/content/human-development-index-hdi.
8 https://freedomhouse.org/report/freedom-world/freedom-world-2018.
9 www.transparency.org/research/cpi/overview.
10 www.prsgroup.com/explore-our-products/international-country-risk-guide/.
11 https://en.unesco.org/gem-report/education-all-development-index.
12 www.legatum.com/philanthropy/investing-in-policies-ideas/the-prosperity-index/.
13 Sakib Sherani, 'Institutional Reform in Pakistan', report commissioned by and submitted to Friedrich Ebert Stiftung, Islamabad, 2017.

18

Praetorian bureaucratization of the political system and politicization of bureaucracy

Shahid Najam

The chapter comprises five parts. The first sets the context; the second the historical evolution of the troika of bureaucracy, the military establishment and the political system; the third dwells on the nature of interface and the impact of the troika on the governance and power structure under various governance paradigms; the fourth gives a succinct comparative analysis of the evolution of the role vis-à-vis India and Bangladesh; and the fifth part tries to draw some conclusions.

Part 1

The power and governance dynamics in Pakistan are inextricably connected to the troika of the three major actors, namely the political system, the bureaucracy and the military establishment. Expediency, the 'doctrine of necessity' and the prevalent political dictates, rather than the mandated role delineated by the Constitution, seem to have determined the troika's respective roles in conducting the business of government. The interface and interaction of the troika in the post-1951 period has been particularly intense. A conjunctive scan of their institutional role in the power nexus ever since the creation of Pakistan, as such, is imperative in order to avoid partial analysis and to draw conclusions on the functioning and governance of the state apparatus in the country.

The bureaucracy in Pakistan as a post-colonial country had distinct legacy and heritage features in that it inherited an administration-driven rather than politically governed system. The political landscape during the pre-independence era was occupied by the traditional land-based rural elite, tribal and aristocratic chieftains who were dependent upon official patronage, favours and support to seek and sustain their local power and prestige. On gaining independence in 1947, the ruling elite accordingly was an alliance between landlords and nascent industrial bourgeoisie supported by the military and a relatively sturdy bureaucracy.[1] This elite political class made no overt effort to strengthen the weak political system and the civil society institutions.

The initial formative years up until 1958 witnessed the supremacy of the bureaucracy due to the frailty and instability of the political institutions. The military acted as a junior partner in conducting state affairs. Later, cognizant of the emerging influence of the military and its overt praetorian designs, the bureaucracy quickly redefined its role in the power nexus between the military, the bureaucracy and the politicians. The military, from its position of junior partner, progressively asserted and expanded its role, first to achieve an equilibrium with the bureaucracy's techno-managerial-Civil Service of Pakistan (CSP) cadre during the period 1958–68 and then to finally assume the role of senior partner especially from 1977 to 1988 and from 1999 to 2008. This unique blend of the bureaucracy and the military in the absence of a strong political tradition occupied the decision making and political space to the detriment of the development of robust political institutions. The post-1971 democratic periods of popularly elected governments between 1971 and 1977, 1989 and 1999 and 2008 to the present day not only lacked a serious effort to consolidate political institutions but also progressively politicized the bureaucracy.

Part 2

This section briefly dwells on the post-1947 development of the three entities of the troika.

a Bureaucracy

The Government of India Act 1858 marked the beginning of the British rule. The Viceroy was responsible for the implementation of imperialist policies through a strong 'steel frame'- hierarchical administrative apparatus comprising permanent secretaries, provincial governors and the district officers. The objective was to strengthen imperial rule and enforce its effective writ throughout the colonial territories. The Imperial Civil Service which later became the Indian Civil Service (ICS)[2] was set up and comprised an elite group of exceptionally talented, highly motivated and competent individuals of integrity and commitment.

The Indian National Congress right from its establishment in 1885 strived to steadily 'Indianize' the bureaucracy.[3] By 1945 remarkable progress had already been made to indigenize the Indian bureaucracy with the top leadership of the National Congress fully engaged in shaping the contours of public administration in free India. An effort of the same size and scale on the part of the Indian Muslim League for public administration was, however, not discernible.

On independence, Pakistan consciously opted for 'path dependency' to adopt the same structure and functional orientation of the bureaucratic institutions. This goes to explain why the civil servants in the initial years bureaucratized the political system and demonstrated their inertia by not responding to the changing realities. This institutional inertia was further solidified by lackadaisical attempts by different governments, whether democratic or military, to advance their myopic power retention interests. In the process, the praetorian dictatorial influence and politicization[4] of the administrative institutions crept in progressively to dilute the core values of merit and efficiency. To exacerbate the situation, under the guise of purging the bureaucracy, successive regimes resorted to deterrent measures to make the bureaucracy more vulnerable.[5] Even the constitutional guarantees for the civil servants were withdrawn while a system of lateral entry was introduced by Zulfikar Ali Bhutto in the name of 'professionalizing' the civil service through the induction of specialists and experts in various cadres. This piece of reform was not only abused to bring in politically loyal persons to assume key positions but also eroded the internal cohesion and *esprit de corps* of the civil service. General Zia ul-Haq institutio-nalized the induction of army officers directly into the civil service at 20 per cent of the intake. General Pervez Musharraf's devolution, deconcentration and decentralization plan truncated the time-tested district-level system by abolishing executive magistracy, replacing the Police Act of 1861 with Police Order 2002, and bringing the entire district administration under the control of an elected mayor, thus further politicizing the civil service.

As a result, the bureaucracy suffered huge institutional decay, lost its core values of meritocracy and integrity and became vulnerable to serve the narrow interests of politi-cians and military. The politics of patronage, loyalism[6] and servility[7] formed the criteria for appointments and promotions. During the last six to eight years of their service senior civil servants go out of the way to prove their personal loyalty to the regime in power and compromise their professional integrity in order to protect their tenure. The survey also revealed that political affiliations are key factors for lucrative postings and career growth.[8] The senior bureaucrats use their organizational and professional expertise to legalize or provide ex post facto justifications for the illicit actions and corruption of the ruling elite and to support the 'godfather' culture. Indeed, the administrative apparatus is in a state of serious crisis.

b Political system

Pakistan inherited a weak civil society and political institutions owing, *inter alia*, to the colonialists' legacy of bureaucratic supremacy over political process; the fragmented and scanty efforts on the part of the Muslims during the independence struggle to develop robust political tradition and democratic value systems; and the ideological content of the freedom movement which overwhelmed its political character.

Right from the beginning of the Imperial Raj, by design, a client-patron relationship was forged between the bureaucracy and the native upper-class Indians, rich businessmen, feudal lords, religious leaders and tribal heads. They were accorded preferential access to the ICS officers who, in return, made full use of the power and positional influence of these locals to ensure social stability and a smooth flow of revenues for the Raj. This elite fully occupied the limited political space created by the imperial rules and subsequently by the Indian Councils Acts of 1892 and 1909. The Legislative Councils and the Legis-lative Assemblies, especially from 1937 until independence, more or less comprised representation of the upper or upper-middle class. This symbiotic relationship and socio-political power structure prevented the development of a robust political ethos.

There was also a huge structural disconnect in the local and provincial arenas of poli-tics and the communally compartmentalized and geographically dispersed electorates. The provincial particularism strongly subdued the all-India perspective of the Muslims as a separate political category. Even the 1934 resuscitation of the All-India Muslim League under Jinnah's leadership was motivated largely by the efforts of politicians in the min-ority provinces which were apprehensive of the forthcoming constitutional arrangements. In the 1937 elections, the Muslim League performed poorly because of its failure to integrate the fragmented and localized structures and garnered 21 oer cent of the Muslim seats. The Muslim League's organizational machinery was indeed weakest in the areas which ultimately became part of Pakistan. On independence, it was Jinnah's leadership and stature as Governor-General that guaranteed the integrity and centrality of authority in Pakistan.

Moreover, the focus of the independence movement was on ideology to secure socio-political rights and constitutional guarantees for the Muslims which created unity and solidarity among Muslims. This commitment to ideology and its fervent expression to safeguard Muslim interests severely constrained the development of political culture and forums to channelize and institutionalize the Muslims' political will. The obvious outcome was neither the development of a truly democratic polity nor the assertation of the supremacy of the political system.

To make the things worse, Pakistan recycled a host of politicians in its early days who were corrupt, keenly interested in maintaining their political power and lacked the will to represent the popular voice for establishing democratic traditions, distributive justice and responsive administrative apparatus. This created a political vacuum for the military-bureaucratic oligarchy to rule Pakistan while parliament remained marginalized.

The introduction of martial law in 1958, the Elective Bodies Disqualification Order of 1959 and the institution of basic democracies further stifled the political process and empowered civil bureaucracy to influence electoral politics. Thereafter, the democratically elected Z. A. Bhutto, Benazir Bhutto and Nawaz Sharif, as heads of the established Pakistan People's Party (PPP) and the Pakistan Muslim League (Nawaz, PML–N), respectively, squandered the opportunity to build organizational and democratic structures including the development of a decentralized and well-knit leadership within their parties. Instead, both manipulated the party as an instrument to consolidate their personal rule and espouse an autocratic style of governance. Even the Charter of Democracy of 2006 which embodied PPP-PML–N affirmation and commitment, *inter alia*, to the undiluted democracy, parliament and constitutional supremacy, independent judiciary, a neutral civil service and curb on periodic military takeovers has been respected more in breach than compliance. Political polemics, confrontation, polarization and truculent tussle to retain power continue to bedevil the country.

c Army

On gaining independence in 1947, the army initially continued with the colonial tradition, doctrines and ethical values of an 'officer and gentleman' that were physically and socio-economically distinct from the mainstream society and totally extricated from political pursuits. However, for the first time, General Ayub Khan imposed martial law in 1958 which laid the foundations for praetorian ventures into politics. In order to legitimize his rule, he formed the Convention Muslim League of which Z. A. Bhutto was a devout member.[9] He was succeeded by General Yahya Khan (1969–71) whose regime led to the dismemberment of Pakistan and symbolized gross mismanagement of national affairs with lack of understanding of the political realities. Bhutto took over on 20 December 1971 and ironically became the first civilian Chief Martial Law Administrator and President of Pakistan.[10]

The second major intervention was General Zia ul-Haq's coup known as Operation Fair Play to dethrone Bhutto, who was hanged after a staged judicial trial for conspiracy of murdering a political opponent. To seek political legitimacy, Zia craftily introduced a doctored political system 'Majlis-e-Shoora' (consultative assembly). Subsequently, he held a farcical national referendum to become elected President of Pakistan. The 1985 elections brought a semblance of democratic order to the political landscape of Pakistan but later the elected Prime Minister Muhammad Khan Junejo (PML) was dismissed on charges of incompetency and economic stagflation.[11] In reality, Junejo's relations with

President Zia deteriorated due to the initiation of a parliamentary inquiry on the Ojhri Camp disaster and the signing of the Geneva Accord in 1988.[12] Co-politicians, including novices like Nawaz Sharif, connived with the army establishment to depose Junejo. Zia also fomented an institutionalized expression of ethnicity in national politics in order to build his political constituency besides unleashing a branded wave of Islamization which led to serious sociopolitical and radicalization implications. His era is also known for its pervasive drug and gun culture as a consequence of his ill-conceived modus operandi at the behest of the United States to fight the Soviet invasion of Afghanistan.

Third time, it was General Musharraf who overthrew an elected government in 1999 on his sacking by the Prime Minister due, *inter alia*, to differences on the Kargil war and Sharif's attempt to surreptitiously appoint an army chief of his own choice. Sharif was exiled under an agreement facilitated by Saudi Arabia with a commitment not to take part in politics in Pakistan for the next 21 years. In June 2001 Musharraf became the President of Pakistan after winning a controversial referendum which awarded him five years of presidency. He also introduced the Local Government System in August 2001 to establish democracy at a grassroot level. He also formed the Pakistan Muslim League–Q (PML–Q) to consolidate his political position which won the 2002 general election. The Constitution was reinstated in the same year; however, in 2007 it was held in 'abeyance' by Proclamation of Emergency. These actions were also validated by the Supreme Court[13]. Musharraf stepped down as President in August 2008 to avoid possible impeachment.

Within the bureaucracy, a number of military officers were inducted during his regime into senior positions. The higher education institutes around the country during the Musharraf era were tasked in particular to revise the national curriculum to give a positive image and to glorify the history of the military.[14]

Over the years, the army has developed an extremely good network of training institutions, research facilities and strategic think tank functions which surpass those of their civilian counterparts.[15] The army believes that it has the constitutional mandate to act in aid of the civilian government and that it had to impose martial law in 1958, 1977 and 1999 in order to maintain law and order and to safeguard national interests. The fact is that only once since 1947 has an elected government completed its full tenure and handed over power smoothly to another party.

Post-Musharraf the army seems to have decided not to dabble in politics. Three successive Chiefs of Army Staff Kayani, Raheel Sharif and the present incumbent, Qamar Bajwa, have steadfastly stuck to a policy of non-interference in order to eschew the political scene; uphold the rule of law and the Constitution; and support the development of robust democratic and political institutions. However, politicians continue to entice military to intervene. In 2014 Prime Minister Sharif appealed to the generals for help in resolving the political crisis created by the *dharna* (sit-in), the Pakistan Tehreek-e-Insaf and the Pakistan Awami Tehrik although army remained neutral and confined its role only to protect key installations as per Article 245 of Pakistan's Constitution. As recently as November 2017, the military's help was again sought to strike a deal with the religious *dharna* in Islamabad although Government itself was for the blame for amending the 2017 Election Act and the Conduct of General Election Order 2002 pertaining to the finality of prophethood.

Part 3

This section discusses, in chronological order, the nature of the interface between the troika of the bureaucracy as an institution, the army as an entity and the political system, the evolution of their respective roles within the power nexus, and their impact on governance since 1947.

a Institutional transition to indigenization (1947–51)

At independence in 1947, Jinnah preferred the governor-general system over parliamentary democracy. He took advice from the governors[16] and senior secretaries in the absence of well-developed political institutions and skills competence of elected representatives. The country confronted two major governance challenges, namely a huge euphoria of freedom and associated optimism for progress, prosperity, distributive justice and good governance; and, the urgency to address the considerable needs of millions of refugees and the paucity of human, financial and organizational resources. The former entailed rapid and equitable development, the latter immediacy of action to settle the refugees and establish a well-endowed governance structure and state apparatus. Jinnah, and after his death, his successor Liaqat Ali Khan, focused on the need to accelerate development and settle the refugees for which the public bureaucracy was entrusted with the task. Both Jinnah and Liaqat relied heavily on the bureaucrats and encouraged direct communication with them on matters of vital interest. In 1950 seven of the top civilian officials were still British. The few Muslims who were there in the top echelons of power came to possess and wield all the administrative authority of the state. This eventually strengthened the position of the bureaucrats, although under Jinnah and Liaqat the supremacy of the political leaders over bureaucracy was obvious.

The CSP – the lineal descendant of the ICS in Pakistan – dominated the institution of bureaucracy and maintained an extraordinary *esprit de corps*, meritocracy and commitment to the rule of law.

The process of needs assessment for development planning, in the initial years, lacked the input from the political system and as such the civil service played a predominant role in the broad areas of socio-economic deve7lopment. This perpetuated the colonial functional and institutional culture and prevented the emergence of a new class of professionals and responsive managers. The civil servants exercised the resource allocation function to oblige the political elite to the exclusion of people-oriented activities. 'From that role, the civil service emerged as larger than life.' Thus, the super-bureaucrats were born.[17]

However, this period also marked *the smooth transition and complete indigenization of public administration* in Pakistan and the full use of the techno-professional capacity and meritocracy of the bureaucracy to successfully deal with (a) the colossal challenges of administrative machinery building; (b) the rehabilitation and resettlement of millions of destitute refugees; (c) the smooth functioning of the commercial and business operations in the urban centres; and (d) the uninterrupted continuation of businesses vacated by the Hindus.

b Bureaucratization of the political system (1951–58): bureaucracy-military axis paradigm

This period was characterized by a close alliance between the civil bureaucracy and the military establishment when Ghulam Muhammad and Chaudhry Muhammad Ali from the civil bureaucracy on the one hand, and Iskandar Mirza (army officer-turned-bureaucrat) and General Muhammad Ayub Khan from the army on the other, dominated the political landscape. Following the assassination of Liaqat Ali Khan in 1951, Khwaja

Nazimuddin took over as Prime Minister. Ghulam Muhammad, a bureaucrat and serving Minister of Finance, was appointed as Governor-General. This precipitated the rapid colonization of the Muslim League by the bureaucrats. Despite a vote of confidence by the Constituent Assembly, Ghulam Muhammad dismissed the Nazimuddin government in April 1953 for its inability to effectively deal with the language movement in Dacca and the religious riots in Lahore. The same Constituent Assembly passed another vote of confidence to approve the appointment of a new Prime Minister, Muhammad Ali Bogra, who was nominated by the Governor-General. In 1954 the first Constituent Assembly tried to establish checks on the Governor-General's powers in the Constitution, Ghulam Muhammad dismissed the Assembly, an action which was ratified by the Supreme Court. Ghulam Muhammad then assembled a 'cabinet of talents' which included for the first time, Gen. Muhammad Ayub Khan, the Army Chief of Staff, to further erode the apolitical character of the army. In 1955 Ghulam Muhammad removed Prime Minister Muhammad Ali Bogra on the pretext of the deteriorating law and order situation. The political body, namely the Constituent Assembly, was merely relegated to proxy status by the powerful bureaucratic and military interests.

Ghulam Muhammad was forced to relinquish the post of Governor-General in 1955 by the then Minister of the Interior, Iskander Ali Mirza, yet another bureaucrat, due to the former's deteriorating health. Another civil servant, Chaudhry Muhammad Ali, who was the Minister of Finance, was elected as Prime Minister by the Second Constituent Assembly. During Ali's tenure the first Constitution of Pakistan was formulated in 1956. With the Constitution in vogue, Iskandar Mirza became the first President of Pakistan on 23 March 1956. However, his rule came to an end by the promulgation of martial law in 1958 by General Ayub Khan.

As is palpably evident from the above, this period witnessed the *bureaucratization of the political system and the emergence of a bureaucracy-military axis* in the wake of huge political vacuum, lodging and dislodging of different Prime Ministers, and the lack of effective political articulation. The non-representative bureaucracy filled the power vacuum, arrogated direct political authority to stifle the growth of already weak and limping political institutions and became the de facto rulers of Pakistan.

However, on a positive note, bureaucracy as an institution, the infractions of the senior-most bureaucrats aside, performed exceedingly well on the economic front. Merit, the highest standards of conduct, result-oriented performance, and techno-managerial professionalism constituted their kernel to drive the country through this difficult period reasonably well. Economic planning and development programming frameworks formulated during this period continue to serve as a robust basis for economic development not only in Pakistan but also in other developing countries, notably the Republic of Korea, Malaysia and Indonesia.

c Praetorian bureaucratization[18] of the political system (1958–71): command-obedience paradigm[19]

General Ayub Khan usurped the power by a *coup d'état* in 1958. This inflicted a heavy blow to the already fractured and feeble political process. He tried to legitimize his regime by contriving an innovative civilian-political experimentation – a system of 'basic democracies' in 1959 to serve as a political vehicle for the indirect election of the President by the electoral college of popularly elected local representatives. This was simultaneously an attempt to institutionalize bureaucratic control over the political process and to perpetuate the power structure of the rural and urban elite entrenched firmly in the 'baradri' system, which favours people from the same ethnicity. With heavy reliance on the senior civil servants, Ayub fortified the central authority and neutralized the potential constraints of the provincial support base of the political parties.

The historical client-patron dependency relationship between the feudal and urban elite and the bureaucracy was fully exploited by the regime to make use of local clans and power groups to support and sustain Ayub's political and governance system. The politicians allowed themselves to remain subservient to the dictates and directions of the bureaucracy-military duo; acquiesced to the bureaucratic manipulation for local elections; and conferred a much needed semblance of legitimacy to the government. The country experienced the saga of the *praetorian bureaucratization of the political system* through an amalgam of military command-obedience modus operandi aided by the techno-professional bureaucracy and the cooptation of elite political interest. Political autonomy and political institutions, for all intents and purposes, were not allowed to develop.

Ayub Khan ultimately resigned in 1969 and ceded powers to Gen. Yahya who ruled the country from 1969 to 1971. During Yahya's government the relative ascendancy of the military over the civil bureaucracy in conducting the national affairs was established. The 'military hegemonic system' persisted until the dismemberment of the country. A mass movement led by the PPP of Zulfikar Ali Bhutto culminated in the replacement of army rule by a civilian administration.

The corporate ethos of the bureaucracy during the Ayub-Yahya regime, however, remained intact and was not marred by pervasive corruption. The merit- and performance-based criteria were respected by the military regime for postings and positions. The civil bureaucracy had considerable autonomy and discretion and was heavily relied upon to manage economic and development planning. Average annual growth of 5.9 per cent during 1958–70, the green revolution in the agricultural sector, and the industrial development of the era still ricochets loudly in Pakistan's development history. The Planning Commission, the Mangla and Tarbela Dams and the industrial estates with their accompanying encouraging policy and strategic frameworks for investment speak volumes of the success and performance of the bureaucracy.

d Politicization of bureaucracy (1971–77): democratic selective patronage paradigm

Zulfiqar Ali Bhutto was a popularly elected politician who assumed the reins of government at a time which witnessed (a) a huge erosion of military supremacy as a result of the infamous surrender during 1971 in what was then East Pakistan; and (b) the weakening and demoralizing of the bureaucratic institutions during Yahya's regime. The general hope was that the political system would finally transform from frailty to robust maturity with constitutionally balanced roles for the legislature, judiciary and executive and full civilian oversight of the security apparatus including that of the military. Contrary to expectations, the period witnessed a rapid replacement of democratic process by the autocratic politicization of the state governance apparatus. Bureaucracy was the worst affected to the extent of changing the character of service The dismissal of 1,300 civil officers without due process on the grounds of corruption and misuse of power not only demoralized the bureaucracy but also created a vacuum in senior positions which made it possible for Bhutto to appoint his specially chosen loyal civil servants. This also initiated the ignominious *process of politicization of the bureaucracy* with far-reaching implications which are being countenanced by the bureaucracy today. The system of lateral entry and horizontal mobility, was used as a short circuit mechanism to penetrate the bureaucracy by recruiting and/or appointing political loyalists to key decision-making positions. The political patronage,[20] nepotism and cronyism were deployed selectively to hire and appoint unqualified and corrupt officials to lucrative posts. Through the administrative reforms, the power and stature of the elite CSP class were greatly eroded and the constitutional guarantee of the civil servants withdrawn. It was also regularly denied its role to facilitate informed decision making and provide techno-professional input to the policy and development processes which resulted in the haphazard nationalization of industry, structural distortions in the economy and poor economic performance with gross domestic product (GDP) decreasing from around 6 per cent in the previous regime to less than 4 per cent.

Furthermore, Bhutto encouraged politics of ideological and regional centre-state conflicts and smothered the politics of bargaining, compromise and accommodation. He grossly mismanaged the political movement initiated against him by the Pakistan National Alliance in 1977 which led to his downfall. He had a unique opportunity to rectify the institutional imbalance and reconstitute the state institutions but he failed to forge a balance between the parliamentary representatives and non-elected institutions.

As for the military, his aspiration to exercise personal absolute control over it rather than constricting its institutional role as per the constitutional arrangements did not yield sustainable results in terms of counteracting the praetorian propensity to venture into the political arena.

e Authoritarian pluralism (1977–88)

General Zia ul-Haq became President after deposing Bhutto in a military coup in July 1977. He successfully consolidated the military's institutional power over the next decade through skilful cooptation of powerful interests and a coterie of politicians in the management of state affairs. The Majlis-e-Shoora, comprising political representatives established at the national and provincial level, was intended to give legitimacy to the regime. In reality, this *authoritarian pluralism* [21] curbed the expression of genuine pluralist and political interests. The military continued to dominate the political and policy domains. He also embarked on the Islamization of Pakistan which in practice encouraged the unintended proliferation of the organized influence of many distorted versions. Later, his regime manipulated the politics of Karachi to subdue opposition and incited for the first time the institutionalized expression on ethnic and linguistic. This invariably led to the diluting of the Federation and of the national perspective to the ubiquitous emergence of provincialism, ethnic and linguistic political culture.

Zia, in 1985, lifted martial law and held general elections on a non-party basis and installed Junejo as Prime Minister. During the interregnum period between the setting up of the Majlis-e-Shoora and elections, however, a new breed of politicians had emerged to dominate the political arena. Some of these were directly patronized by the President, the most prominent protégé being Nawaz Sharif who was first inducted as Minister for Excise Government of Punjab in 1981 and subsequently became the Chief Minister of Punjab 1985. These politicians continued to remain subservient to the military's will and bureaucratic dependence. An exorbitant allocation of development funds and loans were dished out to the assembly members to cement their loyalty. The Prime Minister was rendered ineffective by amassing presidential power through the Eighth Amendment to the Constitution. His government was dismissed and fresh elections announced for November 1988. Zia's death in a plane crash in August 1988 ended his regime.

The bureaucracy, which experienced significant setbacks during Bhutto's regime, was resuscitated as a functional institution with a well-defined role under the military. The civil service confidants[22] were allowed full access to participate in decision making. The policy, planning and programming processes were supported by the techno-professional and senior cadres of the civil service who helped to formulate robust policy, planning and development frameworks without much interference from the military hierarchy. The consequent privatization of the nationalized enterprises, industrialization and deregulation set at naught the deleterious repercussions of Bhutto's nationalization policy. Pakistan recorded the highest GDP growth rate, of 6.3 per cent, since its creation and became the fastest growing economy in the entire South Asian region.

f Benazir Bhutto (1988–90 and 1993–96) and Nawaz Sharif (1990–93 and 1997–99). The politicization of bureaucracy: democratic patronage and loyalism

The sudden death of Zia in an air crash in August 1988 was supposed to usher in a new era of strong, democratic order in the political history of Pakistan. The PPP government came to power in 1988 under the liberal leadership of Benazir Bhutto as a result of a general election. Ghulam Ishaq Khan, a seasoned bureaucrat-turned-politician, became the President of Pakistan under the PPP platform. The political scuffle between the President and the Prime Minister began with the latter's attempt to push for a bill to reverse the Eighth Amendment[23] to the Constitution. The deepening economic crises, the worsening law and order situation and massive corruption gave the President a plausible excuse to dismiss Benazir's government.

At the ensuing elections in 1990 Nawaz Sharif, a leader of the right-wing conservative alliance Islami Jamhoori Ittehad and allegedly supported by the military intelligence services, succeeded Benazir as Prime Minister. However, problems between the President and Prime Minister Sharif surfaced, *inter alia*, on the appointment of a new Chief of Army Staff, following the sudden death of General Asif Nawaz in January 1993. The Prime Minister resented the lack of consultation and consequently attempted to repeal the Eighth Amendment. Eventually, the President used very same Amendment to dismiss Sharif on charges of corruption, but he was reinstated by the Supreme Court which adjudged the use of Eighth Amendment by the President as illegal. The stalemate between the President and the Prime Minister was resolved by the powerful Army Chief who ultimately prevailed upon both to bow out. Benazir again emerged victorious in the 1993 elections. Her government was, however, marred by a plethora of controversies including the murder of her brother Murtaza, an abortive *coup d'état* in 1995 and unbridled bribery scandals attributed to her husband Asif Ali Zardari. Her government was also dismissed by the President Farooq Leghari, again another bureaucrat-turned-politician, on the allegations of rampant corruption in 1996.

Sharif won the general election and became Prime Minister in 1997 with a sweeping majority of nearly 50 per cent of the vote and 66 per cent of the seats. Being the product of the Establishment, he ought to have 'worked' smoothly with it and paid more heed to building the political power base to eventually mitigate the dominance of the military. However, his second term was likewise replete with a number of problems with the judiciary and army. He stripped the President of the constitutional power to dismiss the parliament. He also provocatively forced General Karamat to relieve the command on latter's proposal to constitute a National Security Council comprising representatives from the services, the bureaucracy and the cabinet to deal with a wide range of issues. He replaced him with Musharraf in 1998. Later in 1999, as stated above, Sharif was deposed by the army.

The intermittent rise and fall of democratic governments from 1988 to 1999 clearly indicates the pervasiveness of overt or covert interference by the army and bureaucrats-turned-politicians wishing to influence the political process in Pakistan. The historical institutional dominance of the military-bureaucracy could not be diluted by the political governments because of their lack of ability to establish and strengthen the political and pluralist structures for governing the country. Both Benazir and Sharif squandered opportunities to create an organizational structure for their respective parties, democratize the process of leadership selection and establish a strong tradition of consensual framework for the government-opposition relationship.

With regard to the bureaucracy, during the democratic regime, Bhutto and Sharif both had their own 'team' of civil servants who were *patronized and promoted not on merit but on their perceived loyalty* to their respective political masters. Appointing senior officers known for their political affiliation rather than their professionalism, Bhutto and Sharif crossed all limits to *politicize* the bureaucracy and pursued a deliberate policy of forming 'coalitions' of corrupt politicians and civil servants to advance their personal gains.

At the same time, in order to appease the military, the democratic governments embarked on the renewed induction of army officers to civilian posts which is self-evident from the fact that, for instance, during 1992–93 over 100 coveted civilian appointments were held by senior Pakistani military officers. This allowed the armed forces to 'capture' positions of power outside military organizations.[24]

In a nutshell, while the period 1988–99 was ostensibly democratic in nature, the weak political order and the astigmatic aim of the politicians to cling to power were insidiously manipulated by the military establishment in collaboration with the civil bureaucracy to shape the course of political events in Pakistan.

g Musharraf's rule (1999–2008): dictatorial techno-professionalism

After consolidating his dictatorial rule, Musharraf eventually held local government elections in 2001 on a non-party basis pursuant to his devolution plan to build grass-roots political leadership and institutions. A general election was held in 2002 which brought to power the army-sponsored and -backed PML-Q. Both the elections were an abundant manifestation of the covert designs of the military to engineer the political process and create a pro-military and Establishment-dependent cadre of politicians. This, in fact, was a continuation of the military perspective on the nature of democratic order in Pakistan ever since Ayub's martial law of 1958. He also restored the Constitution in 2002 which was heavily amended by his Legal Framework Order. In 2007 he stuck a deal with Benazir Bhutto and promulgated the National Reconciliation Ordinance (NRO)[25] which granted amnesty to politicians and bureaucrats who were accused of, *inter alia*, corruption, money laundering and terrorism. The NRO allowed Benazir to return to Pakistan without any legal consequences for pending 'politically' motivated corruption cases. She was later assassinated but her party, the PPP, won the 2008 election and retained Musharraf as President. However, his successive actions that were in flagrant violation of fundamental human rights (e.g. forced disappearances and the kidnapping of human rights activists, etc.) and his attempt to subdue the higher judiciary in order to seek validation of the government's arbitrary actions, including the privatization of the state-owned enterprises, attracted serious criticism from the civil society, particularly from the lawyers' community. The unconstitutional suspension of the Chief Justice of the Supreme Court in March 2007 on the frivolous charge of lack of performance and misconduct was highly resented by the Supreme Court Bar Association. The lawyers accordingly initiated the Movement for the Restoration of Judiciary which immediately elicited active support from senior judges, several political parties and civil society forums. His situation became untenable and in order to avoid possible impeachment in 2008, Musharraf resigned.

During his presidency five different Prime Ministers served with Musharraf, including a technocrat, Shaukat Aziz. He is alleged to have struck four insidious deals to consolidate his position: one in 2001 with the Saudi Arabian royal family for the release of the then Prime Minister Nawaz Sharif; another with Benazir Bhutto in 2007 in the form of the NRO; a deal with Asif Zardari in 2008 to allow him safe exit from the country and no trial; and finally his own departure from the country into permanent exile in order to avoid pending legal cases. In itself this is indicative of the degree of political infirmity, the politics of exigency and the avarice of power-hungry politicians of whom he made full use in order to manipulate the political process and validate his actions.

With regard to the civil bureaucracy, he initiated a series of reforms and established numerous institutions including the National Reconstruction Bureau and the National Accountability Bureau besides completely truncating the district-level administrative machinery and making it subservient to locally elected 'Nazim' (councillors) through Local Government Ordinance 2001. This further impaired the bureaucracy as a neutral institution; established undue dominance of the political institutions at the district level; and led to further politicization of bureaucracy and its unholy alliance with the politicians. The military also exercised oversight and monitoring of the civil bureaucracy, but in reality arrogated all operational control for the conduct of government business. Meanwhile, the Police Ordinance 2002 was introduced which emancipated it from the check-and-balance system enshrined in the erstwhile Police Act. The institution of a Deputy Commissioner with its vertical connect both up and down the hierarchy was deconcentrated and replaced by a weak and politically vulnerably institution of District Coordination Officer. This cock-eyed tinkering to undo the Deputy Commissioner institution deprived the marginalized segments of a very potent interest articulation, interest mediation, interest aggregation and interest integration mechanism for district-level development planning. The Police Ordinance as well as the abolition of the Office of Deputy Commissioner/District Magistrate were to have serious implications for the citizens who were denied the pivot for the peaceful resolution of disputes and conflicts and exposed them directly to the coercive power and boots, batons and guns of the state. Above all, almost all of the major civil service institutions were headed by the military officers. Musharraf himself came up with a strong, sophisticated apologia: *'If you want to keep the army out, you have to bring it in'*.

He, however, achieved some success on the economic front thanks to his reliance on the techno-professional advice of the bureaucracy. The economic liberalization and investment-friendly policies yielded an increase of around 50 per cent in GDP at an annual average rate of 6.3 per cent, the emergence of a more assertive middle class, and an increase in the income per head of the population of nearly 25 per cent.

h Democratic rule (i) political patronage and politicization of bureaucracy (2008–13), (ii) bureaucratic servility (2013–17)

The end of the Musharraf era was followed by the politics of compromise characterized by political adjustments *tour de passe-passe* between the two bigger parties, i.e. the PML–N and the PPP. Both the major political parties pursued their usual agenda of demeaning their opponents rather than building and strengthening the political institutions. They brought to the key positions bureaucrats of their choice and loyalty. The political process as well the bureaucracy suffered as a result and lost what little prestige, honour and professionalism remained.

As stated earlier, the PPP won the 2008 elections and formed a four-party coalition. Yousaf Reza Gilani became Prime Minister and Musharraf President as a part of the NRO deal. He struck another deal with the PPP under the leadership of Zardari, which allowed him a safe exit from Pakistan. Zardari became President. In December 2009 the NRO, which granted amnesty to corrupt politicians, was adjudged by the Supreme Court as unconstitutional, being contrary to the national interest and the spirit of the Constitution. This threw the country into political instability and uncertainty for fear of the possible prosecution of prominent politicians including President Zardari on corruption charges. The government was paralysed, but the PPP muddled through a period of existential threat and serious inter-institutional confrontation involving the government and the judiciary. Prime Minister Gilani was convicted of contempt of court over the NRO.[26] He was forced to resign and Raja Pervez Ashraf took over as Prime Minister. However, for the first time in the history of Pakistan a political government completed its full tenure of five years.

The PPP accomplished some landmark achievements including the passage of the Eighteenth Amendment of the Constitution in April 2010 to denude the President of his extraordinary power to dissolve Parliament unilaterally – a move which marked the first gesture in Pakistan's history when a sitting President parted with his powers voluntarily to establish the supremacy of the parliament; the increase of provincial autonomy through the seventh National Finance Comission award; the announcement of the Aghaz-i-Huqooq-i-Balochistan poverty alleviation package to address the sense of political and economic alienation in the province although it did not yield the desired result; significant enhancement of internal autonomy for the Gilgit-Baltistan region; and rehabilitation of the terrorism-stricken tribal area.

With regard to the civil bureaucracy, the 2008 elections initially brought a wave of hope as over 300 officials who had been laterally inducted by Musharraf were repatriated to their parent departments allowing the civil bureaucracy to work more independently and out of the shadow of the army's monitoring mechanism. However, that hope soon turned into despair as the new PPP government brought in its own team of bureaucrats at the national and provincial level . The PPP pursued a policy of patronage, sycophants and submissive officials as evidenced by a 'you serve us and we will serve you' dictum to influence and politicize the bureaucracy. Indeed, the institutionalized alliance of 'corrup-tomaniacs' and coalition of vested interest amplified the governance dysfunction to its limits. Accordingly, the party confronted its worst defeat in the 2013 election.

Under Sharif, the PML–N won the 2013 election with a thumping majority. The party also formed provincial governments in Balochistan and Punjab. However, Sharif did not learn any lessons from the acrimony of his political exile and the bliss of his emergence as a popular political leader. His person-centred, coterie-driven style of governance was worse than his autocratic rule of 1997–99. He demanded unconditional political loyalty, bureaucratic servitude and personal control-influence over the state institutions, which generated considerable tension and confrontation especially with the judiciary and the military. The 'Dawn leaks' affair, which involved the disclosure of the sensitive internal deliberations of a high-level security meeting, created an overt rift between the military and the political government. The political economy of unprecedented external borrowing

(US $83 billion in July 2017), mega-projects and wanton corruption[27] played havoc with the economic and fiscal health of the state. The 'Panama case' involving mega-corruption named Sharif's family on suspicion of money laundering and led to an investigation by a Joint Investigation Team formed by the Supreme Court in 2017. Sharif was disqualified by the Supreme Court on 28 July 2017, *inter alia*, for non-disclosure of an asset arising out of Iqama. The Court also directed the National Accountability Bureau to proceed against the family on corruption charges. He was succeeded by his nominee, Shahid Khaqan Abbasi as titular Prime Minister, while he continued to control major decisions.

In short, the divisive politics and a culture of *tour de passe-passe* between the PML–N and the PPP characterized the conduct of parliamentary business since the restoration of democracy in 2008. The absurdity of the political process is self-evident from the blatant abuse of the parliamentary majority when the Elections Act 2017 was passed to enable the disqualified Sharif become the leader of the PML–N.

As for the bureaucracy, on assuming the office of Prime Minister, Sharif shuffled over a dozen federal secretaries, and assigned important positions to officers who were loyal to his brother's government in Punjab. He demanded complete obedience, servility and loyalty from the civil servants at all levels of government. In order to cement their loyalty, Sharif dished out perks and lucrative emoluments to officers of his choice.[28] The large-scale politicization of the bureaucracy and the inculcation of a culture of servitude had a considerable impact on the performance and output of the civil servants who did not hesitate to flout the law, rules and ethics in carrying out the illicit orders of the regime.

Part 4

A comparative analysis

A comparative analysis of the role of the troika, namely the bureaucracy, the military and the political system in Pakistan, with that of India and Bangladesh will be interesting since all three countries have, more or less, a similar legacy and heritage emanating out of the British colonial period. However, each seems to have charted its own course in shaping the power nexus of the troika for governance and public administration.

In India, the founding fathers and the politicians were committed to parliamentary democracy. The Constituent Assembly adopted the Constitution in November 1949 and this came into effect in January 1950. The new role of the civil service was clearly laid down in the Preamble, namely 'to secure for all citizens justice'. Mindful of its superior quality and meritocracy, it decided to continue with the inherited model but to introduce significant improvements for a functional parliamentary system and the undoubted primacy of the political executive and elected representatives. While over the years the Indian administrative system has been subjected to 'political patronization' based on clients, kin, caste and informal connections, its core in terms of meritocracy, professionalism and neutrality has not been diluted in deference to the Indian Constitution and political stability.

As far as Bangladesh is concerned, the civil service is well-institutionalized with its own set of values owing to its strong historical legacy stemming from the British Raj and then during Pakistan period. After gaining independence in 1971, its development was marred by an unstable political environment and a prolonged period of military and quasi-military rule. Bangladesh opted for a Westminster model of parliamentary democracy, which, in 1975, was converted into a one-party dictatorial presidential system of personalized rule.

The Awami League (AL) attempted in 1971 to make the bureaucracy subservient and loyally subordinate to the political masters and as such personal ties and group affiliations tended to prevail over well-defined institutional norms. Two consecutive military regimes, that of Begum Khaleda Zia (1975–81) and Lt-Gen. Hussain Muhammad Ershad (1981–90), over a period of 15 years, witnessed the presidential form of government with an all too powerful executive which weakened the supremacy of the politicians. The civil-military bureaucrats emerged as a potent alliance of governance.

During the 1990s democratic order was restored, but because of the assiduous tussle, dissent and conflict between the political parties, the reins of government were shared with the bureaucrats. However, bureaucracy as an institution was confronted with major challenges, including the decline of meritocracy, the loss of an *esprit de corps*, and the undue dominance of politicians enforcing personalized and party values in order to regulate their career development. Political connections and affinity with the ruling class are the dominant criteria for the promotion of civil servants, and this has started the politicization of the bureaucracy and has severely compromised its much cherished values of neutrality and justice in carrying out state functions.

Against this backdrop, some of the distinctive and differentiating features are as follows:

- Since its establishment in 1864 the Indian National Congress consistently fought for the greater participation of Indians in the civil service and played a major role in the 'Indianization' of the civil service.[29] The Muslim League, on the other hand, did not play a proactive role in carving out an indigenous civil service.
- India witnessed a very long period of stable parliamentary democracy and constitutional supremacy which guaranteed that the state institutions, including the bureaucracy and the military, do not violate the legally prescribed mandate. On the other hand, during its first 70 years as a nation-state Pakistan experienced the recurrent abrogation and/or suspension of Constitutions, military takeovers, limping democratic governments, shifting political loyalties and politics of NROs to ascend to and retain. Bangladesh also had a protracted 15 years of army rule but with a strong presence of the executive, military and bureaucracy.
- India has matured democratically, and from the 1990s Bangladesh pulled ahead of Pakistan in terms of achieving democratic maturity, while Pakistan continues to be infested with dynastic and dysfunctional democracies that prevent the emergence of strong political institutions.
- In India, corruption is as rampant as it is in Pakistan. However, the accountability of the executive and oversight by an independent judiciary for infractions and administrative abuses serve as powerful deterrents. In Pakistan, on the other hand, dictatorial regimes defy accountability or resort to selective accountability. During democratic eras the accountability mechanisms are not allowed to function independently.
- In India, the bureaucracy stays away from politicking. In Bangladesh (especially post-1990s), the bureaucracy is being politicized, but in Pakistan overt and unflinching support by a section of the bureaucracy for the ruling political party has assumed alarming proportions.
- However, the commonality between bureaucracies in Pakistan, India and Bangladesh is represented by insensitivity to popular demands; status quo orientation and resistance to positive changes; a great deal of red tape and excessive adherence to rules and regulations; and rampant corruption and bribery.

• India and Pakistan inherited similar British colonial traditions, doctrines and ethics with respect to the role of military. However, in the post-independence period the role played by Pakistan's armed forces and that of Bangladesh after cessation from Pakistan has been diametrically different. While the Indian army remained subservient to the political will and respected the constitutional supremacy of the parliamentary democracy[30], [31], Pakistan witnessed an attempted *coup d'état* as early as 1951 and military takeovers in 1958, 1977 and 1999. Bangladesh had two consecutive military regimes from 1975–81 and 1981–90, which had lasting effects on the civil-military relations as well as n public administration and civil bureaucracy.

Conclusion

Since its foundation 70 years ago, the bureaucracy in Pakistan has vacillated from one extreme to another. From an elite public administration and the 'steel frame' of the country based on meritocracy and neutrality in 1947, it has descended to being totally subject to the will of the politicians, especially since 2008 and even more so since 2013. In the process, it bureaucratized the political system in the days of Pakistan's infancy and did not allow strong political traditions and institutions to be established. During the post-1971 period it allowed itself to be politicized and reduced to the status of a mere tool in the hands of politicians and military rulers to serve their ends. The army also progressively expanded its role, in defiance of its constitutional limits, to capture political and bureaucratic space through the intermittent *coup d'états* of 1958, 1977 and 1999. During the course of army rule the military subjected the political system to praetorian bureaucratization and continues to exercise significant influence on the course of political events.

Be that as it may, while there is a preponderant propensity to bedevil the bureaucracy and the military for impeding the development of political institutions, in reality the political elite and the political parties in particular are equally responsible for constraining the development of a political culture and building the state and civilian institutions required for a truly democratic polity. They have failed to articulate and implement a democratic vision based on balance of power, accountability, civilian oversight of the security apparatus and state-citizen synergy. They continue to espouse a culture of 'family dynasties' based on personal gain, nepotism, avarice and rampant corruption at the cost of serving the national interest. Their inability to deal with the enormity of development challenges including poverty, disease, ignorance, widening regional disparities and distributive justice are a source of continuous disillusionment and alienation of the people and are etiological factors for protestation, exodus, violent extremism and rebellion. The disorder, chaos and asymmetry in politics results in pervasive dysfunction in government, economy and society.

The troika of power nexus of the political system, the military and the bureaucracy has consistently, for the last 70 years, exploited and deprived the people of their fundamental rights to exercise and expand their political, economic, social, cultural and environmental choices. Despite this state of affairs, the people of Pakistan have, on many occasions, shown significant political maturity and sagacity and have expressed an informed collective will to articulate their perspectives on national, regional and international issues. The downfall of the dictatorial regime of Gen. Ayub Khan-Yahya Khan in 1971; the shifts of power between the PPP and the PML–N in 1988, 1990, 1993, 1997, 2008 and 2013 through democratic elections; the restoration of the judiciary and the mass movement against Musharraf in 2008; and the recurrent protests against mass corruption and governance failures from 2014 to 2017 speak eloquently of the strong commitment of the people to democracy. It is unfortunate that this reservoir of collective political maturity, energy, consciousness and ability to give it undeterred expression has been denied a robust democratic outlet in the absence of true political pluralist institutions and historically entrenched systemic constraints.

Notes

1 Akmal Hussain, 'The Dynamics of Power: Military, Bureaucracy and the People', Internal Conflicts in South Asia, London, Thousand Oaks and New Delhi, SAGE Publications, 1996, pp. 39–54.
2 Satyendranath Tagore, a Hindu Bengali, was the first Indian to join the ICS in 1857. See John Michael Compton, 'Indians and the Indian Civil Service, 1853–1879: A Study in National Agitation and Imperial Embarrassment', Journal of the Royal Asiatic Society vol. 99, no. 2, 1967, pp. 99–113.
3 The declaration by the British in 1917 to ensure the increasing association of Indians in every branch of administration, the reforms of 1919 to recruit ICS officers in India, the Lee Commission recommendations for greater share of Indians in ICS, and the autonomy to the provincial governments granted under the Government of India Act 1935 amply testify to that effect.
4 Politicization is the action of causing an activity, event or entity to become political in character. The politicization of the bureaucracy is, by design, the manipulation and submissiveness of the bureaucracy to compliance to the directions of politicians for advancement of political and personal gains. It involves the use of state machinery and resources and influencing the conduct and performance of civil servants in defiance of the legal and policy frameworks which negatively affect autonomy, objectivity and neutrality of the civil service and foments a lack of accountability.
5 Ayub Khan dismissed 1,300 civil servants in 1959 by a single order; Gen. Yahya did the same by dismissing 303 civil servants in 1969; and in 1973 the democratically elected Prime Minister, Z. A. Bhutto unceremoniously dismissed as many as 1,400 civil servants, including senior officers.
6 Loyalism is a civil servant's blind allegiance to the established government, political party, or rulers in support and adherence to their cause, ideology, programmes, decisions and dictates without exercising independent decision and judgement and without due regard to the laws, rules and procedures prescribed for the conduct of state business.
7 Political servility is the unconditional, wilful submissiveness or obsequious bondage of the civil servants to the political rulers to make use of all the state machinery and institutional resources, in servile obedience to their dictates and directions and without any regard to prescribed law, rules or ethics, in order to advance and perpetuate the power and authority of the political leader.
8 Nasera Ayesha and and Iqbal Zafr, 'Performance Management in the Public Sector: A Case Study of the Civil Service in Pakistan', South Asian Studies Research Journal, 2016 (Jan.–June).
9 He later became Pakistan's first democratically elected Prime Minister.
10 In 1974 he tasked the Pakistan army with eliminating the Baloch factions who were desirous of independence or greater provincial rights instead of resolving the issues politically through dialogue.
11 Junejo's government was noted for its austerity measures, the reduction of the budget deficit and the repeal of emergency laws to acilitate the freedom of press and media in the country
12 The Ojhri Camp disaster was the explosion of an ammunition depot for Afghan Mujahideen in Rawalpindi in April 1988; and the Geneva Accord was signed between Pakistan and Afghanistan with the United States and the Soviet Union as guarantors which provided for non-interference, the Afghan refugees' voluntary return, and a timeline for the withdrawal of Soviet troops from Afghanistan.
13 These judges had earlier taken oath under the Judges (Oath of Office) Order, 2007, issued by Musharraf.

14 Some 34 out of 74 civilian institutions were headed by military personnel with over 800 retired army officers in different positions in education.

15 Hussain, 'Dynamics of Power: Military, Bureaucracy and the People', pp. 39–54.

16 Three out of four of whom were British ICS officers: Sir Francis Mudie (Punjab), Sir Frederick Bourne (East Bengal) and Sir George Cunningham (NW FP).

17 Saeed Shafqat, director of the Centre for Public Policy and Governance at Forman Christian College.

18 Praetorian bureaucratization is the steady, sustained and compulsive intrusion of the military in the civil bureaucracy and its institutions over the years and emergence of military as dominant partner in the military-bureaucracy duo to exercise excessive influence over the political system, to provide selective support to the political parties, factions or interests and to control the state governance apparatus.

19 The command-obedience paradigm is the submission of civil servants to the hierarchical command and control structure of the military by abrogating self-responsibility and self-judgment and assuming limited accountability in carrying out the orders and decisions of the superior chain of command while conducting state functions and business.

20 Political patronage is the use of state resources, authority or engagement by the political party or rulers to directly appoint, transfer or promote the public officials inside and outside government in violation of the prescribed laws, rules or ethical codes to achieve personal and political interests and gains. It promotes nepotism and cronyism to pressurize and influence civil servants' performance and conduct.

21 Authoritarian pluralism is characterized by a concentration of power and influence in a strong centre with clearly imposed constraints on state institutions and civil rights, and selective cooptation of the pluralist institutions, elites and interest groups in the decision-making process to provide legitimacy to the ruling authoritarian regime.

22 Ghulam Ishaq Khan, Ruedad Khan, Mahbub ul-Haq, Ijlal Hiader Zaidi and Agha Shahi.

23 The Eighth Amendment to the Constitution empowered the President to dissolve the parliament.

24 Bidanda M. Chengappa 'Pakistan: Military Role in Civil Administration', *Strategic Analysis* vol. 23, no. 2, 1999, 299–312.

25 The Ordinance aimed at 'promoting national reconciliation, fostering mutual trust and confidence amongst holders of public office and removing the vestiges of political vendetta and victimization, and to make the election process more transparent'.

26 He was convicted for refusing to revive graft cases against PPP President Asif Ali Zardari.

27 The PML–N government was accused of scandalous corruption in some of its highly acclaimed development projects, including the yellow cab scheme, the National Debt Retirement Programme, the sasti roti scheme, the Nandipur power project, LNG and other power projects, the Metro-bus and the orange line.

28 For example, the allotment of more than one residential plot in government housing schemes, heavy incentive and dual salary packages.

29 INC efforts at self-governance in 1917, reforms in 1919 of the civil service examination to be held in India; Lee Commission Recommendations for provincialization of Indian Services. Historically the INC spearheaded the process in shaping the Indian administrative apparatus.

30 However, since Modi's BJP government, its increasing glorification of army and the provocative and politically coloured statements of Modi's handpicked man Bipin Rawat, the Chief of Army Staff on situation in occupied Kashmir, concerns are being expressed for army eschewing its apolitical image.

31 It is of considerable concern that for the first time the traditional practice of seniority was disregarded by sidelining two highly regarded generals to appoint Rawat as Chief of Staff. See Latha Jishnu, 'Embedding the Army in Politics', *Dawn*, 20 November 2017.

Part IV
Social underdevelopment

19

Getting technology to work for social development

Ayub Ghauri

There was a time when the world's nations wanted to expand their population base, and used to attract settlers; at that time the resources available were far greater than those needed for a good standard of living to be enjoyed by the populace. Initially it took many years for the global population to reach the 1 billion mark, but now it has grown seven-fold, and currently it stands at about 7.6 billion. Today, the world at large is experiencing an unprecedented level of population growth which is of considerable concern to the policy analysts, for the greater the population, the more shrewd and responsible must be the budget allocations and channels of expenditure.

The substantial population increase has been driven to a great extent by the surge in the number of people reaching reproductive age, along with factors such as dramatic urbanization, a huge rise in the rate of women's fertility, and considerable rural-urban migration. This has led to a plethora of socio-economic problems that have an adverse effect on a country's inhabitants in terms of economic outcomes and their well-being.

The deteriorating condition of the facilities offered by medical centres is much debated, and the talk of the reforms needed to improve them quite repeatedly make the rounds, but very little of it is substantiated and translated into action that would help to improve the health and sanitation conditions in the majority of the world's nations.

If we look more closely at the provision of health care in Pakistan, we can see that the country has a mixed health system that includes both public and private health care, along with parastatal, civil society, charitable contributors and donor agencies. In Pakistan, health care delivery to the consumers can be broken down into four sections, including the preventive, curative, rehabilitative, and promotive services.

To highlight the gravity of the situation further, 50 million people are reported to be suffering from common mental disorders, and to make matters worse, there are only 400 trained psychiatrists who are available to offer their medical expertise to these patients. Unfortunately, the current local health care practices are not sustainable and this further aggravates the situation.

As a signatory to the United Nations (UN) Sustainable Development Goals, Pakistan is dedicated to the alignment of its development planning towards a low-carbon footprint for the next 13 years. However, many have their doubts and strongly argue that results stemming from the 40 Millennium Development Goals indicators suggest that Pakistan's ability to achieve the SDGs is limited. That being said, the solution that is being proposed is that states should not adopt the one size-fits-all policy and should work on the identification of targets based on the resources at their disposal, and endeavour to attain them. SDG goal 3 seeks to ensure healthy lives and promote well-being for all at all ages, including the attainment of various goals: alleviating poverty and hunger, a plan to put an end to the epidemics of AIDS, malaria and other communicable diseases by the year 2030. Furthermore, there is a commitment to achieve global health coverage, and to make effective medicines and vaccines readily available for everyone.

According to the latest report published by UNICEF, although there have been a great many improvements over the past two decades, Pakistan regrettably ranks low compared to other countries in regard to infant and neonatal mortality. Hence, this explains why close to 44 per cent of all children in Pakistan are physically challenged, while a further 9.6 million are sadly experiencing abject nutrition deprivation.[1]

Living in close proximity with so many citizens in a state of deplorable health, we have for instance pneumonia taking away the lives of approximately 92,000 children per annum. The Maternal Mortality Ratio Index indicates that Pakistan slipped from 147th position in 2014 to 149 in 2015, recording a disconcerting number of 276 deaths per 100,000 births. The index shows that, with the exception of Afghanistan, other states in the region have much better health indicators than Pakistan.

According to a 2018 UNICEF report on child mortality Pakistan has the worst newborn mortality rate in the world. In order to more accurately articulate the level of social development, the mortality rate among the children are analysed. Since this is very high, it highlights the level of nutrition children receive, their parents' academic background, and the provision of health services.

If we extrapolate and analyse the impact of the Benazir Income Support Program, Pakistan's flagship social protection programme, targeted at the poorest households, we see that it targets women surviving in incessant poverty. Regardless of the loopholes in the system, the programme has had a major impact on indicators concerning the aforementioned factors.

Pakistan has undergone a process of devolution of its services in the public sector, including health following the enforcement of the 18th Amendment in its Constitution, effective from 28 June 2011. With the dissolution of Federal Ministry of Health, responsibility for health services policy, direction and formulation has been assigned to the provinces, thus consolidating their provincial autonomy.

Currently, Pakistan is suffering from the following challenges related to Human Resources for Health (HRH) other than the above-mentioned factors. This list is by no means exhaustive:

- Rural/urban uneven distribution of health workers;
- Lack of strong HRH management system;
- Acute shortage of HRH, especially in rural areas;
- 'Brain drain' of health experts to other nations;
- A non-regulated private sector that essentially operates in urban sectors;
- Weak quality control and standardization of care;
- Lack of a coordination mechanism for HRH stakeholders.

After a close examination of the National Health Vision, it can be established that the socio-economic commitments are given the due weighting. However, it serves as a potential and crucial reminder that unless the public sector has the approval and commitment of the nation, the public-owned health sector will move further down the spiral of the deterioration in health facilities. Without the element of global medical care, the overhaul and revamping of the health sector will not produce the results that the government wishes to achieve, so yes, by positioning health on top of the national priority list will not do the job, and it would require new investment streams, formidable and effective cross-sector synergies and medical training, if the National Health Vision is to be properly executed.

Within the government's development budgeting and policy frameworks, essential for socio-economic progress, Vision 2025, which was the focal point of the Nawaz Sharif government, was to be executed alongside the SDGs. In all honesty, sustainable development should be the key to development, and is achievable through the system of devolving power, which is already in place but needs further extension. If the process of implementation goes efficiently, the SDGs will potentially meet the requirements of the people by bringing those who should be held accountable, and those with the decision-making authority, within the provincial realm.

It is highly likely that by 2030 the degree of poverty eradicated may not be significant, and that the government may fail to feed around 215 million children, and may be unable to ensure the well-being of them all. However, the modification of the programmes necessitates setting them in alignment with the demographics of various, distinct geographical regions and studying any evidence of success with a view to improving the efficiency of delivery.

The lack of proactive action on the part of the public sector health care system in Pakistan has generated space for the private sector, and has incentivized it to penetrate, grow and expand its operations in the health care market, despite its doubtful quality, high cost and unreliable medical practices. The private sector without any doubt can help to develop the much needed health care framework, and can operate to plug the gaps in the delivery of the health care facilities to those who need them urgently. Yet without any jurisdiction on its operations and a strict system of accountability the private sector remains largely unregulated and unsupervised.

Despite having profit maximization as its chief goal, the private sector has played an active and extensive role in the areas of both preventive and curative services. The private sector has been undertaking the task of providing a quality service to consumers, hence it has been able to build up a level of trust with those both willing and able to purchase 'health care' and therefore it is a significant portion of their income. There is most certainly a massive potential for the engagement and the involvement of the private and other non-public-owned set-ups in the health care system. Thankfully they are expanding their horizon of operations as well as their capacities, and are installing regulatory frameworks in order to provide a convenient access to health care facilities for those belonging to the lower strata of the society.

Major challenges

- Restructuring of the HRH regulatory function and creating linkages and coordination between the federation and the provinces to formulate and regulate the HRH policies and decisions at the federal level.
- Maintaining HRH liability as a consequence of devolution at the federal level.[2]

Health conditions in Pakistan

1   The significant improvement in some health indicators is mainly a result of the efforts of the public-private programmes and the contributions made by the non-governmental organizations.

2   Despite this health profile of Pakistan, it is deeply rooted and manifested with a high population growth rate, infant and maternal mortality rates, and dual onus of transmittable and non-transmittable diseases.

3   The paper by Nishtar[3] pointed out that malnutrition is particularly rife in the rural region of Sindh, while in Balochistan 20–30 per cent of children are stunted in growth, and the high infant mortality there is the outcome of malnutrition and diseases such as diarrhoea and pneumonia.

4   Moreover, less than 50 per cent of infant deliveries take place under the supervision of skilled birth attendants, and the surge in the high maternal mortality rate is linked to a high fertility rate, the lack of nourishment and barely any access to the urgently needed emergency services.

5   Current versus ideal ratios:

1:1300–1:1000 (physician to patient)
1:2.7–1:4 (physician to nurse)
1:10–1:20 (nurse to patient)

6   There is an expanding pharmaceutical industry which meets 80 per cent of the nation's medical demands and 20 per cent is imported. The bigger chunk of the health budget is spent on medical products and pharmaceuticals. in 2017 there were 411 registered manufacturing divisions and 30 multinational companies across the country.

The budget is an extremely significant policy statement of the government, which highlights the direction that the state machinery wishes to pursue through its policies and reforms. It defines the various modes of revenue collection, the priority list of the expenses, and sheds light on the budget surplus/deficit, aiding in the preparation of the counter-effect of the budget deficit.

The Ministry of Health announced a budget of 54 billion rupees for health care and services for the tax year 2017–18; this reflects an increase of 80 per cent compared with the previous year's budget of 30 billion rupees.[4] It was alleged that amount originally allocated to the sector was 27 billion rupees, but there were concerns that a number of important programmes would not be properly implemented or were performing poorly. Hence the budget allocation was increased on the orders of the Minister of Finance. The federal government announced that the allocated amount of 54 billion rupees would be invested in both the old and the new development projects related to the health sector in the year 2017–18.

An epidemic of polio was looming over the country and as a result the Ministry of Health allocated a considerable budget of 7.4 billion rupees for the Expanded Programme on Immunization designed to combat vaccine-preventable diseases, under the umbrella of the Public Sector Development Programme. A further 7 billion rupees were set aside for the Prime Minister's National Health Programme which was working to provide cost-free quality health care for those in need.

Meanwhile, the National Programme for Family Planning and Primary Healthcare was allocated 16.4 billion rupees, whereas the National Maternal Programme and the

Neonatal and Child Health Programme were to receive approximately 1.04 billion rupees for their operations.

In that year the government also pledged 684 million rupees for the Prime Minister's National Health Programme to prevent and control malaria, 3 million rupees of which initially were allocated. Some 7.705 billion rupees were to be invested in the Population Welfare Programme that serves the provinces, as well as an additional 273 million rupees for the benefit of the population of Azad Jammu and Kashmir. Moreover, 1.187 billion rupees were allocated for Gilgit-Baltistan, and about 79 million rupees were kept aside for the benefit of the Federally Administered Tribal Areas.

It was reported that the state plans to construct 46 new hospitals in various districts of the country under the National Health Programme. The government pledged funds for the programme under various heads, for instance 8,000 million rupees were allocated for the Prime Minister's Programme for New Hospitals, whereas funding of about 1.317 billion rupees were allocated for the programme to construct new hospitals, for the specialized design and planning, medical assistance equipment, and for the construction supervision services, which would be used to build 500, 200 and 100 bed hospitals all over Pakistan.[5]

The government also designated funds for 12 new health projects in Islamabad, under the auspices of the Public Sector Programme, which essentially means that the allocation is for the Capital Administration and Development Division.

In total, the government set aside about 7.635 billion rupees for both new and old projects. Of this sum, 1.90515 billion rupees were pledged for 14 old and new development projects for the country's two largest government-run hospitals. Furthermore, the amount of 2.03 billion rupees were pledged to pay for recurring costs of the Polyclinic while 3.7 billion rupees have been set aside for the Pakistan Institute of Medical Sciences (PIMS). The government allocated 400 million rupees for the extension of the cardiac centre bloc at the PIMS and 250 million rupees for the establishment of a neuroscience centre at the same hospital.

Other projects included the construction of a female doctors' hostel at the PIMS, for which the government earmarked 100 million rupees. In addition, the government pledged 199.76 million rupees for the establishment of a shredding, sterilization and medical waste disposal unit, as well as 198.13 million rupees to upgrade the non-radiation diagnostic services at the PIMS. Finally, the government allocated 167 million rupees for the extension, feasibility studies and upgrading of the existing power supply to the Polyclinic.

There is indeed a dire need for the health care sector to step up its game, so that the provision of health care facilities can be conveniently provided to the nation's large population.

Across all the developed nations, technology is most certainly considered as the driver of change and improvement, and it is through this that massive breakthroughs in the health care sector are achieved. If we look at the rate of change and comprehend the variations in the status quo by the recent innovations, we can undoubtedly conclude that technology is the solution to most of our current health problems.

One can safely conclude that technology is has a huge influence on the various aspects of our lives as there are developments in data collection and research which have allowed the medical providers to make good use of the new, advanced tools and come up with even more effective ways of treating patients, and carry out the medical practices.

Analysts across the globe share consensus that the accessibility of treatment is one of the significant ways that technology has influenced health care. Health information technology (IT) opens up a great many streams of exploration and research and development, allowing medical specialists to make health care more consumer-centric and diversified in attending to the array of users' needs.

Another area that can be constantly improved is patient care. With the adoption of IT the improvement in patient care has risen by several notches, and has led to greater reliability. It has been observed that health care specialists and health care workers who are primarily working on the frontline, now routinely use hand-held computers to keep track of real-time patient data, which can be shared conveniently and quickly with colleagues or used to update already existing patient histories.

Such devices make it easier to gather and collate laboratory test results in one place, and to track important patient data. The presence of this technology should help to reassure patients when they are considering using the services of a particular medical facility.

Having an efficient data collection system in place means that a vast online resource of patient history serves as research fodder to scientists, as well as policy analysts who are able to generate new ways to examine trends and to accelerate advances in the health care sector. This would also improve liaison between the medical service providers and those residing in the rural settlements.

Through digitalizing the entire health care set up the various issues can be identified; for example, WHO is capable of identifying illnesses, and what are the causes and symptoms of illnesses. Answers could be sought by tapping into a vast database that easily encompasses more than 14,000 individual codes.

This helpful resource makes it easier for medical professionals and researchers to keep a record of, retract and make good use of the valuable data that has been gathered in the effort to control disease, and to have efficient and improved health outcomes.

Software tends to play an integral role in keeping a record of procedures and using billing methods which does not require a great deal of paperwork, and tends to keep it to the basic minimum. Moreover, it allows the medical practitioners to utilize the collected data to improve the quality of care provided, as well as the efficiency of the tasks undertaken.

Physicians report that they are deriving enormous benefits from the drive towards a total system of electronic medical records, while patients like the fact that the introduction of software has created a greater degree of transparency in the health care system.

Thus, it can be argued that the recurrent innovations in health care have facilitated smoother communications within health care organizations. Medical professionals can now use media such as video, online discussion platforms and real-time meeting facilities to communicate and advance the spread of knowledge in the field. Having electronic medical records in-house means that they are accessible by all the relevant departments and care providers. This results in improved case management, treatments and patient recovery.

Previously, medical information resulting from patient visits to their GP, medical specialist, allied health professionals and dentist was held at separate locations with different health practitioners and hospitals. Electronic medical records allow all patient histories, test results, diagnoses and relevant information to be stored centrally in one online location. The data allows for more focused and accurate care as well as the ability to see health trends for each individual. Medical billing systems allow hospitals, clinics and medical practices to run much more smoothly.

Tele-health service providers offer a large range of services which includes video-conferencing that fortunately is a cost-effective way to complement local health services. It is particularly beneficial to those who living in the rural areas which fall outside of the urban periphery, as well as in the remote communities who need regular access to their GPs or medical specialists who are not close by. Usually patients are able to access the services of a GP, regular medical practitioners, midwives, and other health workers, who provide face-to-face medical services to the user while they are engaged with the specialists to make sure that the procedures which are carried out are the correct ones and that they are properly implemented. Tele-consultations have proved to be very useful to the source of medical help, which are the health care workers based at their specified locations, since skilled practitioners can offer their valuable medical education and training via a digital platform.

As for the mobile software applications, they are clearly needed to create the linkage between the skilled practitioners and the users in need of the health services. Mobile apps have conveniently allowed users to manage their well-being; this essentially covers almost all aspects of health care, from ensuring that users to get regular check-ups, to extracting essential medical information or able to easily access test results online at any time of the day without having to book an appointment with a physician, or waiting for an undefined time period (usually) for test results. Meanwhile, the health care professionals can swiftly access information which is relevant to various diseases and drugs, along with the images that are available regarding clinical matters, and educational updates.

The profound impact that the technology ought to bring to the health care sector is that it is devoid of ambiguity. Hospitals whose systems have been digitalized enjoy the benefits of being up to date with the dynamic trends and constantly upgraded innovations. The transition to the digital world promises a higher level of care and encourages the use of cutting-edge online platforms. It also promises greater operational efficiency and would offer automated administrative and clinical processes which would reduce labour cost. It would facilitate the initiation of collaborations. Finally, it would immensely reduce the expenditure stream, it would boost the profits for the businesses involved, and it would work favourably for the medical users in the form of lower medical expenses.

Hence, the use of health IT in therapeutic facilities enhances medicinal services by giving precise patient records and enables specialists to better comprehend the patient's medical history. Having a complete patient history helps specialists to treat diseases more effectively and avoid the mis-use of medications which can be deadly. Without the availability of medical records, physicians have to rely upon the patient's memory, which can result in errors owing to absent-mindedness, complex medication names, and infirmities influencing the patient's memory.

There is an clear need for integration and synergies between the public and non-public health care sectors in order to revolutionize the health sector and digitalize it. Currently, the sector is plagued by poor administration and powerless public accountability that lacks the necessary powers (problems common to most low-salary nations). A market-centric arrangement of medicinal services, with its inherent responsibility system, is a practical alternative – not to the perfect public sector, but rather to the one we find in reality. The government should assist the private sector in the process of penetration and into the health sector, and should ensure that the non-public sector is fully regulated and is made accountable for its errors and omissions. Not only will this facilitate the delivery of high-value services, but it will also help to fill the gaps that the public sector is unable to occupy due to financial constraints and a lack of effective management.

Notes

1 www.unicef.org/pakistan/Stop_Stunting.pdf.
2 *Annual Progress Report Pakistan*, submitted by the Health Services Academy to the Alliance, 2012.
3 Sania Nishtar, Peter Gluckman and Timothy Armstrong, 'Ending Childhood Obesity: A Time for Action', *The Lancet* vol. 387, no. 10021, 2016, pp. 825–27.
4 https://tribune.com.pk/story/1420327/health-budget-80-budget-fiscal-year-2017-18/.
5 https://tribune.com.pk/story/1420327/health-budget-80-budget-fiscal-year-2017-18/.

20

Akhuwat

New microcredit stories

Muhammad Saleem Ahmad Ranjha

Introduction

Microfinance is a rapidly growing sector across the world. One of the main reasons for this is a gap in the market, namely financial services' provision for the poor and financially marginalized. According to the World Bank, in 2017 approximately 750 million people were living on just US $1.90 per day. Perceived as high-risk and not credit-worthy, such people are excluded by mainstream conventional financial service providers, including banks.[1]

As a result, microfinance has emerged as an economic development tool that can help to meet the financial needs of the economically marginalized and the unbanked. The Grameen Bank of Bangladesh, ACCION International bank in the United States and PRODEM, BancoSol's predecessor in Bolivia are few examples of the success stories of such microfinance innovations.[2]

In Pakistan, over the past two decades, many microfinance institutes have initiated Islamic microfinance window operations, thereby introducing financial services in compliance with Islamic Law. Akhuwat, the world's largest interest-free microfinance institution, is among the largest dedicated Islamic microfinance practitioners and offers *Qard-e-Hasan* (interest-free loans).

This chapter aims to explore the rationale behind Akhuwat that has evolved into an organization credited with producing 'new microcredit stories' – stories of hope, financial sustainability and social empowerment.

The first section briefly identifies the need for Islamic microfinance in Pakistan and its subsequent significance for the local economy. The following two sections relate the history of Akhuwat, charting its progress to an archive of two million microcredit stories, and they shed some light on the core philosophy of the organization in which its operations are embedded in. Sections four and five analyse the impact of Akhuwat and its value creation along a socio-economic nexus. The final section brings together the message of Akhuwat and its structural presence to explore what Akhuwat symbolizes as a larger social message, a tool that has moulded new microcredit stories for the world.

Microfinance and the Islamic microfinance sector in Pakistan

Microfinance is essentially the provision of financial services, usually in the form of small-sized financial transactions, to the 'unbanked' – those without access to the formal, conventional financial sector, including commercial banks. The main reason attributed to this status is the absence of a credit history, without which people are labelled as high-risk by service providers.

Islamic microfinance differs from conventional microfinance because it complies with *Sharia* (Islamic law). A simplistic view would be the provision of microfinance services on an interest-free and partnership-based model. Islamic microfinance utilizes a diverse range of models to avoid those elements that are forbidden or prohibited under *Sharia* law such as interest (*riba*), financial uncertainty and deceit (*gharar*). Therefore, all its financial instruments are designed to provide funds in a manner that avoids interest payments and also takes into consideration the need to cover overheads as well as the cost of financing the microfinance institution in a sustainable manner.[3]

History and background

After the inception of Grameen Bank in Bangladesh in 1984, which was the first formal microfinance bank in the world, microfinance has become widely recognized as an important tool for poverty reduction at a global level. A strong correlation has been identified and studied between the availability of microfinance services and poverty alleviation. Grameen Bank's success in serving the financial needs of the poor segment of society on a sustainable basis has made the bank a role model for private as well as public sector institutions in other countries.

During the 1990s the importance of microfinance was widely recognized in international forums; more importantly international financial institutions started providing funds for the development of the microfinance sector. The enhanced international emphasis on microfinance, in particular the increased funding from microfinance institutions, encouraged both the public and private sectors to develop a microfinance sector in Pakistan as well. Hence, following the escalating focus at the international level, microfinance started gaining in importance in Pakistan towards the end of 1990s. The significant increase in the international funding in 1990s enabled non-government organizations (NGOs) in Pakistan to expand their operations. This funding also served as a major driving force for the establishment of specialized microfinance institutions, such as microfinance banks, in the formal sector.

Khushali Bank, the first specialized microfinance bank, was established in 2000 under a special ordinance in Pakistan. However, in order to promote microfinance in the formal sector, the most significant step taken by the government of Pakistan was to pass the Microfinance Ordinance in 2001 that regulates the establishment, business and operations of microfinance institutions. Its aim was to promote the establishment of microfinance institutions to provide organizational, financial and infrastructural support to the poor, particularly women, as well as to mitigate poverty and promote social welfare and economic justice through community building and social mobilization and to provide for matters connected therewith. Moreover, microfinance has also been recognized as an important tool for poverty reduction by the government of Pakistan in the Poverty Reduction Strategy Paper.[4]

Current prevalence and importance of Islamic microfinance in Pakistan

Realizing the need for and the importance of microfinance as a tool for poverty reduction and social mobilization, the government of Pakistan has accelerated its efforts to establish strong foundations for microfinance in the formal sector and has extended considerable support to the informal sector (e.g. NGOs) as well. The development of the microfinance sector has become one of the main pillars in the poverty reduction strategies adopted by many developing countries, including Pakistan. It is envisaged that the potential market for microfinance in Pakistan could be as many as 12 million households, which is approximately one-third of the country's total households.[5] In a nutshell, Pakistan is considered a promising market for Islamic microfinance, with 98 per cent of the population of approximately 208 million being Muslim and a strong cultural focus on a just and fair economic system.[6]

The need for interest-free microcredit in Pakistan

Despite offering many benefits, microfinance institutions (operating on conventional microfinance) have faced a lot of challenges that have limited their reach, especially in predominantly Muslim countries. The high cost of borrowing (approximately 25–60 per cent) is a problem for customers but one of the major challenges that these institutions have faced while catering to Muslim customers has been the provision of microfinance services under *Sharia* law. This is because Islamic law prohibits the charging of interest on loans. Although conventional microfinance has been successful in Muslim countries such as Bangladesh, where the Grameen Bank alone has 8.3 million customers, there remain many people who could potentially benefit from this service but who do not take advantage of it because it is not compliant with *Sharia*.

High unemployment, poverty and low levels of financial access in Muslim countries continue to create a strong demand for microfinance.[7] While conventional microfinance has successfully reached large numbers of financially marginalized people in Muslim countries (most notably in Bangladesh and Indonesia), there is evidence to suggest that there are many potential clients of microfinance that categorically reject products that do not comply with Islamic principles.

According to a 2009 case study of Pakistan, the vast majority of Muslims across the globe refrain from using conventional microfinance services because the element of interest is considered repugnant to *Sharia*. As a result, there has been an increasing recognition of the role that Islamic, *Sharia*-compliant microfinance could play in reducing poverty in Muslim communities.[8] Hence, Islamic microfinance offers an alternative paradigm for millions of poor people who are not served by conventional microfinance. Akhuwat, as a depiction of that alternative paradigm, has served the needs of two million families in Pakistan.

An introduction to Akhuwat

The word 'Akhuwat' is derived from the Arabic language, and means 'brotherhood'. It is deep-rooted in Islamic history and was conceived when the Prophet Muhammad established a bond of brotherhood between the people of Madina and the immigrants fleeing persecution in Mecca. Each local 'adopted' an immigrant as a brother and thereby assumed responsibility for his needs.

Akhuwat, an NGO that was established in Pakistan in 2001, is conceptually embedded in the same historical incident. Interest-free microcredit services are provided to the poor segment of society in order to improve their standards of living, thus establishing a bond between the donors and the borrowers.

According to this model, the rich help their poorer brethren to get on their feet and become self-sufficient. As it is a loan and not charity, it instils a sense of responsibility in the poor. It empowers them to shape their own lives without any social stigma attached to it as happens with most charities. The whole concept of Islamic microfinance is to incorporate faith into the financial sector, because in countries like Pakistan faith is deeply entrenched in all aspects of life.

History and emergence of Akhuwat

In 2001 Dr Muhammad Amjad Saqib, a former civil servant and philanthropist, established Akhuwat, a microfinance institution that was to evolve into a mission to alleviate poverty in all its forms in the space of just 15 years. As background context, a widow refused to take charity, preferring instead to take out a loan (*Qard*). She used this to purchase two sewing machines and later on she established a small boutique at her own house by taking out a similar loan. Her dedication and hard work paid off, enabling her to repay the loan within the allotted period of six months. She also managed to marry off one of her daughters with the income that she had earned. It was this poor widow who became an inspiration for the establishment of Akhuwat, and became its first success story.

Objectives of Akhuwat

Since its inception, the fundamental purpose of Akhuwat has been to help financially marginalized people by providing interest-free loans so that they can become economically self-sufficent. The average size of loans offered by Akhuwat is US $200.

The major objectives of Akhuwat can be summarized as follows:

- Providing interest-free microcredit services to poor families and hence enabling them to become self-sufficient and self-dependent.
- Promoting Akhuwat's *Qard-e-Hasan* or interest-free loans as a viable model as well as a broad-based solution to poverty alleviation.
- Providing social guidance, capacity building and entrepreneurial training to its members.
- Institutionalizing the spirit of brotherhood, compassion and volunteerism among its members.
- Transforming Akhuwat's borrowers into donors.
- Making Akhuwat a sustainable, growth-oriented and replicable organization.

The philosophy of Akhuwat

Akhuwat envisions a poverty-free society built on the principles of compassion and equity. Its philosophy is derived from the concept of *Muwakhaat* which means solidarity. Akhuwat strives to alleviate poverty by creating a mutual support system based on the tradition of the Holy Prophet. For this purpose, the organization has specifically adopted Islamic microfinance as its operational strategy in accordance with the doctrine of interest-free loans.

In order to accomplish its vision and objectives, Akhuwat is currently operating two types of programmes; a *microfinance programme* which aims to enhance the income of the poor segment of society and a *social development programme* which aims to improve their standards and quality of living via an integrated approach to poverty alleviation. The microfinance programme constitutes group-based loans, individual loans and rural credit programmes. When Akhuwat was initiated in 2001, it started by offering group-based loans before gradually introducing individual loans in 2003.

Five core values

The five principles of Akhuwat are:

- To disburse interest-free loans rather than charging high interest rates in the manner of conventional commercial banks.
- To use religious centres such as mosques and churches from which to disburse loans in order to instil a sense of brotherhood and to build cordial community relations.
- To instil a spirit of volunteerism: Akhuwat hires its workers from the very community that it operates in and also lends to. Hence, it tells its employees (both current and prospective) that working for Akhuwat should be seen as volunteering work or a service rather than as an income-generating activity. Akhuwat's board of directors is made up of capable as well as well-qualified philanthropists and social workers.
- To transform borrowers into donors: every borrower receives a small donation box when he or she receives a micro-loan. The borrower displays the donation box in shops where customers can see it. Whenever the borrower or his customers put money in the donation box, they become Akhuwat donors. The borrower takes the box and its contents to Akhuwat when he visits to repay the loan instalment. This 'borrower as donor' concept is highly successful and strengthens the belief of borrowers that they can also do good deeds for the community.
- Non-discrimination on the basis of caste, colour, creed, political affiliation or faith.

The ground-breaking model followed by Akhuwat

There are three modes of expansion that have been followed by Akhuwat as it has risen in prominence, namely self-expansion, replication and partnership.

Through *self-expansion* Akhuwat has tried to either expand its presence in new cities or towns or to further enhance its presence in cities or districts in which it already has offices. In the scenario of improving presence, the process that the company has followed is that it judges the demand for funds coming to a branch and if it assesses that the demands and applications are too high for the efficient disbursement by a single branch then the directors decide to open a new branch within that region. In identifying a new region, the institution first receives some sort of indication as to whether their organization is demanded in the area. Then a feasibility study is done to assess whether this new branch would be productive or not. If yes, then a suitable location near or adjacent to a religious building is found and the training of the new recruits commences. As soon as the new recruits are suitable for fieldwork the new branch can start operating.

Through *partnership* Akhuwat collaborates with other institutions in order to expand. According to this model, the partner institute provides the funds and Akhuwat provides the manpower necessary for running the operations. Initially, the branch is led by one of Akhuwat's experienced employees, but later the branch is handed over to the new employees for operations.

Akhuwat is based largely on charitable funding, with its primary product being *Qard-e-Hasan* (an interest-free loan with long repayment periods). Akhuwat is unique because the model was developed on the concept of community and most branches have been set up in mosques and churches. As Akhuwat has no profit margins on these loans, the institution relies heavily on donations and subsidies, which may have the potential to hamper sustainability in the long term. However, since its inception there has been no shortage of donors, which is strong evidence of the success of this model.

Akhuwat is one of the few institutions in Pakistan that offers a fully *Sharia*-compliant product. Islamic scholars believe that interest (*riba*) is inherently exploitative and that money should be used purely a means of transferring funds and has no intrinsic value. Thus, it is unlawful to make a profit from money itself.[9]

What makes Akhuwat different?

Akhuwat is distinguishable because it violates all the generally accepted or conventional rules of microfinance but has still survived and grown phenomenally. In the current crisis of controversial opinions affecting the reputation of microfinance, not only in Andhra Pradesh and India, but also globally, Akhuwat serves as proof that there is another way to finance loans, and it may even be a better way.[10]

Akhuwat's alignment with Islamic principles extends beyond its interest-free loan mechanism. Akhuwat's linkage with religious space is something that sets the institution apart from its counterparts. Loan introduction programmes and loan disbursements are conducted at mosques or churches to raise awareness of Akhuwat among poor localities. This also increases transparency and accountability while taking advantage of under-utilized space and cutting down on overhead operating costs. Instead of financial penalties and danger of destruction of social capital (normal mechanisms on which other microfinance institutions are based), Akhuwat exploits normative pressures that are connected to faith and religion. By using mosques and churches for the purpose, it actually reinforces this concept while also helping to break down any associated religious barriers and taboos such as the ban on women and non-Muslims entering mosques.

While the organization is founded on Islamic ideals, no individual is discriminated against on the basis of religion or gender. In keeping with Akhuwat's religious philosophical commitments, a central pillar of the organization is that 'it is essential to look beyond oneself'. Saqib, the founder of Akhuwat, expects today's borrowers to become tomorrows' lenders. Akhuwat's success in converting its borrowers to donors is another key aspect that distinguishes it from other institutions of its kind. The growth in donations that Akhuwat has received since the initiation of its Member Donor Programme in 2008 is nothing short of a phenomenon.[11]

Akhuwat's reliance on local donors means that unlike other donor-dependent microfinance institutions it is not under any sort of pressure to scale up quickly. This means it can work with greater due diligence and monitoring. The absence of interest also means that the organization is genuinely interested in helping its clients rather than defrauding them – this being a common perception of many other microfinance institutions.

Where Akhuwat stands today

Akhuwat is an ever-evolving institution. Following its consistent growth year-on-year, Akhuwat has been successful in establishing its presence throughout Pakistan in all four provinces. From its first branch in 2001 it has now expanded to 700 branches in 350 towns and cities in Pakistan.

Global outreach

Over the years, Akhuwat's operational strategy has shifted from being purely based on philanthropy and donations to a public-private partnership model, and it is now working with the federal and state governments of Pakistan for the provision of interest-free loans. Its model of microfinance has been replicated locally in Pakistan and became operational in African countries including Uganda and Kenya in financial year 2017–18. The impact of Akhuwat has been validated by circles from across the globe including the prestigious Harvard Kennedy School as well.

What Akhuwat symbolizes

Akhuwat has adopted a well-integrated and comprehensive approach to poverty elimination. This is the reason why despite providing basic microfinance loans, it has been able to make a positive influence on the lives of millions of poor people across Pakistan because the approach that it has chosen in order to deal with poverty eradication is different from those of other microfinance institutions in terms of social impact and welfare.

Hence, Akhuwat believes in an integrated approach, using microfinance as one of the tools that needs to be complemented by a holistic approach which involves intervention in social welfare projects.

With an average loan of US $200, people who borrow from Akhuwat are able to engage in small-sized ventures as tailors, street vendors, car mechanics, hairdressers, and so on. In short, they become more productive members of society. Consequently, on a social nexus, they can afford to send their children to school and provide them with a better standard of living that includes basic utilities such as electricity.

Poverty is also reflected in the increasing gap between the different segments of society. The widening economic and social gap results in indifference and apathy among the population. That is 'emotional poverty'. In Pakistan, Akhuwat saw this emotional poverty as a challenge and decided to channel it into a social opportunity. For example, the Akhuwat Clothes Bank, which in 2017 was in its third year of operation, had successfully disbursed 1.5 million clothes in the form of a gift to any family rated as vulnerable and extremely poor on the national poverty index.

The opening of Akhuwat College (Lahore) was the one of first steps on the road to achieving Akhuwat's goals. Since October 2015 it has been providing free education and accommodation to 250 students from underprivileged backgrounds irrespective of their religion, race or ethnicity. In addition, 300 primary public schools have been outsourced to Akhuwat by the government of the Punjab – in 2017 the total enrolment rate in these schools stood at 50,000. Akhuwat now intends to extend its education services by providing free higher education. In order to achieve this goal, Pakistan's first fee-free university, which in 2018 was still under construction, will provide a world-class education to students.

Similarly, the transgender community in Pakistan is unfortunately among the most marginalized, socially, economically and politically. They are deprived of basic civil rights.

Given Akhuwat's goal of creating a poverty-free society based on the principles of compassion and equity, it is seeking to achieve the social inclusion of transgender people in a bid to lift them out of economic poverty. Therefore, Akhuwat, in collaboration with Fountain House, launched the Khwajasira Support Programme in 2011 for the transgender community. Besides advocacy participation, transgender people are also given health insurance, vocational training, a monthly stipend and employment opportunities with Akhuwat's network of partners.

Conclusion

In sum, Akhuwat represents what is best in society, namely the willingness, commitment and enthusiasm of members of society to assist one other during difficult times and also to make certain sacrifices. Akhuwat bases its actions on these principles and considers that it has a moral obligation underpinned by religion to encourage people to help one other out but without any prejudice and without any form of coercion. It also aims not only to help others financially but also to transforming their perception of the world in which they live. It is a model that all social entrepreneurs can ignore only at their peril.

Notes

1 World Bank, The World Bank Annual Report 2017: *End Extreme Poverty, Boost Shared Prosperity*, main report (English), Washington, DC, World Bank Group, 2017. Available at http://documents.worldbank.org/curated/en/132951507537966126/Main-report..

2 Mahboob ur-Rashid, The *Role of Microfinance in the Context of Islamic Banking:* A *Study of the Products Offered by Banks in* Pakistan, Institute of Management Studies, University of Peshawar, 2012.

3 Kajia Hurlburt, *What Is Islamic Microfinance?*, Shuraako.org, December 2012. Available at http://shuraako.org/sites/default/files/documents/What%20is%20Islamic%20Microfinance.pdf.

4 Poverty Reduction Strategy Papers are prepared by member countries through a participatory process involving domestic stakeholders as well as engaging development partners, including the World Bank and International Monetary Fund.

5 World Bank, The State of Pakistan's Economy, 2nd quarterly report for FY06, Washington, DC, 2006. Available at https://data.worldbank.org/topic/poverty?end=2014&start=2008.

6 Juliana S. Beall, 'Akhuwat: Potential for a Sustainable Islamic Interest Free Microfinance Model', *BusinessWire*, 2016. Available at www.businesswire.com/news/home/20160713005857/en/Global-Microfinance-Market-Grow-15.56-2020–.

7 M. Khaled, Building a Successful Business Model for Islamic Microfinance, Consultative Group to Assist the Poor, 2011.

8 Hurlburt, *What Is Islamic Microfinance?*

9 Beall, 'Akhuwat'.

10 M. Harper, 'Akhuwat: It Sometimes Makes Sense to Break the Rules', conference proceedings, 24 March 2011.

11 Beall.

21

Private sector in education

Shahid Kardar

Introduction

Pakistan has one of the world's worst profiles in human development owing to its chronic neglect of social factors. Out of the 775 million illiterate adults globally 50 million are from Pakistan – the third highest level of illiteracy in the world,[1] with a literacy rate of 60 per cent for those aged 10 years and above. Indeed, the country's illiterate population of 15 years and above today is more than the population of the country at the time of independence.

The participation rates at all levels of education are low relative to other South Asian countries and others with similar levels of per head income. The 2017 Global Human Capital Report ranks Pakistan's Human Capital Index as low as 125, compared with India at 103, Bangladesh at 111, Sri Lanka at 70, Nepal at 98, Vietnam at 64, Kenya at 78 and Myanmar at 89.

Around five million children of primary school age are not enrolled in education, while 60 per cent at the secondary level are not in school (resulting in 22.6 million children between the ages of five and 16 being out of school).[2] Thus, the proportion of the population aged 15 years and above with a secondary education is 25 per cent in the case of Pakistan, compared with an average of 59.5 per cent for South Asia and 54.5 per cent for low-middle-income countries,[3] while the university-level participation rate is below 5 per cent. Furthermore, the drop-out rate is high, with almost 34 per cent of the budget spent on children dropping out before completing the primary education cycle.

Background to the rise in private education

The principal reason for these outcomes has been the weak political commitment to human development, reflected in the poor prioritization of education in the profile of government expenditure. In 2012 education in Pakistan was allocated 2.1 per cent of gross domestic product (GDP) compared with an average of 2.35 per cent of GDP for South Asia and 3.4 per cent of GDP in the case of low-middle-income countries (compared with UNESCO's recommendation of 4 per cent of GDP). Consequently, the government has been unable to keep pace with the needs of a population swelling at 2.4 per cent per annum, address the helplessness of the less well-heeled segments of society in developing their abilities through the public education system to enable their social and economic mobility, the increasing social demand for education owing to improvements in returns to education and a growing upwardly mobile middle class thirsty for better-quality education. However, the low level of spending on education is a lesser issue than matters pertaining to governance which is a particularly debilitating factor when it comes to the delivery of basic social services.

With the public sector failing to deliver decent-quality social services effectively and at reasonable cost, the nostrum that the government should not be engaged in economic and commercial activities such as running airlines, steel mills and banks, and should hand over these operations to the private sector, but should be focusing its energies and limited financial and human resources instead on the delivery of social services like education and health, is seemingly misplaced in the Pakistan context.

The public delivery of education services continues to suffer from legal and political economy predicaments in the shape of non-existing schools and teachers (more popularly referred to as 'ghost schools and ghost teachers'), teachers playing truant (either not showing up for duty or not fulfilling their responsibilities), teachers not recruited on merit, poor-quality human capital unable to adapt to changing global dynamics, quality differentials with the learning outcomes of children enrolled in private schools (see below), and political interference in the area of teacher recruitment and placement.

A major constraint to the delivery of quality education by the system is the protection accorded to teachers by politicians owing to their role as polling agents during elections and the weak accountability systems that facilitate the blackmailing of governments by powerful teachers' unions if they try to open proceedings against those guilty of rampant absenteeism. It is almost impossible to dismiss civil servants in Pakistan, especially teachers who do not turn up for duty let alone those who do turn up but who fail to perform the services for which they have been engaged. Rights are seemingly only the preserve of the service providers and not of the service recipients. Moreover, from their announcements and actions governments also tend to indicate that their primary interest is in the provision of jobs and not in the number of children they hope to educate through the induction of these teachers.

Disappointed by the quality of services delivered through publicly managed schools, households with school age children have begun to look for options. The private sector stepped in to tap this demand and, understandably, chose the schooling system as the first point of entry.

Growth of private sector managed schools

Whereas high fee-charging schools had been catering to the more privileged sections of society for some time, private schools began increasingly to be sought by less affluent households. And contrary to popular perceptions the private sector services all sections of the population with the vast majority charging less than US $5 per month to accommodate children from less prosperous families. Again, contrary to generally held opinions about low-income households they are conscious of factors generally perceived to be related with quality education.

The urban areas have experienced a rapid increase in the number of private schools which, despite their often limited facilities and otherwise meagre resources of adequately qualified personnel, have come to be identified with a certain level of quality education, and a large number of poor and low-middle-income households are sending their children to private schools. The decision of parents to enrol their child in a private school, even when there is a government school in the vicinity of their residence, indicates the exercising of a considered choice based on their assessment of the quality of education provided by private schools, as opposed to that offered by government-run schools.

Unsurprisingly, the private sector has been active where the environment is more lucrative, e.g. the relatively more affluent areas of Punjab and the main cities such as Karachi, Hyderabad, Sukkur, Peshawar and Quetta.[4] Hence, more than 50 per cent are spatially concentrated in 10 districts (less than 10 per cent of the total number of districts), with the poorest households in the less developed parts of the country left with no choice other than poorly functioning government schools.

That parents have begun to vote with their feet, and are rejecting the services provided by the government, is reflected in Punjab, for example, which has close to 60,000 private schools,[5] more than those run by the government. Even as far back as 1999/2000 the share of the private sector of GDP was 0.66 per cent with 36,000 institutions (95 per cent of which provided co-education), enrolling 6.1 million school children. By 2007/08 their share of enrolment nationally was 34 per cent.[6] In 2011/12 the overall participation rate in private schools for the age group 6–10 years was 22 per cent (Punjab 27 per cent, Sindh 18 per cent, Khyber Pakhtunkhawa 16 per cent and Balochistan 3 per cent with their share of enrolment being 43 per cent in urban areas and 13 per cent in rural areas); close to 95 per cent are of the low fees category, charging monthly fees of less than US $25, with 20–25 per cent of students on scholarships in 2017.[7] By 2015/16 their share in enrolment was approximately 42 per cent, with a share of 39 per cent in primary schools and 35–37 per cent in secondary and higher secondary schools. Punjab's share of private schools was around 69 per cent, with a share of 62 per cent of the enrolment in the privately run institutions.[8]

An important reason for the rise in number of these private schools has been the demand for schools offering English as the medium of instruction, which is generally perceived to be a key instrument in the development of a capability for securing a more remunerative job, thereby gaining social and economic mobility.

The government and multilateral and bilateral donors, however, continued to ignore this overwhelming evidence. They contended that parents were not enrolling their children in government schools because these institutions did not offer desirable facilities such as toilets, boundary walls and an adequate number of classrooms. Investments were made in infrastructure with limited success in enhancing enrolment in government schools, while the share of private schools both in the number of schools and in the numbers enrolling in them continued to grow at a healthy pace.

Having analysed these results, both the government and donors revised their strategy arguing for (a) more qualified teachers (although the comparable private schools have significantly less academically qualified teachers who get paid one-third of the salary of a government school teacher); (b) recruitment on contracts (that could be terminated if the teacher was frequently absent or did not perform his/her duties diligently); and (c) teachers being tied to a school so as to make them accountable for service delivery. But, again, little difference was observed in enrolment in government schools. Moreover, all contract teachers have been regularized, and fully imbibe the culture and work ethics of those enjoying 'permanent status'. In other words, despite the customer rebuff,[9] which should have been acknowledged as a testimony to the failure of government service delivery, donors continued to press for more dedicated resources resulting in the pouring of yet more money into a dysfunctional system.

Study after study has demonstrated conclusively that better-quality education is being provided by private schools at a significantly lower cost than that which the government spends to educate a child in its own schools. Annual Status of Education Reports (ASER) reveal that the differential between the learning outcomes of children in private schools located in rural areas and those enrolled in government schools was more than 20 percentage points in tests administered in the subjects of English and mathmatics despite the much higher academic qualifications of government school teachers. In the case of schools in urban areas the differential in the same subjects was in excess of 17 percentage points.[10]

The cash subsidy concept pioneered by the Punjab Education Foundation

In recognition of the evidence depicting better learning outcomes of children enrolled in private schools I conceived and pioneered an approach under the auspices of the Punjab Education Foundation (PEF) in 2004/05 to attract disadvantaged children to school; in 2017 it was educating more than 1.5 million children. The contract between the PEF and the private entrepreneur was designed for the delivery of education-related services of a defined quantity and quality at an agreed price.

The implementation of the underlying concept demonstrated that better-quality education can be provided than that being delivered by government schools through public cash subsidies at the rate of 550 rupees per child to mixed gender schools. The partner school becomes completely free for enrolled children (the subsidy being less than half what it costs the government to educate a child in the public schooling system – excluding the cost of land and amortization of the school building and the cost of administration by the provincial Education Department). Furthermore, this financial assistance is made conditional upon minimum acceptable performance of children in standardized academic tests conducted regularly. It administers these tests in languages, mathematics and sciences.

Private sector at the tertiary level

Introduction

Education is generally viewed as a public good (the total economic and social returns to society are greater than the sum of the gains of individuals) that produces a wide variety of benefits for its consumers who in turn confer a part of these gains onto those not acquiring it directly themselves. It is, therefore, argued that improving access to education, and specifically higher education, through subsidies will not only raise the national income of a country but more importantly lead to large, albeit not fully quantifiable, social benefits. Some of the positive spillovers include improvements in health, reductions in poverty, population growth and crime, improvements in income distribution, and strengthening of democracy and civil liberties. Hence, by taxing those who receive these benefits indirectly through the provision of subsidized education, the welfare of the society as a whole can be increased. This subsidy for higher education is also advocated on the premise that it is the duty of the government to provide all citizens with an equal opportunity to have an education irrespective of their economic and social backgrounds. Therefore, the argument proceeds, the modern state can use subsidies as an effective instrument to ensure equity and provide free education at all levels so as to guarantee equality of educational opportunity.

Another argument in support of public subsidies is that in developing countries imperfect capital markets prevent students from borrowing against the uncertain future returns of higher education. For individuals, the risk of not completing their programme and/or being unemployed in the future is high which diminishes their willingness to borrow in order to invest in higher education. Even lenders (financial institutions such as banks) may be reluctant to lend because of the uncertain future income of the debtors.

Growth of private universities

The lack of adequate physical infrastructure and adequate funding that is critical for expanding the base and quality in the public sector in order to accommodate the rapidly growing population demanding higher education has resulted in the private sector responding to this opportunity. Table 21.1 summarizes the growth in the private sector offering higher education, with 76 institutions accredited by a regulatory body, the Higher Education Commission (HEC), representing 44 per cent of the number of universities with a 16 per cent share in enrolment.[11] Their pace of development has been facilitated by the provision of some key inputs for delivering educational services either free-of-cost or at affordable rates by the HEC.[12]

Contributions of private universities to the higher education sector

Some of the contributions made by private universities during the relatively short period of their establishment are mentioned below:

1 The ratio of students admitted to top-tier universities in the United States, the United Kingdom and the European Union on masters and PhD programmes and their presence in corporate leadership positions is higher for private universities. And there is more than just anecdotal evidence of the feedback of employers about the better quality of graduates of private universities, especially for the social sciences.
2 The private sector improved compensation structures for faculty in general, forcing the public sector also to adjust, thereby making it easier to attract and retain better-quality academics.

Table 21.1 Data showing tertiary level education

	2001–02	*2015–16*
Universities (Number)		
• Total	74	184
• Private	33	76
Enrolment Total (Number) *	276,274	1,393,425
• Private Universities (%)	15.9	19.1
• Female (%)	36.8	45.6
Female graduates with 16 years of education (%)	33	35
Female graduates with 18 years of education (%)	32	39

Source: Higher Education Commission.
Note: *Includes Distance Learning Institutions (DLIs), equivalent to 35% per cent of total enrolments (without DLIs the private share was 29 per cent).

3 Private universities also promote inclusiveness by providing needs-based scholarships worth approximately 10 per cent of their revenues from tuition fees.[13]

4 In the first two years of the Lahore University of Management Sciences Entrepreneurship programme 53 companies have been incubated providing 500 direct and indirect jobs and US $2 million in revenue, with the company valuation of eight of them exceeding US $16 million,[14] while graduates of the school of visual arts at the 10-year-old Beaconhouse National University are getting recognition in the art world and receiving global awards.

Factors constraining private sector growth

State priorities tend to be distorted, reflected in the taxation structure and the rigidity of the regulatory systems.

A key factor tending to restrict private sector delivery of schooling in particular and education in general to low-income households is the regulatory structure established by the government, which is characterized by the lack of clarity of objectives, content and scope. The stipulations that schools have to satisfy are rather loosely worded – giving regulators considerable latitude for interpreting them at their discretion, and giving government officials a great deal of scope for extracting rent by harassing the management bodies of private schools. It is another matter that its intrusive intent is enforced in a benign manner and, therefore, the 'cost of compliance' is low.

The following illustrate the arguments made above with respect to the regulatory requirements:

1 Under the governing provincial legislation and the rules for regulating privately managed educational institutions those seeking registration are required to furnish a lot of information, most of which is irrelevant to the delivery of education, partly because it becomes rapidly outdated and loses its currency.[15] In the absence of institutional arrangements and mechanisms for either periodically updating this information or analysing it for policy or other purposes it is difficult to understand the need and relevance of gathering and collating all this information.

2 The HEC grants accreditation to universities located in cities only if they actually own the land on which their institution is situated and at least three acres of it, and seven acres if the institution is established outside urban limits. Since urban land is expensive this regulation forces institutions to locate away from population concentrations, discouraging private investment in higher education to complement the public provision of tertiary education.

3 The regulatory structure empowers the government to rule on the commercial terms that may apply to school operations, on the proviso that the school should operate as a non-commercial institution. For example, the government can insist that the terms and conditions of employment of teachers (pays, pensions, etc.) should not be less beneficial than those applicable to government teachers, rule on financial discipline issues, and demand that the level of school fees should be reasonable (the term 'reasonable limits' has not been defined – thus opening up opportunities for officials to exercise discretion).

4 Although the government provides neither funding nor incentives to private providers of education it displays a penchant for control (as opposed to regulation). Caps have recently been placed on tuition fee increases (5 per cent at schooling level and 10 per

cent for higher education) irrespective of the rate of inflation, facility provisions and quality-related interventions. This vigour stems from the pressure that is brought to bear by the articulate middle- and upper-income groups, who, having given up on the public sector's ability to provide adequate quality schooling, want the government to rule on the reasonableness of the fees that the private sector charges for delivering education-related services.

5   The regulatory framework provides for disproportionate penalties even for trivial contraventions of the rules. For example, in Sindh, where prior permission is required from the Education Department to increase school fees, failure to register an insti-tution or to run it in contravention of the provisions of the Ordinance or the accompanying rules can result in a one-year prison sentence.[16]

6   The HEC ranking of universities on the basis of a 66-point indicator criteria assigns more weight to quantity than to quality. For example, the criteria focus on the number of students enrolled, the number of teachers and the number of research publications, the ratio of enrolment to total applicants, and the number of PhDs produced. These rankings are also at variance with parental and market perceptions about the quality of education provided by different universities and the choice of the institution exercised by households.

7   There is a continuing battle for turf between the federal HEC and the provincial HECs that were established following the 18th Amendment to the Constitution, under which some functions were delegated to the provinces, who then demanded a larger and more expanded role for themselves, including powers of accreditation of institutions and academic programmes on offer. The resulting fragmentation and duplication of regulatory bodies has created a cumbersome system that absorbs a lot of the time and energy of operators in the sector.

The tax regime

Instead of favouring institutions catering to less privileged households the government's tax policy tends to discriminate against them. For example, the tax liability of teachers or researchers working in a non-profit education or research institution recognized by the mandated regulatory bodies is half that payable by not just another salaried employee earning the same level of income but also by a teacher working in a private school cate-gorized as a commercial, for-profit establishment. This odd treatment that penalizes a teacher for working in a private educational institution that operates along commercial lines has created an anomalous situation whereby a teacher or professor employed by an institution for more privileged households, and drawing, on average, a salary that is 20–30 times higher than that of an ordinary school teacher, gets an income tax concession.

Again, self-occupied educational institutions pay a property tax that is around twice the rate that is applicable to similar sized owner-occupied residential properties in the same locality – a rate that is 40–50 per cent of the tax payable by a similar sized owner-occupied commercial establishment. It is when we compare this apparently soft treatment of educational institutions with that accorded to properties with institutions managed by the government or autonomous institutions colonizing government-owned land (all of whom are exempted from property tax, although they also consume similar services) that the gloss of the concession begins to wear thin. We are, therefore, confronted with another peculiar situation under which non-profit schools or schools charging a fee of US $5 a month, pay property tax, while properties being used by an institution catering to the elite, e.g. the Aitchison College, located in the centre of Lahore, are exempt because the land is owned by the government.

Finally, educational institutions have been denied a zero-rated status for adjusting the General Sales Tax on inputs (with a minimum rate of 19 per cent), thus raising the cost of operations. There is also a continuing threat to withdraw their not-for-profit status for income tax purposes on the argument that they charge 'high fees'.

Other weaknesses

The academic rigour and its currency is weak, especially at the tertiary level, with teaching standards having suffered – particularly in the case of sciences – because of poor subject knowledge of faculty. Moreover, the systems in place are not exploiting the opportunities provided by highly cost-effective technology in general, and by e-learning technology in particular (distance learning, Khan's Academy, Coursera, etc.), which strengthen the quality of instruction at an affordable cost. What does not help is a dysfunctional tax structure that protects inefficient producers, rendering the need for professional inputs unnecessary for improving competitiveness, thereby affecting the demand for high-quality human capital.

Recommendations

The rapidly growing private sector presents important opportunities that can complement the efforts of the public sector in improving access to education. To take advantage of this opportunity, an effective regulatory policy and incentives in the form of a financing support structure and a more benign tax regime are required to maximize service provision from non-government institutions in general, and schools in particular, in a manner that is equitable, does not disadvantage the poor, but manages to provide quality education. The system should not unnecessarily burden the costs of service provision which could result in the pricing out of the less privileged segments of society, whose interests the government attempts to protect and promote through the framework that it has installed to regulate the private delivery of education.

Since, as argued above, service delivery adjustments will be difficult in government-managed institutions (especially schools) in the foreseeable future, the wide range of institutions offering education of a quality to match the spending power of the multiple tiers of households presents an opportunity that can be exploited gainfully. To begin with it should allow the market to determine fee levels based on the services and facilities that each institution provides. However, what may need to be addressed is transparency at the time of admission, so that at the point of enrolment parents should clearly be able to ascertain all the components of the charges that the school will levy. This means that parents should know at the outset what they are required to pay as an admission fee, security deposit, tuition fee, etc. Other information that should be made available to parents is the rate by which the total fees have been increased in each of the last three years.

The government is finding it difficult to discharge this obligation, particularly in urban areas where the latent demand for education is the strongest but where publicly owned land for establishing schools is no longer available and land prices are prohibitive. Hence, the segment of the private sector providing educational facilities to the less affluent members of society is performing a function that is the prime responsibility of the public sector – improving the access of low-income households to education.

The discussion above suggests that the best way forward is for the government to ensure that children get free schooling (this is its constitutional responsibility as well as its moral obligation) using the private sector as an instrument/institution for service provision, i.e. it should be financing the provision of schooling, instead of providing the service itself. Moreover, in order to strengthen quality-related interventions additional financial support to private schools can be linked to improvement in rankings in tests conducted by PISA/TIMS.

The PEF experiment, while supporting the recommendations shown above for government financing of private sector delivery of education, also suggests that in most areas the government should not set up new schools in future. It should fund the private provision of education such that children get free schooling, making the continuing availability of funds to such schools contingent upon decent learning outcomes of the enrolled children. And the role of the government should be to promote healthy competition and in particular support those private schools being accessed by low-income households. It should also include in its role the publishing and publicizing of results of all schools so that parents can make an informed choice at the point of entry.

Notes

1 United Nations Educational, Scientific and Cultural Organization, 'Education for People and Planet, Global Education Monitoring Report, UNESCO, Paris, 2016.
2 Pakistan Education Statistics 2015/16, National Education Management Information System (NEMIS), Academy of Educational Planning and Management, Government of Pakistan, 2017.
3 World Development Indicators, World Development Report, World Bank, 2017.
4 The variety of functioning private schools includes those set up by philanthropists, with the largest number operating under the banner of 'The Citizens Foundation', with around 1,050 purpose-built campuses educating 150,000 children (approximately 50 per cent of them being girls) through 7,000 female teachers, who are provided a free of cost transport service to school.
5 With around 35 per cent located in urban areas.
6 The National Education Census, 2005, NEMIS report 2007/08 and Pakistan's Education Statistics 2013/14 estimated that there were a total of 62,216 registered private schools in the country. The inclusion of unregistered private schools was estimated to be 16 per cent by Access to schools more than 73,000.
7 It is estimated that presently at the primary level 68 per cent of enrolled children are attending private schools in urban areas compared with 34 per cent in urban areas.
8 Pakistan Education Statistics 2015/16, National Education Management Information System (NEMIS), Academy of Educational Planning and Management, Government of Pakistan, 2017. Approximately 80 per cent of the schools in Punjab are either providing primary or elementary level education.
9 The clear message from consumers is their rejection of the schooling on offer from the government owing to its poor quality. This message is echoed even by teachers at government schools who are enrolling their own children in private schools.
10 Annual Status of Education Report (ASER), Pakistan, 2015 and 2016.
11 The share of the provinces of Sindh and Punjab in private universities is 42 per cent and 32 per cent, respectively. There are another 165 non-HEC recognized institutions (with 102 in the province of Punjab, 38 of them in Lahore alone).
12 These include IT-related equipment (data centres, computers, UPS, etc.), internet-related services, digital libraries, 162 software applications, including Windows-related licenses, and, in some cases, funding for needs-based scholarships to more than 6,700 disadvantaged students, thus enabling them to enrol on different programmes offered by public and private universities.
13 Also an HEC guideline.
14 Sohail Naqvi, 'The Resurgence of Higher Education in Pakistan', *QS Showcase 2017, Asia Country Features.*

15 Examples of such redundant information sought include enrolment in each grade, the names and salaries of teachers, details of the playground and sports facilities, the teaching aids, the equipment in the science laboratories, books in the library (with titles), registers maintained for recording receipts and expenditures, details of assets held (including the number of chairs, desks, blackboards, wall clocks, relief maps, stocks, mats and cupboards – stating separately the number of wooden and steel cupboards), students admitted, names of school leavers, attendance record of teachers and students, the name and qualifications of the school's registered medical practitioner, etc.

16 In 2017 the Department of Education in the Punjab was proceeding against schools that had raised their tuition fees by more than 5 per cent annually.

22

Educating and employing women

Nasreen Kasuri

When Nobel Peace Prize Laureate Malala Yousafzai was designated as a United Nations Messenger of Peace by the UN Secretary-General António Guterres in April 2017, the highest honour to have been bestowed on a global citizen, it underscored the importance of girls' education. While the story of resistance and courage of this particular girl has inspired the world and is symbolic of the struggle for education, particularly of females, it is not uncommon in Pakistan.

The landscape of educated and accomplished women widens and deepens by the day even as the figures and statistics darken that horizon every time a new study is completed and made public. Physicists, microbiologists, fighter pilots, neurosurgeons, bankers, army generals, urban planners, psychiatrists, industrialists, mountain climbers – the list keeps growing. Yet we know that they come out of an inverted pyramid. Government statistics for 2014–15 show that the literacy rate for 10 years and above was 70 per cent among the male population and 49 per cent among females. Not unexpectedly, there was a major difference between the urban and rural population. Female literacy in rural areas was 38 per cent compared to male literacy at 63 per cent, and in urban areas the figures were 69 per cent for females and 82 per cent for males. However, it is generally agreed that these figures do not represent the actual state of the nation's education levels.

The 2016 UN Global Education Monitoring Report[1] does not mince its words. It claims that Pakistan is fully half a century behind its primary education targets and 60-plus years behind its secondary education targets. The report grimly points out that Pakistan has 5.6 million out-of-school children of primary school age and 5.5 million out-of-school children of secondary school age. The report also dwells on the disparities and gaps between rich and poor, between rural and urban and, most importantly, between boys and girls in the population. The official data, about which educationists are always sceptical, claims that the literacy rate among underprivileged rural males is 64 per cent, but only 14 per cent for females in the same population.

Pakistan was a member of the global Education For All (EFA) movement, with the noble objective of addressing the problem of gender disparity in primary and secondary schools and eliminating this by 2015. Jointly launched in 1990 by the UN Educational, Scientific and Cultural Organization (UNESCO), the UN Development Programme,

UNICEF and the World Bank, the movement gave participating nations a set of six key education goals to meet in the learning needs of all children, youth and adults by 2015. Among these six goals was the elimination of gender disparities in primary and secondary education and the achievement of gender equality by 2015. There was an emphasis on ensuring that the girl child received full and equal access to good-quality basic education.

Pakistan, however, failed to achieve this goal and the disparities continue to plague its education sector. This was confirmed by UNESCO's Atlas of Gender Inequality in Education Report[2] which showed that girls continue to be the first victims when it comes to being denied the right to education.

Schools for boys far outnumber schools for girls, including both public and private sector schools. For the five-year period from 2011 to 2016 enrolment figures show an increase of less than 1 per cent at primary school level and a decrease of 1 per cent at middle school level. The figures for high schools suggest a slightly more hopeful trend. In 2011–12 high school enrolment was 1.06 million boys and 0.72 million girls. By 2015–16 the enrolment figures for boys stood at 1.25 million, while for girls it was 0.90 million – an increase of 15 per cent for boys but a healthier 20 per cent for girls.[3] This may also suggest that once girls reach a particular stage of schooling, there is greater motivation for them to stay on and pursue their educational goals. In other words, the inverted pyramid is asserting itself and the girl child is beginning to make the most of the slender opportunities afforded to her.

It is undeniable that the girl child's greatest impediments to accessing education are historical and social determinants. It is only very recently that economic imperatives have begun to prevail upon the family unit, creating incentives for girls to be educated.

As a keen observer of policymaking in education, I have always hoped for a wider and more in-depth discussion on allocations and available resources. The EFA stresses that international funding agencies also need to pay greater attention to the most excluded and least accessible people in any country. This inevitably implies the female population. I have found that, while awareness of the need exists at almost every level of policymaking, the formulation of project proposals focusing on gender disparity has not been satisfactory and an energetic engagement with the problem has yet to happen.

Although available statistics vary, approximately 127,000 of schools providing basic primary level education are located in rural areas. Less than half of these are dedicated to females. This is a major drawback when it comes to acceptability in conservative rural areas.

Poor rural families are less likely to educate the girl child than the male child. Even when families may be inclined to send the girl child to school, the school may be inaccessible, located far from home. Sending a female child to a distant location is simply not an option.

Furthermore, the health of the females has to be considered when discussing education. Studies show that the school-going female child is more malnourished than school-going boys of the same age and this physical disadvantage can make females less motivated, less active, and less attentive, eventually underperforming compared to their male counterparts. However, it is against this backdrop that the success stories emerge to inspire and encourage the community.

The cost implication for poor families in rural areas is another impediment to education for females. When the family weighs the benefits of withdrawing the female child from substantial tasks at home, it is not a decision taken lightly. Girls look after their siblings, tend to animals, fetch water and fuel, help to cook meals and deliver them to male members of the household at work. Although government schools are supposedly free or low cost, the investment may still be beyond the financial resources of the family unit. Uniforms, school books and stationery are beyond the resources of most rural families subsisting with no cash outlays.

Linked to the issue of accessibility of schools is the equally critical question of availability of a workforce of teachers. The gender of the teacher can be yet another impediment in setting up a girls' school when need and intent are not lacking.

It is fair to point out that there have been focused attempts to look at the problem of teachers for girls' schools. The Punjab government introduced teacher training programmes, which recognized the problem of mobility for the female teacher. In 1984–85 teacher training units were started in rural areas, attached to secondary schools.

Locating these training units close to the residences of would-be teachers was hugely effective in raising the numbers of female teachers. Parental opposition receded as female teacher trainees were able to travel from home each day to their centre. But their trainers were only educated up to the secondary level and, although they added significantly to the pool of trained human resource, the impact at the grassroots level for the child remained critical.

Teaching and the practice of medicine are the two jobs considered 'acceptable' for educated females. While medicine is a much coveted and often unattainable option, teaching remains the economic mainstay of women with access to education. The transition from housework to a paid job has gained ground despite the many practical impediments. The most significant among those is the mobility of the female teacher. In her study on female labour supply in Pakistan,[4] Hadia Majid explores the larger question of women in the labour force in Pakistan, the sectorial distribution, types of employment and the effect of gender on incomes.

However, in her conclusion she mentions the often negative portrayal of the working woman in the media. This is in spite of the very clear-cut relationship between 'economic wellbeing and participation linked with educational achievement'.[5] The study reinforces other research which finds that parental demand for girls' schooling is affected by school distances and facilities, and this is echoed in the predicament of women subsequently taking up employment as teachers.

The greater focus on an increase in school enrolment for the girl child and the incentives to make her continue sometimes overshadows the attention required for the equally important issue of improving the working experience of female teachers, who will after all develop the girl child in the public school. The two concerns are interlinked, as affirmed by Jackie Kirk, whose recommendation is to 'increase policy and programming attention to women teachers'.[6] She does, however, also point out that women teachers are constrained because their 'opportunities to participate in school or ministry level decision-making processes are often limited'.[7]

This observation is in the wider South Asian perception, but can be read as being particular to Pakistan. Gender policies regarding the employment and working guidelines for males and females tend to be discriminatory.

There are specific needs which are not prioritized when viewed against the advocacy required to enlarge the workforce of female teachers. This includes childcare, health benefits and career paths leading to promotion and leadership positions. This may be due to many factors but the most likely one would be that the teachers themselves did not have effective or quality training in the subjects.

Dilshad Ashraf points out that academics, educational researchers and policymakers are agreed that increasing the number of female teachers is an effective strategy in improving the emolument and participation of females in education.[8] The female teacher is seen as a positive role model in patriarchal communities and this encourages parents to enrol girls in schools.

An interesting point made by Ashraf is how closely the school set-up mirrors that of the home, i.e. the head of both the home and the school is usually the male patriarch. Despite many pressures and difficulties faced by these teachers in balancing their various roles at home and at work, it has remained their favoured paid occupation. When other options became available such as with non-governmental organizations which offered higher salaries and facilities, the women would not take up these upwardly mobile offers because they were thought to be 'culturally inappropriate'. Many were located in areas far from home and involved interaction with too many employees.

An added dimension was the school being seen as an extension of the domestic space with children being the major component. Breaking out of this circle of home and its 'related' space was to make one vulnerable to criticism and social stigma. The harmonization of the teaching role with the woman's role in the home is constantly stressed by the women in the case studies. The favourable working hours and annual vacations provide solace for the female teacher who is vocal about her 'right' to this profession.

One aspect of their role in the administration structure suggests that their tasks are gender-specific, posing professional limitations. The head teacher, often a male, decides a division of labour and delegation of responsibilities. Women's leadership is rarely nurtured, nor does it surface with any frequency. Effective management, which includes interaction with the community and attending meetings with authorities, is generally considered the male's domain.

Only one of the five women in the study was able to face and overcome the obstacles in her ascent to her leadership position of headmistress. A detailed description of the tasks that this particular woman leader undertook, which were quite routine for a male counterpart but highly unusual for a female, indicates the extent of risk-taking and risk management in which the male members of her family were fully involved, otherwise it would not have occurred. It highlights the prevailing realities of the social order and its tenacious nature despite subtle shifts and changes.

The most noticeable change in the educational landscape and, by implication, in female education had come about not through state intervention but because of rising awareness, demand and market forces. This has occurred because the state failed to deliver and has abdicated its role, providing spaces at various levels for the market to respond. Hence the phenomenal and steady growth of private schools across the country allowing greater access to the girl child, but even more significantly for the female teacher.

A major study was carried out by Tahir Andrabi in association with a team of researchers over an extended period of 15 years, in which they tracked households across Pakistan.[9] The most ambitious and sustained survey and research study of its kind, it threw up many unexpected facts, trends and concerns, which are still being absorbed and analysed.

The study points out the interesting relationship between the growth of private schools to the setting up of government schools for girls in the 1980s. The authors note that

> the teacher's gender matters because females are the cheaper source of labor. It is the lower cost of female teachers that allows private schools to spring up in villages where such a teacher supply exists and the private school provision increases the density of schooling in rural areas thus reducing the distance to school for students.[10]

In the popular imagination in Pakistan, and indeed elsewhere, the notion of the 'private' school is one of high fee-charging 'English medium' schools located in urban areas. Government crackdowns on rising fees and other regulatory issues have not seriously focused on the distribution of private schools, and there the numbers actually lie. At one time, certainly, the number of children serviced by such schools was limited, as was the number of girls benefiting from them, but the data now in evidence paints a very different picture.

The study shows that the increase in the number of private schools in rural areas equalled that of those being established in urban areas. The role of the female teacher is marked in both rural and urban populations and may be the single most important factor to consider. The study highlights the fact that in both the North-west Frontier Province and Punjab there are differences of nearly 20 per cent in overall female enrolment in villages with private schools, compared to those without. There is thus a critical role being played by the private school, staffed by female teachers, in reducing the gender gap.

The research data in the Learning and Education Achievement in Punjab Schools (LEAPS) study[11] suggests a strong connection between enrolment patterns for females in places where private schools exist – in contrast to those places where there are no private schools. There is a 29 percentage point increase in female enrolment compared to a 21 percentage point increase for male children. This is a very interesting finding which seems to imply a greater confidence in the private school even though the household is now paying for the education received.

In their aptly titled essay, 'A Dime a Day',[12] the authors claim that the monthly fee of US $5.00 a month, or 'less than a dime' a day, is affordable for those living on the poverty line of $1 per day. Of course, these low fees are wholly dependent on the presence of low-paid teachers in large numbers. The marked difference between the average pay for the female teacher in a government school and that in a private school is astounding.

The data from the study reveals that salaries for public (government) school teachers are commensurate with their educational training and specific to their gender. Thus, public sector teachers have the advantage of being compensated for qualifications, experience and training. The private sector, on the other hand, does not necessarily compensate for these factors. The data reveals that remuneration in the government and private sectors are based on very different factors. There are well-defined pay scales in the government sector which are based on officially recognized parameters.

These are unconnected to labour market conditions. The private sector schools, although not unappreciative of teacher training or educational achievements, are cognizant of the options in the labour market and take advantage of such options accordingly.

As indicated earlier in this chapter, the labour force participation for women in rural areas is very low compared to men. What is significant, however, is that 80 per cent of this input is in agricultural work and only 8 per cent is in the service sector, of which education is a part.

The authors of the LEAPS study are of the opinion that market-based hiring does not prioritize training or better education since it does not necessarily add value to the labour force. The teachers, being overwhelmingly female in this sector of the labour market, are thus hired for less than they would be entitled to in government schools.

Due purely to market forces, women have played a significant role in contributing to the spread and growth of school enrolment for both genders in Pakistan. It must be stressed, however, that this is at the primary level across the country and is integrally dependent on local women teachers servicing private schools, which are multiplying at a phenomenal rate. It is only one segment of the educational sector and only one segment of the labour market.

The LEAPS study highlights this fact:

> the more consistent presence of female teachers at private schools may more than compensate for their lower qualifications since a primary school teacher who has a higher level of formal education will have less impact if she shows up for work less often.[13]

My own extensive experience in the field of education and as an employer (primarily of women), in many ways reflects the broader issues touched upon in this chapter.

The project I started as a modest, almost personal, venture more than four decades ago, grew far beyond what was initially envisioned. It became one of the largest school systems in Asia with over 286,200 students in 35 cities throughout Pakistan and overseas, and a staff of over 17,000 in eight countries in the world. Considering the fact that the organization today, in its many enterprises, employs more than 11,000 women, both in Pakistan and in other countries, certain conclusions and inferences can be drawn which may be relevant to the issues examined previously.

For the record, it is worth noting that the first school in this enterprise, set up in 1975, was in fact to accommodate the male children in the family. Les Anges Montessori Academy, as it was named, was based in the upper story of my grandmother's house and had 19 students. The primary motivation was to provide an ideal educational environment to nurture the basic needs for children's development and discovery of the world around them.

Family needs and family approvals were intertwined in this endeavour to do what was best for the child. The activity was modest but it reflected a wider unspoken desire to explore and understand the intricacies of educational development and learning methodologies for young children. The unassuming establishment known as Les Anges was limited in its aspirations and was close to the original impulse to give a specific group of children the benefit of learning opportunities which were not generally available in the wider 'market'. Barely three years later, the venture blossomed into a school – an acknowledgment of an increasing need and a welcoming market.

In an interesting and oblique way, the history of the Beaconhouse Group echoes the scholarly findings of the in-depth studies of Andrabi, Das and Khwaja. Although their data does not focus on the so-called elite end of private schooling in Pakistan, the motivations, experiences and dependency on the female workforce are not dissimilar. While the researchers attribute the 'dramatic rise of private schools that has reshaped the educational landscape of Pakistan since the mid-1990s' to the fact that they charge low fees, it is obviously not applicable to the Beaconhouse enterprise. However, other prevalent circumstances have been the same.[14]

The single most critical factor has been the constant decline of publicly funded schools, which were not a desirable option for middle-class families looking for better educational opportunities for their children. The emerging need within our expanding professional class was for quality education incorporating a vision in consonance with the growing mobility of families. The factor which was crucial at this economic level was precisely that which was prevalent across the board, i.e. the availability of well-educated females willing to take up paid employment which was 'respectable' in the eyes of family and community and did not strain relations within the domestic sphere and, as it turned out, also provided a sense of self-worth to the woman.

In 1978 the Beaconhouse School was well on its way, with no notion that it was to evolve in a manner inconceivable at its inception. Beaconhouse was to be the elite grooming and learning environment which was the demand of educated, progressive parents increasingly interested in participating in their children's education. It soon became apparent that, while this profile may have been welcomed by parents, the demand for a school for girls was equally pressing. Thus, the girls' branch of Beaconhouse was set up to accommodate what was an unavoidable necessity. Inevitably, these developments, although welcomed in the community, were viewed with some trepidation in the home. What had commenced as a harmless 'hobby' in the domestic sphere was quickly burgeoning into an unforeseen challenging enterprise. The tensions and concerns articulated by women in the teaching profession in the academic studies referred to elsewhere do mention the added responsibility of ensuring that the family needs to be placated, and household commitments met.

The juggling of roles, contending with competing loyalties and management of time, was an exciting, exhausting and often difficult involvement. In this, the female teachers at a grassroots level and the female management are no different. The female in her primary role as nurturer of children finds herself split and propelled in divergent directions.

After 45 years as an employer primarily of women in education, I have experienced these divergences at first hand. Professional parameters evolved over time – as did systems, procedures and practices – but always in the context of living in Pakistan and being a part of its specific social and cultural milieu.

The educational sector which has established its growing dependence on women entering the labour force has contributed in a vital way to this educational project. The mutual relationships which have unfolded over these years have clearly demonstrated the capabilities of women in managerial positions. Their predisposition to multi-tasking and problem-solving in a conservative, yet rapidly changing, social order has provided the means for transformation and innovation in education. Within this Beaconhouse project, all aspects of employing and educating women have been experienced, observed, gathered and drawn upon. The accumulation of knowledge based on hands-on observation and practice to widen and deepen the understanding, not just of education as an occupation but also as a process, has been a challenging learning curve.

As expectations and demands multiplied, so did the awareness of the complexity of the field and the tasks in hand. Multiple facets associated with the enterprise emerged on an urgent basis, for example general administration, curriculum, teacher training, etc. The pace of expansion was gaining momentum, as was the need for greater in-house expertise and refinement of skills.

Teachers were hired initially on the basis of a basic degree, facility with the English language, and the ability to fit the template of a motivated individual from a 'respectable' family. This in itself laid out a set of guidelines for both the employer and the employee, which evolved over the years into an identifiable teaching and learning culture.

In her paper entitled 'A Journey to Remember', on the historical and cultural evolution of the Beaconhouse organization, former Director of Studies of the Beaconhouse School System Roohi Haq traces both the administrative and educational expansion over four and a half decades. The maturing of the enterprise was marked by several phases, characterized not only by the physical growth, but by layers of proficiency, judgement, critical expertise and engagement necessitated by the process itself.

It became apparent very early on that this was a venture which was predominantly dependent on a workforce consisting of women. Thus, all the determinants which ruled women's lives would be facets interwoven into management, systems and programmes.

While a trained labour force was not in place, it was evident that enhancement of skills would need to be undertaken to ensure quality education. In conjunction with this recognition was the consciousness of the need for investment in human resources which was the backbone of the school community. It was also a fact that women as employees, quite contrary to popular perceptions, were adaptable, multifaceted, dependable and resourceful. In the highly patriarchal context which defines Pakistan, women were continually able to navigate social norms, and occasionally defy them, in a bid to shape an image of themselves as individuals. The pride taken in the workplace strongly reinforced the sense of accomplishment in the domestic sphere. The right to their own income was not a minor aspect of this process, which provided the majority of these female employees their first encounter with personal economic viability and a measure of independence.

The vast majority of Beaconhouse employees are female; their male counterparts are less than half their number. At the risk of generalization, the positive effect of the female presence in the workplace can be discerned. The frame of reference being the specific domain of education, a modicum of urbane, courteous affability in the environment is assured. Both by definition and by tradition, teaching is accepted as a 'noble' profession. As underscored in the studies referred to in this chapter, from the most basic school in a semi-urban environment to one in Karachi, the school teacher speaks of it as 'a respectable profession' requiring 'full attention and full devotion.'[15]

A slow but noticeable social transformation has occurred in Pakistan over the past 45 years, which is reflected in all areas of women's employment and development. Social attitudes in education are no longer so patronizing, but the effort to secure and uphold the women's hard-won status is still far from easy. A manifestation of this has been the enactment of the workplace harassment law which was passed in 2010. Organizations are now required to have mechanisms which can investigate complaints and implement the law in its spirit.

An articulated objective is to ensure an atmosphere of equality and fairness for female employees, when the dignity of labour for both men and women has yet to be ingrained in society.

In order to guarantee a measure of professional competence and to provide quality education, it became imperative to ensure 'value addition'. It was obvious that advancement in the quality of human resources was only possible through teacher training, and taking the workforce to the next level of competence.

Teacher training colleges in the public sector emerged as early as the 19th century. Beaconhouse initiated the first phases of its training programmes in 1992 and by 1995 they were well established. These academic development plans were a milestone in the enhancement of human resource development in education in Pakistan and focused on seven areas, which included instruction training of head teachers, research, curriculum development, assessment systems and evaluation. Within 10 years, a forum had come into being where a whole community of educators and managers could discuss methodologies, philosophies and implementation strategies.

The impact of any professional enhancement on the community at large is undeniable. The ripple effect generated by a particular school system is often a quickly multiplying phenomenon which is taken for granted once it is in place. It breeds similar initiatives as the market expands and demand exceeds supply. A successful model and economic imperatives provide incentives of many kinds for women and an established combination of educator and entrepreneur proliferates with amazing ease and speed.

The challenges and impediments, however, remain the same. Women as employees are embodiments of their aspirations, ambitions and status in a rapidly changing society.

Most have encountered discrimination and stereotyping from the outset and it is a constant struggle to find opportunities for education and for self-esteem.

The development of a work culture which is conscientiously fair to both genders and which balances the influences embedded in the socio-economic fabric is not instantly attainable. It evolves through a process which is both hands-on and reflective. The maturing of the process has been intertwined with the philosophical and pedagogical underpinnings of the Beaconhouse enterprise, which have run parallel to its other facets. The woman, being the 'lesser voice' in this society (even in the most progressive of institutions), has been encouraged intellectually and in practice. This does not occur with the facility that one might imagine, but is an ongoing, unfolding process both accelerating and stalling as circumstances demand.

From experience, I believe that organizations led by women will be more sensitive to these struggles and will ensure a culture which protects and enables women. In an environment which is only just beginning to allow women to find their voice, education is their primary ally and their ultimate insurance policy.

Notes

1 United Nations Educational, Scientific and Cultural Organization, 'Education for People and Planet, Global Education Monitoring Report, UNESCO, Paris, 2016.
2 Edward B. Fiske, *World Atlas of Gender Equality in Education*, UNESCO, Paris, 2012.
3 Author's estimates based on data released by the Government of Pakistan.
4 Hadia Majid, 'Female Labour Supply in Pakistan: Mapping the Last Three Decades', Department of Economics, Lahore University of Management Sciences, 2016. The paper was prepared as part of a project on female labour supply and the escape from poverty; new evidence from household data at University of Sussex and founded by ESRC-DFID.
5 Ibid.
6 Jackie Kirk (ed.) *Women Teaching in South Asia*, New Delhi, Sage Publications, 2008, p. 5.
7 Ibid., p. 18.
8 D. Ashraf, 'Schools Are Like Our Home': Women in Teaching and School Leadership in Northern Pakistan.', in J. Kirk (ed.) *Women Teaching in South Asia*, New Delhi, Sage Publications, 2008, pp. 34–55.
9 Tahir Andrabi, Jishnu Das and Asim Ijaz Khwaja, 'A Dime a Day: The Possibilities and Limits of Private Schooling in Pakistan', *Comparative Education Review*, vol. 52, no. 3, 2008.
10 Ibid., p. 331.
11 Tahir Andrabi, Jishnu Das, Asim Ijaz Khwaja, Tara Vishwanath and Tristan Zajonc, 'Learning and Educational Achievements in Punjab Schools (LEAPS): Insights to Inform the Education Policy Debate', World Bank, Washington, DC, 2007.
12 Andrabi *et al.*, 'A Dime a Day', pp. 329–55.
13 Ibid., p. 352.
14 Ibid.
15 Jackie Kirk, 'Impossible Fiction: The Lived Experience of Women Teachers in Karachi', *Comparative Education Review* vol. 48, no. 4, 2004, 374–95.

Part V
Energy and the environment

23

The downward spiral of the quality of life in Pakistan

Is control possible, or even desired?

Kulsum Ahmed

In 1947 Pakistan was predominately a rural country, Data from 1951 indicated a population of 34 million in West Pakistan and 42 million in East Pakistan (now modern Bangladesh), with the former being 18 per cent urban and the latter 4 per cent urban, resulting in 10 per cent of the total population residing in urban areas.[1] The 1951 census also showed the comparison with 1941, when all the cities, in what is now Pakistan and Bangladesh, had a population of well under one million. Indeed, even in 1951 the only city with a population of over one million was Karachi, which had grown exponentially from 387,000 in 1941 to 1,068,000 in 1951. The preliminary data from the 2017 census put the population of what was West Pakistan at approximately 207 million, and lists 10 cities with at least one million inhabitants. Meanwhile, there is still controversy on whether the urban-rural ratio has been correctly classified, and what is the actual size of the population of Pakistan's largest city, Karachi.[2] According to World Bank data, the urban population of Pakistan grew from 22 per cent in 1960 to 39 per cent in 2016.[3] The data is revealing, as it reflects a very high rate of growth in population and urbanization. Today, Pakistan is the most urbanized country in South Asia.[4]

High population growth and rapid urbanization, coupled with poor use of resources and weak institutions, have meant that Pakistan has continued to struggle with the provision of basic infrastructure, such as that needed for clean water and sanitation. It is telling that only 36 per cent of Pakistanis have access to a safely managed drinking water source according to 2015 data, despite 55 per cent piped water coverage.[5] There has been progress on some fronts, such as a steady increase in rural sanitation coverage. In 1990 over 90 per cent of the rural population did not have access to modern sanitation facilities, and over 70 per cent resorted to open defecation. However, 2015 data indicates that at least 48 per cent of the rural population have access to basic sanitation and that open defecation has decreased to 19 per cent in rural areas. At a country level, in 2015 there was 58 per cent overall basic sanitation coverage, and 60 per cent basic hygiene coverage.[6] However, according to the United Nations Development Programme (UNDP), despite a remarkable increase in the proportion of the population using an improved water source and an improved sanitation facility, 27.2 million Pakistanis do not have access to safe water and 52.7 million do not have access to adequate sanitation facilities.[7] It is also unclear whether there is 0 per cent coverage of safely managed sanitation in Pakistan or whether the data for this indicator is not available.[8] If the former is the case, this is perhaps an indicator of the quality of sanitation services today, despite increasing coverage. Poor waste management is also a frequent source of discussion in the media, eliciting complaints from citizens about poor-quality service provision and even deaths due to lethal landfill fires.[9]

Urbanization and electrification often result in a reduction in some types of pollution, such as indoor air pollution. But this continues to be a significant problem in Pakistan. On the other hand, rapid urbanization has also created new hazards, such as outdoor air pollution in cities. The World Health Organization (WHO) estimated that the mortality rate attributable to household and ambient pollution per 100,000 population was 87.2 in 2012.[10] With a population of 177.9 million in 2012, that means that 155,000 deaths that year were attributable to indoor and outdoor air pollution alone. This mortality rate rises to 133.8 per 100,000, when it is age-standardized by WHO, taking into account Pakistan's young population. Furthermore, in 2016 WHO collated data for all the major cities in Pakistan which indicated an incredibly high level of particulate matter, less than 2.5 microns in diameter (PM2.5).[11] This pollutant has been correlated with negative health impacts, as the particles are small enough to enter and lodge within the deepest part of the human lung. Data indicates annual mean concentrations of PM2.5 as high as 111 ug/m3 and 107 ug/m3 for Peshawar and Rawalpindi, respectively, and 88 ug/m3 for Karachi, in comparison with the WHO recommended guideline of 10 ug/m3 and Pakistan's own ambient standard of 15 ug/m3. In comparison, Beijing, a city well known for its extreme air pollution, reports an annual mean concentration of 85 ug/m3. This is even more surprising as Beijing is subject to thermal inversions, in which meteorological conditions keep the pollution trapped over the city for extended periods, as is also the case for Lahore. However, Karachi is subject to a sea breeze and the natural clearing of pollution. Khwaja et al. made one of the first attempts to measure the correlation between air pollution and morbidity in Karachi by monitoring the number of hospital and accident and emergency (A&E) visits correlated with increasing PM2.5 levels. The results of this study were consistent with those in other developed countries, indicating that a rise in both hospital admissions and A&E visits occurs along with rises in PM2.5 levels.[12] Indeed, the data seems to suggest that air pollution and its impacts are severely underestimated in Pakistan despite WHO's efforts to highlight this issue as one of the top health hazards in the world, with over 6.5 million deaths globally in 2012 (accounting for about 11 per cent of all global deaths).

The impact on the health and quality of life of Pakistani citizens owing to this deterioration of the physical environment is generally poorly analysed and reported. WHO estimated in 2009, using 2004 data, that 22 per cent of the burden of disease was due to environmental factors.[13] A World Bank report in 2008 estimated the annual cost of the direct and indirect impact of environmental risk factors in 2005 to be almost 9 per cent of gross domestic product (GDP).[14] In comparison, Pakistan's annual GDP growth (not taking into account the cost of environmental degradation) in 2005 was a high 7.7 per cent, according to World Bank data. Using another measure, 62,441 people died in Pakistan as a result of terrorist activities between 2003 and 2017, with the worst year on record being 2009, when 11,704 fatalities occurred.[15] Compare this with the WHO estimate of 155,000 deaths in Pakistan in 2012 from air pollution alone described earlier.

Similar estimates shook governments into action in the People's Republic of China and Mexico to seek to remedy the situation, yet in Pakistan there continues to be poor reporting and understanding of the extent of the problem, and action to address these issues is not commensurate with the size of the problem in terms of its impact on the number of fatalities and citizens' quality of life.

However, it does not stop there. Pakistan is poised for a further downward spiral on the physical environment front. Climate change is already affecting and will further affect the country in the years ahead, primarily on two fronts, water and temperature, which in turn will directly impact food, energy and water security. Specifically, the melting of the Himalayan glaciers, a natural storage mechanism for water, is expected to result in increased early volumetric flow in rivers, and less water during the growing season, thus impacting freshwater supplies. This, coupled with rising temperatures, is projected to negatively impact agricultural productivity and water security. Pakistan's National Policy on Climate Change also projects a considerable increase in the frequency and intensity of extreme weather events, coupled with erratic monsoon rains causing frequent and intense floods and droughts. These, in turn, are expected to result in increased siltation of major dams. Sea level rise is also projected, threatening coastal areas. For many observers, the two catastrophic floods in Pakistan in 2010 and 2012, when more than 20 per cent of the country's land area was covered by water, were a harbinger of things to come.

Germanwatch's Climate Risk Index 2015 analyses the quantified impacts of extreme weather in terms of the number of fatalities as well as the extent of economic losses that occurred between 1996 and 2015. Pakistan is ranked seventh globally in this long-term index, with 133 events taking place during that period.[16] The report specifically notes that most of the affected countries in the bottom 10 of the long-term index have a high ranking due to exceptional catastrophes, but Pakistan appears in both the long-term index and is listed among the most affected countries for the last six years, due to recurring catastrophes. The Pakistan Intended Nationally Determined Contribution (Pak-INDC) submitted for the UN Framework Convention on Climate Change Paris Agreement in 2015 notes that

> studies and assessments undertaken by the National Disaster Management Authority show that extreme climate events between 1994 and 2013 have resulted in an average annual economic loss of almost US$ 4 billion. The last five floods (2010–2014) have resulted in monetary losses of over US$ 18 billion with 38.12 million people affected, 3.45 million houses damaged and 10.63 million acres of crops destroyed. Likewise, over 1200 people lost their lives due to the unprecedented heat wave in Karachi in 2015.[17]

The Food and Agriculture Organization of the UN (FAO) examined the wider impact of disasters across the food value chain, noting that the negative consequences went further than the national economy.[18] The FAO report notes that

> crop production losses caused by the 2010 floods in Pakistan directly affected cotton ginning, rice processing and flour and sugar milling, while cotton and rice imports surged. Agriculture absorbed 50 percent of the $10 billion in total damage and losses, and sector growth dropped from 3.5 percent to 0.2 percent between 2009 and 2010, as did national gross domestic product (GDP) – which is sum of all final goods and services produced within that economy during a specified period – from 2.8 percent to 1.6 percent between the same years.

Any disaster that impacts agriculture also has a direct effect on citizens' livelihoods and food security. In FAO's assessment, the 2010 floods in Pakistan affected 4.5 million workers, two-thirds of whom were employed in agriculture, and over 70 per cent of farmers lost more than half of their expected income. Even more disturbingly, under a business-as-usual scenario of future greenhouse gas emissions recent climate models project that by the late 21st century the densely populated, agricultural Indus river basin will be affected by a lethal combination of humidity and heat.[19] The potential consequences for a population that works primarily outdoors in agriculture, and without the means to enjoy air-conditioning even in their homes, is sobering. We already know the effect of the unprecedented heat wave in 2015 in Karachi.

However, it is water, perhaps more so than any other resource, which best highlights the quality of life story for Pakistan since independence. At independence, Pakistan was a water-rich country, with 5,000 m3/caput of water.[20] Today, it is a water-scarce country, with only 1,000 m3/caput.[21] Division of water across provinces pre-independence created strife. Since independence, despite water-rich times, this strife has only become more magnified, rather than being resolved. The discussion remains focused on India, rather than on what Pakistan can do for itself within the country. Today, 94 per cent of freshwater withdrawal is used for agriculture, despite the greater proportion of urban population, and the overall increase in population.[22] Climate change is projected to further exacerbate the situation, through too much or too little water being available at all the wrong times, as glaciers and snow melt too early for the growing season due to higher temperatures and this results in drought when water is actually needed. This suggests that the country should adopt an approach to water that is Pakistan-wide, not province-focused. In 2017 Pakistan had 30 days' worth of water storage, compared with the United States which has 900 days. Pakistan comes in only above Ethiopia, which has lowest storage capacity globally.[23] When countries are water-scarce, each drop of water is saved, used sparingly, and then cleaned and reused.[24] However, as discussed earlier, Pakistan's infrastructure has not kept up with this challenge. There is virtually no rainwater collection and storage. The maintenance of irrigation canals is very poor and highly subsidized, sending the wrong signals and thereby encouraging water wastage.[25] Water management and governance have not been prioritized. The regulations are still based on a different level of water availability, with provincial irrigation departments relying on procedural regulations set up by the British during the colonial era.[26] Drought-resistant varieties of seeds, encouraging high-value crops to offset the high economic cost of water, encouraging more efficient drip irrigation methods or no-till farming in order to preserve soil moisture do not seem to be a part of the national dialogue.[27] Industries continue to put contaminated effluents into the drainage system, and those households that do get water, use it with abandon. All this suggests that Pakistan has not fully internalized that a lot has changed since independence and that the country is now water-scarce.

The groundwater story is also very unfortunate. Over the past 70 years the country has also been depleting its groundwater reserves faster than they can regenerate. Over 60 per cent of Pakistan's water is pumped from natural underground reservoirs, with no limits placed on how many wells can be drilled or how much anyone can take.[28] Awareness of natural contamination of groundwater, for example with arsenic, has also been slow, resulting in no action being taken to date, despite initial recognition of this problem in 2000.[29] A 2017 study estimates that as many as 50 million people living in the Indus basin may be at risk of arsenic poisoning.[30] Drinking water affects the health and productivity of Pakistani citizens. It is also a resource that affects rich and poor very differently, with the rich able to buy drinking water, and even water for household use, thus avoiding most of the associated health effects. On the other hand, UNDP estimates that approximately 39,000 children under the age of five die every year from diarrhoea caused by unsafe water and poor sanitation in Pakistan.[31] Repeated bouts of diarrhoea and malnutrition in children under the age of two also result in significant reductions in IQ and hence productivity.[32] Thus, the poor and the rich see very different sides of the water story.

Do the Pakistanis want to control this downward spiral?

The first question to consider is whether the Pakistanis want to do anything about this downward spiral of their quality of life. In order to answer this question, one has to first ask whether anybody is aware of this data. Most of the data quoted here is from development agencies' reports and was prepared for and disseminated mainly to relevant government agencies. The majority of the data for these reports is supplied by government agencies. So, this seems to suggest that there are poor internal mechanisms in place to identify national priority issues. In most countries, it is the citizens who speak up when the government of the day does not deliver basic services. In Pakistan's case, with outdoor air quality being the exception in recent years, the wealthy and the politically connected have not felt the impact of this lack of services in the same way as the poor. There also is low awareness of these facts and figures among the general population, and virtually no inclusion of these issues in school and university curricula. A number of institutes and non-governmental organizations (NGOs) are active on these issues, but have failed to shift them to the centre of political attention.[33] Newspaper reporting of these issues, however, has increased in recent years, even though it is still far from being a central part of the national dialogue. In 2014 a sub-committee of the Senate Functional Committee on Human Rights launched the country's first media manual for journalists covering the environment and climate change in order to improve reporting.[34] The environment features widely in the Quran, indeed more so than in any other holy book of the Abrahamic faiths, and yet this aspect does not seem to be highlighted by the mullahs or in Friday sermons, despite the context of Pakistan being an Islamic Republic.[35]

As has happened in other countries, it is the extreme disasters and the tragedies that catch national attention, rather than the realities of day-to-day life, even though in Pakistan's case, these are much greater in number and impact. Indeed, Pakistan is one of 19 countries whose citizens are aware of global climate change, viewing it as the main global threat.[36] Yet in the 1990s the Supreme Court clearly established the rights of Pakistani citizens with respect to a clean environment. An important milestone in that regard was the 1994 ruling of the Supreme Court in the landmark case of *Shehla Zia and others vs. WAPDA* (the Water and Power Development Authority), in which the Court concluded that the right to a clean environment is a fundamental right of all citizens of Pakistan covered by the right to life and right to dignity under Articles 9 and 14 of the Constitution.[37]

Industry's awareness of environmental issues has primarily been driven by environmental standards and licensing requirements, as well as by parent company requirements for multinationals. As a result, the larger companies in Pakistan report regularly on their environmental compliance. Some large companies have taken this further through their corporate social responsibility programmes to support efforts to improve environmental quality and related impacts. However, this is not the case for the majority of small and medium-sized enterprises (SMEs), which lack both the awareness and capacity for managing environmental issues. Industrial activities continue to be a significant source of air, water and land-based pollution.[38] More recently, the emphasis of the Sustainable Development Goals (SDGs) on multi-stakeholder responsibility to advance development goals has resulted in a renewed focus on sustainability by large companies through the establishment of a new Centre of Excellence in Responsible Business by the Pakistan Business Council.[39]

So, some people are aware of the data, but not everybody. Does it still make sense to act to control the downward spiral, especially in a country that has so many problems and not enough resources to deal with them? I would argue yes, on three counts. Primarily, it's a moral issue. The poor are disproportionately affected and this aspect affects their health, quality of life and productivity, even if they have a job. The term environmental justice has been used previously to describes a social movement that focuses on the fair distribution of environmental benefits and burdens, but in today's Pakistan, environmental inequality is perhaps a more apt term, although it will not be long, given current outdoor air pollution levels, before the rich are also significantly affected. Ultimately, though, it is a matter of the country's self-respect as well as the way in which it is perceived externally. As noted by the Russian writer, Fyodor Dostoyevsky, 'If you want to be respected by others the great thing is to respect yourself. Only by that will you compel others to respect you.' It is difficult to have self-respect if a country's citizens are falling ill and dying from the very air that they breathe and the water that they drink, if there is rubbish everywhere and if the government is unable to provide even the most basic services to all its citizens.

Second, the world is rapidly moving towards a new set of norms, and if action is not taken soon, Pakistan will be left far behind. In that regard, two important drivers are the SDGs and the 2015 Paris Climate Agreement, to both of which Pakistan is party. Climate change is physically changing the country's water availability, temperature, humidity, sea levels, level of glacier melt, and this is leading it towards very high levels of internal strife. Some have even called it a matter of national security.[40] However, global awareness of climate change has also become heightened, including the investment risks associated with it, and this prompting new behaviour on the part of investors. A 2017 survey suggests that more than two-thirds of institutional investors are planning to increase investments related to tackling climate change, moving 'green finance' from the margins to the mainstream of global markets.[41] Socially Responsible Investing, or impact investing, which seeks to consider both financial return and social good to bring about social change, is an exponentially growing market globally, signifying the direction in which the world is headed.[42]

Third, the country's future growth is affected. This is due to climate risk exposure and whether or not its attractive to future investors, as described above, and therefore the country is at risk of missing opportunities for on future industries. As many countries are realizing, climate change offers a real opportunity for business. It is guaranteeing a current and future global market for energy and water efficiency services and products, as well as alternative (non-fossil fuel) energy products, such as solar energy, wind power and electric cars. In response, the transformation at breakneck speed of the energy industry is similar to that of the information technology (IT) revolution. India's call for only electric cars by 2030, prompting Tesla to commit to a new battery factory in India is another example of this early jostling by countries to be the first movers in these new markets.[43] So, given all of the above – moral obligation, keeping up with the new norms and positioning Pakistan to be a player in future markets – it makes sense to act.

Pakistan's governance and institutional frameworks to improve quality of life

Before getting into a discussion of what to do going forward, it is also important to discuss the governance and institutional frameworks needed to manage these quality of life issues and their evolution. In 1983 the Pakistan Environmental Protection Ordinance established the requirement to prepare an Environmental Impact Assessment for development projects, and in 1993 the National Environmental Quality Standards (NEQS) were issued, eventually becoming effective in 2000.[44] However, the cornerstone of environmental legislation is the Pakistan Environmental Protection Act of 1997, which established the general conditions, prohibitions and enforcement for the prevention and control of pollution, and the promotion of sustainable development. It also assigned responsibility to the Pakistan Environmental Protection Council (PEPC), originally established in 1993, at the federal level with the Prime Minister as chairperson for approving environmental policy across sectors, the Pakistan Environmental Protection Agency (Pak-EPA) for proposing and enforcing the NEQS and deconcentrated provincial EPA departments. A Ministry of the Environment was established in 2002. The Pak-EPA went on to issue ambient standards in 2010.[45] As such, up to 2010 Pakistan's institutional framework was consistent with those of other countries around the world, albeit with a poor record of action and poor technical capacity. The PEPC, given its role as the apex environmental body, met only irregularly, for example meeting only once between 2005 and 2010, and the EPA offices lacked sufficient technical skills and capacity.[46] Furthermore, there was, and still is, a very poor general understanding of the need for of standards, namely to ensure that air, water and soil conditions are safe for human and ecosystem health.

Other milestones for putting in place an environmental policy framework have included (over time) the adoption of the National Conservation Strategy in 1992, a National Environmental Action Plan in 2001 with the stated objective of alleviating poverty through environmental projects, and the National Environmental Policy in 2005, which provides broad guidelines to the federal, provincial and local governments in addressing environmental concerns and cross-sectoral issues such as poverty, health, trade and local governance.[47] The National Sanitation Policy of 2006 which envisioned the creation of an open defecation-free environment through the safe disposal of liquid and solid waste and the promotion of health and hygiene practices recognized the benefits of a community-led total sanitation approach. This was another important milestone, as was the National Drinking Water Policy of 2009, which aimed to provide an adequate quantity of safe drinking water to the entire population at an affordable cost and in an equitable, efficient and sustainable manner.

However, in 2010 major changes in the organizational framework resulted in a significant weakening of environmental governance frameworks. The 2010 18th Amendment to the Constitution absorbed the Ministry of the Environment into the Ministry of National Disaster Management, renaming it the Ministry of Climate Change in 2012. This was downgraded in 2013 to a division. This resulted in significant downscaling of the Pak-EPA's work. The 18th Amendment also devolved the responsibility for environmental management to provincial governments. This forced a completely new start on the institutional front, despite severe capacity constraints. Furthermore, these federal laws had to be re-enacted again at the provincial level. Since then, there has been variable and slow progress on environmental management functions. On the air quality front, only Punjab has a project in place aimed at continuing air quality monitoring efforts.[48] It has also made the most progress on issuing provincial environmental standards. At the same time, the *Punjab Gazette* notification date for the ambient air standard was 15 August 2016.[49] On sanitation, the Sindh government was the first provincial government to approve its sanitation strategy in 2015, one of the first states to introduce a regulatory framework after the 18th Amendment moved the responsibility for sanitation management to the provinces, and culminating in the 2017 Sanitation Policy.[50]

Today, international best practice on environmental governance calls for 'an apex central ministry or agency, with a number of technical and action-oriented agencies designating and implementing public policies, and enforcing regulations'.[51] Decentralization is important too, but, as usual, it is a balanced approach with a central agency playing a coordination role to ensure uniformity that leads to the best results.[52] In addition, many countries confronted by significant environmental challenges have explored additional environmental bodies for periods of time to facilitate environmental mainstreaming or sustainable development in other sectors, such as Mexico's Sustainable Development Council in the President's Office and Colombia's inclusion of an Environment Unit in its Planning Ministry. These efforts require a continued focus, and adequate resources, if they are to be successful. Today, the SDGs integrate the concept of environmental sustainability directly into sectoral development. Nonetheless, in Pakistan, there is still a general perception that the environment is hindering economic growth, rather than accompanying sustainable growth, and this suggests that there may still be a need for an additional institutional mechanism to facilitate sectoral-level sustainable development.

Is control of the downward spiral possible, and what will it take?

This leads us to the third question; namely, can we do anything about this downward spiral or is it already too late? From other countries' examples, we learn that controlling the downward spiral is indeed difficult, but it is certainly possible. Consider the examples of China and Colombia. China is a great example of a country acting in a focused way to reduce environmental degradation prompted by economic and health concerns, but also shows how difficult it is to clean up if it is left too late. Initially, acid rain (from poor air quality) affected crops and damaged buildings in the 1980s, becoming much more prevalent by the 1990s, and causing sufficient alarm for the Chinese government to consider air quality seriously.[53] The impact of air quality on human health was only just being understood better at the time. Some remarkable efforts followed, including the Chinese putting in place strict sulphur emissions regulations for their coal power plants, realizing that this was an important cause of the pollution. Due to domestic demand, this created a huge market for flue gas desulphurization technology, which the Chinese took on, significantly reducing the global price for this technology.[54] The air quality problem has continued to get worse resulting in the Chinese putting in place even stricter standards for coal plant technology (such as supercritical power plants) and also investing in other renewable technologies. They also continue to cancel planned coal power plants as well as those under construction.[55] Air quality management is a continuous battle in China, given the extent of locked-in coal-based power generation, keeping China on its toes, even more so these days as the world, and China's own citizens, better understand the effect of poor air quality on their health. To their great credit, the Chinese have kept this at the forefront in many ways, including their active championing of the Paris Climate Agreement, shifting away from a position of highlighting their low per head carbon emissions and the 'right' of all Chinese people to own a car. In doing so, China has put itself clearly in a high moral position, advocating for a better quality of life for its own citizens as well as becoming a global champion. At the same time, Chinese technology continues to actively help to reduce the cost of certain renewable technologies, such as solar photovoltaic cells, thus making it a market leader.

Colombia's story is a different one. During a period of considerable strife and violence there was conscious acknowledgment by the government in 1991 that it had transitioned from a predominantly rural country to a primarily urban country, requiring a new governance framework for urban environmental matters.[56] Subsequently, a number of laws were enacted facilitating decentralization, empowering municipalities, putting in place a new regulatory framework for urban environmental management (where cities with over one million inhabitants were directly responsible for urban environmental management and the Ministry of Natural Resources was expanded to include urban environmental management), facilitating private sector participation for service provision, and strengthening citizen participation in decision making. Ten years later, it was noted that on some fronts, this had led to positive outcomes, such as greater accountability by municipalities, wider local participation, significant increases in solid waste treatment and collection and water supply. There was mixed progress among municipalities on other fronts. Bogotá, for example, implemented a successful approach to urban transport to reduce congestion, travel time and pollution, through a bus rapid transit system, the *Transmilenio*, whereas other cities lagged behind. There were also negative outcomes, such as poor service quality, inefficient financial management by the municipalities and poor basic service coverage of poorer segments of the population. Subsequently, Colombia introduced further structural reforms. Successful approaches in some cities were also replicated, such as the effective *Transmilenio* in Bogotá. Politicians also played a greater role standing on environmental platforms, such as air quality improvements, thus raising attention to these issues.[57] Yet at the same time, urbanization provided a real opportunity to more efficiently deliver urban services to citizens. There is now almost universal access to basic services in Colombian cities, and the focus has shifted to how Colombian cities can contribute to broader national economic growth and foster greater efficiencies by coordinating better on regional infrastructure investments (thus shifting away from extreme decentralization).[58]

The Colombian example shows again that there is no silver bullet, but rather a conscious effort to keep the environment high on the agenda, and to monitor and adjust approaches and solutions over time to address changing needs. It also highlights the potential pitfalls of an extremely decentralized system for revenue generation, suggesting that a certain level of centralization is important to ensure that the poor are not left behind and to facilitate collaboration and hence greater efficiency.[59] On urban environmental management, the country's balanced framework, with an apex agency, as well as decentralized responsibility for cities with over one million inhabitants in 1991 seemed to work well.[60] Between 2002 and 2004 there was a shift, merging most of the functions of the Ministry of the Environment with those of the Ministry of Planning, Development and Reform, and a phasing out of the Environmental Directorate in the Planning Ministry in 2004.[61] However, in 2011 a new central Ministry of the Environment and Sustainable Development was established.[62]

So, it is possible to control the downward spiral, but how can one tackle a seemingly intractable problem, and what are the possible pitfalls? Here we can learn a lot from Pakistan's recent efforts to increase its power capacity. A crucial step has been Pakistan's clear announcement of its needs and desire to increase its power capacity, namely to address the consistent shortfall of 5,000–6,000 MW. This has mobilized action on many fronts to address this issue. Some examples include the large industrial companies in Pakistan setting up power plants as independent power producers, neighbouring countries like China and Tajikistan supporting Pakistan through the construction of power plants in Pakistan linked with the China–Pakistan Economic Corridor or by supplying power through purchase agreements through the CASA-1000, development agencies such as the World Bank Group and the Asian Development Bank supporting Pakistan to develop wind power and other renewable projects, and so on. As is often the case, others step in with their products and support, if there is a match with the priority that is set. For Pakistan to ensure that it gains the maximum benefit, it also needs to develop a coherent Energy Sector Strategy and Plan, so that it can avoid potential longer-term pitfalls related to these offerings and thus maximize gains. The lack of adequate planning to ensure sufficient capacity in the transmission system to fully benefit from the power generated from some of the recent wind projects or the potentially devastating future effects of the air pollution from coal power plants, due to the country lacking environmental emissions standards for PM2.5 for coal power plants, are just two obvious examples. Another less obvious example is the government's focus on grid connected power, thus effectively slowing down possible innovation on distributed power options, and preventing smaller local companies from entering this space. Another possible gain that has not been maximized is the tapping of considerable global climate money to improve energy efficiency and to harness methane from landfills for energy, thereby also helping to address the separate issue of waste management. In fact, the approach in the PAK-INDC is very much of a country that boasts about its low carbon emissions per head, rather than one taking steps to address even the low emissions. This stance ultimately harms the country only from accessing resources to address its local needs, such as sufficient power.

A strategy and action plan, at the end of the day, is just a report. It is the formulation and then the implementation of the strategy and plan that is important. Experience from other countries and the development literature shows that the process of developing the report is key.

In today's world, where information is easily accessible and social networks empower all groups, why not mobilize all these groups to contribute towards a common goal for all, namely improved quality of life? [63] If one agrees with this hypothesis, then the federal government's role in formulating and implementing a strategy and action plan is very clear. It boils down to eight principle actions, the first of which is to be clear that 'improving quality of life for all' is a goal and it is important to stick with it for the long term. [64] It also means putting in place the necessary governance framework to facilitate the implementation of such a goal.

Second, a cornerstone of good management is to put in the best people to lead this effort and instruct them to prepare a strategy that takes a Pakistan-wide look at the problem, not a geographical look at provinces or individual cities. Why is this? On energy, water and food security, three potential crises facing Pakistan that are linked to climate change, the diversity that the country's provinces bring becomes a potential strength in the context of developing a resilient system. Taken together, Punjab's food production capacity, Sindh's wind power and rainwater storage capacity, Khyber Pakhtunkhwa's micro hydropower plants and ability to protect watersheds upstream through managing deforestation, as well as solar power from Balochistan, will helps Pakistan to move towards a more efficient national system. The very different conditions mean that each province can both contribute and benefit through a network of reliance that helps to create a safety net for all citizens and result in more than the sum of the parts. A major challenge that will have to be overcome to move towards such a solution is the current Pakistani political system which remains anchored in provincial political parties, leading to suspicion (whether true or not) of government actions and a culture of mistrust. Poor and uneven provision of services in cities also enhances inequality and creates further fissures between political parties. Shifting to a more coherent country-wide approach on improving quality of life for all Pakistanis will also help to foster more confidence on the part of citizens in their government.

Third, the government, at all different levels, needs to invite a wide set of stakeholders to contribute to the thinking on the plan. This should help to create greater ownership, foster communities, and also encourage a broader set of ideas to be put forward. Achieving results will also require multi-sectoral participation, as most issues discussed above, are linked with multiple sectors. Take for example, respiratory illnesses which are due to a variety of factors, ranging from poor urban air quality as a result of vehicular emissions, emissions from factories, burning of municipal waste, dust, and poor indoor air quality as a result of lighting fires using fuel wood or other solid fuels inside the home, without adequate ventilation. The vehicular emissions in turn are due to two-stroke auto rickshaws and obsolete diesel buses and trucks, poorly maintained roads, poor traffic management, poor quality fuel, poorly tuned car engines, dust from unpaved roads, among other factors. As you can see, we have highlighted the health, transport, energy, education, urban, and other sectors in tackling this challenge, without even covering each topic. Improving 'quality of life' means there is a role to play by SMEs, NGOs, academia, the judiciary, as well as the government. It is also important for the government not to be too prescriptive with solutions, but instead to enable underlying systems to contribute towards the goal of improved quality of life, for example by encouraging green businesses, but also encouraging different government departments as well as city and provincial departments to offer Pakistan-wide solutions, and equally encouraging offers of third-party monitoring by NGOs. Experience clearly shows that there is no such thing as a easy fix: the very successful bus rapid transit system of Bogotá, Colombia, was considered 'a wasteful use of public resources' and abandoned when an audit indicated that the social and economic benefits were less than that of the bus lane in Guangzhou, China.[65] Over time, the solutions offered by each of these groups may well change. It really does not matter. Ultimately, what matters is the progress towards the goal, and central monitoring and reporting of this progress, with a conscious effort to document and transparently report on how the solutions are contributing to the goal.

Fourth, it is important for the federal government to be clear who is accountable at the federal, provincial and municipal government level for improving different facets of 'improved quality of life', and precisely for what they are responsible, including the updating of related legislation. In assigning responsibility, it is also important to identify what are the sources of revenue they can generate and how progress will be measured. As with other things, progress indicators need to be monitored, and be made transparent, and adjustments made as needed, depending on what actually happens in practice, as was done in Colombia. Fifth, it is imperative to encourage greater environmental sustainability in the business sector, innovation in the development of green businesses, as well as to enable the participation of the private sector in basic infrastructure and service provision, allowing for a more financially sustainable model of service delivery right from the outset for basic services. But principle number six means that the government has to particularly keep an eye out for the poor, who may not be able to pay for these services. This may mean subsidizing the services for the poorest and encouraging different service models from private companies that are more commensurate with the purchasing power of these groups, but that will still ensure basic service provision. One example may be communal waste collection facilities rather than door-to-door collection. Another example is facilitating the development of less polluting urban public transport options.

Seven, data should be gathered and made available to the public. The accurate gathering of data by the government and using it to make informed policy choices for the benefit of citizens is paramount.[66] Putting data forward transparently will help to move out of the past into the present, putting everyone on the same page about the nature of the challenge and the context as the plan is developed, but also helps to shift behaviours. How one shares the data is also important, so that it can reach a wider audience. For example, by widely broadcasting through the media, key pollution data and resulting health impacts, such as levels of PM2.5 in cities, the government can promote greater awareness as well as behavioural change on the part of Pakistani citizens. The choice of indicators is also key. For example, it is not sufficient to merely monitor data of ambient conditions or service coverage, but also data related to understanding the sources of pollution so that ambient conditions can be better addressed, as well as the coverage of basic services by each income group so that there is a better understanding of which areas need additional focus. Gathering, sharing and updating data constantly over the long term is a key action for central governments to facilitate.

Finally, eight, Pakistan needs to ask for help from other countries. A possibility would be asking China to help with air quality improvements, since most of Pakistan's cities are as polluted (or worse) than theirs.

This leads to the obvious question: where are the resources for such an effort? In that regard, Pakistan's army provides an excellent example. For a poor country, Pakistan has a first world army. Why is this? It may well be because security has been a national priority for the last 70 years of the country's existence. Money always shifts to the priority. More often than not, the real issue is not a lack of resources but rather a conscious prioritization of existing resources to other issues. Most countries do this immediately when they face a national disaster or security risk. Results-on-the-ground also foster more revenue generation. It is only human nature to pay taxes more readily when you can actually benefit from the public goods being financed. It is necessary to think about resources in a wider context. One very relevant and real resource is Pakistan's burgeoning youth population. As noted in Chapter 1 in this volume, the youth population in cities may be as high as 75 per cent of the population, and has access to better education opportunities. Why not harness modern technology, and challenge them to find solutions and build businesses to change their own and everyone else's quality of life? Fostering innovation is key to achieving growth, and growth and continuous greening go hand in hand.[67] The IT revolution is a force of change in many countries today. By encouraging start-ups focused on green business, civic technology and social entrepreneurship, Pakistan could rely on the youth to be a force of change, helping up to leapfrog to new approaches to improve quality of life. Given that these issues are equally pressing for other South and East Asian countries, and that there is a distinct early movers advantage in this area, the future market for Pakistan's home-grown green businesses is potentially much wider.

In Pakistan's case, a very similar approach appears to have been employed in the context of the Vision 2025 Plan, prepared by the Ministry of Planning, Development and Reform. The Vision, however, lacks in one very important aspect. It does not take into account the carrying capacity of the physical environment, including potential climate impacts, in advancing many of the pillars discussed, perhaps given the lack of a voice on these issues in the form of an apex central agency. The obvious example is the effect on air quality of expanding coal-fired power coverage. Another example is the focus on food availability, without considering sanitation coverage, when the two go hand-in-hand in malnutrition impacts. A third example is the focus on only centrally driven solutions, like water treatment plants, to provide clean water for all, without consideration of the local environment, such as groundwater withdrawal, nor the accompanying sanitation and hygiene improvements necessary to achieve health improvements, which are now provincial responsibilities. Yet, at the same time, Vision 2025 and the way its implementation is envisaged could provide a win-win situation on many fronts to both significantly improve quality of life and meet Pakistan's 2025 goals.

In that regard, a final policy recommendation would be to consider expanding the mandate of the Ministry of Planning, Development and Reform to include the function of encouraging and overseeing the greening or sustainable development of different sectors. Given the emphasis on the SDGs in Vision 2025, perhaps the Ministry of Planning and Sustainable Development could be a more apt title. Such a Ministry of Planning and Sustainable Development could encourage the use of policy Strategic Environmental Assessments by sectoral ministries to help to change the culture and bring the sustainability dimensions into sectoral policies and plans.[68] It could also help to provide the impetus to include environment and climate change in school and university curricula, as well as to encourage youth innovation and entrepreneurship linked specifically with addressing Pakistan's physical quality of life. For example, Vision 2025 youth debate forums could specifically elicit ideas to improve physical quality of life and actively engage this crucial stakeholder group to innovate through technology to produce solutions, and possible new start-up companies, which could subsequently be funded by the private sector. On the other hand, a well-regarded and resourced Ministry of the Environment and Sustainable Development could also play such a role, in addition to the role of developing national policy, legislative and regulatory frameworks, and enforcing them. Ultimately, whatever arrangement is set up, it will need to have 'teeth' to have any impact.

In conclusion, from a quality of life perspective, thinking about Pakistan's future is both sobering and exhilarating. Sobering, because the country is on a downward spiral that could lead to much worse devastation than can currently be imagined, and in order to control it the country will have to start to behave very differently, people must think and act as members of communities, and learn to focus more inwardly to improve conditions for its own people. Yet it is also exhilarating because the country still have choices that if made could halt the current path and take it in a very different direction, ultimately to a country that is more resilient, because it is more united and actively works to promote better quality of life for all its citizens. The future is still, to a large degree, in the hands of its people.

Box 23.1   Controlling the downward spiral: eight key actions

1   Declare that 'improving quality of life for all' is a broader multisectoral goal for the long term (even beyond 2025) and put in place an organizational framework accountable for its implementation.

a   Create a Ministry of the Environment and Climate Change responsible for setting national environmental and climate policies, preparing and implementing related legislative and regulatory frameworks, and enforcing them.

b   Put in place a mechanism to encourage integration of sustainable considerations into sectoral policy and plans and to raise general awareness of quality of life issues, perhaps through a Planning and Sustainable Development Ministry applying policy Strategic Environmental Assessments.

2   Prepare a 'Quality of Life' Strategy focused on the physical environment and potential climate impacts and solutions, that takes a Pakistan-wide look at the problem.

3   Invite a wide set of stakeholders to contribute to the plan to maximize ideas and options and ensure wider ownership.

4   Clarify accountabilities, responsibilities (including legislative updates), revenue generation and progress indicators at the federal, provincial and municipal government level for improving different facets of 'improved quality of life'.

5   Partner with the private sector to encourage greater environmental sustainability, innovation in the development of green businesses, and enable financially sustainable model of basic service delivery.

6   Keep an eye out for the poor, ensuring that they too have access to basic services and that their environmental rights are secure.

7   Gather data on progress towards the goal, and make it available to the public, e.g. set up air quality monitoring networks and report data to the public on a regular basis, prepare an annual state of the environment report for the public and use it to inform future policies.

8   Ask for help from other countries, e.g. China on air pollution.

Notes

1 Census of Pakistan, 1951, Urban and Rural Population and Area, Tables 1 and 1A, Census Bulletin No. 3. Available at http://121.52.153.178:8080/xmlui/handle/123456789/14515 (accessed 7 September 2017).

2 There has been considerable uproar in the press and social media specifically about the alleged size of Karachi, which the 2017 census put at 15 million. On the other hand, Wendell Cox infers a population in Karachi of 22 million in 2012, based on the 2011 house count; see 'World Urban Areas Population and Density: A 2012 Update', *New Geography* vol. 5, 2012. According to the 13th annual edition of *Demographia*, Karachi is one of the 10 largest cities in the world, with a population that is a similar size to Shanghai, at about 23 million. See Wendell Cox, 'The 37 Megacities and Largest Cities', *Demographia World Urban Areas*, 2017. A number of factors seem to be at play here, from the classification assigned by the government to rural versus urban areas, to the accurate accounting for migrant workers, both of which appear to be inconsistently handled across provinces, to the lack of inclusion of refugees, who are primarily Karachi-based.

3 See   https://data.worldbank.org/indicator/SP.URB.TOTL.IN.ZS?locations=PK   (accessed   11 September 2017).

4 See section on Pakistan in *The Little Green Data Book*, Washington, DC, World Bank, 2017, p. 164. The information presented here was taken from World Development Indicators 2017, Washington, DC, World Bank. Data is presented by country with side-by-side comparisons with the average data for the region, as well as for the group of similar income-level countries globally.

5 See https://washdata.org/data#!/pak (accessed 11 September 2017). The World Health Organization and UNICEF Joint Monitoring Programme define a safely managed water source as being accessible on the premises, available when needed, with water free from contamination.

6 For 1990 figures, see WHO/UNICEF Joint Monitoring Programme for Water Supply and Sanitation, *Pakistan: Improved Sanitation Coverage Estimates (1980–2008)*, March 2010. Available at www.wssinfo.org/resources/documents.html?type=country_files (accessed 13 August 2010).

7 UNDP, 'Development Advocate Pakistan, Water Security in Pakistan: Issues and Challenges', vol. 3, no. 4, December 2016.

8 WHO/UNICEF, 'Progress of Drinking Water, Sanitation and Hygiene: Update and SDG Baselines', 2017. Available at https://washdata.org/data#!/pak (accessed 11 September 2017). The report notes that 'Improved sanitation facilities are those designed to hygienically separate excreta from human contact. There are three main ways to meet the criteria for having a safely managed sanitation service (SDG 6.2). People should use improved sanitation facilities that are not shared with other households, and the excreta produced should either be treated and disposed of in situ, or stored temporarily and then emptied, transported and treated off-site, or transported through a sewer with wastewater and then treated off-site. If the excreta from improved sanitation facilities are not safely managed, then people using those facilities will be classed as having a basic sanitation service (SDG 1.4).'

9 The *Dawn* newspaper, 5 March 2017 published a heartbreaking story about Shameem and Mohammed Umair losing their three children to a lethal landfill fire. See www.dawn.com/news/1318581.

10 See http://apps.who.int/gho/data/node.sdg.3-9-data?lang=en (accessed 11 September 2017).

11 See WHO Global Urban Ambient Air Pollution Database (updated in 2016). Available at www.who.int/phe/health_topics/outdoorair/databases/cities/en/.

12 Haider A. Khwaja, Zafar Fatmi, Daniel Malashock, Zafar Aminov, Ambreen Kazi, Azhar Siddique, JahanZeb Qureshi and David O. Carpenter, 'Effect of Air Pollution on Daily Morbidity in Karachi, Pakistan', *Journal of Local and Global Health Science*, 2013, p. 3.

13 See www.who.int/quantifying_ehimpacts/national/countryprofile/pakistan.pdf (accessed 11 September 2017).

14 See World Bank, *Environmental Health and Child Survival: Epidemiology, Economics, Experiences*, Washington, DC, World Bank, 2008. The Pakistan case study in this report estimated the cost of disease, in terms of loss of productivity, early mortality and health costs associated with environmental factors, such as lack of clean water, inadequate sanitation, poor waste disposal, indoor and outdoor air pollution, vector borne diseases, such as malaria, and problems arising from industrial chemicals and wastes. It also included malnutrition-mediated indirect effects of environmental risk factors. In today's Pakistan, this is likely to be a significant underestimate given the significant deterioration of the physical environment and related indicators since 2005, particularly related to outdoor air pollution.

15 See www.satp.org/satporgtp/countries/pakistan/database/casualties.htm (accessed 11 September 2017).

16 Sönke Kreft, David Eckstein, Lisa Junghans, Candice Kerestan and Ursula Hagen, Global Climate Risk Index 2015, Who Suffers Most from Extreme Weather Events, Weather-related Loss Events in 2013 and 1994 to 2013, p. 1Á31.

17 See Pakistan's INDC (PAK-INDC) at www4.unfccc.int/Submissions/INDC/Published%20Documents/Pakistan/1/Pak-INDC.pdf (accessed 12 September 2017).

18 FAO, *The Impact of Disasters on Agriculture and Food Security*, Rome, 2015. Available at www.fao.org/resilience/resources/resources-detail/en/c/346258/.

19 Eun-Soon Im, Jeremy Paal and Elfatir Eltahir, 'Deadly Heat Waves Projected in the Densely Populated Agricultural Regions of South Asia', *Science Advances*, 2 August 2017, vol. 3, no. 8. Available at http://advances.sciencemag.org/content/3/8/e1603322.full (accessed 12 September 2017).

20 Sajjad Ashraf, *Pakistan's Water Woes*, East Asia Forum, 12 September 2013. Available at www.eastasiaforum.org/2013/09/12/pakistans-water-woes/ (accessed 13 September 2017).

21 See ibid. and UNDP, 'Development Advocate Pakistan, Water Security in Pakistan'.

22 See Pakistan in the *Little Green Data Book*.

23 See UNDP, Development Advocate Pakistan, Water Security in Pakistan, p. 3.

24 Singapore provides an example of this at one end of the spectrum, see, for example, Singapore's efforts with NEWater at http://www.legco.gov.hk/research-publications/english/1516fsc22-newa ter-in-singapore-20160226-e.pdf, and at www.pub.gov.sg/watersupply/fournationaltaps/newater (both accessed 13 September 2017).

25 See Ashraf, *Pakistan's Water Woes*, and UNDP, 'Development Advocate Pakistan, Water Security in Pakistan'.

26 Nasir Hayat, 'Water Governance in Agriculture', in UNDP, Development Advocate Pakistan, Water Security in Pakistan.

27 See PAK-INDC.

28 See www.nasa.gov/feature/jpl/nasa-data-used-to-track-groundwater-in-pakistan (accessed 13 September 2017).

29 World Bank, *Towards a More Effective Operational Response: Arsenic Contamination of Groundwater in South and East Asian Countries*, Washington, DC, World Bank, 2012. Available at http://documents.worldbank.org/curated/en/610191468101990398/Towards-a-more-effective-operational-response-arsenic-contamination-of-groundwater-in-South-and-East-Asian-countries.

30 See, for example, *Dawn*. Available at www.dawn.com/news/1353482 (accessed 12 September 2017).

31 UNDP, Development Advocate Pakistan, Water Security in Pakistan.

32 Malnutrition and environmental infections are inextricably linked. Repeated infections, especially diarrhoea and helminths, caused by poor environmental conditions in early childhood, lead to underweight and stunted children. These growth-faltering effects, in turn, make individuals more predisposed to infections and even to chronic diseases later in life. See World Bank, *Environmental Health and Child Survival: Epidemiology, Economics, Experiences*, Washington, DC, 2008.

33 Prominent NGOs and institutes in Pakistan drawing attention to environmental issues include WWF-Pakistan, IUCN, SHEHRI, Arif Hasan's Urban Resource Center, SDPI, and LEAD-Pakistan, among others.

34 See www.pakistanpressfoundation.org/senate-body-to-launch-media-manual-on-environment/ (accessed 13 September 2017).

35 It is interesting to contrast this with the statements and the encyclical (Laudato Si) of Pope Francis.

36 Pew Research Center Survey, 2015. See www.pewglobal.org/2015/07/14/climate-change-seen-as-top-global-threat/ (accessed 13 September 2017).

37 World Bank, *Pakistan: Strategic Country Environmental Assessment*, Report No. 36946-PK, Washington, DC, 2006. In addition, see UNEP/UNDP/Dutch Government Joint Project on Environmental Law and Institutions in Africa, 1998, Compendium of Judicial Decisions on matters Related to Environment: National Decisions, vol. 1. Available at www.unep.org/pa delia/publications/Jud.Dec.Nat.pre.pdf (accessed 25 August 2010). Three cases from Pakistan are presented in this volume, all dating from 1994, the first of which was *Shehla Zia and others vs. WAPDA*.

38 See Ernesto Sanchez-Triana, Dan Biller, Ijaz Nabi, Leonard Ortolano, Ghazal Dezfuli, Javaid Afzal and Santiago Enriquez, *Revitalizing Industrial Growth in Pakistan: Trade, Infrastructure and Environmental Performance*, Washington, DC, World Bank, 2014.

39 See http://pbc.org.pk/research-initiatives/centre-of-excellence-in-responsible-business-cerb/ (accessed 13 September 2017).

40 See, for example, www.dawn.com/news/1354456/planets-warning (accessed 13 September 2017).

41 See 'Big investors to Put More Money into Tackling Climate Change', *Financial Times*, 12 September 2017. Available at www.ft.com/content/0c485f68-96eb-11e7-a652-cde3f882dd7b (accessed 13 September 2017).

42 Globally, there are now US $22.89 trillion of assets being professionally managed under responsible investment strategies, an increase of 25 per cent since 2014, according to the Global Sustainable Investment Review, 2016. Available at http://www.gsi-alliance.org/wp-content/uploads/2017/03/GSIR_Review2016.F.pdf (accessed 13 September 2017).

43 See http://money.cnn.com/2017/06/03/technology/future/india-electric-cars/index.html (accessed 13 September 2017).

44 Ernesto Sanchez-Triana, Santiago Enriquez, Javaid Afzal, Akiko Nakagawa and Asif Shuja Khan, 'Cleaning Pakistan's Air: Policy Options to Address the Cost of Outdoor Air Pollution', in *Directions in Development: Energy and Mining*, Washington, DC, World Bank, 2014. See also *Pakistan: Strategic Country Environmental Assessment*, Report No. 36946-PK, Washington, DC, World Bank, 2006.

45 Pakistan's original NEQS were emission standards and did not take into account ambient conditions. Typically, countries have both emission and ambient standards, as the purpose of standards is to ensure that the quality of the physical resource (air, water, soil) does not deteriorate below a level that is hazardous to human health and the health of the ecosystem. Ambient standards are also typically measured and reported. Emission standards are used to determine what are permissible emissions from a new point source, so that the ambient conditions do not deteriorate below acceptable levels.

46 Sanchez-Triana *et al.*, 'Cleaning Pakistan's Air'. See also Ernesto Sanchez-Triana, Santiago Enriquez, Bjorn Larsen, Peter Webster and Javaid Afzal, 'Sustainability and Poverty Alleviation: Confronting Environmental Threats in Sindh, Pakistan', in *Directions in Development: Environment and Sustainable Development*, Washington, DC, World Bank, 2015.

47 See also World Bank, *Pakistan.*.

48 See Sanchez-Triana *et al.*, 'Cleaning Pakistan's Air', p. 92.

49 See http://epd.punjab.gov.pk/system/files/Punjab%20Environmental%20Quality%20Standards% 20for%20Ambient%20Air.pdf (accessed 22 September 2017).

50 See Ernesto Sanchez-Triana, Santiago Enriquez, Bjorn Larsen, Peter Webster and Javaid Afzal, 'Sustainability and Poverty Alleviation: Confronting Environmental Threats in Sindh, Pakistan', in *Directions in Development: Environment and Sustainable Development*, Washington, DC, World Bank, 2015, p. 129; and also the Sindh Sanitation Policy, May 2017 at www.sindh.gov.pk/ dpt/phe/2017_05_23_11_41_00.pdf (accessed 22 September 2017).

51 Sanchez-Triana *et al.*, 'Cleaning Pakistan's Air'.

52 Ibid., pp. 89–91. See for an excellent discussion of functions at the central and decentralized levels for environmental management.

53 Sarath K. Guttikanda, Todd M. Johnson, Feng Liu and Jitendra Shah, *Programs to Control Air Pollution and Acid Rain*, 'Urbanization, Energy and Air Pollution in China: The Challenges Ahead, Proceedings of a Symposium in 2004', National Academies of Science, Engineering and Medicine, Washington, DC, 2017. Available at www.nap.edu/read/11192/chapter/7#89 (accessed 14 September 2017).

54 One report from 2009 notes that the McIlvaine Chinese Utility Plans database shows that 'China is operating 379,000 MW of scrubbers compared to only 130,000 MW in the US. China has these FGD scrubbers on 67% of its coal-fired plants which is a higher percentage than in the US. China is also the largest supplier of many types of air pollution control equipment and several Chinese companies are the world's leading suppliers of electrostatic precipitators. According to McIlvaine, in recent years, suppliers of FGD systems have grown rapidly and ten of these [Chinese] companies are among the 20 largest FGD companies in the world.' Mark Holmes, 'Flue Gas Desulfurization Increases in China', *Filtration and Separation*, 24 June 2009. Available at www.filtsep.com/oil-and-gas/news/flue-gas-desulphurisation-increases-in-china/ (accessed 14 September 2017).

55 In January 2017 China cancelled 103 planned and under construction coal power plants, amounting to 120 GW capacity. See www.nytimes.com/2017/01/18/world/asia/china-coal-p ower-plants-pollution.html?mcubz=0 (accessed 14 January 2017).

56 Thakoor Persaud and Alexandra Ortiz, 'Urban Development', in Marcelo Giugale, Olivier Lafourcade and Connie Luff (eds) *Colombia: The Economic Foundation of Peace*, Washington, DC, World Bank, 2003.

57 Kulsum Ahmed and Ernesto Sanchez-Triana, 'Using Strategic Environmental Assessment to Design and Implement Public Policy', in Kulsum Ahmed and Ernesto Sanchez-Triana (eds) *Strategic Environmental Assessment for Policies: An Instrument of Good Governance*, Washington, DC, World Bank, 2008. See https://openknowledge.worldbank.org/handle/10986/6461 (accessed 14 September 2017).

58 Taimur Samad, Nancy Lozano-Garcia and Alexander Panman, *Colombia Urbanization Review: Amplifying the Gains from the Urban Transition*, Washington, DC, World Bank, 2012. See

http://documents.worldbank.org/curated/en/527041468025227166/Colombia-urbanization-revie
w-amplifying-the-gains-from-the-urban-transition (accessed 14 September 2017).

59 See See Ehtisham Ahmad, 'Political Economy of Tax Reform for SDGs' (G24 Background
Paper), August 2017, which advocates for a package approach.

60 See World Bank, *Colombia: Urban Environmental Management Project*, Washington, DC, World
Bank, 2003. Available at http://documents.worldbank.org/curated/en/972291468744059871/pdf/
26147.pdf (accessed 22 September 2017).

61 See Ernesto Sanchez-Triana, Kulsum Ahmed and Yewande Awe (eds), 'Environmental Priorities
and Poverty Reduction: A Country Environmental Analysis for Colombia', in Directions in
Development: Environment and Sustainable Development, Washington, DC, World Bank,
2007, p. 23.

62 See http://theredddesk.org/countries/actors/ministry-environment-and-sustainable-development-co
lombia and https://en.wikipedia.org/wiki/Ministry_of_Environment_and_Sustainable_Developm
ent_(Colombia) (both accessed 22 September 2017).

63 Ahmed, Kulsum, *Getting to Green: A Sourcebook of Pollution Management Policy Tools for
Growth and Competitiveness*, Washington, DC, World Bank, 2012. See http://documents.
worldbank.org/curated/en/560021468330349857/Getting-to-green-a-sourcebook-of-pollution-ma
nagement-policy-tools-for-growth-and-competitiveness (accessed 14 September 2017).

64 Kulsum Ahmed and Ernesto Sanchez-Triana (eds), *Strategic Environmental Assessment for
Policies: An Instrument of Good Governance*, Washington, DC, World Bank, 2008. See https://op
enknowledge.worldbank.org/handle/10986/6461 (accessed 14 September 2017).

65 Xinghou Yuan, 'BRTs and Investment Fads: Civic Engagement and Fiscal Discipline', in
Ahmad Ehtisham, Meili Niu and Kezhou Xiao (eds) *Fiscal Underpinnings for Sustainable
Development in China: Rebalancing in Guangdong*, Springer, Singapore, 2018.

66 Unfortunately, the recent 2017 preliminary census data does not set a good benchmark, and
suggests that this is an area in need of much reform.

67 Shahid Yusuf (ed.), *Five Cities Going Green: How Are They Doing It?* Washington, DC, Growth
Dialogue, 2013.

68 China requires SEAs for all sectoral plans by law, as does the European Union. See Kulsum
Ahmed and Yvonne Fiadjoe, 'A Selective Review of SEA Legislation: Results from a Nine-
Country Review', Environment Strategy Paper No. 13, World Bank, Washington, DC, 2006.
For a discussion on policy SEA, particularly apt for Pakistan given its governance short-
comings, see Ahmed and Sanchez-Triana, *Strategic Environmental Assessment for Policies*.

24

Water problems and solutions

Mahmood Ahmad

Historical perspective

Soon after Partition in 1947, internal as well as external (with India) water issues started to emerge. In 1960, through the arbitration of the World Bank, the Indus Basin Treaty (IBT) was signed which allocated water rights on three eastern rivers to India and three western rivers (Indus, Jhelum and Chenab) to Pakistan. To compensate for the loss of the eastern rivers, Pakistan built two large dams (Mangla and Tarbela) and 12 link canals under the Indus Basin Project. Total water and power investments during the 1960s exceeded US $2.5 billion and accounted for more than 50 per cent of total public development spending.[1] Another notable investment took place with the support of the United States through Salinity Control and Reclamation Projects involving the use of public tube wells to lower the water table and solve the problem of waterlogging and salinity. This was an era of water supply enhancement.

After the completion of the Indus Basin Project, inter-provincial conflict emerged regarding the sharing and use of water for irrigation purposes. A series of high-level commissions were formed and the matter was settled through the Water Apportionment Accord of 1991, which provided a season-wise share to each province. An independent body, the Indus River System Authority (ISRA), was established to implement the Accord. The ISRA worked satisfactorily for a while, but growing water demands and diminishing reservoir capacity have made it increasingly difficult to meet the expectations of the provinces and a politically charged situation continues to prevail.

Institutional reforms

The Water and Power Development Authority (WAPDA) is responsible for construction and operations and maintenance (O&M) of the big, multi-purpose reservoirs and inter-provincial link canals. Provincial Irrigation Departments (PIDs) are responsible for O&M of the distribution systems above outlets (*moghas*). The O&M of water courses and field channels are the responsibility of farmers. Off-farm drainage systems are normally developed by WAPDA and handed over to the PIDs for O&M. The public sector operates the irrigation system above the *moghas*. Each season, the WAPDA of the federal government estimates the water availability for the following season. The PIDs inform the WAPDA of provincial water demands at specific locations. The WAPDA releases water from reservoirs to meet demands as closely as possible. Limited reservoir capacity of the system does not permit the full regulation of rivers used for irrigation purposes. It should be noted that the system was designed to provide 67 per cent of cropping intensity, but now the need is on average for 145 per cent, demanding more water than system capacity.

A major water policy reform proposed by the World Bank and other donors in the early 1990s emphasized that the best option for the Pakistan government was to develop autonomous, commercially oriented public utilities on a canal command that would be financially independent and would have commercial interests. At farm level, fully functioning farmer organizations were proposed. It envisaged a continuous role in water through the distribution of water users, who are responsible for O&M and collection of user charges. The WAPDA would continue to be responsible for overall assessment, coordination and development of water resources. The PIDs should be restructured to develop an administratively autonomous Provincial Water Authority that would be responsible for coordinating and planning the water resources of the provinces. A provincial regulatory commission would oversee the financial affairs of the public utilities, register water rights and settle local water distribution disputes. The strategy called for instituting enabling legislation on water rights, quality and markets.[2] The large investments and proposed institutional reforms carried a mixed record of success, although meeting to a large extent food security needs but failed to add the expected value that water can add to the economy. The reforms were implemented without strong commitment from huge governance bureaucracy put in place over time.

The issues

On a global scale, over the next 15 years, almost half of the world's population will be living in areas that are running out of water.[3] Pakistan is already in this bracket – within our lifespan, the country has moved from excess supply to water deficient – food for thought.

Declining water availability

Pakistan faces a water shortage cycle which is predicted to worsen over time and its availability has a seasonal pattern. One commonly used indicator shows a significant decrease in per head water use from 3,000 cu m in 1980 to 1,300 in 2017, but some estimates put it below 1,000 per cu m, a level considered water scarce (see Table 24.1). The per head water usage is based on population growth, with new estimates at 208 million in 2017; the per head availability will fall sharply and make Pakistan one of the world's most water-scarce countries. With the Indus being a closed basin, meaning that the water cycle is fully utilized, there is not much capacity for additional water. The potential storage facilities often mentioned would not add new water but they would redistribute the existing supply.

The implications are that the gap between water demand and supply is widening, and the challenge to the water sector is how to reduce this gap.

Table 24.1 Per head water availability

Years	Population	Per capita availability in M3	Where we stand
1951	34	5650	Plenty
2003	146	1200	Stress
2010	168	1000	Scarcity
2025	221	800	Scarcity

Source: WAPDA reports.

Water quality

The water quality is affected by a lack of proper management of the watersheds; there has been a denudation of rangelands, and a depletion of forest cover and vegetation resulting in soil erosion and siltation. On the other hand, 38 per cent of Pakistan's irrigated land is waterlogged and 14 per cent is saline; there is now saline water intrusion in the mined aquifers. The quality of groundwater ranges from fresh near the major rivers to highly saline further away, with salinity measured at more than 3000 mg/l TDS. Close to the edges of the irrigated lands, fresh ground water can be found at a depth of 20–50 m.[4] Developing huge irrigation systems without technically sound drainage has turned out to be a costly policy option.

The water quality has been degrading over time due to sewage and industrial effluent discharges, urban and agriculture run-off as well as saline water intrusion that is making the water quality so poor that it might not be safe for public use. A report by the United Nations Development Programme (UNDP)[5] highlights the fact that water pollution caused by organic matter, pathogenic agents and hazardous and toxic wastes are serious issues. Pollution loads discharged into inland water bodies have been estimated to double by 2025.

A large part of the country's population is deprived of improved access to safe drinking water and sanitation; 27.2 million people do not have access to safe water and 52.7 million do not have access to sanitation, while more than 39,000 children under the age of five die every year from diarrhoea caused by drinking unsafe water and poor sanitation.[6] A growing demand for water for domestic use, urban development and China–Economic Corridor (CPEC) projects will put extra pressure on water availability.

The solution lies in introducing and implementing better regulations to tackle point and non-point pollution – proper treatment of sewage and industrial toxic waste necessary to improve the water quality. There are cost-effective ways to treat water which can be used for commercial activities. Furthermore, a proper ground water management and drainage system are key to solving the issue. However, education and public awareness, especially among young people, are needed to prevent pollution at source.

Ground water depletion

The increase in the number of tube wells in the Indus Basin has been phenomenal, and are now estimated at 1.5 million units, accounting for half of all farm irrigation requirements and supplementing the 34 million acre feet of surface water that reaches farmlands. This conjunctive use of surface and groundwater has helped to spur the green revolution and plays a crucial role in the socio-economic development of the country. This massive growth is leading to groundwater depletion in urban, peri-urban and rural areas, resulting in a drop in the water table, with rising availability and quality problems expected to intensify in future which might be irreversible if a policy of unsustainable water use continues. Farmers go deeper and deeper to keep their agriculture, but only large farmers can afford these operations – this reflects a complete institutional failure to regulate and monitor the sustainable use of groundwater. The drop in the water table is significant in Karachi and Lahore, and in many cases there has been intrusion of saline groundwater into previously freshwater resources.[7] The situation is particularly serious in Balochistan where unsustainable extraction is leading to changes in its ecology and very recently a drop in soil levels. In areas with high groundwater tables, poor drainage is contributing to waterlogging, salinization and alkalinity problems, especially in Sindh and Punjab. Improving the quality of polluted aquifers is often prohibitively expensive and sometimes technically impossible.

Further effects on health are often not accounted for, and pollution from poor sanitation, mining, industry and agro-chemicals (pesticides and fertilizers) together with naturally occurring contaminants (arsenic, fluoride and iron) reduce not only the 'effective' groundwater supply but make water consumption unfit for human use. According to the Swiss Federal Institute of Aquatic Science and Technology, results from samples taken from 1,200 wells in Pakistan show that up to two-thirds of these wells are supplying water contaminated with arsenic, indicating a level above 200 micrograms per litre, far higher than the World Health Organization's global standard of 10 micrograms per litre and the Pakistan government's limit of 50 micrograms per litre. This should be of serious concern to policymakers who continue to closely monitor the unregulated and heavy use of chemical fertilizers and pesticides, raw sewage irrigation, and improper disposal of industrial effluents into water channels, all of which have contributed to the leaching of toxins and arsenic in the groundwater supplies.[8]

What are the main drivers of this tragedy? They include a weak legislative and regulatory framework; the fragmented and sometimes conflicting roles and responsibilities of various agencies supporting groundwater management; and development at the central, provincial and local levels. Furthermore, water demand management policies have not been even considered, let alone adopted. On the other hand, cheap drilling and pumping technologies and energy subsidies are the main 'pull' factors. Poor water supply and irrigation service delivery from surface water have compelled farmers and other users to opt for access to groundwater that provides supply on demand. Other factors include the limited capacity of groundwater departments (if they exist at all); the inadequate coordination of groundwater management and development with other related sectors (drinking water, energy environment, health, etc.); and the limited knowledge base and poor understanding of this precious resource.

So, what is the best solution to address this serious issue? Pricing irrigation groundwater is politically infeasible and so is any increase in electricity prices. A number of researchers argue that the best solution is to allocate groundwater shares or quotas to each farmer according to the farm size and historical cropped area. Oman's case is illustrative where 40 farms have benefited from the installation of intelligent energy and water meters. The objective is to reduce the cost of monitoring, to introduce monitoring on a weekly/monthly basis of the groundwater extraction and to send alerts to those farmers who exceed their allocated water quota in a preventive way. India provides a good example of a success story that can be of interest to regions/countries facing groundwater depletion. The successful farmer-managed groundwater systems initiative, Andhra

Pradesh Farmer Managed Groundwater Systems, offers useful lessons on participatory groundwater management.[9] Collective action has resulted in sustainable groundwater management, reduction in cost, and growing high-value crops. Pakistan continues to promote rice and sugar cane; neither crop can be justified under water-scarce conditions unless water use is rationalized in agriculture and more specifically for these two water-thirsty crops.

Climate change: a new worry

Pakistan receives snowfall only in the northern areas during winter. Frozen reservoirs in the upper country release large amounts of meltwater into many of the major rivers. The impact of climate change can already be seen in Pakistan. During the last few decades there has been a rapid retreat of glaciers, resulting in an enhanced water supply in the river system. This can be attributed to global temperatures that are projected to rise over the next three to eight decades. There follows a brief analysis for Pakistan, using fresh-water outflow to the sea as an indication of the total river flow for the period 1976–2013.[10] During the period 1975–90 (following the construction of the Tarbella Dam) the average flow into the sea measured 35.17 million acre feet (MAF) per year. However, during the period 1990–2000, this flow was recorded at been 51.50 MAF per year, i.e. about 42 per cent greater. However, during the period 2000–13 there was a significant decrease in in outflow, to just 13.20 MAF per year, indicating the possible impact of climate change. This is already having a significant effect on both water availability and agriculture sustainability.

The possible impacts on agriculture are summarized below:

- Reduced yield
- Uncertain outputs due to reduction in rainfall
- Higher frequency of droughts
- Degradation of natural grazing areas
- Decline in per head share of water for all uses
- Tremendous decline in livestock rearing in general, and in sheep rearing in particular
- Limited data on climatic changes
- Greater rural poverty, fewer jobs and ensuing rural migration to urban areas.

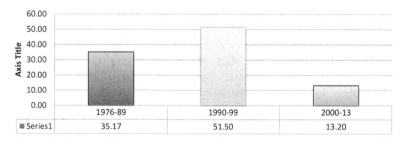

Figure 24.1 Escapages below Kotri to sea: indicator of climate change (annual discharge – MAF)
Source: Author's elaboration from I. Ahmad, A. Sufi and I. Tariq, Water Resources of Pakistan, paper no. 711, Centenary Celebration, Pakistan Engineering Congress, Lahore.

The analysis

The problems of water scarcity, groundwater depletion, sedimentation, waterlogging and salinity and climate change discussed above are symptoms of a much deeper problem embedded in policy, institutional and market failures for the development and management of water resources in Pakistan[11] – highlighting very well the 'three Es' in water management: economic efficiency, environmental sustainability, and equity, offering a useful framework with which to analyse these issues.

Policy failure

Policy failure is largely reflected in attributing a low value to water, in spite of the fact that it is now considered a scarce resource. Two-fold arguments are often provided, for this. First, water is critical to national food security, a low price of water would keep farmer's profitability and incentive to grow low-value security crops such as wheat, rice and sugar cane. Second, the government needs to price water in accordance with the need for mobilizing adequate funds for water development and infrastructure maintenance. The present price regime of water neither meets the financial needs (cost of O&M) nor the efficiency criteria (marginal cost) of allocating the resources. When comparing canal water charges to average annual per hectare groundwater costs, which range in price from 5,000 rupees to 6,500 rupees, this signifies the degree of distortion or policy failure.

Institutional and market failure

Arrangements to deliver water at different levels of distribution are inefficient, inadequate, inequitable, and full of corruption with low public participation. Too many organizations are serving the water sector and often lack the coordination required for water supplies to the end users. The worst case is the disconnect between the Ministry of Water/Irrigation (the water provider) and the Ministry of Agriculture (the water user). A large part of the budget is spent on administration (usually salaries) with very little left over for O&M. On the other hand, only about 50 per cent of the O&M costs of the government-run irrigation facilities are recovered through irrigation service fees, and many existing water distribution systems for irrigation are deteriorating rapidly. Another problem is that water charges are not linked to O&M needs and level of service delivery. The revenues are collected by the Irrigation Departments and become part of the general revenue. It appears that the government's approach is to 'build-neglect-rebuild',[12] a policy dilemma that seems hard to change.

Market failure in the water sector is prevalent due to three aspects: (1) water being treated as a public good; (2) lack of policy reforms in creating water rights and markets; and (3) non-recognition of environmental externalities associated with water. At the heart of the water problem for policy makers/institutions is how to allocate water among competing uses when water scarcity is increasing. Broadly speaking, water can be allocated through pricing mechanisms or through administrative mechanisms. Contrary to many other countries, in Pakistan water is allocated through a well-established mechanism which is better than many other countries;[13] a transboundary agreement with India has been well tested, at the provincial level the water accord provides a working mechanism. However, a new set of problems are testing the established system to its limits and in some cases it is breaking down.

It is often suggested that the creation of water rights and a water market would alleviate the problems of water allocation, availability, accessibility – but would it lead to water conservation? This is true especially where water rights are not well defined or enacted. Pakistan provides an interesting case. Water markets are illegal, but at least 70 per cent of all farmers trade water on the watercourses in order to meet scarcity and improve supply.[14] In Pakistan, given the way that society is organized, it is of particular concern that legalizing the trade in water would add to the existing inequity between upstream and downstream users, and therefore putting a value on the water rights is not desirable. It is difficult to curb the illegal water markets for urban supply because there is a greater willingness to pay for water for use in urban areas than for agricultural purposes. Even if regulatory regimes are set up that could mitigate the open sale of water, underground markets will spur on this activity (see Box 25.1). One has to weigh up these negative externalities against the expected benefits from the shift in policy, keeping in view the facts on the ground. The focus needs to be on whether water rights should be tied to the land or whether they can be traded separately.

In the case of the transboundary water agreement with India, water experts from both India and Pakistan regard the Indus Water Treaty as a success story on water cooperation. However, because the treaty was designed in 1960 it does not provide for changes in water availability due to climatic changes, increasing demands, environmental flows, groundwater development and technological advancements. These all have changed considerably since 1960 and there is a need to strengthen and extend the treaty, particularly the sections on future cooperation. It will not be in the interest of both India and Pakistan to reopen the treaty or challenge its validity, instead, a serious and sincere dialogue is needed, with new spirit to resolve issues in light of a new dimension of water policy, for example the needs of environmental flows.

On market failure the externalities (unpaid cost) generated from point and non-point sources are quite dominant in the industry and agriculture sectors. Underinvestment in watersheds is a huge cost borne by downstream users in terms of high siltation loads. The lining of water courses and canals negatively affects return flows, meaning a that poor and reduced amount of water is available for downstream users. The solution lies in improved regulations and their implementation to tackle pollution, i.e. the proper treatment of sewage and industrial toxic waste is necessary to improve the water quality. There are cost-effective ways to treat water which can be used for economic activities. Furthermore, a proper groundwater management and drainage system is key to sreolving the issue. However, education and public awareness, especially among young people, are needed to prevent pollution at source.

Box 24.1   Water markets: the case of Karachi

The water allocation system is also breaking down as demand for competing use increases and water transfer especially around within growing cities rises. Water market and trade is common and a lucrative business charging a high price for water sales recurring water crisis in Karachi is classical case where water transfer and rent-seeking is enormous. It is alleged that the water tanker mafia charge 3,000–8,000 rupees per tanker, when the official price for 1,000 gallons of water is fixed at 1,000 rupees, even though the rates may vary from one locality to the other. On the other hand, it is often argued that urban poor cannot afford even this price, price of water from tankers is completely beyond their means. Furthermore, the quality of such water often does meet international standards. It is also very clear that consumers are willing to pay for water so long as they get a reliable supply which the public service has failed to provide. The fact is that the private sector (water market) is capturing the revenue that which in reality the local water utility (Karachi Water Supply Board) should have been collecting by improving the level of service. The water markets will continue to supply water, as long as KWSB fails to provide water and the services needed by consumers.

Source: M. Ahmad, 'Water Crisis in Karachi', *Business Recorder*, 2015.

Which policy actions are needed?

Better water management and allocation strategies (sharing, equity and pricing)

The existing legal framework for water resources allocation and management lacks a water policy that integrates both the development and management of this valuable resource. At 2018 neither Pakistan's long-awaited National Water Policy nor its Ground Water Policy had yet to be completed. The National Drinking Water Policy and the National Sanitation Policy were still at the preliminary stage and it is too early to ascertain their effectiveness.

With rising and competing demand for water, given that agriculture uses 96 per cent of the available water the sector would be under pressure to reduce its share for growing water demand for domestic (4 per cent) and industrial (2 per cent) use in times of water crisis, when, as is the case already, the low-use sectors would get higher priority as opposed to agriculture. The CPEC would put additional pressure on demand.

Agriculture has to produce more but with less water. That water use in agriculture must be rationalized is inevitable, but little has been said on this issue in the many workshops and conferences dealing with water that largely put emphasis on water conservation in a sector which uses only 2–3 per cent of the water, and therefore increasing water productivity for agriculture needs to be fully explored.

Water pricing as a tool to conserve water might have a limited impact on inter-sector water allocation and conservation, but can be very useful for intra-sector water allocation among high- and low-water delta crops. It is also needed to raise revenue to the meet the cost of O&M of the huge irrigation infrastructure.

Using technology to save water has been adopted in a piecemeal approach and with limited take-up as it is perceived as an opportunity for subsidy. Farmers will not adopt modern and costly technology as long as the cost of water is low and not a profitable investment. The equitable distribution of water among the provinces is important, but it is equally important to share water benefits with equity and fair distribution within provinces i.e. between those who have first access to the water pipe, those second in line, and those at the end of that pipe.

Reforming institutions

There are 18 agencies serving the water sector in Pakistan, yet no single organization is responsible for the integrity of water resources in the Indus River Basin. Institutional reform necessitates a shift from a business-as-usual scenario to benefit-sharing mechanisms between provinces so that the needs and priorities of all the provinces are met by the new water management frameworks.

The water problem needs to be redefined in terms of unbundling the land and water rights, of head, middle, and tail farmlands in irrigated areas, and in terms of other methods of water resource management in non-irrigated rain-fed and arid areas where groundwater use is critical. Non-traditional sources of water should be boosted such as water harvesting, recycling waste water in agriculture and other sectors and the use of solar energy to desalinate water along coastal belts where tourism is expected to grow as a result of the CPEC.

Reducing environmental externality

Gilgit-Baltistan is the water bank of Pakistan; it preserves the watershed and has a hugely valuable environment which protects the quality and quantity of water. There is a complete neglect and lack of awareness of the importance of what an appropriate watershed management can contribute.

Climate change is putting additional stress on ensuring environmental flows as greater demands are placed on water. There must be regulation and licensing for extracting groundwater; an inventory of groundwater resources and monitoring of changes over time; and the promotion of solar-operated pumps where feasible that require initial large investments but have marginal costs, that can lead to over-pumping, unless regulation is effective.

Notes

1 BIPP, Annual Report, Agriculture and Water, Lahore, 2017.
2 'Pakistan Irrigation and Drainage: Issues and Options', Report No. 11884-Pak, South Asia Region, Country Department III, Agriculture Division, World Bank, 1993.
3 'Nestlé Pakistan Water Plan', in partnership with Lahore University of Management Sciences, LUMS Centre for Water Informatics and Technology, October 2017.
4 S. Kamal, *'Pakistan's Water Challenges: Entitlement, Access, Efficiency and Equity', Running on Empty: Pakistan's Water Crisis.* Washington, DC, Woodrow Wilson International Centre for Scholars Asia Programme, 2009, pp. 28–44.
5 UNDP, 'Water Security in Pakistan: Issues and Challenges, Development Advocate Pakistan', UNDP, December 2016.
6 Ibid.
7 Intizar Hussain (ed.) 'Pro-poor Intervention Strategies in Irrigated Agriculture in Asia: Poverty in Irrigated Agriculture: Issues and Options, Pakistan. Pakistan Country Report', Colombo, Sri Lanka, International Water Management Institute, 2004. Available at www.iwmi.cgiar.org/prop oor/files/ADB_Project/Project%20Reports/Pakistan.pdf.
8 Daniyal Khalid, 'How Serious Is the Risk to Pakistanis from Arsenic Contamination of Groundwater?' *Dawn*, 29 August 2017.
9 Participatory Ground Water Management in AP Draft Outline of the legal framework emerging following discussions with the Principal Secretary, RD, Government of AP on 10 August.
10 Imtiaz Ahmed, Global Climatic Change and Pakistan's Water-Resources, Chief Executive Secretariat No. 2, Islamabad, Pakistan.
11 M. Ahmad, 'Water Pricing and Markets in the Near East: Policy Issues and Options', *Water Policy*, vol. 2, no. 3, 14 July 2002, pp. 229–42.
12 'Pakistan Country Water Resources Assistance Strategy: Water Economy: Running Dry, South Asia Region, Agriculture and Rural Development Unit Report No. 34081-PK, Washington, DC, World Bank, 2005.
13 Ibid.
14 'Pakistan Irrigation and Drainage: Issues and Options', Report No. 11884-Pak, South Asia Region, Country Department III, Agriculture Division, World Bank, 1993.

25

Ways of solving the energy problem

Ziad Alahdad

Introduction

Critical energy shortages are arguably the most serious impediment to Pakistan's economic growth. It is an established fact, nationally and internationally, that Pakistan's energy sector is in a state of crisis. Virtually everyone, in one way or other, has been affected. The most starkly visible effects during peak demand seasons are power shortages lasting up to 18 hours per day. The silver lining is that, finally, the government has initiated concerted remedial action in collaboration with the private sector, under the umbrella of the China–Pakistan Economic Corridor (CPEC). Few people appreciate that the energy crisis is a common phenomenon in South Asia as a whole, and that it is likely to become even worse given the declining water resources caused by global warming.

One of the unfortunate dilemmas facing the energy sector is the surfeit of self-proclaimed experts – reminiscent of the proverbial elephant in the village of the blind. Everyone who touches a part of the animal thinks he knows what the whole animal looks like. The author of this chapter has spent the majority of his career in the energy sector and would be the first to admit that he is still learning and does not fully understand the whole animal. Energy sector analysis is a highly specialized skill and we need to treat the sector with a degree of humility and the respect that it deserves.

The chapter begins with an outline of the key energy issues Pakistan faces. It goes on to discuss the critical importance of the CPEC, dispelling the myths and focusing on the salient features of its design, which is based on an integrated approach to energy policy and planning. It then introduces the integrated approach as the essential starting point to address the country's energy issues. It traces the turbulent history of the integrated approach, which has been buffeted by political and ideological interference. Focusing on Pakistan, it shows how the integrated approach provides the essential framework to resolve critical issues. The chapter concludes with a vision of the future in which CPEC is implemented in letter and spirit, within the framework of the integrated approach. Throughout the chapter, references to the CPEC and comparisons with India which (dimensions aside) is confronting very similar issues, provide a regional context and emphasize the immense potential benefits of regional energy trade – an important by-product of the integrated approach.

Pakistan's key energy issues: a synthesis

How do we present the long list of burning issues in Pakistan's energy sector in a concise form? The following 13-point list has been synthesized from a plethora of background material. Most importantly, the common thread running through each of the points is the critical need to build capacity and improve governance.

1 Growing energy deficit despite a substantial energy resource base, a paradox which is not uncommon.
2 Endemic issues in each sub-sector, involving system management, maintenance and operations, losses, collection performance, etc.
3 Spiralling circular debt with emphasis on bailouts rather than solving endemic issues.
4 Exclusion of non-commercial energy with serious repercussions on sustainable and inclusive growth, poverty levels and the environment. Absence of an integrated forestry/fuelwood policy.
5 Need to establish appropriate level and structure of pricing, subsidies and regulations for balanced energy development, poverty alleviation and mobilizing private investment.
6 Institutional weaknesses within subsectors.
7 Fragmented policy-level institutional structure causing overlap, confusion and lack of coordination (part of broader civil service reform).
8 Ad hoc, crisis-driven policy and investment decisions, frozen in the short-term.
9 Stop-go reform implementation and repeated reversals.
10 Need for a comprehensive optimum energy strategy from source to consumption, with projections and scenarios.
11 Inadequate provision for a pro-poor and environmentally friendly energy policy.
12 Inability to quantify (i) cost penalty of suboptimal policies; and therefore (ii) penalty of deviations from optimum.
13 Legacy of lost opportunities. Lessons from history are critical with the advent of the CPEC.

This seems to be a formidable list. But the good news is that it reflects the situation in most developing countries and even in many developed countries. The difference in Pakistan is that the magnitude of the problems has grown out of control and needs to be reined in to make it manageable. That, in short, is the statement of the problem and the approach to its solution. This chapter takes up each of the issues in more detail later.

In seriously affected countries such as Pakistan, many observers would maintain that the energy sector, and by extension, its effect on the economy, are difficult to reverse. This claim is completely unsubstantiated. If every crisis presents an opportunity, Pakistan with its many crises should also have as many opportunities. This should be the starting point for resolving the crisis. The story of the energy sector is symptomatic of all sectors of the economy. Like the financial sector, energy pervades the entire economy; so much so that analysts have referred to energy as the currency of the economy.

How do we begin to solve all this? A solution is needed that addresses all the above issues and looks at the sector as a whole – an integrated approach. The acronym IEP

(Integrated Energy Planning and Policy) is used in this chapter. The approach is called by many names in different countries. Some do not even give it a name; they consider it the normal way of doing business in the energy sector, as is the case of the People's Republic of China. Acronyms or names do not matter – it is the principles that count.

Pakistan is finally moving in this direction with support from the United States Agency for International Development (USAID) and the Department of Energy.[1] Interestingly, China has always been a strong advocate of the integrated approach and it is likely that this will be reflected in the design and implementation of the CPEC energy programme. However, in these initiatives there are inherent risks which could jeopardize the endeavour and take Pakistan's energy sector back to square one - hence the timeliness of this topic.

The critical significance of the CPEC

If one follows the general rhetoric prevalent in Pakistan including that found in the media, the CPEC is characterized as an all-important, highly visible, highly praised yet highly controversial and highly criticized initiative. It is largely touted as payback from China for allowing it access to the Arabian Sea. The fact that there is no consensus on the narrative indicates that the message from the authorities is either not convincing enough for a sceptical audience or has not as yet taken root.

The CPEC Progress Report of January 2015 summarizes the CPEC portfolio[2] as having an overall investment of US $46 billion, of which the energy sector claims the lion's share of $27 billion. The rest of it ($19 billion) covers the construction of roads, railways, the Gwadar Port and its transportation links (sea, air and land), fibre optic cable systems, and urban mass transportation schemes. Since the programme is expected to be implemented over a 10-year period, the list of projects can only be taken as indicative of the overall size of the programme and it is assumed that there will be many changes as individual components in each of the broad categories are designed and developed. In fact, the updated list of projects[3] as of January 2017 is estimated to cost $54 billion, of which $35 billion is for energy projects. A relatively small but not insignificant portion of the financing, $11 billion, is disbursed through the Exim Bank of China on concessional terms (2 per cent interest with 20–25-year repayment), the China Development Bank, and the Industrial and Commercial Bank of China. The bulk of the financing, including all the energy projects, will be on commercial terms and therefore depends on the strength of individual projects, the quality of the reform agenda and country risk, among other contingent factors.

If the CPEC is implemented as envisaged, it would add 2–2.5 per cent to gross domestic product (GDP), and add projects valued at 17 per cent of Pakistan's 2015 GDP, equivalent to all direct foreign investment since 1970.[4] These are impressive figures, the likes of which Pakistan has never encountered throughout its economic history. During 2018 ongoing projects were largely being implemented on schedule and some are even ahead of schedule. In November 2016 the first consignment from China through the CPEC corridor was delivered to Gwadar Port for onward shipment to Africa and Western Asia.

One aspect does seem clear. The CPEC is not about concessional handouts but, more importantly, it is implicitly calling on Pakistan to catch up on the backlog of reform actions, improve governance, enhance security and build its capacity to enable it to mobilize commercial funding for the individual projects, presumably with guidance from Chinese authorities and experts. If this is the case, the CPEC can be said to be a well-thought out initiative designed to develop Pakistan rather than increase its dependence on handouts – the kind of programme that Pakistan needs for its long-term well-being. In effect, China is holding Pakistan's feet to the fire, to persuade Pakistan just what it must do to secure its transition to an economically powerful nation. In serving its own strategic interest, China is also implicitly investing in the CPEC's success.

Hence, if managed correctly, the CPEC could turn the country around. If not, it could become a liability of immense proportions. There seems to be no middle ground. With the limited options available to the country, this is an opportunity it cannot afford to squander.

Notwithstanding the inevitable changes over the 10-year programme period, a number of features stand out. The CPEC is the largest consolidated programme of energy investment in Pakistan and is expected to eventually add over 17,000 MW of power capacity, thus nearly doubling the existing grid of 22,500 MW. It focuses on indigenous energy sources and therefore is designed to reduce dependence and enhance energy security. It introduces solar and wind power on a scale never before envisaged in Pakistan. Looking at the individual components, there is clearly a balance between environmentally benign renewable energy resources (hydro, solar and wind) and a polluting fossil fuel (coal), the reserves of which are too large to ignore. China has extensive world-class expertise in each of these areas from manufacturing, project design, installation through to operation. It is the world leader in research and development (R&D) in solar and wind technology. The CPEC list of projects includes one of the largest solar farms in the world located at Bahawalpur, with an eventual capacity of 1,000 MW, of which the first stage of 100 MW is already operational. In light of these facts, the programme is clearly well-conceived and has been put together in the context of an integrated energy planning approach, tempered by strategic and energy security considerations, much like China's own energy plans. Early progress is indicative of an implementation performance surpassing the lacklustre norm of the last few decades. If managed correctly, the CPEC energy programme could prove to be a windfall and turning point for Pakistan's energy sector.

Building capacity

Through several national planning cycles, policymakers in Pakistan have ably articulated policy objectives for the energy sector to support the economy. The problem is not a lack of clarity on *what* needs to be done but *how* it is to be done. Rather than to offer prescriptive solutions, this chapter advocates building capacity to enable policymakers to make their own informed decisions – an essential ingredient for ownership. State-of-the-art findings of the World Bank Institute[5] conclude that capacity must be built concurrently at three levels: individual, institutional and policy. The individual level implies building skills; the institutional requires restructuring to meet objectives; and the policy environment provides incentives and governance structures. All three levels are necessary and all three must be mutually compatible. Even if one level is missing, capacity-building efforts will not bear fruit.

The IEP concept

In many developing countries, despite claims to the contrary, energy plans are largely confined to short-term remedial measures within individual energy sub-sectors. What is lacking is the ability to bring together all options for each sub-sector through a robust mechanism which establishes relative priorities. This encapsulates the concept of IEP. The objective is a programme of policy and investment options within each country's financial and capacity constraints. The mechanism must also prevent short-term decisions which deviate from a longer-term vision or, even worse, are launched without a clear vision. Pakistan's energy plans have yet to go beyond the short term and have therefore continued in a state of crisis. The CPEC energy programme is addressing this very concern. An example is Pakistan's preoccupation with the power sub-sector – this is only the visible tip of the energy sector iceberg. It is a result of the country's inability to emerge from a short-term approach. In the energy sector, where projects are typically highly capital-intensive with long lead times, cost-penalties of suboptimal decisions are prohibitive. Paradoxically, defining that long-term vision is an immediate requirement and adhering to it through the short and medium term is an imperative.

In its most sophisticated form IEP could be rather daunting for a non-technical readership. Hence, it is important to simplify and demystify the concept. IEP deploys the three essential levels of capacity building discussed above – individual, institutional and policy environment – and has two essential components:

- analysis that feeds the decision-making process; and
- an institutional structure at the policy level which facilitates sound decision making.[6]

IEP integrates energy sub-sector plans and policies to support national objectives providing a range of policy scenarios which are tested for impact on the economy, as illustrated in the diagram below.[7]

It employs a five-stage iterative process. Starting with quantified national socio-economic objectives, the IEP process determines energy demand, identifies supply options,

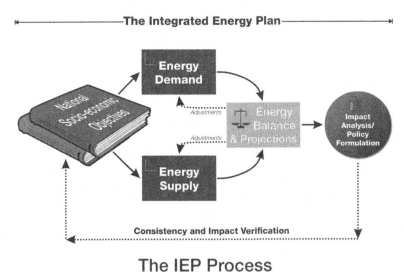

Figure 25.1 The IEP Process

prepares energy balance projections, and carries out an impact analysis of interventions (policy and investment) which is then fed back for impact verification. The most sophisticated part is the construction of an 'energy balance'. The flow chart shown below,[8] developed over several years from a number of sources, gives an idea of the logic, sequence, type of inputs and computations required, starting from energy supply through its processing, conversions and transmission, to its consumption.

IEP operates in three tiers: linking the economy with the energy sector; integration of energy sub-sectors within the overall sector; and planning within each sub-sector. IEP addresses short-, medium- and long-term issues and identifies the policy tools to address issues and remove bottlenecks. The short-term effectiveness needs to be emphasized. Many developing countries have favourable long-term prospects but to get there they need to navigate the troublesome short term. Then there is the erroneous preconception that IEP serves the long term only. In fact, its short-term tools are the most effective because they ensure that the long-term view is not compromised. Also, by definition, short-term data is more reliable and therefore lends itself to more accurate analysis. Very importantly, the effective implementation of IEP requires a separate energy ministry with overarching responsibility for the sector and access to top policy levels. That is vital. As an interim measure, the effort can be located within a neutral agency such as a national planning ministry.

Examples of policy objectives which IEP can help to achieve include determining energy needs to achieve national growth while maintaining environmental standards; optimizing the energy supply mix; identifying and prioritizing energy conservation measures; enhancing energy security through diversification and reducing dependence;

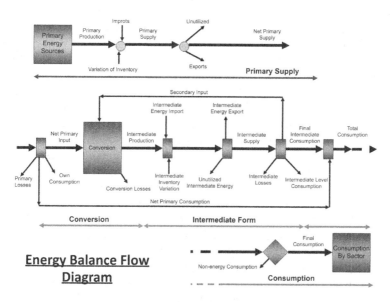

Figure 25.2 Energy balance flow diagram

meeting energy needs of the poor; saving foreign exchange; reducing trade deficits; and raising revenues for sustained energy sector development. Without IEP, the default energy situation drives the outcome in each of the areas mentioned. With IEP, policymakers are able to influence these often conflicting economic objectives.

Brief history and international experience

The history of IEP at the international level reveals some critical lessons for the way forward. IEP was introduced in the 1970s. In the United States the seminal work of Amory Lovins could be construed as a starting point.[9] It was successful in transforming energy planning in many developing countries. The World Bank's involvement emanated from two programmes. The first was the Energy Sector Assessment Programme introduced in the late 1970s and early 1980s assessed energy issues and options for some 70 countries using the integrated approach. This gave rise to the Energy Sector Management Assistance Programme providing policy and pre-investment advice which, in four years, had expanded to 45 countries with IEP as one of its flagship activities.

In the early 1990s there was a major setback. Following the collapse of the former Soviet Union, IEP suffered a reversal, largely triggered by the international development community's reluctance to encourage anything that might be construed as supporting a central planning ideology. In 1993 the World Bank sought to introduce market-based reform in the world's largest upstream oil sector via the Russia Oil Rehabilitation Project.[10] While the operation had an ambitious policy reform agenda, IEP was conspicuously absent. The IEP nomenclature was largely dropped, and its principles, while not entirely eliminated, were expected to re-emerge through free market reform, i.e. the free market would determine appropriate policy choices. In hindsight, this was, at best, a premature assumption since the free market would take a long time to mature. At worst, it was a serious mistake.

Interestingly, the former Soviet Union's newly independent states, while assimilating market reform principles to varying degrees, retained the essence of the IEP approach. Perhaps the reason for this was that the initial euphoria of independence rapidly gave way to the common sense of economic integration among the new republics.[11] The new states maintained at least a modicum of a regional integrated approach in their energy sector planning. However, many other countries dropped IEP. They then began to regret their mistake and eventually started clamouring for its return. Finally, in response, the Bank energy strategy[12] accorded top priority to sector-wide planning. The strategy advocates a holistic engagement to catalyse transformation of the sector in the context of long-term, system-wide planning. It involves system-wide optimization, supply-demand integration and, where justified, expanding the coverage to the regional level. This change clearly signals the triumph of economic common sense over ideology to achieve a practical balance. It is an example of the World Bank learning from its mistakes and adjusting accordingly. It also demonstrates the unfortunate cost of delayed action. Through it all, China steadfastly upheld the principles of IEP in developing its own energy policy. There is every reason to believe that this approach will be supported by China under the CPEC initiative, provided Pakistan endorses it.

In general, in countries where energy development has been well managed, the two key characteristics of IEP have been maintained: (i) robust integrated analysis; and (ii) well-coordinated institutional arrangements at the policy level. The latter take the form of a separate energy ministry/agency or an integrated energy department in a central ministry.

Examples include Belarus, Bulgaria, Cambodia, the Czech Republic, Hungary, Indonesia, Kazakhstan, Kyrgyzstan, Malaysia, the Philippines, Poland, Romania, the Russian Federation, Slovakia, Tajikistan, Thailand, Turkey, Uganda, the Ukraine, Uzbekistan and Vietnam.[13] Two of these countries, Turkey and Kazakhstan, which have integrated line ministries, are good models for Pakistan.

India-Pakistan energy trade

Given appropriate policies and incentives, trade between India and Pakistan should be able to expand exponentially, simply because of their common long border and the shared heritage. A report published in 2013 by the Woodrow Wilson Center[14] conservatively estimates that the present level of trade of US $2.5 billion could be readily increased to $40 billion, under normalized conditions. And a significant portion of this would be energy trade. Trade prospects are currently hampered by perceived or real security issues often unduly amplified for political reasons. Trade and security present a chicken-and-egg situation. Given the potential benefits there for the taking, the two countries do not have the luxury of waiting for the security situation to normalize before expanding trade, the more so since trade often leads to the improving of security. Therefore, the approach strongly advocated is to build trade and peace will follow. But, in order to maximize the mutual benefits of such a future, both countries clearly need to give more consideration to the nature of their relationship.

Size and characteristics of the energy sector

Figures 25.3 and 25.4[15] give an idea of the dimensions of Pakistan's energy supply and consumption in 2015.

Total primary energy supply in Pakistan is 70 million metric tons of oil equivalent (MTOE), which can be broken down thus: natural gas 43 per cent, oil 36 per cent, hydropower 11 per cent, coal 7 per cent, and nuclear, LPG and imported power 3 per cent. Pakistan imports 30 per cent of its energy, mostly in the form of crude oil and related products, at a cost of US $15 billion annually. Energy consumption in that year was 40 MTOE, industry being the dominant consumer with 35 per cent of the market, followed by transport (32 per cent) and household (25 per cent).

The figures from India[16] shown below, while not entirely compatible with those of Pakistan, do serve the purpose of this discussion. Two years are represented below, 2015 and 2012.

The figures for 2012 are given below. For 2012, the figures included an explicit provision for biofuels which was excluded in the 2015 figures.

India's primary supply is 680 MTOE, 43 per cent from coal, 24 per cent from biofuels, 22 per cent from oil, 8 per cent from natural gas. The dominant consumer is the residential sector (40 per cent) followed by industry (39 per cent) and transport (14 per cent). In 2017 oil imports stood at US $80 billion per annum.

Inherent in these figures is a key lesson that Pakistan's analysts and policymakers can learn from India. India's figures, unlike Pakistan's, include biofuels. This will be discussed later in this chapter.

In both countries, a strong correlation between growth rates for energy consumption and GDP[17] confirm that energy fuels the economy and, conversely, its shortage impedes economic growth. Energy shortages have resulted in prohibitive losses in both

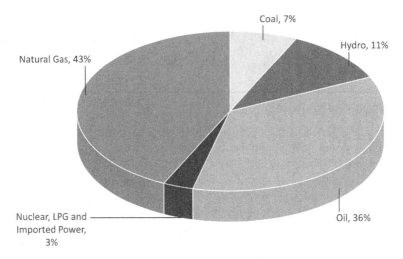

Figure 25.3 Primary commercial energy supply totalling 70 MTOE, 2015

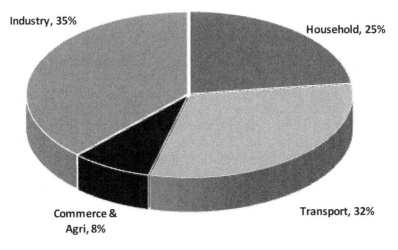

Figure 25.4 Commercial energy consumption totalling 40 MTOE, 2015

countries. In Pakistan's industrial sector alone, power outages depress GDP by 2.5 per cent.[18] Energy consumption per head,[19] at less than one-third of the world average in both countries, reflects the state of development and the incidence of poverty. Energy consumption per dollar of GDP growth,[20] three times the world average, indicates low energy-use efficiency. In a constrained supply situation, efficiency gains mean increased supply.

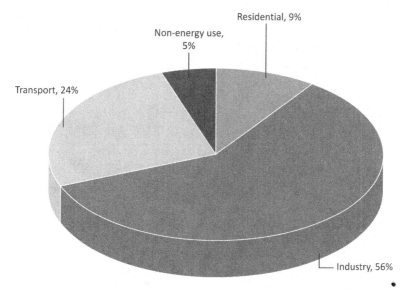

Figure 25.5 Primary commercial energy supply, totalling 769 MTOE, 2015

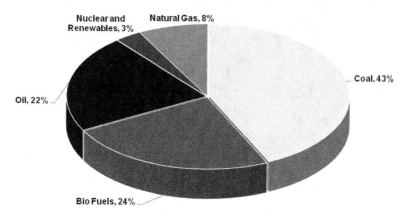

Figure 25.6 Energy consumption by sector, totalling 484 MTOE, 2015

IEP in Pakistan: history and prospects

As mentioned earlier, on the analytical side of IEP, the most sophisticated aspect is the energy balance. The Hydrocarbon Development Institute of Pakistan produces the *Energy Yearbook* which includes comprehensive energy balances – testimony to the excellence within Pakistan despite the brain drain and a source of hope for the future.

IEP is therefore not unknown in Pakistan. It was introduced in the early 1980s.[21] The government of the day was firmly committed to introducing IEP. It established a planning unit within the Directorate General of Energy Resources with the intention of moving this to a central neutral location in the Planning Division. Administrative orders[22] were issued, budgets were approved and the necessary Gazette Notification[23] was published – all in a matter of a few weeks. An Energy Policy Board, with top-level representation

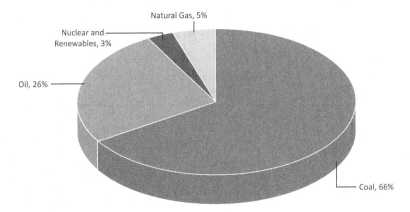

Figure 25.7 Primary commercial energy supply, totalling 680 MTOE, 2012

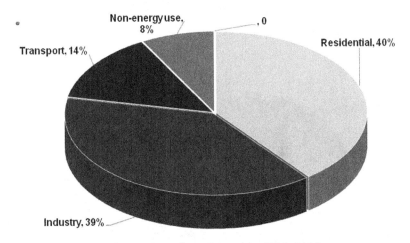

Figure 25.8 Energy consumption by sector, totalling 422 MTOE, 2012

from energy-related ministries, was instituted to facilitate integration with national plans and policies. In bureaucratic parlance, this meant a done deal.

A noteworthy start – but unravelling was inevitable. There was no follow-through on the necessary organizational changes. Instead of moving to a simple integrated structure, there was a gradual fragmentation of policy institutions, compounding the complexity, confusion and overlap of responsibilities. Instead of one integrated ministry there are now over 15 agencies and ministries,[24] making coordination impossible. The situation in India is similar. Separate federal ministries exist for coal, power, renewables, and petroleum and natural gas, and there are a host of regulatory agencies with overlapping mandates.

There are two main reasons for the unravelling and both are related to serious governance issues. The first is the power of vested interests within and outside the country, always wary of sound analysis that exposes their efforts to promote suboptimal schemes. If nothing else, increased 'rent' would have to be paid to push through schemes in the face of compelling evidence that says otherwise. The second is the expected inertia of the bureaucracy to resist change particularly involving authority shifts or downsizing.

Restarting IEP and potential pitfalls

Going forward, while bureaucratic wrangling, turf battles, job protection and efforts by vested interests can be expected, with political and administrative resolve, the situation can be remedied rapidly. The steps to start IEP in Pakistan have been taken before. Necessary records are retrievable. The sophisticated analytical component is, paradoxically, easy to handle. The Planning Division already has the capability of preparing energy balances using advanced modelling techniques. There are, however, questions about the accuracy of input data and the conspicuous absence of non-commercial energy. But these are details and can be addressed by acquiring requisite data and analytical skills. However, the greater problem is that the information generated does not find its way to the country's policymakers. A new Ministry of Energy, which incorporates all the energy sub-sectors, will go a long way to address this. To signal political will, the intention to form the new ministry must be officially announced. Not doing so increases the risk of unravelling. As an interim measure, the new initiative can be housed in a central neutral location such as the Planning Ministry. The Ministry of Energy can then be phased-in gradually to minimize organizational disruption.

The Nawaz Sharif government formed a Ministry of Energy by merging the Ministry of Petroleum and Natural Resources with the Ministry of Water and Power. However, hydropower was transferred to another Ministry of Water Resources – a retrograde step that once again increased fragmentation. This legacy of 'one step forward, two steps back' must be checked. Fragmentation can also take the form of subnational energy plans, e.g. in 2015 the Pakhtunkhwa Province called for tenders for a provincial integrated energy plan – again a retrogressive step.

A promising start is now being made by the Khan government's Planning Ministry to reintroduce IEP on a national scale with support from USAID/Department of Energy. As this activity proceeds, care needs to be taken not simply to upgrade the analytical capability, which is the relatively easy task but, more importantly, to galvanize the necessary institutional changes at the policy level to facilitate implementation. Failing to do so could result in yet another study relegated to the shelf. Another word of caution is that efforts to reintroduce IEP must not start everything from scratch but take into account the useful work that is already being done such as data collection and collation. The gaps in the process would need to be identified and the requisite capacity built up to fill the gaps.

Addressing Pakistan's energy issues through IEP

In showing how IEP can address energy issues, the 13 issues identified earlier have been combined into five sets of issues, primarily focused on Pakistan, and comparisons made with the situation in India. While this is not a comprehensive 'issues and options' exercise, in all likelihood the issues raised would be given high priority in such an undertaking.

The first set: A key benefit of IEP is its ability to quantify the cost penalty of pursuing suboptimal plans – vital for a cash-strapped economy confronted with poverty and inequitable income distribution, where access to and affordability of energy are critical concerns among the urban and rural poor.

No country adheres to the optimum. Departures will be necessary. However, the degree of departure from the optimum marks the difference between success and failure of energy policy. Knowing the cost of deviation is vital for informed decision making. Without IEP, the optimum remains undetermined as does the cost of deviations.

Pakistan purports to have a pro-poor energy policy. Poverty reduction relies on economic growth coupled with social protection. Poverty eradication requires a long-term vision. In Pakistan the vision is drowned out by immediate concerns, resulting in prohibitively expensive short-term measures with little relevance to the poor. Recent examples include rental power plants, an extremely expensive option; diesel back-up generators for individual households, an improper choice of fuel; development of compressed natural gas for transport without assessing long-term availability and a lack of coordination within the same sub-sector; skewed subsidy arrangements that favour the wrong segments of the population; and bailouts to resolve circular debt without addressing endemic issues.

Concerning poverty and the state of the energy sector in India, Charles Ebinger says,[25]

> Of its nearly 1.2 billion people, approximately 820 million live on less than $2 per day ... Access to energy in India is still the preserve of a small minority. 404 million people lack even rudimentary access to electricity, and 855 million are dependent on biomass and other traditional sources for cooking.

Social protection is therefore an inescapable requirement. This involves subsidies in the short term. Subsidies can be a powerful tool if they are:

- targeted at the deserving groups only – and this implies means testing;
- affordable – no country can give what is does not have without incurring penalties such as deficits, depreciation of currency, etc.;
- transparent – and not buried in some quasi-fiscal transactions;
- consistent with a long-term view; and
- the moral hazard of encouraging waste is minimized.

By measuring the impact of energy subsidies on the economy, IEP enables informed choices. It provides the essential tool to assess the types, extent and cost of subsidies to alleviate poverty in the short term, within the confines of the resource envelope.

The second set: A substantial resource potential and a large, expanding deficit are two contradictory characteristics of the region's energy sector. In Pakistan, the deficit was 20 MTOE in 2017

and is predicted to increase to 120 MTOE by 2025.[26] In India, to support its growing economy, the country's current power capacity of 200 GW would need to be doubled by the year 2035, an equally daunting task.[27] These figures also underscore the vast economic potential for energy exchange between the two countries or collaboration in energy import from outside the region.

Pakistan's large-hydro potential is 41,700 MW with only 16 per cent harnessed.[28] A mere 4 per cent of the 1,500 MW small-hydro potential has been tapped.[29] Solar and wind resources remain virtually untouched. Wind regime studies estimate a potential of 41,000 MW.[30] These are large figures bearing in mind that the total installed power capacity in Pakistan is 22,500 MW. The Thar coal deposits, the world's fifth largest, remain largely unexploited with only 1 per cent proven reserves.[31] Petroleum potential remains under-evaluated due to low drilling density (one-fifth of the world average)[32] despite impressive success rates (seven times the world average).[33] In Pakistan's vast pro-spective basin (830,000 sq km), less than 4 per cent of probable oil reserves and 19 per cent of gas reserves have been confirmed.[34] And then there are the potentially large unexploited shale gas deposits. Had these resources been developed Pakistan would not be focusing on huge import schemes such as CASA 1000, TAPI, the Iran Pipeline or LNG import terminals. The latter would perhaps have been export terminals.

The combination of prohibitive deficits and abundant resources tempts policymakers to promote all forms of energy. This is a common trap that is wasteful and unaffordable. IEP can prevent this by striking an affordable balance. Both countries have the advantage of drawing on the experience, good and bad, of more advanced countries. Take, for example, Germany's faltering renewable energy programme[35] – a case of politically influenced reform. Power shortfalls due to inadequate solar and wind technology neces-sitated the recommissioning of coal-fired plants. So, while achieving the 25 per cent target of renewables in its fuel mix, emissions actually increased. In retrospect, one can treat this situation as a learning curve. For Germany, it has set in motion a firm policy direction which, while falling short of its initial target, will inevitably yield future economic benefits as the technology improves. For others, the enthusiasm for developing wind and solar photo-voltaic resources must be tempered with economic and technological reality.

CPEC energy projects are focused on power generation using renewables and coal. Both energy sources deserve special comment. As energy specialists maintain: renewable energy is free but not cheap. While R&D expenditure in wind and solar generation in China, Germany, Spain and other countries is resulting in lowering costs, under present suppressed oil price regimes, the economic crossover point of fossil fuel generation versus wind and solar, has inevitably been delayed. The strategy for Pakistan should be to posi-tion itself for a major push at the time of the crossover. In the meantime, it should restrict itself to pilot schemes or to investments mainly in areas remote from the power grid and where it makes clear economic sense. Economic viability and timing would need to be carefully assessed on a case-by-case basis. Partnership with China under the CPEC should help in this regard as China is the world's leader in R&D in solar and wind technology.

Common rhetoric labels Thar coal as very low quality with high ash, sulphur and moisture content. Therefore, for coal-fired power generation, pollution levels would be high and purification costs prohibitive. However, for such large potential deposits, the amount of exploratory work done so far is negligible; far greater efforts are needed before we can come to a reliable conclusion. Moreover, 80 per cent of current atmospheric pol-lution levels in Pakistan are attributable to transport, according to a World Bank report.[36] This is mainly due to existing environmental standards not being enforced. It is worth examining that, if these levels were reduced appreciably, how much coal-fired gen-eration would become feasible within the same pollution envelope? Therefore, coal-based power generation is indeed worth pursuing provided emission standards for transport are enforced and, as is being done under the CPEC, clean coal technologies are deployed.

It is the management of resources, not their abundance, that marks the difference between success and failure of economies. IEP provides the management tools which enable resource management, as well as monitoring and forecasting of technological innovation.

The third set: the convoluted problem of circular debt is the result of payment-arrears of power utilities, their suppliers and their clients. Revenues are insufficient and produc-tion costs too high. Endemic issues relate to system management and structure, stop-go reforms, plant replacement and maintenance, operational efficiency, system losses (25 per cent of net generation) including theft, and tariff collection (30 per cent outstanding).[37]

Similarly, in India, the utilities in Mumbai and Delhi were facing losses of 30 per cent in 2016. Pakistan's installed capacity is around 22,500 MW and the peak demand is around 15,000 MW of which only 70 per cent is being met.[38] Consequently, less than half of Pakistan's installed capacity is effectively utilized. This is too low even considering the prevailing mix of thermal and hydroelectric generation, which is sensitive to seasonal fluctuations in water levels. For independent private power producers (IPPs), the take-or-pay contractual arrangements in place and the inability of public power utilities to pay, severely restricts the power output of the IPPs.[39]

Instead of focusing on the endemic issues, the solution has been a series of unconditional bailouts which present a major moral hazard. IEP would address endemic issues and rely less on stop-gap bailouts. No amount of bailout will improve the situation without time-bound conditions for tackling endemic issues and that is what IEP brings to bear.

Given the potential of significant IPP investments in the power sector from China,[40] IEP becomes even more critical as a means of addressing endemic problems. Without it, the new power plants, transmission and distribution lines will eventually sink into the same endemic quagmire and the incremental capacity could fade as rapidly as it came on stream.

The fourth set: as reflected in *Energy Yearbook* statistics, Pakistan's policymakers have neglected non-commercial/traditional energy. Commercial energy is a key ingredient of national growth and warrants the lion's share of attention from policymakers under pressure to jump-start the economy. There is an inherent fallacy here. While commercial energy stimulates GDP growth, neglect of non-commercial consumers retards growth over the longer term. Consequent unregulated and unchecked practices and technologies have disastrous effects on the eco-system and on poverty. Integrating non-commercial energy through IEP changes the picture dramatically, as shown below.

Biofuels head the list by a large margin and households become the primary consumer, as is the case with India. The most egregious aspect of the omission is that traditional energy accounts for half of the overall demand.[41] An integrated picture will drive major shifts in emphasis. More efficient household cook-stoves will have greater impact than industrial energy conservation. Environment and poverty impacts will be brought to the very forefront. This is the crucial impact of IEP analysis without which such factors remain unaddressed or, at best, are tackled on a sporadic basis.

The fifth set: missed opportunities have contributed significantly to the decline of the energy sector. One of many examples relates to Central Asia in the early to mid-1990s.[42] The new republics, under immense internal economic pressures, actively pursued the route through Pakistan to export surplus energy to the energy-starved South Asian market and to gain access to the Arabian Sea. This was long before the security situation had begun to deteriorate. Given the high stakes, competitors were promoting alternative routes. This development clearly warranted a coordinated effort from Pakistani and Indian authorities, both public and private, rather than the lukewarm and uncoordinated response. The rest is history. One can only surmise how the trade corridors would have transformed the region. Benefits from trade, energy transport tariffs and increased energy supplies would have brought prosperity to Afghanistan, Pakistan and India. Interdependence and economic uplift of neglected areas would have helped to mitigate, even prevent, the conflict which engulfs the region today. IEP, had it existed, would have signalled the need to aggressively pursue southern corridor projects as a regional policy imperative.

The important thing is to learn from these mistakes. Pakistan has been offered yet another chance with the CPEC. This new opportunity, perhaps the best yet, needs to become a success story.

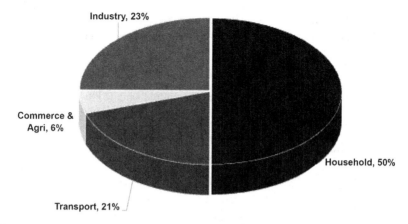

Figure 25.9 Energy consumption: commercial and non-commercial

A glimpse into the future

The vision, and indeed a comprehensive energy plan will emerge through IEP analysis and the realization of the vision through its implementation. But we can make some tentative predictions for a post-IEP future. Oil and gas exploration and production will be enhanced. Small and large hydropower schemes will be implemented. Thar and other coal deposits will be developed keeping environmental trade-offs in mind with enforcement of transport emissions regulations; solar and wind power will be harnessed as the economic crossover with fossil fuels occurs. Integrated forestry practices will maintain a maximum allowable cut, thus containing environmental degradation while securing fuelwood and agricultural residue supplies. Nuclear power enhancement will provide energy security. Regional energy projects (import and export) will be operational. Appropriate subsidy policies will provide an affordable level of social protection. Energy conservation, especially in the domestic, industrial and transport sectors, will add to the supply mix. Producer and consumer pricing, taxation, and business incentives will be streamlined, allowing for balanced development with optimum supply and utilization patterns. With the exception of strategic assets, most of the sector will be in private hands, under well-defined regulations managed by independent regulatory agencies. The Ministry of Energy will implement IEP and formulate energy policies in consultation with all stakeholders.

All this will be done within the confines of the resource and capacity envelope at least cost to the economy. Pakistan will be a net energy exporter and the country will be gaining financially and economically from export earnings and revenues from a vibrant private sector.

How rapidly this scenario unfolds depends on implementation which, in turn, depends on political will. But, if the will is there, improvements will be visible within a year of IEP start-up.

Conclusion

IEP should once again become the centrepiece of the energy reform agenda of Pakistan as a core component of the CPEC initiative. Policymakers can then go beyond what needs to be done to how it needs to be done. The strengthened policy environment will be capable of addressing the most serious energy issues and promoting regional energy trade, essential prerequisites for the successful implementation of the CPEC. The revival of the energy sector will fuel enhanced inclusive economic growth. The time to act is now and, with the CPEC there to help it along, Pakistan must take the initiative.

Notes

1 Technical assistance support has been initiated for reintroducing IEP by the Planning Commission of Pakistan. Consultants have been engaged under USAID funding and are due to commence their work shortly.
2 CPEC Progress Report, Planning Commission, January 2015.
3 CPEC Planning Commission Updates, 2016.
4 Ibid.
5 'Developing Capacity Interventions at Three Levels', Annual Report, Washington, DC, World Bank Institute, 2005.
6 IEP concepts and principles are based on Ziad Alahdad, 'Pakistan's Energy Sector: Putting It All Together', in *Pakistan's Interminable Energy Crisis: Is There Any Way Out?* Washington, DC, Woodrow Wilson Center, 2015; Ziad Alahdad, 'Pakistan's Energy Sector: From Crisis to Crisis—Breaking the Chain', PIDE Monograph Series, Pakistan Institute of Development Economics, Islamabad, 2012. Available at www.pide.org.pk/pdf/publications/Monograph/Pakistans%20Energy%20Sector%20From%20Crisis%20to%20Crisis-Breaking%20the%20Chain.
pdf; Ziad Alahdad, 'Turning Energy Around', in Maleeha Lodhi (ed.) *Pakistan beyond the Crisis State*, New York, Columbia University Press, 2011; and Mohan Munasinghe, 'Integrated National Energy Planning in Developing Countries', *Natural Resources Forum*, vol. 4, pp. 359–74. Available through World Bank Reprint Series, no. 165).
7 Diagram developed by the author based on Mohan Munasinghe, 'Integrated National Energy Planning in Developing Countries'.
8 Flow diagram developed by the author over several years from various sources.
9 Amory Lovins, 'Energy Strategy: The Road Not Taken', *Foreign Affairs*, October 1976. Document ID E77–01.
10 At the time, the author was task manager for the Russia Oil Rehabilitation Project, the World Bank's largest investment operation and the first in the Russian Federation.
11 At the time, the author was the deputy chief and coordinator of energy operations at the World Bank's Regional Mission in Central Asia. He was a member of the team which established the Mission.
12 World Bank Group, 'Toward a Sustainable Energy Future for All: Directions for the World Bank Group's Energy Sector', 2013. Available at www-wds.worldbank.org/external/default/WDSContentServer/WDSP/IB/2013/07/17/000456286_20130717103746/Rendered/PDF/795970SST0SecM00box377380B00PUBLIC0.pdf.
13 Ziad Alahdad, 'Pakistan's Energy Sector'.
14 Michael Kugelman, 'The Pakistan India Trade Relationship: Prospects, Profits and Pitfalls', in *Pakistan-India Trade: What Needs to be Done? What Does It Matter?*, Washington, DC, Woodrow Wilson Center, 2013.
15 *Pakistan Energy Yearbook 2013*, Hydrocarbon Development Institute of Pakistan, Ministry of Petroleum and Natural Resources, April 2014.
16 'Energy Statistics', Central Statistics Office, Ministry of Statistics and Programme Implementation, Government of India, New Delhi.
17 Federal Bureau of Statistics, Government of Pakistan, Islamabad; 'Energy Statistics', Central Statistics Office, Ministry of Statistics and Programme Implementation, Government of India, New Delhi.
18 'State of the Economy: Pulling Back from the Abyss', Third Annual Report, Institute of Public Policy, Beaconhouse National University, Lahore, 2010. Available at http://ippbnu.org/AR/3AR.pdf.
19 Derived from Akhtar Awan, 'Renewable Energy and Pakistan', presentation at Pakistan government Planning Commission, Islamabad, 2008; 'Energy Statistics', Central Statistics Office, Ministry of Statistics and Programme Implementation, Government of India, New Delhi.
20 Ibid
21 At the time, the author was the World Bank's adviser on energy projects in Pakistan.

22 'Administrative Approval and Expenditure Sanction in Respect of Energy Planning and Development Project (ENERPLAN)', Planning and Development Division directive, Government of Pakistan, number Energy/ENP/19(1)PC/84, 1 October 1984.
23 Gazette Notification number 12 (29–1) Energy/PC/83, Government of Pakistan, 26 September 1984.
24 Alahdad, 'Pakistan's Energy Sector'.
25 Charles K. Ebinger, *Energy and Security in South Asia: Cooperation or Conflict*, Washington, DC, Brookings Institution, 2011.
26 'Medium-Term Development Framework: 2005–10', Pakistan Planning Commission, government of Pakistan, May 2005.
27 Ebinger, *Energy and Security in South Asia*.
28 Awan, 'Renewable Energy and Pakistan'.
29 Ibid.
30 Ibid.
31 *Pakistan Energy Yearbook 2013*.
32 'Successful Past and a Brighter Future', in *Opportunities in Pakistan's Oil and Gas Sector*, Ministry of Petroleum and Natural Resources, Government of Pakistan, 2009.
33 Ibid.
34 Oil and gas theoretical/probable reserves come from 'An Overview of Fossil Fuel Energy sources of Pakistan', Ministry of Petroleum and Natural Resources, 2008. Confirmed/proven reserves and production figures come from *Pakistan Energy Yearbook 2010*, Hydrocarbon Development Institute of Pakistan, Ministry of Petroleum and Natural Resources, 2011.
35 Holman Jenkins, 'Germany Reinvents the Energy Crisis', *Wall Street Journal*, 8 November 2013. Available at www.wsj.com/articles/SB10001424052702304448204579185720802195590.
36 World Bank, 'Policy Options to Address the Cost of Air Pollution in Pakistan', Non-Lending Technical Assistance Draft Report, May 2011.
37 Achilles G. Adamantiades and Vladislav Vucetic, 'Power Sector Reform in Pakistan: Issues and Challenges', in Robert M. Hathaway, Bhumika Muchhala and Michael Kugelman (eds) *Fueling the Future: Meeting Pakistan's Needs in the 21st Century*, Washington, DC, Woodrow Wilson Center, 2007. Available at www.wilsoncenter.org/sites/default/files/Asia_FuelingtheFuture_rptmain.pdf.
38 Ebinger, *Energy and Security in South Asia*, p. 81; and Adamantiades and Vucetic, 'Power Sector Reform in Pakistan', p. 110.
39 Julia M. Fraser, 'Lessons from the Independent Private Power Experience in Pakistan', Energy and Mining Sector Board Discussion Paper No.14, World Bank, Washington, DC, May 2005. Available at http://info.worldbank.org/etools/docs/library/240338/Lessons%20from%20the%20Independent%20Private%20Power%20Experience%20in%20Pakistan.pdf. With take-or-pay contracts, the bulk buyer of electricity (the utility) is obligated to pay for an agreed minimum power offtake from the producer, irrespective of whether the buyer has actually taken that minimum level.
40 CPEC Province-wise List of Energy Projects, 1 May 2015. This list was compiled by BIPP based on its analysis of data released by the Ministry of Planning, Development and Reform, Government of Pakistan.
41 S. Qureshi, 'Energy, Poverty Reduction and Equitable Development in Pakistan', in Robert M. Hathaway, Bhumika Muchhala and Michael Kugelman (eds) *Fueling the Future: Meeting Pakistan's Needs in the 21st Century*, Washington, DC, Woodrow Wilson Center, 2007. Available at www.wilsoncenter.org/sites/default/files/Asia_FuelingtheFuture_rptmain.pdf.
42 At the time, the author was the deputy chief and coordinator of energy operations at the World Bank's Regional Mission in Central Asia. He was a member of the team which established the Mission.

Part VI
Conclusion

26

The last word

Shahid Javed Burki

The 10th general election after the adoption of the 1973 Constitution was held on 25 July 2018 and saw Imran Khan, the cricketer-turned-politician, become Pakistan's 22nd Prime Minister. His party, the Pakistan Tehreek-e-Insaf (PTI), formed a coalition with a number of smaller parties to gain a majority in the National Assembly. The long-established Pakistan Peoples Party (PPP) and the Pakistan Muslim League (Nawaz) (PML–N) were forced onto the Opposition benches and the Khan group was able to elect the Speaker and Deputy Speaker of the Assembly from its ranks. What would this political earthquake produce for Pakistan?

The future is hard to predict for a country such as Pakistan where so much remains unsettled even after more than seven decades of its existence as an independent state. According to Philipp Tetlock and Dan Gardner in *Superforecasting*, the future can indeed be foretold, at least in the short term. Their definition of the 'short term' is about a year or two. They show that prophecy is not a divine gift, but a skill that can be practised and improved. Following the British philosopher Isaiah Berlin, they divide those who speculate about the future into two categories: hedgehogs, whose understanding about the future depends on one or two big ideas; and foxes, who think the world is too complicated to boil down into a single conclusion.[1] I count myself among Berlin's foxes.

In discussing Pakistan's future, it is fair to say that the country has been through some unusual experiences from the time of its birth more than 70 years ago. To borrow Naseem Taleb's phrase, Pakistan has had many 'black swan' moments in its past and the likelihood of the country being shocked again cannot be ruled out. Usually, a 'black swan' moment is the one that is actually very unlikely to occur, but the country has already experienced several such moments in the course of its history.[2] More may hit Pakistan in the years to come.

Given that, what predictions can be made about Pakistan's future? Will the already charged political situation become more unmanageable following the election in late 2018 of Imran Khan as Prime Minister? Will this encourage the military to intervene once again and dispense with democracy? Will the separatist movement in the restive province of Balochistan put even more pressure on the political integrity of the Pakistani nation-state? Will the loosening of the fiscal strings in preparation for the elections take the country towards bankruptcy? Will relations with India deteriorate further with confrontation between the two nuclear states to extend beyond the Line of Control in the disputed territory of Kashmir? Will the redefined American effort in Afghanistan fail, leading to that country's disintegration into mini-Islamic and -tribal states?

Since 2016 there have been a number of significant changes on the global scene. These were the consequences of many developments, two of which will be consequential for Pakistan. The first was the impact that the presidency of Donald Trump would have on the global system. The second was the continuing economic rise of the People's Republic of China. The country has increased the size of its economy 32-fold since 1980 when it began to open up to the outside world. China now expects to see its economy expand at an average annual rate of 6 per cent in the next decade, and could become the world's largest economy, thereby overtaking the United States, the current leader. A weakened United States under Donald Trump, its maverick President and a strengthened China under assertive President Xi Jinping have resulted in pushing Pakistan into the Chinese orbit. In the years ahead, Pakistan will undoubtedly move closer to Beijing.[3]

The period following the election of Khan in 2018 should provide some indication of the political direction in which Pakistan is headed. The main political parties agreed to use the preliminary results from the population census conducted in 2017 to demarcate the constituencies for the national and provincial assemblies. At the national level, Punjab lost nine seats and these were to be divided among the remaining provinces.

One issue that was solved and remains of critical importance for the country's future concerns the treatment of the federally administered tribal areas, the FATAs. For the last 70 years they have been treated separately for administrative purposes. The British-era Frontier Crimes Regulations were used for maintaining law and order in the region. Criminal as well as civil cases are settled by *jirgas* – councils of elders – over which the local tribal chiefs exercised a great deal of influence. The judicial system that administers justice in other parts of the country has no role in the FATAs.

Development work was also handled by the tribal chiefs. Government grants for this purpose were handed over to them to be used mostly at their discretion. This further added to their authority. The separateness of the FATAs made it difficult for the governments in Islamabad and Peshawar, the capital of the province of Khyber Pakhtunkhawa (KP). A committee set up by the National Assembly recommended the merger of the FATAs into the KP. Its recommendation was accepted and the tribal areas joined the province. This was an importnat development since this long-neglected area of the country may be able to make economic and social progress, denying the insurgent groups such as the Taliban of the sanctuaries they have enjoyed for years.

There are many reasons for being optimistic about the country's future. In *Pakistan: A Hard Country* Anatol Lieven remarks on the resilience of the Pakistani people.[4] They have successfully dealt with many 'black swan' moments. Overall, 2017 was a remarkable year in politics. There are not many examples – certainly not in the Muslim world – of a powerful prime minister backed by a solid parliamentary majority being forced to leave office following a carefully deliberated verdict by the Supreme Court. But progress was not confined to politics. The economy rebounded; the growth rate in 2018 reached 5.7 per cent. The Chinese investment began to flow in under the China–Pakistan Economic Corridor initiative and may add another percentage point to the rate of growth. The private sector is now even more involved in promoting social development in the country. According to this way of looking at the country, this fox believes that the future looks promising for Pakistan.

Pakistan's future also depends on the way the country is perceived by the rest of the world. The country's narrative needs to change. It is viewed negatively by the world at large in part because of the way Pakistanis themselves view their present and their future. An American journalist who writes frequently about Pakistan commented that when Pakistanis talk about their country, their views are mostly negative, as though they have given up hope for their country. The journalist was right; I hear the same kind of talk whenever I visit Pakistan. Even the large Pakistani diaspora in the United States, of which I am a part, has negative views about their country of origin.

The Western press has indeed contributed to the development of this narrative. There are two subjects that cause it to draw negative attention to Pakistan. One is the way in which women are treated in the Islamic world and the other is how Muslim countries deal with religious minorities. Stories related to these subjects make the headlines even if they are positive. In 2017 the *New York Times* and the *Washington Post* carried positive stories about women and minorities in Pakistan. The former featured an analysis of the decline of Pakistan's film industry since the days of the military dictator, President Zia ul-Haq. Journalist Mehreen Zahra-Malik wrote that a 'film about a rape victim who fights to bring her politically powerful attacker to justice has rankled Pakistani censors but emboldened women to speak about sexual assault in a country where the discussion of such topics is discouraged'.[5]

The film, *Verna*, was banned by Pakistan's Central Board for its 'edgy content' that 'maligned state institutions'. However, public outcry, fuelled by extensive news coverage and a social media campaign, led to the lifting of the ban by the appellate board. Zhara-Malik reminded her readers that this controversy was the result of General Zia following the practices in Saudi Arabia that did not allow the public showing of movies. The movies made by the exceptionally devout Muslim leader who was happy to impose his views about religion on the citizenry destroyed Pakistan's once-vibrant film industry. In 1981 Pakistan was one of the top 10 film-producing countries in the world, producing more than 100 movies a year. It had more than 1,000 movie theatres. Now the country makes about 20 films a year and only 45 screens show movies. But the situation is changing. Since 2018 Saudi Arabia has allowed the opening of movie theatres.

Pamela Constable reminded readers of the *Washington Post* about the acts of terrorism committed by radical Islamists against the country's Christian community that numbers three million among a population of approximately 208 million. A week before Christmas in 2017 nine people died and 57 were injured when a church in Quetta was attacked by two suicide bombers. On Easter Sunday in 2016, Taliban suicide bombers killed 72 people and wounded more than 300 in a park in Lahore. In September 2013 a suicide attack at a church in Peshawar left 80 people dead. In March 2011 Shahbaz Bhatti, a Christian and federal minister for religious minority affairs, was assassinated. But this time people reacted against these acts of terrorism. Constable remarked, 'Across Pakistan church volunteers got bust decorating trees and placing wreaths on pews … Urban bazaars that had been lit up December 1 to celebrate the birthday of the prophet Muhammad glowed with Christmas lights, illuminating displays of plastic fir trees and tinsel imported from China'.[6] Acts such as these can improve the narrative about Pakistan which will contribute to ensuring a better economic future. Potential investors will be drawn to the country and bring in badly needed capital.

During his campaign for the presidency, Donald Trump promised that he would 'make America great again'. This he would do by following an 'America first' policy. He kept his promise during the first few days he spent in the Oval Office following his inauguration.

He withdrew the United States from the Trans-Pacific Partnership (TPP) agreement; banned the entry into the country of citizens from seven Muslim-majority countries; and recruited people into several senior positions who were committed to downsizing the agencies they were to lead.

Trump's attack on the TPP was made without understanding that the deal concluded by Barack Obama, his predecessor in the White House, would have been good for the United States. The withdrawal followed two years of painstaking negotiations with 11 countries located on either side of the Pacific Ocean. The agreement was aimed at pre-empting China and establishing a new order that would have adopted global trading rules covering everything from data flows to the behaviour of state-owned enterprises. Trump, the deal-maker par excellence, did not have any interest in multilateral negotiations. The 'art of the deal' was to squeeze the other party in what was seen as a zero-sum game. It did not occur to the new President that economically small powers such as Pakistan would not like to sit across the table and conclude deals with a very large and powerful country such as the United States. As one commentator noted, 'the issue is particularly acute for the country's tech companies, which were counting on US trade negotiations to enshrine, core principles, such as free flow of data across borders'.[7]

Notes

1 Philip Tetlock and Dan Gardner, *Superforecasting: The Art and Science of Prediction*, New York, Random House, 2015.
2 Nassim Nicholas Taleb, *The Black: Swan: The Impact of the Highly Improbable*, New York, Random House, 2010.
3 See Shahid Javed Burki, *Rising Powers and Global Governance: Changes and Challenges for the World's Nations*, New York, Palgrave Macmillan., 2017.
4 Anatol Lieven, *Pakistan: A Hard Country*, New York, PublicAffairs, 2012.
5 Mehreen Zahra-Malik, 'A Pakistani Film, Banned and then Revived, Strikes a Timely Nerve', *New York Times*, 26 December 2017, p. A6.
6 Pamela Constable, 'Christmas Spirit Shines in Pakistan Despite Church Attack', *Washington Post*, 26 December 2017, p. A12.
7 Shawn Donnan, 'Globalization Marches on Without Trump', *Financial Times,* 7 November 2017, p. 9.

27

Postscript

Shahid Javed Burki and Asad Ejaz Butt

Shahid Javed Burki, Asad Ejaz Butt and Iftekhar Ahmed Chowdhury, the co-editors of this book, invited their Pakistan-based contributors to a review meeting. Several attended. The meeting was held at the office of the Shahid Javed Burki Institute of Public Policy (BIPP) in Lahore on 29 March 2018. The aim of the meeting was to review the final manuscript, discuss the utility of the work, reflect on how the main conclusions reached in the book could be disseminated once it had been published, and to contemplate on how the country could improve the narrative that had developed around it.

The meeting coincided with the launch of the BIPP's annual report, the 10th in the series begun in 2008.[1] The 2017 report focused on the China–Pakistan Economic Corridor (CPEC), a programme of infrastructure improvement launched by President Xi Jinping of China during a visit to Pakistan in 2015. The CPEC is a part of a Chinese initiative aimed at improving the country's connection with the world to its west including the landlocked countries of Central Asia as well as Europe and Africa. Called the One Belt, One Road initiative, the BRI programme is expected to cost the Chinese government several trillions of dollars and to improve the country's links with five dozen countries. At the meeting the contributors discussed at some length what the CPEC and the BRI would mean for Pakistan.

One issue that came up for discussion was the role played by migration, both internal and international, in Pakistan's political and economic life as well as its in relations with the rest of the world. This issue was not dealt with as an individual topic by any of the contributors to this book. Perhaps it should have been, since in many respects Pakistan's experience is unique. This discussion should go beyond the 'counter-factual' related to the arrival of Urdu-speaking refugees from India to Karachi. To this migration was added the arrival of millions of people from the provinces of Punjab and Khyber-Pakhtunkhwa to work on hundreds of construction sites in Karachi, Pakistan's first capital. Having chosen a capital, the government then had to build offices and housing for the thousands of workers it was recruiting. As is usually the case with any large-scale migration, the new arrivals formed their own communities in their own geographic space. This led to the establishment of such Pashtun colonies as Sohrab Goth on the city's outskirts. The Soviet Unions' attempted conquest of Afghanistan and the Pashtun resistance to that occupation in the 1980s generated another wave of migration. Between four and five million Afghan refugees crossed the porous border between Afghanistan and Pakistan. The efforts to contain them in refugee colonies built along the border were only partially successful. Millions escaped and took up residence in Pakistan's large cities. Karachi's Pashtun colonies proved to be very welcoming with the result that Karachi is now the world's largest Pashtun city.

The authors agreed that Pakistan is undergoing a massive transformation in terms of its economy, its political system and its relations with the outside world. Not only is it rapidly changing but it is also changing in the right direction. Clearly, there are irritants and challenges including the prevalence of corruption, bad governance and poor competence of the ruling elite that was voted out of office in the 25 July 2018 elections, but there are also hopes attached to the new government that took office in August 2018. The administrations that will take office following the 2018 elections might be able to build on the number of positives identified by the contributors to this book.

It was inevitable that the authors' thoughts about the book would lead to a discussion of the current political and economic issues as well as the country's relations with the outside world. Will Pakistan grow stronger after the elections of 2018? The authors were inclined to say 'yes' to the question, notwithstanding the impression of a fairly large segment of the thinking populace in the country that has serious concerns about the direction in which Pakistan is moving. These concerns are not confined to politics; there are also worries about the developing economic situation and the country's relations with the outside world. The one area where there was some comfort was the security situation in the country. But that must also have been shaken by the assassination attempt on Ahsan Iqbal, the then Minister of the Interior, on 6 May 2018.

After meandering aimlessly in the political field for decades – a subject well covered in several chapters in the book – Pakistan seems to have finally embarked on the constitutional path. But conventional wisdom is a powerful force. It can produce the feared results. The attack on the minister will add to the negative view many hold in the country about its political future. It appears that the major players in the political system – politicians, people holding senior positions in the military, the judiciary and the highly energized media – have not found a way to work together within the constitutional framework. To these the authors added a fifth player: the Pakistani youth.

In examining where we are today, how we have arrived at the current point, and where we might be headed, the authors' discussion was concerned only with politics. That said, it is worth pointing out that of late – and by that we mean over the last decade or so – economists have begun to realize that the main assumption on which they had structured their thinking was at best weak. Psychoanalysts invaded their domain and established that human beings do not always behave rationally. Most of the time they fashion their behaviour based on biases and experience. Political scientists had already forced economists to recognize that the two disciplines in which they worked interacted with one another. Pakistan's economic future, therefore, will be determined by the way its political system develops. In contemplating that development, most thinking people have concluded that our politics is headed towards prolonged instability. That impression has been created by past history as well as by a number of recent events.

For the past 70 years, Pakistan has adjusted its politics to deal with recurrent crises. The result was that the boundaries of the areas in which various institutions should have worked were never clearly defined. The military should have focused on ensuring security, but instead it interfered in politics in the belief that it could manage the crisis of the day better than its civilian counterparts. Four times it intervened directly and established itself as the unchallenged ruler. Even when it was not in charge, it continued to wield considerable influence. Politicians did not constrain their involvement in governance by clearly defining the rules they would follow. This would have meant taking the Constitution seriously. But the Constitution is a living and dynamic framework that evolves as circumstances change. This is where the judiciary enters the picture. For decades, the Superior Court assigned a passive role to itself, hiding behind what it called the 'doctrine of necessity'. Under the doctrine, it justified actions by the executive and the military that were clearly unconstitutional. The media, the fourth pillar in a well-functioning political system, was able to work without constraints after General Pervez Musharraf, the country's fourth military leader, freed it from government control. The number of private television channels soared and aggressively competed with one another. But the expanded electronic media did not always act responsibly.

What makes democracy the system that should produce positive results is its ability to correct the mistakes various groups within the citizenry often make in conducting themselves. Winston Churchill's famous conclusion was that democracy constituted the 'worst form of government – except for all those other forms that have been tried'. According to Boris Johnson, the former British Secretary of State for Foreign and Commonwealth Affairs, Churchill 'was not succumbing to pessimism; on the contrary, faced with an array of unappetizing options, there is a deep wisdom in choosing the one with the smallest downside and then fixing its limitations'.[2]

This fixing comes through periodic elections in which the voters give their views about the people who are asking for their support. While the people of Pakistan have voted in elections ten times since the country adopted the 1973 Constitution, real choice was exercised only four times: in 1970 and again in 2008, 2013 and 2018. In 1970 some of those who held the reins of power refused to accept the election's verdict. The obvious outcome should have been to transfer power to the Bengali leader Sheikh Mujibur Rehman and his political party, the Awami League. But that was not done. Mujib and his party were the clear winners but Zulfikar Ali Bhutto's Pakistan Peoples Party had won the majority in West Pakistan. His convoluted political logic led to the civil war in East Pakistan and the break-up of the original concept of Pakistan. On the three other occasions, the electorate voted to bring about decisive changes. This was not just in facilitating the transfer of power from one political party to another but in establishing the simple but important fact that the will of the people will prevail. Elections, therefore, serve to cleanse the political system.

But when our contributors talked about the 'people', they were not using an abstract notion. They were referring to those whom the law of the land recognizes as legitimate voters, namely people above the age of 18. Demographic movements bring about changes that are not always appreciated or comprehended by the political establishment. The most telling transformation that came about in the five-year period between 2013 and 2018 was the entry of some 20–22 million newcomers to the electorate. This is the youth who will want their aspirations to be recognized. Some years ago, Anatol Lieven suggested that the remarkable resilience of the people in the country lay in their reliance on local systems for support. The best known of these is the 'baradari system'.[3] That may have been the case in the past but with the demographic tilt in favour of the youth, these old alliances are no longer at the centre of political processes. Political parties have now established themselves at the heart of the system. Now there are some 105 million people below the age of 24, the country's median age. In the large cities, 75 per cent of the population is below that age. These people have political and economic aspirations; they want systems of governance that are inclusive, not exclusive. They will vote for those that can satisfy these demands.

The attempt on the life of the former minister points to one area of unfinished business in terms of placing the country under the rule of law. In spite of the successes achieved by the military to improve the security situation in the country, there are still people who believe that the use of violence is the right option to force their views on the rest of the citizenry. The 22-year-old young man who attempted to kill the minister belongs to a group that believes passionately in the doctrine of *khatam-e-nabuwat*, the finality of pro-phethood. 'This menace of hatred will destroy everything', tweeted former Minister of Foreign Affairs Khawaja Asif. 'We have to work together for our country'. In another tweet, Afrasiab Khattak, a retired senator, warned, 'weaponizing religion is a path to horrible disaster'.[4]

'Rule of law' is a generic-sounding term but the 2018 elections provided an opportunity to reaffirm it. Under this form of governance, government actors are both limited by it and accountable to it. While the Constitution is the basic document that defines it, the courts interpret it, and the media watches the way it is operated. The way the system is developing, the military has assumed the role to ensure that these three actors stay the course.

After discussing the political situation, the contributors told the co-editors of this volume that some of their thoughts could perhaps be included in a second edition, perhaps post-2023 when the PTI and Imran Khan, the new Prime Minister, would go back to the electorate and test how their performance in office had been viewed.

Notes

1 Shahid Javed Burki Institute of Public Policy, *Tenth Annual Report, 2017: The State of the Economy, China-Pakistan Economic Corridor*, Lahore, 2018.
2 Boris Johnson, 'Don't Scuttle the Iran Nuclear Deal', *New York Times*, 7 May 2018, p. A31.
3 Anatol Lieven, Pakistan: A Hard Country, New York, PublicAffairs, 2012.
4 Quoted in Pamela Constable, 'Shooting in Pakistan Highlights Muslim Groups' Rising Influence', *Washington Post*, 8 May 2018, p. A9.

Index

Page numbers in **bold** and *italics* reference Tables and Figures, respectively.

Printed in the United States
by Baker & Taylor Publisher Services